READINGS ON

J.R.R. TOLKIEN

OTHER TITLES IN THE GREENHAVEN PRESS LITERARY COMPANION SERIES:

BRITISH AUTHORS

Jane Austen
Joseph Conrad
Charles Dickens

BRITISH LITERATURE

Animal Farm
Beowulf
Brave New World
The Canterbury Tales
Frankenstein
Great Expectations
Hamlet
Heart of Darkness
Julius Caesar
Lord of the Flies
Macbeth
The Merchant of Venice
Othello
Pride and Prejudice
Romeo and Juliet
Shakespeare: The Comedies
Shakespeare: The Histories
Shakespeare: The Sonnets
Shakespeare: The Tragedies
A Tale of Two Cities
Tess of the d'Urbervilles
Wuthering Heights

THE GREENHAVEN PRESS
Literary Companion
TO BRITISH AUTHORS

READINGS ON

J.R.R. TOLKIEN

Katie de Koster, *Book Editor*

David L. Bender, *Publisher*
Bruno Leone, *Executive Editor*
Bonnie Szumski, *Series Editor*

Greenhaven Press, Inc., San Diego, CA

Every effort has been made to trace the owners of copyrighted material. The articles in this volume may have been edited for content, length, and/or reading level. The titles have been changed to enhance the editorial purpose. Those interested in locating the original source will find the complete citation on the first page of each article.

Library of Congress Cataloging-in-Publication Data

Readings on J.R.R. Tolkien / Katie de Koster, book editor.
   p.   cm. — (The Greenhaven Press literary companion to British authors)
   Includes bibliographical references and index.
   ISBN 0-7377-0245-1 (lib. bdg. : alk. paper). —
ISBN 0-7377-0244-3 (pbk. : alk. paper)
   1. Tolkien, J.R.R. (John Ronald Reuel), 1892–1973—Criticism and interpretation. 2. Tolkien, J.R.R. (John Ronald Reuel), 1892–1973. Lord of the rings. 3. Tolkien, J.R.R. (John Ronald Reuel), 1892–1973. Hobbit. 4. Fantasy fiction, English—History and criticism.
5. Middle Earth (Imaginary place) I. De Koster, Katie, 1948–   . II. Series
PR6039.032Z798   2000
828'.91209—dc21
                                        99-34336
                                        CIP

Cover photo: Liaison Agency, Inc.

Copyright © 2000 by Greenhaven Press, Inc.
PO Box 289009
San Diego, CA 92198-9009
Printed in the U.S.A.

> **I write things that might be classified as fairy-stories not because I wish to address children . . . but because I wish to write this kind of story and no other.**
>
> —J.R.R. Tolkien

CONTENTS

FOREWORD

*"'Tis the good reader that
makes the good book."*

Ralph Waldo Emerson

The story's bare facts are simple: The captain, an old and scarred seafarer, walks with a peg leg made of whale ivory. He relentlessly drives his crew to hunt the world's oceans for the great white whale that crippled him. After a long search, the ship encounters the whale and a fierce battle ensues. Finally the captain drives his harpoon into the whale, but the harpoon line catches the captain about the neck and drags him to his death.

A simple story, a straightforward plot—yet, since the 1851 publication of Herman Melville's *Moby-Dick*, readers and critics have found many meanings in the struggle between Captain Ahab and the whale. To some, the novel is a cautionary tale that depicts how Ahab's obsession with revenge leads to his insanity and death. Others believe that the whale represents the unknowable secrets of the universe and that Ahab is a tragic hero who dares to challenge fate by attempting to discover this knowledge. Perhaps Melville intended Ahab as a criticism of Americans' tendency to become involved in well-intentioned but irrational causes. Or did Melville model Ahab after himself, letting his fictional character express his anger at what he perceived as a cruel and distant god?

Although literary critics disagree over the meaning of *Moby-Dick*, readers do not need to choose one particular interpretation in order to gain an understanding of Melville's novel. Instead, by examining various analyses, they can gain numerous insights into the issues that lie under the surface of the basic plot. Studying the writings of literary critics can also aid readers in making their own assessments of *Moby-Dick* and other literary works and in developing analytical thinking skills.

The Greenhaven Literary Companion Series was created with these goals in mind. Designed for young adults, this unique anthology series provides an engaging and comprehensive introduction to literary analysis and criticism. The essays included in the Literary Companion Series are chosen for their accessibility to a young adult audience and are expertly edited in consideration of both the reading and comprehension levels of this audience. In addition, each essay is introduced by a concise summation that presents the contributing writer's main themes and insights. Every anthology in the Literary Companion Series contains a varied selection of critical essays that cover a wide time span and express diverse views. Wherever possible, primary sources are represented through excerpts from authors' notebooks, letters, and journals and through contemporary criticism.

Each title in the Literary Companion Series pays careful consideration to the historical context of the particular author or literary work. In-depth biographies and detailed chronologies reveal important aspects of authors' lives and emphasize the historical events and social milieu that influenced their writings. To facilitate further research, every anthology includes primary and secondary source bibliographies of articles and/or books selected for their suitability for young adults. These engaging features make the Greenhaven Literary Companion series ideal for introducing students to literary analysis in the classroom or as a library resource for young adults researching the world's great authors and literature.

Exceptional in its focus on young adults, the Greenhaven Literary Companion Series strives to present literary criticism in a compelling and accessible format. Every title in the series is intended to spark readers' interest in leading American and world authors, to help them broaden their understanding of literature, and to encourage them to formulate their own analyses of the literary works that they read. It is the editors' hope that young adult readers will find these anthologies to be true companions in their study of literature.

INTRODUCTION

Readers generally do not need to be encouraged to enjoy reading J.R.R. Tolkien's most famous works, *The Hobbit* and *The Lord of the Rings*. They are drawn into the pages, engaged by the stories, reluctant to put the books down, and sad when they reach the end.

Like any good mythology—which is what Tolkien was consciously creating—the books can be enjoyed on many levels. They resonate differently and offer different views and shades of meanings depending on what the reader brings to the experience. But beyond understanding the tale of the quest, for example, or the religious significance of The One, or the nature of heroism, there is another asset of great value in Tolkien's work that can be mined painlessly: language.

Not "languages," such as Quenya, the High-elven tongue, but the mastery of language. Tolkien was a prose poet who loved words, loved how words work together, and who had a master's understanding of the underpinnings of how we communicate with words. His command of the language is such that the reader will be tempted to simply dive in and allow the rush of words to flow and surge. But once in a while, stand back and look at what Tolkien has wrought. See how he puts the words together. Observe the precise use of grammar and punctuation as well as nouns and verbs. Appreciate the shadings and nuances as he creates an entire mythology with words that seem to come alive. There has been no one else like him, and may never be again.

J.R.R. TOLKIEN: MAKER OF WORLDS

The birth of John Ronald Reuel Tolkien in Bloemfontein, South Africa, was quite an event. With his eyes of English blue and a bit of very fair hair topping an unusually high brow, he was such a curiosity that his parents' houseboy, Isaak, "borrowed" him for a while to take him into his village and show him off. Since Isaak's excursion with the baby was unauthorized, it caused quite a bit of turmoil. Fortunately for Isaak, the Tolkiens—especially young Ronald's mother—were understanding. In gratitude for their tolerance, Isaak named his own son Isaak Mister Tolkien Victor.

MABEL AND ARTHUR TOLKIEN

Both of Ronald's parents were from Birmingham, England, where financial conditions were difficult at the end of the nineteenth century. Arthur Reuel Tolkien's family had once manufactured pianos, but they had lost the firm and Arthur's father had gone bankrupt. Mabel Suffield's father had owned a drapery business, but he too had suffered bankruptcy. Thus when Arthur proposed to Mabel shortly after her eighteenth birthday, her father objected to their betrothal both on grounds of her youth (Arthur was thirteen years older than she was) and because Arthur's position in the Birmingham branch of Lloyd's Bank did not pay well enough to support a family. The couple wrote letters to each other in secret—Mabel's sister Jane acted as go-between, making the exchange with Arthur on a train platform on her way home from school—while waiting for her to reach the age of twenty-one, when her father would no longer be able to forbid her to marry.

Although John Suffield, Mabel's father, would not allow them to announce a formal betrothal, Mabel had accepted Arthur's proposal. With this new incentive to succeed, he sought a banking position with better prospects, and soon accepted a position with the Bank of Africa. By the end of 1890 he was manager of the branch in Bloemfontein, the capital of the Orange Free State, now part of South Africa. It provided not only an adequate income but also a home, Bank House on Maitland Street, with servants. Mabel turned twenty-one in January 1891 and shortly afterward sailed for South Africa to marry Arthur. They were married in Cape Town on April 16.

After a short honeymoon, the newlyweds made the grueling seven-hundred-mile rail journey to their new home in Bloemfontein. The town was an oasis of civilization in the veldt, where wolves and jackals roamed just a few hundred yards from the houses. The extremes of temperature in summer and winter were far from what they were used to, and even the winters were dry and dusty. When Mabel wrote home, she described the place as " 'Owlin' Wilderness! Horrid Waste!" But Arthur was happy there, if not as healthy as she would have liked, so she tried to settle in, realizing unhappily that they would not be eligible for "home leave"—a chance to visit England—for another three years.

Arthur was often busy—when not at the bank, he was often studying Dutch, the language of business and government in colonial South Africa, or cultivating useful acquaintances to help his bank succeed in its rivalry with the native National Bank. Mabel became pregnant almost immediately, and her first son was born on January 3, 1892. They named him John, for Mabel's father; Reuel, after Arthur's middle name; and Ronald, which was what his family came to call him. John Ronald Reuel Tolkien was christened in Bloemfontein's Anglican cathedral on January 31.

FROM AFRICA BACK TO ENGLAND

Toddlers in Bloemfontein were exposed to a variety of rather exotic dangers. Tolkien biographer Humphrey Carpenter reports that a neighbor's pet monkeys climbed over the wall and chewed up young Tolkien's pinafores, and that the woodshed was a favorite lurking spot for snakes. Carpenter highlights one incident in which, just as he was learning to walk, young Ronald came upon a tarantula in the garden. It bit him and he ran screaming until his nurse caught him and treated the wound. In later years, the author remembered the terror he felt running through the grass on that hot day. Although he said he did not remember the tarantula itself, Tolkien's writings include more than one monstrous spider with a poisonous bite.

By that winter, Mabel was making no secret of her intense

dislike of the living conditions in Bloemfontein; she hated the climate, the tedious social life, and especially the fact that Arthur seemed so happy there, that she feared he would never agree to return to England. She began making plans for their home leave, but had to postpone them when she found herself pregnant again. Hilary Arthur Reuel, Ronald's brother, was born on February 17, 1894.

While Hilary seemed to thrive in South Africa, Ronald did not; the summer heat that year exacerbated the fever of teething, and Mabel became determined to take him to a cooler place for his health. In November she took the two boys to the coast near Cape Town for a vacation. Once they were back in Bloemfontein, with the boys now healthy enough for the long voyage, she began planning their home leave.

Although he wanted to accompany his young family, Arthur would not be able to go with them immediately, for business and financial reasons—he was needed in important railway negotiations, and during his home leave time he would receive only half pay. Mabel and the boys, with a nurse Arthur engaged for the journey, sailed for England in April 1895. Ronald later remembered watching Arthur paint his name on the lid of a trunk they would take with them; it was his only clear memory of his father.

Mabel and her sons stayed with her parents in Birmingham. She was glad to see that Ronald's health improved over the spring and summer, but unhappy that business further delayed Arthur in South Africa. In November he contracted rheumatic fever, which damages the heart, and did not want to attempt the long journey or face the English winter until he was well. By January, when he was still ill, Mabel decided to return to South Africa to care for him. Arrangements for the return trip had been completed when word arrived that Arthur had suffered a severe hemorrhage and died on February 15, 1896, just two days before Hilary's second birthday. He was buried in Bloemfontein.

Grief and guilt had to be put aside as Mabel, called Mab, turned to the problem of providing for her sons. She found a cheap semidetached row house in the village of Sarehole, in the countryside just outside Birmingham, a wonderful place for boys to play and explore. She also began to prepare Ronald for the entrance exams at his father's old school, King Edward VI School in Birmingham, which had an excellent reputation. Mabel was a linguist and taught her son Latin and German (both of which he enjoyed), as well as French (which for some reason did not appeal to him). Mab also taught him drawing and painting and supplied him with plenty of books to read. (He was especially taken with a story in the *Red Fairy Book* by Andrew Lang, about the dragon Fafnir; he later remembered, "I desired dragons with a profound desire.") She taught both boys botany, with disparate results: Ronald became especially good at drawing plants, while Hilary grew up to be a farmer.

ROMAN CATHOLICISM

Mab earned little income after her husband died, but both the Suffields and Tolkiens offered some financial help. However, in 1900, Mab converted to Roman Catholicism, which horrified and outraged both her own family and her in-laws. The Suffields withdrew their financial support and she and the boys became somewhat estranged from her family. Arthur's side of the family also objected strongly, although one of Ronald's uncles did agree to supply the twelve pounds per year needed for him to attend King Edward VI School when he passed the entrance examination on his second try, in 1900.

Mab knew that if Ronald was going to attend university, he would need to do well enough in school to win a scholarship. King Edward School was the best in Birmingham, but it was four miles from their home in Sarehole. Ronald walked to and from school for a few weeks, but with the onset of winter Mab decided to move the family closer to the school. After four happy years in their little cottage, they moved into town, to a house near King's Heath station that was right next to the railroad tracks. The trains were noisy and made the neighborhood less desirable, but Ronald was fascinated by the Welsh names painted on the rail cars that carried coal to the nearby coalyard. Captivated by such words as *Penrhiwceiber*, he added a lifelong love of the Welsh language to his other linguistic enthusiasms.

Although Mab had chosen the King's Heath house in part because of its proximity to St. Dunstan's Catholic Church, she soon decided she did not care for that church and began visiting others in the area. Thus she discovered the Birmingham Oratory, a large church with a community of priests and its own school, St. Philip's, which set lower fees than King Edward's and would provide her sons with a Roman Catholic education. In early 1902, they moved to Edgbaston, where the

Oratory was located, and the boys were enrolled in St. Philip's. The parish priest, Father Francis Xavier Morgan, soon became a good friend of the family, offering affection and a fatherly presence in the boys' lives that had been missing since they had become estranged from their relatives.

Ronald and Hilary were students of very different natures. Hilary was an indifferent student, whereas Ronald outpaced his new classmates so quickly that Mab soon realized he would need to return to King Edward's to get a good education. Mab withdrew them both from St. Philip's and resumed schooling them at home. Ronald won a Foundation Scholarship to King Edward's, returning there in the fall of 1903, while Hilary continued to study at home with their mother.

A Passion for Languages

At King Edward's, Ronald began learning Greek; he later noted, "The fluidity of Greek, punctuated by its hardness, and with its surface glitter captivated me. But part of the attraction was antiquity and alien remoteness (from me): it did not touch home." He found that he disliked Shakespeare, but— guided by medievalist George Brewerton, an enthusiastic teacher who had the students read the *Canterbury Tales*—he found another language to love. Middle English did not have the glitter of Greek or the euphony of Welsh; instead, Tolkien became interested in the language because it was the historical antecedent to his own tongue. He decided to investigate the history of languages.

As 1904 began, though, the entire household was ill. The boys had measles, followed by whooping cough; Hilary also had pneumonia. Although all of these diseases can be prevented or treated today, a century ago there were no powerful antibiotics. The strain of nursing the boys took its toll on their mother; by April 1904 Mabel was taken to the hospital, where she was diagnosed as diabetic.

This was long before insulin was developed as a treatment for diabetes. The illness was so serious that the family's house was closed, the furniture put into storage, and the boys sent to different Suffield relatives. Mab remained in the hospital until June, when she was released with the understanding that she would require a long convalescence.

Father Francis found a place for the three Tolkiens to live together, sharing a cottage with a postman and his wife on the grounds of a country retreat for the Oratory clergy, in Rednal. The setting was much like the happy home they had shared in Sarehole: The Tills, with whom they shared the cottage, saw they were well fed, and the boys delighted in an idyllic existence for the rest of the summer.

When fall arrived, it was time for Ronald to return to King Edward's, but Mab was reluctant to return to their drab existence in Birmingham. Instead, Ronald walked a mile each way to the station and took the train into town. As the days shortened, he would arrive home in the dark, often met by Hilary with a lantern.

The boys did not realize their mother's condition was deteriorating until she suddenly collapsed in early November. Sinking into a diabetic coma, she died on November 14, 1904. Ronald was twelve.

Their mother's death obviously changed the boys' physical circumstances, but it also had several less tangible effects on Ronald. She had introduced him to languages; her death strengthened his love of words, as it honored and maintained a connection with her. Their happiest times had been in rural settings, which became emotionally charged for Ronald after his mother's death. Mab's death also changed him emotionally. He had been a cheerful boy, and after she died he maintained a cheerful face in company. But in private, he developed a profound pessimism; her sudden death, after the idyllic summer, gave him a sense not only of loss, but of impermanence. It made him feel, as his biographer Humphrey Carpenter puts it, "Nothing was safe. Nothing would last. No battle would be won forever."

Life as an Orphan

Mabel had made Father Francis the boys' guardian. At first he did not want the boys to go to live with relatives since some of their kin wanted to contest the terms of her will and send the boys to a Protestant boarding school. Finally, though, Father Francis discovered that one of the boys' aunts, Beatrice Suffield, had a spare bedroom to offer and no strong religious views. Father Francis moved them into her home in Edgbaston.

Unfortunately, Aunt Beatrice, recently widowed herself, had little affection or understanding to offer the boys. The boys made the Oratory their unofficial home, spending as much time there as possible. Hilary was now a student at King Edward's too, so they walked to school together after helping at morning mass. Father Francis supplemented the small funds left by their mother with family money of his own, so they did not lack for material necessities.

Ronald's fellow student Christopher Wiseman became his inseparable companion and friendly rival for first place in their class. They shared interests in Latin and Greek, in rugby, and in discussing everything. They moved up from Fifth Class to First (senior) Class together. It was in First Class that the headmaster, Robert Cary Gilson, introduced them to the study not just of language, but of linguistics. Encouraged by Gilson, Ronald began to study the general principles of language, while the loan of an Anglo-Saxon primer from his Chaucer master, Brewerton, led him not only to the roots of his own language but to the great Old English poem *Beowulf.* Moving forward in time to Middle English, he read the medieval poem-story *Sir Gawain and the Green Knight* and *The Pearl,* an allegorical poem said to have been written by *Sir Gawain*'s author. Reading these classics in their original languages fired his passion; he was soon studying Old Norse so he could read the original tale of Fafnir the dragon, which he had enjoyed years ago in Andrew Lang's retelling of the tale. On his own, he scoured the shelves of the local bookshop, eventually coming across studies of philology (the study of literature and related disciplines) in German that helped him understand the structure of languages.

And then the young author took the next logical step: He began making up languages of his own. At first he used existing languages, such as Welsh and Spanish (a favorite of Father Francis's), as his starting point. After buying a copy of Joseph Wright's *Primer of the Gothic Language,* he discovered that only a few fragments of the written language survived, and he decided to fill in the gaps. He often discussed his efforts with his friend Christopher Wiseman, who was himself involved in studying the Egyptian language and hieroglyphics.

EDITH BRATT

In the meantime, when Ronald was fifteen, Father Francis realized the brothers were unhappy at their aunt's and moved them into a boardinghouse run by a Mrs. Faulkner. Another lodger there was also an orphan, nineteen-year-old Edith Bratt. She was an attractive girl with a gift for music. However, while Mrs. Faulkner encouraged Edith to play the piano at her evening musical soirees, she had no patience for practice arpeggios and scales. Edith spent more of her time in her room, at her sewing machine.

Ronald was sixteen and had been reared almost exclusively in the company of males. Understandably shy, he found it difficult to hold a conversation with a girl, but living in the same boardinghouse quickly broke down his reserve. The two became allies against the landlady (who never seemed to provide enough food to satisfy the growing adolescents). By the summer of 1909, they were in love.

Ronald was supposed to be studying diligently in order to win a scholarship to Oxford University, but he was pursuing other interests instead: inventing languages, thinking about Edith and seeing her away from the boardinghouse when he could, and joining the senior debating society at school. An indistinct speaker whose voice still occasionally squeaked, he had not done much public speaking, but he found joy in forming arguments and confounding his opponents by delivering them not in the Latin they expected, but in Gothic, Greek, or Anglo-Saxon.

Ronald and Edith thought they had been discreet about their relationship, but word of it eventually reached Father Francis, who was appalled. He berated Ronald, both for neglecting the studies that were his only hope for a good education and for carrying on a secret relationship with a girl who lived in the same house. He moved the boys out of the boardinghouse, then became infuriated when the couple began meeting again (although he had not expressly forbidden them to see each other). Eventually Edith decided to move to Cheltenham to live with a family who had befriended her. Father Francis ordered Ronald not to see or write Edith again until he was twenty-one and out of his guardianship, except for one last meeting on the day of her departure to say goodbye. Before she left, though, the two exchanged brief words during a few accidental meetings—the boys still lived nearby—and Father Francis found out. He called Ronald evil and foolish, and threatened to block his entrance to the university. Edith and Ronald would have to wait three years to see each other again, with no communication between them in the meantime.

Father Francis did not intend to be cruel; he felt his orders were in the best interests of his charge and improved his chances for a good education. But he was, perhaps, foolish; he certainly did not understand Ronald well enough to foresee the effect of his decision. For the next three years, Ronald would romanticize his relationship with Edith, focusing his plans and hopes on her. At the same time, since he was promised to her, he avoided other female company, spending

all his time with male friends. In later years, he would com-
partmentalize his relationship with his wife and family from
his camaraderie with his fellow scholars.

OXFORD

Ronald first took the scholarship exams for Oxford during
the height of the blowup over Edith, and he failed to win an
award. He could try again the following year, but in the
meantime he needed to work harder at his studies at King
Edward's. With Edith gone, relations with Father Francis
strained, and depression setting in, he turned all his attention
to school. In 1911 he and Christopher Wiseman, along with
R.Q. Gilson (son of the headmaster of King Edward's) and a
few other boys, founded the Tea Club. They began by having
tea in the library—a forbidden pleasure and therefore a delight. Later they met at the Tea Room in Barrow's Stores, so
they changed the name of their clique to the Barrovian Society. When Wiseman, who was editor of the school newspa-
per, printed a list of students who had excelled in some way,
he noted that their group were "members of the T.C., B.S.,
etc."—and so they became the T.C.B.S. The nucleus of the
group consisted of Ronald, Christopher, R.Q., and later Geoffrey Bache Smith. The members had diverse interests, which
they shared with one another: Christopher favored math,
natural sciences, and music; R.Q. enjoyed studying drawing
and design, Renaissance painting, and the eighteenth century; Geoffrey was interested in "modern" (post-Chaucer)
English studies and poetry. John Ronald, as his friends then
called him, brought his passion for philology and mythology
as well as his command of Germanic languages and Norse
writings.

Ronald's interests were not all cerebral; he loved playing
rugby, even though he suffered a broken nose that was never
quite the same shape again. But most of his time not spent
with the T.C.B.S. was spent in working at languages (his own
as well as historical ones), debating, and studying for the
scholarship exam. On December 17, 1910, he learned that he
had won an award to study classics at Oxford. It was not a full
scholarship, but with help from Father Francis and a fund at
King Edward's, he would be able to go to the university.

He was even able to take a holiday that summer, after the
final session at King Edward's. He and Hilary (who had left
school to take up agriculture) were part of a group that
toured Switzerland on foot. Just before returning to England,

he bought some picture postcards, including one of a painting by J. Madelener called *Der Berggeist* ("the mountain spirit"). The picture shows an old man with a long white beard, flowing cape, and wide-brimmed hat with a white fawn nuzzling his hands. Tolkien kept the card, later writing on the cover he used to protect it, "Origin of Gandalf." He was back in England by early September, and a month later arrived at Oxford.

Money, as always, was a problem, but otherwise he was happy at Oxford. He joined the debating society and played rugby, and started his own club, the Apolausticks ("those devoted to self-indulgence"), which like the T.C.B.S. was a jolly group of male friends who loved to talk. He found himself bored by many of his studies, but discovered that the comparative philology professor was Joseph Wright—the same man who had written the Gothic primer that had so excited him years before. A scholar who had taught himself to read and write when he was fifteen (he had been working in woolen mills, not going to school, since he was six), Wright enjoyed a tremendous enthusiasm for philology, and knew enough to challenge Ronald in ways his other teachers could not.

Ronald found books on medieval Welsh and began to learn the language that had fascinated him since he had first seen the Welsh words on the sides of coal cars. At the same time, he began to draw and paint again, finding that he was gifted in drawing landscapes. His enthusiasm for languages did not abate, though; when he discovered Finnish, he said, "It quite intoxicated me." He began creating a language with strong Finnish elements; this would eventually become Quenya, or the High-elven tongue. As he began reading Finnish mythological poetry, he expressed his wish that English culture had retained more of "that very primitive undergrowth" of myth. It was a lack he would later rectify, as he created a complete new-old English mythology.

COMING OF AGE

Immediately on turning twenty-one, Ronald wrote Edith, declaring his love and asking how soon they could be married. To his dismay, she replied that she was engaged to be married to someone else.

Three years without communication, she explained, had persuaded her that he had probably forgotten her (as Father Francis had probably hoped); she was twenty-four and afraid she would be a spinster all her life if she did not accept the offer of George Field, who had been kind to her. But behind her words Ronald read her true message: that she would prefer to marry him. He took a train to Cheltenham. She met him at the station; and, after a day of walking and talking, Edith declared she would break off her engagement to George and marry Ronald.

This time, he did not keep his intentions from Father Francis; although the priest was no longer his guardian, he was still helping out financially, and the loss of that support would jeopardize his ability to continue his studies. Father Francis seemed resigned to the match, and made no objection. Oddly, Ronald had never mentioned Edith to his friends. As they decided to become formally betrothed, he informed his fellow T.C.B.S. members of the fact (but not of her name). They assured him that little would change among the group.

A greater danger to his studies was his late nights talking with his friends; Ronald found himself ill-prepared for his exams in Classics. He managed to pass Second Class, but the college noted that he had presented a practically flawless paper in comparative philology, due both to Joseph Wright's coaching and the fact that this was where Tolkien's greatest talents lay. The college suggested that since his strongest interests lay in the Germanic languages, such as Old and Middle English, he should consider transferring from Classics to the English School, which he did at the beginning of the 1913 summer term.

Now that he was studying what he really loved, he spent more time doing so. Even though he found his new field unexpectedly challenging, he delighted in Anglo-Saxon religious poetry and the Old Norse Eddas, with their magical repositories of Icelandic myth and legend.

The revived relationship with Edith, however, had hit a snag. While she was away, she had been happily active in the Church of England in Cheltenham. The Jessops, the family with whom she was staying, were staunchly anti-Catholic. While she was willing to convert to Catholicism, she did not want to provoke unpleasantness with her hosts; she said she would wait to renounce the Anglican Church until closer to the time of their marriage. But Ronald insisted that she immediately start attending a Catholic church; if her erstwhile friends persecuted her, he said, it would be just what had happened to his own mother, and thus not unexpected or devastating. Edith reluctantly acceded to his wishes. Just as she had feared, the Jessops reacted angrily, telling her to leave their home as soon as possible. She decided to share accommodations with her cousin, Jennie Grove.

On January 14, 1914, the first anniversary of Ronald and Edith's reunion, she was received into the Roman Catholic Church; shortly afterward, they were officially betrothed.

By late that summer, England had declared war on Germany, and young men across the country were enlisting to fight.

WORLD WAR I

If he managed to gain a First Class degree—and if he managed to survive the war—Ronald knew he would be able to find a good job in the academic world when the fighting was over. On the other hand, if he did not finish this final year and earn his degree, he might never be able to complete his college education. Fortunately, he discovered an army program that allowed him to begin training immediately while still leaving him enough time to finish his studies. He successfully won his First Class degree in June 1915. Shortly thereafter he joined his regiment, the Lancashire Fusiliers, which he had chosen because his friend Geoffrey Smith was a member. He was disappointed when they were assigned to different battalions.

After several months, as reports of the war's heavy casualties made them realize that he might not return from battle, Edith and Ronald decided not to wait until the war was over to wed. They were married March 22, 1916. She faced a moment of panic when she had to put her father's name and occupation on the marriage certificate; she had never told Ronald that she was illegitimate. When she told him later, he wrote her, "I think I love you even more tenderly because of all that, my wife," then said they should both simply forget it. On June 4, Ronald left for France and the Battle of the Somme.

At the end of the first day of fighting, R.Q. Gilson was among the twenty thousand Allied troops who had been killed. The horror of war surrounded the survivors, as life became a nightmare of marches and attacks, boredom interspersed with panic, mud, and dismembered, rotting corpses. During his time in France, Ronald developed little liking for the senior officers, but a great deal of respect for the privates, batmen (officers' servants), and noncommissioned officers of his battalion, who stolidly carried on under the most appalling circumstances. He wrote later that Sam Gamgee of *The Lord of the Rings* was based on "the English soldier, . . . the privates and batmen I knew in the 1914 war, and recognised as so far superior to myself."

Lice spread a disease called trench fever, which causes high fever, rash, headaches, and mental confusion. Ronald came down with the malady, and on November 8, 1916, he was shipped home to a Birmingham hospital. While he was recovering, he learned that Geoffrey Smith had been hit by fragments of a bursting shell and had died of complications of gangrene. Shortly before he was wounded, he had written Tolkien:

> My chief consolation is that if I am scuppered tonight . . . there will still be left a member of the great T.C.B.S. to voice what I dreamed and what we all agreed upon. For the death of one of its members cannot, I am determined, dissolve the T.C.B.S. . . . It cannot put an end to the immortal four! . . . May God bless you, my dear John Ronald, and may you say the things I have tried to say long after I am not there to say them, if such be my lot.

CREATING A NEW MYTHOLOGY

As Tolkien had been creating languages over the years, he had gradually come to realize that his languages must have a "history" in which to develop. He began his history, his mythological cycle, in a notebook on the cover of which he had written "The Book of Lost Tales." The stories he began here would eventually become *The Silmarillion.*

Humphrey Carpenter lists three reasons why Tolkien chose this time to begin his new mythology: Smith's letter; a desire, inspired by the T.C.B.S., to express himself in poetry (including prose poetry); and the wish to create a mythology for his native country. Surely the heightened sense of life engendered by battle had an effect, too, as did a note he received from the remaining one of the "immortal four," Christopher Wiseman, who wrote, "You ought to start the epic." And so he did.

He had time to write, for he spent much of the next two years in various hospitals. For a while, when he was on sick leave at Great Haywood in early 1917, Edith was able to join him. She helped by making a legible copy of the first story he wrote, "The Fall of Gondolin," and they spent their evenings playing the piano, reading poetry, and drawing.

They conceived a child during this respite from the war. When he was posted to Yorkshire, she followed him again, but after repeated transfers she and her cousin Jennie finally moved back to Cheltenham, where she had been happy during the three years of their separation. It was in a Cheltenham nursing home that their first son was born, on November 16, 1917. John Francis (for Father Francis) Reuel was a difficult labor. Edith nearly died, and suffered pain from the labor for many months afterward.

By now it seemed unlikely that Ronald would be sent back to the fighting, so Edith and John moved to Yorkshire to be near him. On his occasional leaves, they would wander together in a small nearby wood, where Edith would sing and dance for him. These precious days formed the basis of the central story of *The Silmarillion:* the mortal man Beren who falls in love with the immortal elven-maid Lúthien Tinúviel, first glimpsed dancing in a wood.

More than a half-century later, after Edith's death, Tolkien wrote to his son Christopher:

> She was (and knew she was) my Lúthien. I will say no more now. But I should like ere long to have a long talk with you. . . . Someone close in heart to me should know something about things that records do not record: the dreadful sufferings of our childhood, from which we rescued one another, but could not wholly heal wounds that later often proved disabling; the sufferings that we endured after our love began—all of which (over and above personal weaknesses) might help to make pardonable, or understandable, the lapses and darknesses which at times marred our lives—and to explain how these never touched our depths nor dimmed the memories of our youthful love.

A BRIEF STINT HELPING WRITE A DICTIONARY

During a period out of the hospital, in October 1918, Tolkien had gone to Oxford to see what employment prospects he might expect at the university when the war ended. The institution was in disarray and could offer little information, but while he was there he saw William Craigie, who had taught him Icelandic. Craigie was on the staff of the *Oxford New English Dictionary*, and he said he would be able to secure a position as assistant lexicographer for his former student. When the war ended the following month, Tolkien obtained permission to move to Oxford while he awaited official demobilization. By late November, he, Edith, baby John, and Jennie had moved into rooms near his new job, researching etymologies, or word origins (he began with *w: warm, wasp, water*). He later said of his stint on the dictionary staff, "I learned more in those two years than in any other equal period of my life." In later years, when he was chided for his spelling *dwarves* when the *OED* specified *dwarfs*, he rather grandiosely responded that he had *written* the *Oxford English Dictionary.*

Work on the dictionary was not expected to fill his entire day, nor to provide his entire income. He began to tutor students in Anglo-Saxon, and by the late summer of 1919 he and Edith could afford to rent a small house and hire a cook-housemaid. By the following spring, Ronald was earning enough from tuition to leave his job at the dictionary. Edith was pregnant again, and Ronald was making progress in his writing. When a position as reader (teacher) in English language became available at the University of Leeds, he applied, expecting nothing to come of it. Unexpectedly, he was awarded the position.

LEEDS

Unlike Oxford, Leeds was an industrial town whose smoke-stacks produced a thick fog of industrial pollutants. It was with some misgiving that he accepted the position and moved there, to the north of England. Edith stayed in Oxford to bear their second child, Michael Hilary Reuel, just as the October term began in Leeds. She remained in Oxford for several months, until early 1921.

Although Leeds was not as prestigious as Oxford, the head of the English Department nevertheless invited Tolkien to create a syllabus that would attract students to philology and give them a sound education in the field. Although the students in this Yorkshire town seemed much less lively than the friends he had cultivated in school, he was surprised and pleased to find that many of them were hard workers capable of achieving at a high level.

He was soon joined by a student he had tutored at Oxford, E.V. Gordon, now a junior lecturer in the language side of the Leeds English Department. The two men decided to compile an edition of the Middle English poem that had fascinated him earlier, *Sir Gawain and the Green Knight,* in an edition that would be suitable for college students. Gordon was industrious and Tolkien managed to keep up with him; their collaborative effort was published in 1925, when it was acknowledged as a major contribution to the study of medieval literature.

He also kept working on *The Book of Lost Tales / The Silmarillion,* but as he drew near the end, he turned to polishing and rewriting what he already had rather than finishing it. His career at Leeds continued to progress; he became a full professor in 1924 at the remarkably young age of thirty-two. That year, he and Edith bought a fairly large house surrounded by fields and had their third child, Christopher Reuel, named for Tolkien's friend Christopher Wiseman. Christopher Reuel Tolkien would grow up to edit his father's voluminous papers, including the posthumous twelve-volume *History of Middle-earth.*

Early in 1925, Tolkien learned that his old Icelandic teacher and Oxford dictionary coworker was moving to America; his position as professor of Anglo-Saxon at Oxford would soon be vacant. Tolkien applied for and won the position, and the family moved back to Oxford.

FINALLY SETTLING DOWN AT OXFORD

Humphrey Carpenter writes of this time,

> And after this, you might say, nothing else really happened. Tolkien came back to Oxford, was Rawlinson and Bosworth Professor of Anglo-Saxon for twenty years, was then elected Merton Professor of English Language and Literature, went to live in a conventional Oxford suburb where he spent the first part of his retirement, moved to a nondescript seaside resort, came back to Oxford after his wife died, and himself died a peaceful death at the age of eighty-one. . . . And that would be that—apart from the strange fact that during these years when "nothing happened" he wrote two books [*The Hobbit* and *The Lord of the Rings*] . . . that have captured the imagination and influenced the thinking of several million readers.

The Tolkiens settled into a comfortable house on Northmoor Road in 1926. In 1929, when their fourth child and first daughter, Priscilla Mary Reuel, was born, a larger house next door became available, and they decided to buy it. They moved in 1930, and finally stayed in one place until 1947.

In 1926 C.S. Lewis joined the English faculty. Tolkien invited him to join the Coalbiters, a group that met to read Icelandic sagas, and they soon began a long friendship. Lewis listened as Tolkien read from the manuscript of *The Silmarillion,* and urged him to complete it. Tolkien helped Lewis struggle with his religious doubts and explorations; when he explained his view of the story of Christ as a myth that had really happened, he helped Lewis find a new Christian faith. Lewis went on to write such overtly Christian writings as *The Screwtape Letters,* as well as the *Chronicles of Narnia* and many other works.

Lewis and Tolkien were two early members of the Inklings, a group that took the place of the Coalbiters once that group had finished reading all the principal Icelandic sagas. The original Inklings group was founded by an Oxford undergraduate, Tangye Lean, to bring together scholars to read and criticize unpublished manuscripts. When Lean left, the name stuck to a group of men, mostly dons at the university, who gathered around Lewis and met regularly. The Inklings were an early audience for Tolkien's readings from *The Hobbit* and *The Lord of the Rings*.

Tolkien had begun *The Hobbit* in 1930, as a story for his children, but abandoned it when they were no longer interested in an evening "story time." In 1936 a friend and a former student mentioned the manuscript to Susan Dagnall, a representative of publishers Allen and Unwin, who subsequently read it and encouraged him to finish it. Her enthusiasm was echoed by that of Rayner Unwin, the ten-year-old son of the publisher, who wrote a favorable report of it for his father. The book was published the following year, and was popular enough that publisher Stanley Unwin suggested he write a sequel. None of the stories he had already begun would do; they wanted more hobbits.

TOLKIEN'S EPIC IS PUBLISHED

It would be twelve years before he finished *The Lord of the Rings* in 1950. In a 1971 BBC radio interview, he recalled, "I remember I actually wept at the denouement." He went on to say, "But then of course there was a tremendous lot of revision," and he made a joke about errors that remained in the manuscript:

> I suppose I'm in a position where it doesn't matter what people think of me now—there were some frightful mistakes in grammar, which from a Professor of English Language and Lit are rather shocking. . . . There was one where I used *bestrode* as the past participle of *bestride!* [laughs]

In 1965, U.S. publisher Ace Books, taking advantage of a loophole in U.S. copyright laws, issued an unauthorized edition of *The Hobbit*, which sold especially well on college campuses. Rather than sue (Ace was legally able to refuse to pay Tolkien any royalties), the author started a quiet campaign pleading for "courtesy to living authors." The resultant outcry persuaded Ace to pay Tolkien a royalty for every copy sold and to promise not to print any more copies. This provided a boon for the authorized U.S. publisher, Ballantine, which profited by the attention and enthusiasm the Ace edition had stirred up.

With the success of *The Hobbit* and *The Lord of the Rings,* Tolkien could afford to retire from teaching and turn his attention to *The Silmarillion*—a daunting prospect, since he had been accumulating and revising it in bits and pieces for forty years. However, between attending to family obligations and responding to questions from readers all over the globe, he made little progress in bringing this massive project to fruition. He finally made an agreement with his youngest son that, should he die before completing the book, Christopher would complete it, a promise that eased his mind.

Tolkien was visiting friends in Bournemouth in late August 1973 when he became ill and was taken to the hospital. At first doctors felt he would recover from the acute bleeding gastric ulcer that had incapacitated him, but he developed a secondary infection and failed rapidly. He died at the age of eighty-one on September 2, 1973.

A SON'S PROMISES

Christopher Tolkien kept his promises to his father. Ronald was buried next to Edith. Their tombstones bear their names, birth and death years, and the names Ronald had given to his *Silmarillion* lovers: Lúthien on hers, Beren on his.

His larger promise—to edit and publish the mass of work his father left—has taken decades. A glance at this book's chronology for the years after Ronald's death will give an idea of the degree to which Christopher has devoted himself to fulfilling his father's plans and dreams.

CHAPTER 1

The Hobbit

READINGS ON
J.R.R. TOLKIEN

The Hobbit Is Rooted in the Tradition of Classic British Children's Novels

Lois R. Kuznets

In comparing *The Hobbit* to Lewis Carroll's *Alice's Adventures in Wonderland* and other works that are considered classic British children's novels, Lois Kuznets points out that Tolkien's work is rooted firmly in that great tradition. Authors of such classics deal similarly with time and space, use an obtrusive narrator, and create characters with whom children can identify. Kuznets, author of *When Toys Come Alive: Narratives of Animation, Metamorphosis, and Development*, has also written a study of Kenneth Grahame, whose *The Wind in the Willows* is often compared to Tolkien's writing.

If there is anything left to say about *The Hobbit*, it is this: no matter how Tolkien wished to deny it, to repudiate those very qualities that confirm it, his first novel is solidly based on the great tradition of the British children's classic.[1] For that reason above all, Tolkien's *The Hobbit*—like Lewis Carroll's *Alice's Adventures in Wonderland*, George Macdonald's *The Princess and the Goblin* and *The Princess and Curdie*, and Kenneth Grahame's *The Wind in the Willows*—still deserves critical consideration.

My aim here is to show how, in *The Hobbit*, in contrast to *The Lord of the Rings*, Tolkien employs a "rhetoric of childhood" highly influenced by these writers, Grahame and Macdonald in particular. I use the word "rhetoric" as Booth does in *The Rhetoric of Fiction*, to designate the means that the literary artist uses to persuade the reader to dwell, at least momentarily,

Excerpted from Lois R. Kuznets, "Tolkien and the Rhetoric of Childhood," in *Tolkien: New Critical Perspectives*, edited by Neil D. Isaacs and Rose A. Zimbardo. Copyright © 1981 by The University Press of Kentucky. Reprinted by permission of The University Press of Kentucky.

within a "realistic" or "fantastic" world totally created and controlled by the writer.[2] The writer exercises rhetorical control largely through means technically known as voice (that is, point of view or narrational stance), but also through style in general as well as through choice of character, characterization, and manipulation of time and space.

The classic rhetoric of childhood combines the following characteristics: an obtrusive narrator, commenting, addressing the reader, and using richly descriptive prose; characters with whom preadolescent children can comfortably identify and who develop and change as they do; an emphasis on the relationship between time and development within a compressed narrative time scheme; a circumscribed geography and a significant concern with the security or danger of specific places in the setting.

I will discuss these rhetorical devices beginning with time and space, moving on to the more problematic point of view and associated stylistic matters, and ending with the complexities of characterization and their implications.

TIME AND SPACE

The Hobbit covers about a year and emphasizes seasonal changes; movements in space are also correlated with changes in season. Baggins, Thorin, and company make major changes in position on solstices and equinoxes. Simple age-old seasonal associations are conventionally exploited: spring is the time of hopeful starting out; summer signals the ripening of adventure; autumn brings despair; winter is total war and death; spring is peace and joyful return. Generally, in children's literature, seasons are also specifically equated with developmental cycles: spring is associated closely with growth and exploration of the outside world, winter with a kind of hibernation or growth plateau. Sharing this common pattern are the openings of *The Hobbit* and *The Wind in the Willows*. Bilbo and Mole emerge from their respective holes in the spring of the year; they return only after much growth and development have taken place. Their spring beginnings contrast with the autumn beginning of *The Fellowship of the Ring*, which heralds another kind of development in Frodo that leaves him without the impulse ever again to respond to spring in Middle-earth.

The three-volume "interlaced" *Lord of the Rings*, covers about one year too, but in *The Hobbit* Tolkien tells the story straightforwardly and quickly, in digestible portions, with a feeling of some closure at the end of each incident. Children, like adults, are capable of delight in suspense and the unexpected, but they cannot for long patiently sustain a sense of incompleteness. Bilbo, in very childlike fashion, having already traveled for months, can hardly stand the short wait (in days) "on the doorstep"; child readers have barely a page of waiting before the light beams on the keyhole. As in this instance, children's literature both divides and compresses time and, therefore, good children's books are episodic despite their underlying unity.

Again in contrast with the trilogy, Tolkien's landscape in *The Hobbit* is a circumscribed bifurcated one with lowlands to the west and forested lands to the east of the central and longitudinal mountains and river. This spatial representation quite neatly divides the world into safe and dangerous sides. Grahame's geography in *The Wind in the Willows* is roughly similar, if less graphic; there the safe field and rich river cultures oppose the Wild Wood, which lies on the other side of The River. Such simple geography not only emblematically indicates outside good and evil but also represents inner states and relative psychic disturbance. So Mole is threatened and experiences sheer psychological "Terror of the Wild Wood" just as Bilbo and the dwarves experience Mirkwood. . . .

In the matter of maturing adventures underground, Carroll's *Alice* is the recognized children's literature exemplum and is, like *The Hobbit*, amenable to both Freudian and Jungian interpretation.[3] *The Hobbit* is also much like other children's classics in its depiction of this highly significant space. On the one hand, no one—certainly not Tolkien—beats Grahame in the detailed description of what one might call the secure "domestic underground": comfortable accommodations for gentlemen of limited (Mole) and extensive (Badger) means.[4] On the other hand, Macdonald shares with Tolkien a fascination with the dangerous "foreign underground": the wonder of mountain caves, their terrors, treasures, and the characteristics of their degenerate inhabitants. The following passage, for instance, is part of Macdonald's long introductory description of the "beautiful terror" of mountains: "But the inside, who shall tell what lies there? Caverns of the awfullest solitude, their walls miles thick, sparkling with ores of gold or silver, copper or iron, tin or mercury, studded perhaps with precious stones—perhaps a brook, with eyeless fish in it, running, running ceaselessly, cold and babbling, through banks crusted with carbuncles and golden topazes, or over a gravel of which some of the stones are rubies and emeralds, perhaps diamonds and sapphires—who can tell?"[5]

As Robert Wolff points out in his study of Macdonald, this passage from *The Princess and Curdie* (1882) and others like it from the totally cave-oriented *The Princess and the Goblin* (1871) closely resemble the writings of the nineteenth-century German Romantics Novalis, Hoffmann, and Tieck.[6] Tolkien's cave descriptions, both in *The Hobbit* and in *The Lord of the Rings*, belong to a long literary line which Macdonald, not Tolkien, introduced into children's literature. Tolkien does, however, combine and relate the safe with the dangerous undergrounds as Grahame and Macdonald do not.

NARRATIVE VOICE

In point of view as in use of time and space Tolkien, in *The Hobbit*, belongs with these writers. The rhetorical element that distinguishes *The Hobbit* most immediately from his later books, is the obtrusive narrator. In *The Hobbit*, the narrator is constantly addressing the reader and is thus involved in a kind of "talking to children," as Tolkien himself regretfully points out.[7] This is, indeed, the most usual voice in all the great classics of British children's literature. A rhetorical convention like any other, the obtrusive narrative voice can be used well or badly. When it is well used, the voice can steer the child along the course of a complicated narrative, Socratically raise certain questions in his or her mind, and point to implications beneath the surface of behavior or events. Abused, it can be cloyingly didactic.

In the work of better children's writers, the obtrusive narrator is the instrument of emotional sensitivity, moral perception, and playfulness. Lewis Carroll is working within this convention when he writes: "'Well!' thought Alice to herself, 'after such a fall as this, I shall think nothing of tumbling downstairs. How brave they'll all think me at home! Why I wouldn't say anything about it even if I fell off the top of the house.' (Which was very likely true.)"[8] C.S. Lewis, who readily admits the influence of the rhetoric of childhood, also uses that convention. He writes, in *The Lion, the Witch and the Wardrobe*, after the sacrifice of Aslan: "I hope no one who reads this book has been quite as miserable as Susan and Lucy were that night; but if you have been—if you've been up all night and cried till you have no more tears left in you—you will know that there comes in the end a sort of quietness. You feel as if nothing was ever going to happen again."[9] Tolkien uses it particularly skillfully when he comments dryly, "You are familiar with Thorin's style on important occasions, so I will not give you any more of it, though he went on a good deal longer than this" (p. 203), or notes about Bilbo's approach to the dragon's lair: "Going on from there was the bravest thing he ever did. The tremendous things that happened afterwards were as nothing compared to it. He fought the real battle in the tunnel alone, before he ever saw the vast danger that lay in wait" (pp. 225f.).

The continued practice of reading aloud to children partly accounts for the persistence of the obtrusive narrator, with its explicitly oral quality. But this convention has always been more than just mechanical; it can be a special gift from adult author to child reader. The obtrusive narrator implicitly promises protection and companionship even when one is reading alone (or when childlike characters are left without protectors like Gandalf). One trusts the voice, at least, to desert neither the characters nor the reader, to say when one should be afraid and therefore alert and prudent and when one—either character or reader—can safely venture on or lay oneself down to sleep. This voice is the voice of a benevolent anthropomorphic god—not only the creator but the guardian of the imaginary universe in which it persuades the reader to dwell. . . .

SENSORY DETAIL

Other aspects of Tolkien's style . . . reveal that the rhetoric of childhood did not come as naturally or as richly to him as to some of his predecessors. Particularly noticeable to the reader of other great children's books is Tolkien's lack of sensory detail. In *The Hobbit*, characters like to eat but when they get a chance to do so they never seem to taste or smell their food; it's all dreams of bacon and eggs. Contrast Tolkien's eating dreams or scenes with Grahame's evocative prose: "When the girl returned, some hours later, she carried a tray, with a cup of fragrant tea steaming on it; and a plate piled up with very hot buttered toast, cut thick, very brown on both sides, with butter running through the holes in it in great golden drops, like honey from the honeycomb. The smell of that buttered toast simply talked to Toad." [10] The visually intriguing sport of smoking pipes and blowing smoke rings is conveyed by Tolkien with far more reality as an oral satisfaction than is eating. The sense of touch, exploited by Macdonald and C.S. Lewis after him is not indulged; sensory discomforts—with which children are unfortunately very familiar—are mentioned but minimized.

Tolkien thought of himself as having "a very strong visual imagination" that was "not so strong in other points." He revealingly doubted "if many authors visualize very closely faces and voices." [11] This suggests not only that lack of sensory imagination already noted but also the nature of Tolkien's visual imagination: he doesn't see things close up very clearly—unlike many children and writers for children—but has a much longer visual span; he is able to reproduce total landscapes and see relationships among landmarks; he is basically uninterested in interior or decorative details. Tolkien is figuratively farsighted rather than nearsighted.

Tolkien's lack of sensory detail and his long view are not particularly characteristic of the rhetoric of childhood, but in other stylistic matters, he is again among the masters. In *The Hobbit*, there is plenty of one thing Carroll's Alice wanted: "conversation." Characters talk to each other naturally and with differentiation among their speech patterns. They do not make speeches much or tell seemingly interminable "digressive" tales, as they are wont to do in the trilogy. They also make up words, like "bebother" and "confustication," and use constructions like "miserabler" as Carroll does. They engage in verbal trickery and combat, riddle games, and raillery—remnants of ancient verbal pastimes that also appear in Macdonald's and Carroll's works. Neither of the latter has characters play the riddle game as straightforwardly as Tolkien does in the Gollum chapter; however, Macdonald's Curdie taunts the goblins in much the same way that Bilbo taunts the spiders in Mirkwood. Another of Macdonald's characters, Diamond in *At the Back of the North Wind*, brings back poetry from other worlds and spiritual experiences, inspired in a Caedmonian fashion [Caedmon: 7th-century Anglo-Saxon poet], as many of Tolkien's characters are. The general interspersion of verse and song in the prose narrative is another remnant of an earlier tradition that has remained longer in children's fiction than in adult and is exploited by all of the authors mentioned. Tolkien's most original touch in the matter of dialogue and the like is to have Gollum talk the true "rhetoric of children," narcissistic baby talk; one wonders whether children don't catch on to this faster than adults.

CHARACTERS AND RELATIONSHIPS

The physical and emotional traits of Tolkien's characters and the relationships among them are well within the rhetoric of childhood. The invention of the beardless, three-to-four-foot-tall hobbit is especially so. In beardlessness, and size (roughly the height of the four-to-seven-year-old child), the hobbit evokes the most primitive type of identification on the part of children. Children's literature abounds with characters from Tom Thumb to Alice whose size is in some fashion contrasted with the demands of the world around them. These characters have, in various ways, to use the power of the psyche to overcome or to take advantage of the limits of their physical power (which is reflected, on a deeper level, by the male characters' lack of a beard).

Significantly, the other notable characteristic of the hobbits, their hairy feet, is virtually ignored in the trilogy. These feet symbolize a relationship to the animal kingdom that often appears in children's literature—where childlike characters are animals, or where children have special relationships with animals from whom they receive uncritical affection and toward whom they can feel superior and grown-up. The hobbits' hairy feet are, however, a vestigial trait related to much less conscious identification with animals on the part of children. Bettelheim, in *The Uses of Enchantment*, describes a whole cycle of animal transformation stories as having a repulsion-recognition-integration theme, through which the child first tries to rid himself of his "animal" instincts, especially sexuality, then recognizes them as part of himself, and finally integrates them into his personality and so controls them.[12] The hobbits' hairy feet are constant reminders of both the good and bad aspects of one's relationship to animals; hairy feet are somewhat repulsive but also allow more freedom of self-expression than even bare feet do. The child in me is both repelled by the grotesquerie and attracted to the freedom of those hairy feet. After all, to wear shoes is one of the continuing restraints and privileges of being grown-up and "civilized."

The hobbit species is truly an original and inspired sub-creation. Certain other creatures or features seem less original when one compares, for example, Tolkien's wily chatty dragon with Grahame's "reluctant dragon." And Gollum of *The Hobbit* is preceded by strange, degenerate animal creatures that live in the caves of Macdonald's *The Princess and the Goblin* and *The Princess and Curdie.* The conception of physical and moral degeneration of both species and individuals living away from fresh air and light is also a prominent theme of the two *Princess* books. Macdonald too uses savior birds and in the great battle at the end of *The Princess and Curdie* a battalion of pigeons rescues the outnumbered forces of good.[13]

The character of the hero or heroine is a central issue in the rhetoric of childhood. In contrast to Frodo [in *The Lord of the Rings*], Bilbo is the typical hero of children's literature with the typical quest. Bilbo and Frodo are exactly the same age at the beginning of their respective quests, but Bilbo is youthful and inexperienced, Frodo much more mature and relatively learned. In addition, the nature of Frodo's quest is not to find himself but to lose himself and so to find himself on another, other-worldly level. Self-integration of Bilbo's type, not self-transcendence of Frodo's type, is *the* quest of children's literature.

RELATIONSHIP BETWEEN THE HERO AND THE CHILD

More specifically, Bilbo, like many heroes of children's literature, displays all the outer traits and needs of the period that Freud designates as latency, when Oedipal and sexual conflicts are temporarily at rest. This period corresponds roughly to the elementary-school years. Erikson identifies it as the "fourth age of man" in which the main conflict is one between "industry and inferiority." This is the period when the child must learn the "fundamentals of technology" and become "ready to handle the utensils, the tools, and weapons used by the big people."[14] That is, among other things, what Bilbo is doing: discovering that he has not only inner resources but outer skills—seeing clearly, moving quietly, throwing stones, as well as developing power to wield the sword—that make it possible for him to function in a world less protected than his home.

The break at that particular period of life from home to public school was the most significant trauma for many an

English schoolboy, as we see not only in adult memoirs but in children's literature of the schoolboy variety (slang from which sometimes surfaces in the prose of *The Hobbit*). The struggle to become one of the boys is present in *The Hobbit* although not so blatantly as in these realistic novels.

Present too, in the fantasy element of the work, is the desire to *repress* rather than express competitive conflict and much of the other psychological conflict of childhood. This repression is characteristic of another kind of children's book: Lili Peller, a child psychologist, calls it "the early tale." The stories that she so designates have in common a denial of conflicts inherent in the dichotomies of male-female, old-young. She notes: "In each story we find a group of loyal friends and we find a Protector who can work magic.... Every member of the group has unique gifts and skills and foibles.... The magician-Protector stays offstage or near the wing and the friends' actions and their feelings really carry the story.... Family relations of all kinds are nonexistent or they are at the very fringe of the story.... Most of them [the characters] belong to different species. Who will compare a monkey with a toad?" [15] Tolkien's story exhibits many of the repressive elements of "the early tale." One might note especially here the absence of contact with "the opposite sex"—a trait that *The Hobbit* shares with the major portion of *The Wind in the Willows*. Without reference to the clear misogyny of *The Lord of the Rings*, even a feminist might find Bilbo, as a character in *The Hobbit*, androgynous rather than misogynous in his bachelorhood. Either male or female children may, therefore, finally come to identify with him. [16]

BILBO'S DEVELOPMENT

One element of Peller's early tale that Tolkien does not replicate is a static quality in terms of the growth and development of the characters. This growth and development in Bilbo is the major theme of the story. But what Tolkien regarded as the end product of that growth and development in 1937 is quite different from what he tried to make it later, by changing the Gollum chapter after he began the trilogy. [17] In the early version, the high point of Bilbo's moral development can only be construed as an expanded concept of *justice* that goes beyond selfish desires to acknowledge Bard's claims: "Now these were fair words and true, if proudly and grimly spoken; and Bilbo thought that Thorin would at once admit what justice was in them" (p. 275).

Bilbo's subsequent renunciation of the Arkenstone perhaps foreshadows his later renunciation of the ring but is well within the morality of fairness and sharing inculcated in children at an early age. This morality is synonymous with justice to them; therefore, a child might be capable of what Bilbo is capable of at the high point of his moral development in *The Hobbit.*

Mercy, however, is not a concept of childhood, as many, including Tolkien himself, have been at pains to point out.[18] Tolkien attempted to write the concept of mercy into Bilbo's development when he revised *The Hobbit* in the 1950s. The moment in "Riddles in the Dark" when Bilbo has a flash of understanding of Gollum's fallen state—"a glimpse of endless unmarked days without light or hope of betterment, hard stone, cold fish, sneaking and whispering" (p. 78)—is not part of the original story nor of the usual rhetoric of childhood.

The "mercy passage" is really connected with the very unchildlike sacrificial development of Frodo's personality and his acknowledgment of his relationship to "it," his shadow, Gollum. In *The Lord of the Rings*, Frodo practically goes mad and the three small creatures—Frodo, Gollum, and Sam—who move across the devastated landscape are emblematic not only of man's state in general, but also of the struggle in the divided psyche among superego, id, and ego.[19] Sam, the ego figure, survives, but he is not, after all, prominent even among the several "heroes" of the narrative.[20]

Bilbo's resourcefulness and basic sanity are honored in *The Hobbit,* not overshadowed by saintliness, as Sam's similar qualities are in the trilogy. The contrast between Bilbo and Frodo as heroes recalls Chesterton's distinction: "In the fairy tales, the cosmos goes mad, but the hero does not go mad. In the modern novels, the hero is mad before the book begins and suffers from the harsh steadiness and cruel sanity of the cosmos."[21] In most good children's literature, as in fairy tales, the hero or heroine appears to represent the healthy developing ego with its capacity for just action and for survival in *this* world. Bilbo lives. And Bilbo joins Alice, Curdie, Mole, Rat, and Toad in the gallery of such sane and down-to-earth protagonists. In this way, as in others, *The Hobbit* belongs to the great tradition of "the rhetoric of childhood."

NOTES

Note: Unless otherwise indicated, quotations from *The Hobbit* are from the Houghton Mifflin edition (Boston, 1938).

1. In an early foreword to *The Fellowship of the Ring,* Tolkien seems to concede that *The Hobbit* was composed for his children: "Since my children and others of their age, who first heard of the Ring, have grown older with the years, this book speaks more plainly of the darker things which lurked only on the borders of the earlier tale" (New York: Ace Books, n.d.), p. 9. In a late interview with Philip Norman, Tolkien denies that *The Hobbit* is a children's book and repudiates "anything that in any way was marked out in 'The Hobbit' as for children instead of just for people." "The Prevalence of Hobbits," *New York Times Magazine,* Jan. 15, 1967, p. 100.

   This is in clear contrast to C.S. Lewis who chose the children's story because it was "the best art-form" for those things he had to say. Lewis, "Three Ways of Writing for Children," in *Of Other Worlds, Essays and Stories,* ed. Walter Hooper (New York, 1966), p. 23.

2. Wayne Booth, *The Rhetoric of Fiction* (Chicago, 1961).

3. The most famous of these analyses of Alice is William Empson's "The Child as Swain" in *Some Versions of Pastoral* (New York, 1950). Randel Helms does the same for *The Hobbit* in "The Hobbit as Swain," *Tolkien's World* (Boston, 1974), pp. 41–55. See also Dorothy Matthews, "The Psychological Journey of Bilbo Baggins" in *A Tolkien Compass,* ed. Jared Lobdell (La Salle, Ill., 1975), pp. 29–42, and Marion Zimmer Bradley, "Men, Halflings and Hero-Worship," in *Tolkien and the Critics,* ed. Neil D. Isaacs and Rose A. Zimbardo (Notre Dame, Ind., 1968), pp. 109–27.

4. We are introduced to Badger's home thus: "He shuffled on in front of them, carrying the light and they followed him, nudging each other in an anticipating sort of way, down a long, gloomy, and to tell the truth, decidedly shabby passage, into a sort of central-hall, out of which they could dimly see other long tunnel-like passages mysterious and without apparent end. But there were doors in the hall as well—stout oaken comfortable looking doors. One of these Badger flung open, and at once they found themselves in all the glow and warmth of a large fire-lit kitchen." Another paragraph is devoted to describing that kitchen, ending with: "The ruddy brick floor smiled up at the smoky ceiling; the oaken settles, shiny with long wear, exchanged cheerful glances with each other; plates on the dresser grinned at pots on the shelf, and the merry fire-

light flickered and played over everything without distinction." Kenneth Grahame, *The Wind in the Willows* (1908; rpt. New York, 1969), pp. 58–59.

5. Macdonald, *The Princess and Curdie* (1882; rpt. London, 1964), p. 11. Sharing my sense of Tolkien's debt to Macdonald in this and other ways are both Hugh Crago and Robert L. Wolff. See Crago, "Remarks on the Nature and Development of Fantasy," in J.S. Ryan, *Tolkien: Cult or Culture?* (Armidale, Australia, 1969), Appendix D, esp. pp. 216–20, and Wolff, *The Golden Key: A Study of the Fiction of George Macdonald* (New Haven, Conn., 1961), p. 9.

6. Wolff, pp. 170–71.

7. Tolkien says, "'The Hobbit' was written in what I should now regard as a bad style, as if one were talking to children." Norman, p. 100.

8. Carroll, *Alice's Adventures in Wonderland* (1865; rpt. Baltimore, Md., 1946), p. 25.

9. Lewis, *The Lion, the Witch and the Wardrobe* (New York, 1950), p. 128.

10. Grahame, p. 135.

11. Norman, p. 102.

12. Bettelheim, *The Uses of Enchantment: The Meaning and Importance of Fairy Tales* (1975; rpt. New York, 1977), pp. 227–310 and passim.

13. Tolkien's very use of the word "goblin" in *The Hobbit,* which he changes to "orc" in the trilogy (and in his revision of the Gollum chapter), perhaps subconsciously reflects his debt to Macdonald.

14. Erik H. Erikson, "The Eight Ages of Man," *Childhood and Society,* 2nd ed. (New York, 1963), pp. 247–74, esp. 258–60. Bilbo also at first resembles the third son or "Dummy" in fairy tales that Bettelheim analyzes, p. 75.

15. Peller, "Daydreams and Children's Favorite Books," in *The Causes of Behavior,* 2nd ed., ed. Judy F. Rosenblith and Wesley Allinsmith (Boston, 1970), pp. 469–75.

16. Bettelheim claims that for children the sex of the protagonist comes not to matter, p. 59.

17. For an analysis of the changes Tolkien made in *The Hobbit* see Bonniejean Christensen, "Gollum's Character Transformation in *The Hobbit,*" *Tolkien Compass,* ed. Lobdell, pp. 9–28.

18. Tolkien, "On Fairy-Stories," p. 44. See also Bettelheim, p. 144.

19. Compare Tolkien's portrayal of the Frodo-Gollum-Sam struggles with Freud's description of the close relationship between the Superego and the Id and of the Ego's struggles to serve, mediate, and temper both their excesses while developing and strengthening itself in relation to the outside world. See Sigmund Freud, *The Ego and the Id*, trans. Joan Rivière (New York, 1960).
20. Merry and Pippin come closest to being children's heroes.
21. G.K. Chesterton, "The Dragon's Grandmother," *Tremendous Truths* (New York, 1927), p. 126.

Adult Themes in a Tale to Be Read to Children

Paul H. Kocher

Although *The Hobbit* uses such child-pleasing devices as direct address and sound effects meant to be read aloud, Tolkien treats several issues that can only be comprehended by adults, writes Paul H. Kocher. Although the story is suitable for children, it operates throughout at two separate levels of maturity. Besides *Master of Middle-earth: The Fiction of J.R.R. Tolkien* (from which this essay is excerpted) and a book on Tolkien's *The Silmarillion*, Kocher has also written on Elizabethan England and Christopher Marlowe.

The beginning of wisdom in understanding *The Hobbit* is to think of Tolkien, or another adult, in a chair by the fireside telling the story to a semicircle of children sitting on the floor facing him. From the opening paragraphs hardly a page goes by in which the narrator does not address the children directly in the first person singular. Since the breed of hobbits has just sprung freshly minted from his brain, he loses no time in telling his young listeners about how they look and behave, notably their shyness "when large stupid folk like you and me come blundering along," and he ends his description by, "Now you know enough to go on with. As I was saying. . . ."[1] Sometimes he uses the direct address technique to create anticipation, as in introducing Gandalf: "Gandalf! If you had heard only a quarter of what I have heard about him, and I have only heard very little of all there is to hear, you would be prepared for any sort of remarkable tale." Sometimes his remarks to the child audience take on a genial, joking tone, as in pointing out the flaw in Bilbo's

1. All references are to *The Hobbit* (Boston: Houghton Mifflin Co., 1967).

plan for freeing the captive dwarves by putting them into barrels (his inability to put himself into one): "Most likely you saw it some time ago and have been laughing at him; but I don't suppose you would have done half as well yourselves in his place." Then, there are jocular interjections of no special moment, but aimed at maintaining a playful intimacy: "If you want to know what *cram* is, I can only say that I don't know the recipe; but it is biscuitish. . . ."

Tolkien also makes the technique work for him expositorily in making clear to the youngsters important shifts in the plot sequence. Normally he describes every scene from Bilbo's point of view, and describes none in which Bilbo himself is not present. But Chapter XIV diverges to report what happened at Lake-town, while Bilbo and the dwarves were shut inside Erebor, when Smaug the dragon attacked the town and was killed by Bard the archer. So Tolkien opens the chapter with the sentence: "Now if you wish, like the dwarves, to hear news of Smaug, you must go back again to the evening when he smashed the door and flew off in a rage, two days before." Incidentally, this careful score-keeping of days elapsed at every stage of his tale is typical of Tolkien. Having narrated events at Lake-town he steers his young audience back to their hero with the words, "Now we will return to Bilbo and the dwarves." And, on occasion, in order to remind them of an important fact, already explained some time before, which they may have forgotten, he repeats it. Thus when the Master in Lake-town judges Thorin's claim to the treasure by inheritance to be a fraud Tolkien reiterates what Gandalf and Elrond acknowledged earlier: "He was wrong. Thorin, of course, was really the grandson of the king under the Mountain. . . ." This care in keeping the plot crystal clear is adapted to the possible squirmings and short attentiveness of the children he is speaking to.

DEVICES AIMED AT A YOUNG AUDIENCE

Also for their benefit is Tolkien's method all through *The Hobbit* of prefacing the introduction into the story of each new race with a paragraph or so setting forth in plain words whatever needs to be known about its looks, its habits, its traits, and whether it is good or bad. He has started this practice off with the hobbits. He extends it to trolls, dwarves, goblins, eagles, elves, and lakemen as each of these makes its entry. These little capsules of racial qualities are enlivened usually with personal interjections: "Yes, I am afraid trolls do behave like that, even those with only one head each"; or "Eagles are not kindly birds," but they did come to the rescue of Bilbo's party, and "a very good thing too!" Goblins are wicked and bear a special grudge against dwarves "because of the war which you have heard mentioned, but which does not come into this tale." Elves are hunters by starlight at the edges of the wood and are "Good People." After such set pieces no small auditor will be in any doubt as to which people he should cheer for. The whole tale gives him a very firm moral framework by which to judge.[2]

Another minor but persistent device in the manner of its telling likewise is meant to delight childish ears. The prose is full of sound effects, which the eye of the reader might miss but the hearing of the listener would not. Bilbo's doorbell rings *ding-dong-a-ling-dang;* Gandalf's smoke rings go *pop!;* the fire from his wand explodes with a *poof;* Bombur falls out of a tree *plop* onto the ground; Bilbo falls *splash!* into the water, and so on at every turn. Nor are these sound effects limited to the prose. Many of the poems are designed more for onomatopoeic purposes than for content. One prime example is the song of the goblins underground after their capture of Bilbo and the dwarves, with its *Clash, crash! Crush, smash!* and *Swish, smack! Whip crack* and *Ho, ho, my lad.* The elves' barrel-rolling song has all the appropriate noises, from *roll-roll-rolling* to *splash plump!* and *down they bump!* Tolkien knows that up to a certain age children like their stories to be highly audible.[3]

But the question as to what age Tolkien is addressing cannot be long deferred. Probably he himself had no precise answer in mind, but the very nature of the tale and the methods of its telling draw the principal parameters. The children listening to its recital must be young enough not to resent the genial fatherliness of the I-You technique, the encapsulated expositions, sound effects, and the rest, yet old enough

2. Only in the very last paragraph does Tolkien attach this limited framework to a wider cosmic order, foreshadowing the ideas discussed in the next chapter, as Gandalf asks Bilbo laughingly: "Surely you don't disbelieve the prophecies, because you had a hand in bringing them about yourself? You don't really suppose, do you, that all your adventures and escapes were managed by mere luck, just for your sole benefit?" This reference is too fleeting to affect the atmosphere of the tale as a whole and would not, I suppose, mean much to children. 3. On one or two occasions Tolkien's choice of similes is obviously dictated by children's interests: Bilbo laughs at the dwarf Fili wrapped around with spider webs "jerking his stiff arms and legs as he danced on the spider-string under his armpits, just like one of those funny toys bobbing on a wire." But his atrocious punning in describing the origins of the game of golf seems destined for the unlucky ears of adults.

to be able to cope with the fairly stiff vocabulary used on many occasions and to make at least something of the maturer elements that keep cropping up in what they hear. For, although *The Hobbit* is predominantly juvenile fiction, it is not all of a piece. Much of the confusion about it arises from the fact that it contains episodes more suited to the adult mind than the child's.

EPISODES FOR ADULT MINDS

One such is Bard's claim to a share in Smaug's treasure after he has killed the dragon, a claim made not only on his own behalf but also on behalf of the elves and the people of Lake-town. Tolkien has built up here a very pretty conundrum in law, equity, and morals. The treasure consists of a hoard gathered by Thorin's ancestors, but Smaug has mingled with it unestimated valuables belonging to Bard's forebears in the city of Dale. So Bard has a clear legal claim to some unclear fraction. The Lake-town men have no title in law to any portion but rest their case on the argument that Thorin owes them an equitable share because the dwarves roused Smaug to destroy their town, leaving them now destitute; and besides they helped to outfit the dwarf expedition when it was penniless. Bard invokes for them, in fact, the general principle that the wealthy "may have pity beyond right on the needy that befriended them when they were in want." And what of the elves' contention that the dwarves stole the treasure from them in the first place, as against the dwarf reply that they took it in payment for goldsmith work for the elves under a contract which their king later refused to honor? A Solomon might well pick his way gingerly among these claims and counterclaims, especially when faced with Thorin's answer that he is not responsible for Smaug's devastations, and will not bargain under threat of siege by an army anyway. If so, what is even the wise child to make of it all?

Well, Tolkien does not leave his audience, young or old, without some guidance. He comes right out and says of Bard's claim when first uttered, "Now these were fair words and true, if proudly and grimly spoken; and Bilbo thought that Thorin would at once admit what justice was in them." Thorin's refusal is characterized as dwarfish "lust" for gold fevered by brooding on the dragon's hoard. The experienced reader of Tolkien's other writings recognizes here his usual condemnation of the cardinal sin of "possessiveness," which besets dwarves as a race and which indeed is at the core of all the evil underlying the War of the Ring, and much other ill in the world besides. But Bard is a little too eager to resort to arms, being himself somewhat afflicted by the same curse. He has to be rebuked by the elf king, who contrives to conquer the same inclination to greed in his own breast, "Long will I tarry, ere I begin this war for gold. . . . Let us hope still for something that will bring reconciliation." Bilbo tries to break the deadlock by setting a moral example, but one which, oddly, requires an initial act of theft. After hiding in his pocket the great jeweled Arkenstone he steals from the recovered treasure, on the theory that it represents the one-fourteenth share promised him by the dwarves, Bilbo carries it secretly to Bard's camp by night, gives it to him freely to use as a bargaining counter against Thorin, and returns to the dwarves inside the mountain to face the music. For all this he is highly praised by Gandalf, surely a spokesman for Tolkien. Bilbo's self-sacrifice does not work out as planned, however, and open war between the contestants for Smaug's gold is averted only by the unforeseen attack of an army of goblins, which unites them against the common enemy. Tolkien's solution of the complex problem of ownership is finally moral. It comes about through the dying Thorin's repentance for his greed, which leads his followers to a generous sharing of the hoard with their new friends. This strongly fortifies the moral tone of the adventure, which began sordidly enough from motives of profit and revenge. But a good deal of rather adult territory has to be traversed to reach this consummation. One wonders what most child auditors would get out of it beyond the general impression that it is wrong to fight over who owns what. In this climactic spot the story really operates at two separate levels of maturity.

A similar double track seems to run through that other critical episode of Bilbo's encounter with Gollum in the tunnels under the goblin mountain. The riddle game the two play would be fun for audiences of any age, as its prototype was in Norse and Anglo-Saxon literature. But the case may well be otherwise when it comes to the portrayal of Gollum's character, with its mixture of cruelty, greed, and miserable loneliness, and Bilbo's response of horror, fear, and pity. Taken alone, any one of these emotions is as familiar to a child as to his parents, but their skillful blending as achieved by Tolkien requires some sophistication of understanding, which comes only with years. Particularly the pity that causes Bilbo to spare the life of a vile creature whom he hates and fears seems a high moral quality of which Tolkien writes, over the heads of all save a mature audience: "A sudden understanding, a pity mixed with horror, welled up in Bilbo's heart: a glimpse of endless unmarked days without light or hope of betterment. . . ." Tolkien is already looking ahead to that scene of revelation in *The Lord of the Rings* in which Gandalf tells Frodo that Bilbo's compassion in sparing Gollum would later save the world. However that may be, in *The Hobbit* the whole episode is one more example to Tolkien's writing at the same time both for children and for the parents who will often be reading them the tale. A fair enough practice, provided it can be so managed as not to confuse or irritate both parties.

SLY DIGS AT MODERN LIFE

Plenty of other passages of the same double character come readily to mind, frequently in the form of sly hits by Tolkien at some favorite targets in modern life. He pokes fun, for instance, at the stodgy respectability of hobbit (or human) society which brands as "queer" any hobbit who travels to foreign parts or has even mildly unusual experiences. The family of such a black sheep always hastens to hush up the offense. Finding himself "no longer quite respectable" on his return from his adventure, Bilbo "took to writing poetry and visiting the elves." Whereupon his neighbors thought him mad. Tolkien laughs at this same rationalistic rejection of fantasy again in the Lake-town episode when he writes that "some young people in the town openly doubted the existence of any dragon in the mountain, and laughed at the greybeards and gammers who said that they had seen him flying in the sky in their younger days"—this despite the fact that Smaug is snoring on his hoard not many miles to the north. Or, another shaft at modern skeptical materialism: ". . . one morning long ago in the quiet of the world, when there was less noise and more green, and the hobbits were still numerous and prosperous. . . ." Or, more plainly still, Tolkien's usual vendetta against our machine age showing through his remarks about goblins, that they love wheels and engines: "It is not unlikely that they invented some of the machines that have since troubled the world, especially the ingenious devices for killing large numbers of people at once," but in Bilbo's day "they had not advanced (as it is called) so far." Tolkien was ecologist, champion of the extraordinary, hater of "progress," lover of handicrafts, detester of war long before such attitudes became fashionable.

Besides the paramount interest *The Hobbit* can claim in its own right as the earliest specimen of Tolkien's fiction to be published and therefore as showing his art in its infancy, it has also great interest as the immediate precursor—and, to some extent, source—of the far more finished *Lord of the Rings.* In the Foreword to the latter work Tolkien describes *The Hobbit* as being drawn irresistibly toward the materials he had been assembling for several years past to tell the history of the earlier Ages of Middle-earth. So much so that glimpses crept into it "unbidden of things higher or deeper or darker than its surface: Durin, Moria, Gandalf, the Necromancer, the Ring.". . .

THE RING: LINK BETWEEN *THE HOBBIT* AND *THE LORD OF THE RINGS*

Of special import is the use Tolkien makes of the Ring he first described in *The Hobbit* as a prize won by Bilbo from Gollum in the riddle contest. Judging by the text of that story as a whole, Tolkien originally thought of the Ring only as one of those rings of invisibility that abound in fairy tales, wonder-working but harmless. Bilbo puts it on his finger and takes it off frequently as a means of escape from dangers that threaten him from time to time in caves, forests, dungeons, and battles. Yet it does not enslave him or impair his moral outlook in the slightest. On the contrary, he has become a stronger and better hobbit by the time the story ends. After this first version had been completed Tolkien began writing *The Lord of the Rings* as a sequel and only then, it seems, conceived of the scheme of taking over Bilbo's Ring and turning it into the potent instrument of evil around which swirls all the action of the epic. Bilbo's finding of it, which in *The Hobbit* is merely a turning point in his personal "career," was to be magnified into a turning point in the history of Middle-earth. The Ring itself, which *The Hobbit* does not report as belonging to the Necromancer or anybody else, was to be attributed to Sauron as maker and master, in order to account for its malignant power over anyone wearing it.

The Ring, therefore, is the link that inseparably binds the later epic to the earlier children's story. But how to explain the glaring differences between Bilbo's harmless little gold band and Sauron's ruling Ring on which hung the fate of the world? Tolkien does not really try to explain them in any detail, but he does give some hints to pacify the curious reader. In the section of his Prologue to the second (1965) edition of the epic, titled "Of the Finding of the Ring," Tolkien remarks that Bilbo had not told his friends the true story of how he obtained the Ring and that Gandalf had long suspected the falsehood. Such a lapse on the part of a usually truthful hobbit struck Gandalf as very "strange and suspicious" and made him begin to doubt that the Ring was the innocent plaything it seemed on the surface. Of course, Gandalf knew the story of Sauron's Ring. He was starting to wonder what the cause of Bilbo's deceit could be and to connect it dimly with the Ring that had come so mysteriously into his possession.

IT'S A MISTAKE TO TALK DOWN TO CHILDREN

As Tolkien biographer Humphrey Carpenter notes, Tolkien changed his mind about how children should be addressed in a story.

For [*The Hobbit*] *is* a children's story. Despite the fact that it had been drawn into his mythology, Tolkien did not allow it to become overwhelmingly serious or even adult in tone, but stuck to his original intention of amusing his own and perhaps other people's children. Indeed he did this too consciously and deliberately at times in the first draft, which contains a large number of 'asides' to juvenile readers, remarks such as 'Now you know quite enough to go on with' and 'As we shall see in the end.' He later removed many of these, but some remain in the published text—to his regret, for he came to dislike them, and even to believe that any deliberate talking down to children is a great mistake in a story. 'Never mind about the young!' he once wrote. 'I am not interested in the "child" as such, modern or otherwise, and certainly have no intention of meeting him/her half way, or a quarter of the way. It is a mistaken thing to do anyway, either useless (when applied to the stupid) or pernicious (when inflicted on the gifted).' But when he wrote *The Hobbit* he was still suffering from what he later called 'the contemporary delusions about "fairy-stories" and children'—delusions that not long afterwards he made a conscious decision to renounce.

Humphrey Carpenter, *Tolkien: A Biography*. Boston: Houghton Mifflin, 1977.

By this new element prefacing *The Lord of the Rings*, as well as by some textual modifications in the later editions of *The Hobbit*, Tolkien provides for the necessary transition from the latter's mere ring of invisibility to the epic's great Ring of Power. Even so, of course, for the purpose of *The Hobbit* Bilbo's ring continues to be only a toy, useful for escapes and escapades, but having no deeper moral significance. No reader who had not previously read the epic would sense anything malefic about it. The story of *The Hobbit* has its own kind of logic quite different from that of the epic. To confuse them is to do a disservice to both tales. In sum, it is important to see *The Hobbit* as essentially independent of the epic, though serving as a quarry of important themes for the larger work....

If *The Hobbit* is a quarry it is one in which the blocks of stone lie scattered about in a much looser and less imposing pattern than that in which the epic assembles those which it chooses to borrow. For example, Bilbo's enemies are serial, not united under any paragon of evil, as is to happen in the epic. *The Hobbit's* trolls, goblins (orcs), spiders, and dragon know nothing of one another and are all acting on their own. They are certainly not shown to be servants of the nameless and nebulous Necromancer, whose only function in the story is to cause Gandalf to leave Bilbo and company to confront exciting perils unaided for a time. Nor, as has been said, is that magician linked in any way with the Ring, which comes out of nowhere belonging to no one. Also, as there is no alliance on behalf of evil so there is none against it. Dwarves, elves, and men act mainly for their selfish interests, often at cross-purposes, until a coalition is forced upon them by a goblin army hostile to all at the very end. Even then the issue is relatively localized and not worldwide in its ramifications....

THE LEAP FROM CHILDREN'S TALE TO EPIC

The case is the same for the individual characters and the races in *The Hobbit* who will reappear in *The Lord of the Rings*. Tolkien's abrupt leap from a children's tale to an epic of heroic struggle requires a radical elevation of stature for all of them....

Much of this need for upgrading the characters and the plot of *The Hobbit* arises from Tolkien's treatment of them in many situations of that tale as seriocomic. He evidently believes that the children will enjoy laughing at them some-

times, as a relief from shivering in excitement sympatheti-
cally with them at others. In truth, *The Hobbit* is seldom far
from comedy. Tolkien begins by making Bilbo the butt of
Gandalf's joke in sending the dwarves unexpectedly to eat up
all his food, proceeds on to the lamentable humor of the troll
scene, hangs his dwarves up in trees, rolls them in barrels,
touches the riddle scene with wit, makes the talk between
Bilbo and Smaug triumphantly ridiculous, and tops it all off
with Bilbo's return home to find his goods being auctioned
off and his reputation for respectable stupidity in ruins. It
must be acknowledged that the comedy is not invariably successful and that Tolkien's wry paternal manner of addressing
his young listeners does not always avoid an air of talking
down, which sets the teeth on edge. Nevertheless, *The Hobbit*
was never meant to be a wholly serious tale, nor his young
audience to listen without laughing often. In contradistinc-
tion, *The Lord of the Rings* does on occasion evoke smiles,
but most of the time its issues go too deep for laughter.

The Nature of Heroism in a Comic World

Katharyn F. Crabbe

Although Bilbo Baggins is a funny little character who seems to have little in common with the mythic, godlike heroes he admires, he is called to his own kind of heroism in *The Hobbit*, writes Katharyn F. Crabbe. He seems ridiculous in his first comic adventures, but gradually becomes the kind of hero Tolkien respects: the average person, without divine qualities, who is willing to risk his life for others. Besides the full-length study of Tolkien from which this essay is excerpted, Crabbe is the author of a biography of British author Evelyn Waugh.

Rather than being a simple and episodic little adventure story, *The Hobbit* is a carefully structured tale that uses a principle of progression (of journeys to the underworld, of the quality of opponents) to create a sense of working toward a climax.... The journey motif, the "There and Back Again" part of the story, encloses the two progressions in a circular structure which in turn gives the story a sense of completion.

Within the tidy circular structure, Tolkien develops two major and universal themes, both as accessible to children as they are to adults: the nature of heroism in a comic world and the conflict between good and evil. These are typical fairy-tale themes; however, Tolkien's fairy tale is distinguished from most others by the complexity he accords to these issues and by the way he combines them with a far less common theme in children's books, the power of language.

THE NATURE OF HEROISM

A distinctive part of Tolkien's fiction is his vision of what it means to be a hero and what is the nature of heroism. His

Excerpted from *J.R.R. Tolkien*, by Katharyn F. Crabbe. Copyright © 1981 by Frederic Ungar Publishing Company, Inc. Reprinted by permission of The Continuum Publishing Company.

concern with heroism in *The Hobbit* is limited in scope to a kind of hero we may call low mimetic—the hero who is no better than we are, neither in kind nor in degree. And that hero is, of course, Bilbo Baggins. From the first scenes of the book, Bilbo's limitations, his differences from the high-mimetic heroes of myth who are either gods or godlike men, very different from us, are clear. Bilbo is "very respectable," which means he "never had any adventures or did anything unexpected." Gandalf, the wizard, whose machinations set Bilbo in motion, understands clearly that Bilbo is not a mythic hero, and he understands that mythic heroes are high mimetic, but as he points out to the dwarves, "I tried to find one; but warriors are busy fighting one another in distant lands, and in this neighborhood heroes are scarce, or simply not to be found." As in that most typical of British fairy tales, "Jack the Giant Killer," the best possibility for heroism in the Shire is to be found in a burglar.

Bilbo Baggins, then, has possibilities. He is, for example, the son of "the fabulous Belladonna Took" and may through her be descended from fairies. As a result, there is something more to Bilbo, "something that only [waits] for a chance to come out." Furthermore, like many low-mimetic heroes, Bilbo has a taste for real heroes of the high-mimetic kind—he loves "wonderful tales . . . about dragons and goblins and giants and the rescue of princesses and the unexpected luck of widow's sons." That is, even the least likely looking hobbit has by inheritance and imagination some heroic possibilities.

HEROES AND NONHEROES

Just as Bilbo's sense of his own possibilities as a hero increases throughout the story, so does the seriousness of his motives. His first adventure, in which he and all the company are captured by trolls, is strictly a comic event. Bilbo is depicted as a being of limited experience, one whose sheltered life keeps him from understanding the ways of the world, particularly the part of the world where people "have seldom even heard of the King," that is, where the rules differ from those of the Shire. Thus, his naivete, his lack of competence, and his taste for animal comforts, which he shares with the dwarves and the reader, are all roundly ridiculed.

As the book progresses, however, Bilbo's ridiculousness is tempered with quite another quality. By the time he is captured and escapes from the goblins and from Gollum, his determination to return to the goblin caverns and search for his friends has the effect of connecting him with two significant high-mimetic heroes: Christ and Gandalf. The connection with Christ is tenuous but real, resulting from the conjunction of the language of the passage with the New Testament "greater love hath no man than this: that he lay down his life for his friend," as Tolkien writes, "He wondered whether he ought not, now he had the magic ring, to go back into the horrible, horrible tunnels and look for his friends." The connection with Gandalf is less tenuous; it results from Bilbo's willingness to assume the role of shepherd that Gandalf has portrayed so far and is trying to persuade the dwarves to help him portray again: "Gandalf was saying that they could not possibly go on with their journey leaving Mr. Baggins in the hands of the goblins without trying to find out if he was alive or dead, and without trying to rescue him."

"After all he is my friend," said the wizard, "and not a bad little chap." Gandalf and Bilbo, the high-mimetic and low-mimetic heroes, sharing a willingness to return to the "horrible, horrible tunnels" to save their friends, are set apart from the dwarves, who are ruled by their own fears: "If we have got to go back now into those abominable tunnels to look for him, then drat him, I say." Dwarves are not, as the narrator says later, bad people, but they are not heroes.

INFLUENCES BEYOND THE HERO'S CONTROL

Once Bilbo and Gandalf are set up as representing the low-mimetic and high-mimetic sides of the hero, Gandalf may leave to attend to "some pressing business away south." His concern with and responsibility for the world beyond, foreshadowed early in his meeting Thorin's father in the dungeons of the Necromancer and in his decision not to let the Wargs "have it all their own way," looks forward to his return in time for the Battle of the Five Armies with its wider implications for Middle-earth.

Gandalf leaves Thorin and Company with a series of warnings that sound very like Christian's exhortations to himself in *Pilgrim's Progress:* "We may meet again before this is all over and then again we may not. That depends on your luck and on your courage and sense." That is, not everything is foreordained. Both God and man have a hand in shaping all that happens: God through the medium of grace, which Tolkien calls "luck," and man through his physical and rational excellences, bravery and sense, which, at their best, represent the God-like in man.

That Gandalf is only a hero of a higher order or perhaps a messenger of God is suggested by his own limitations—he can be afraid, though he is a wizard and, he admits, his success in bringing the troop through the mountains has depended upon the same forces on which they must rely—"good management and good luck."

THE LONER AND THE SOCIAL HERO

While Gandalf, the high-mimetic hero, is a loner, one particularly important quality in Bilbo's heroism as it develops in the episodes before Thorin and Company reach the city of Esgaroth upon the long lake is its essential socialness. From the moment Bilbo bursts out of his house without his pipe or his pipe-weed, or even a pocket-handkerchief, his movement has always been *toward* the dwarves. Separated from them by Wood-elves, he always moves toward the company of the adventurers. The paradox is that although he always moves *toward*, Bilbo is also always gaining in confidence, competence, and character—all the qualities that lead to self-sufficiency. By the time the dwarves escape from the caverns of the Wood-elves, Bilbo is clearly the leader, and even Thorin must agree to follow him. In doing what he must do to remain a part of the group, Bilbo takes responsibility for it; taking responsibility makes him a leader and sets him apart, isolates him from the group, as illustrated in the description of the escape from the caverns of the Wood-elves: "He was in the dark tunnel, floating in icy water, all alone—for you cannot count friends that are all packed up in barrels."

A WIDER RESPONSIBILITY

By the time of the escape from the Wood-elves, Bilbo has developed as far as is possible in the direction of his small society. Yet the end of the quest has not been achieved. The possibilities for continuing are two: Bilbo may stop in his development (as Mark Twain's Tom Sawyer does) and simply lead the dwarves to the treasure, or he may continue to develop in some way that parallels the continuation of the quest. The first possibility is unlikely, for it would reduce the importance of the final episode to a simple working out of plot. The tale would become mere episodic adventure instead of a unified quest. But if Bilbo is to continue to develop, which direction must he take? The answer is provided in Gandalf's example: As Gandalf's "some pressing business away south" suggests a responsibility to the wider world beyond the company, Bilbo eventually finds that he has a wider responsibility, too—to the men of Esgaroth, to the king of the Wood-elves, to the Five Armies. And yet, Thorin and Company cannot be utterly deserted, for they are a part of that wider world too.

The movement of Bilbo away from the society of Thorin and Company is evident as soon as the party leaves Esgaroth for the Lonely Mountain—and it is here that the sense of making Bilbo a hobbit rather than another dwarf or an elf becomes clear—he is with the company but not of them. Though the company finds the door in the mountain without too much delay, they are quite unable to guess its secret until a day when "the dwarves all went wandering off in various directions. . . . All day Bilbo sat gloomily in the grassy bay gazing at the stone, or out west through the narrow opening." Here the real movement of Bilbo away from the company begins, and it begins in contemplation of the west— the source of wisdom and creativity, though also the symbol of the end.

THE HERO INITIATES ACTION

Tolkien uses structural repetition to demonstrate Bilbo's growth in this episode. Once the door is opened and Bilbo is in the tunnel, the situation is very like that following the escape from the goblins' tunnel when Bilbo was pursued by Gollum: He accepts his duty to do for the dwarves, even though he cannot (and does not) hope that the dwarves will do for him:

> The most that can be said for the dwarves is this: they intended to pay Bilbo really handsomely for his services; they had brought him to do a nasty job for them, and they did not mind the little fellow doing it if he would; but they would all have done their best to get him out of trouble, if he got into it, as they did in the case of the trolls at the beginning of their adventures before they had any reason for being grateful to him. There it is: dwarves are not heroes, but calculating folk with a great idea of the value of money; some are tricky and treacherous and pretty bad lots; some are not, but are decent enough people like Thorin and Company, if you don't expect too much.

There are two important suggestions about Tolkien's view of the nature of heroism in this passage. First, it suggests that heroism is active rather than reactive, because Thorin and Company are steady and brave in rescuing friends in need, as Thorin's reaction when Smaug leaves his den will show. But Bilbo must be the initiator of action, not just a reactor. And he becomes an initiator when he steps into the tunnel and begins, for the first time, to move out away from the company and toward the wide world. As was true when he escaped from the goblins, his most heroic act in this scene is a psychological one: Once out of the horrible goblin caves, Bilbo had decided to go back inside to search for his companions if necessary. Here, once inside the tunnel, Bilbo makes another heroic decision—to keep going further despite the agonizing fear he feels when he hears Smaug's snoring and sees his red glow.

This is an important step for Bilbo, because it transforms him. Smaug's dream, prophetic as it is, features no burglars and no grocers. Instead, it is "an uneasy dream (in which a warrior, altogether insignificant in size, but provided with a bitter sword and great courage, figured most unpleasantly)." In deciding to go on alone, Bilbo becomes the warrior that Gandalf was looking for, and Smaug's dream of a warrior foreshadows the gift of the mithril mail Thorin will give Bilbo in recognition of his bravery.

THE HERO CONTINUES WHEN HOPE IS GONE

In the encounter with Smaug, the confrontation with the men of Dale, and the Battle of the Five Armies, Bilbo demonstrates the final defining quality of his low-mimetic heroism, the ability to go on when there is no hope. Whether the issue is recovering the treasure by getting rid of Smaug ("Personally, I have no hopes at all . . ."), or rescuing dwarves from Wood-elves ("he was not as hopeful as they were"), Bilbo's hopelessness is always short-lived and gives way to hope that springs from plans and action. Though Bilbo's states of hopelessness never last as long as Frodo's will in *The Lord of the Rings*, Tolkien sounds the first notes of the theme in *The Hobbit*.

By the closing chapters of the story, the reader has long understood that Bilbo's capacity for physical bravery is far greater than he thought, so we are not surprised when, in the Battle of the Five Armies, he draws his sword to stand with the Elvenking. But the side of heroism Bilbo reveals in giving up the Arkenstone, the sacrificial act that repudiates the heart of the mountain and the heart of Thorin, is a binding force: It draws men to it and binds them. Bilbo's giving up the arkenstone, that is, his expressing a commitment to the wider world that comes before his commitment to Thorin and Company, unites him not only with Gandalf but also with the high-mimetic hero, Bard.

BEINGS OF HEROIC PROPORTION VS. ORDINARY HEROES

Bard, as the high-mimetic hero Bilbo is not, foreshadows the kind of heroism that will be represented by Aragorn, the king of men, in *The Lord of the Rings*. He is a man of heroic stature, the descendant of kings, and the protector of his people. Thus he is the kind of hero who may be expected to slay dragons, a traditional high-mimetic heroic feat. Furthermore, like Aragorn, Bard is a healer. After Smaug's destruction of Esgaroth, he is quick "to help in the ordering of the camps and in the care of the sick and the wounded," and when he approaches Thorin to demand a portion of the treasure, he asks for it in the name of justice, but also in the name of mercy.

High-mimetic heroism, then, of the kind demonstrated by warrior kings and other men or demigods of heroic proportions appears in *The Hobbit* not so much as a vision of heroism in which Tolkien is particularly interested at this time, but as a background against which the quality of Bilbo's heroism (and by implication, the heroism of which the reader is capable) may be more clearly seen. The viewing of Bilbo's deeds against the assumptions about heroes underlying the heroism of Gandalf and Bard illustrates clearly that the ordinary man, though he cannot work magic or kill dragons, can do what a hero does: He can save us. It also illustrates that the qualities of the low-mimetic hero need not be great strength or great wisdom, but a kind heart, a hopeful disposition, and a love of his fellow beings. As Gandalf reminds Bilbo at the end of the story, "You are a very fine person, Mr. Baggins, and I am fond of you; but you are only quite a little fellow in a wide world after all." Indeed, suggests Tolkien, so are we all.

Psychological Themes in *The Hobbit*

Dorothy Matthews

Although its resemblance to certain nursery tales may keep it from being taken seriously, *The Hobbit* provides some profound insights into the human psyche, writes Dorothy Matthews. Exploring the unbalanced masculine and feminine sides of Bilbo Baggins's personality, Matthews traces the steps he takes to bring the two sides of his character into harmony. Matthews chaired the National Council of Teachers of English Committee to revise NCTE's annotated list of High Interest–Easy Reading books for high school and junior high school students.

Since its publication in 1938, J.R.R. Tolkien's *The Hobbit* has received very little serious critical attention other than as the precursor of *The Lord of the Rings*. It has usually been praised as a good introduction to the trilogy, and as a children's book, but anyone familiar with psychoanalysis cannot avoid being tantalized by recurrent themes and motifs.... Bilbo's story has surprising depths that can be plumbed by the reader who is receptive to psychoanalytic interpretations.

The central pattern of *The Hobbit* is, quite obviously, a quest. Like so many heroes before him, Bilbo sets out on a perilous journey, encounters and overcomes many obstacles (including a confrontation with a dragon) and returns victorious after he has restored a kingdom and righted ancient wrongs. However, this pattern is so commonplace in literature that it is not a very helpful signpost. But it may help in other ways.

Let us first look briefly at *The Hobbit* for its folk ingredients, that is, the common motifs or story elements which it shares with folk narratives. There are, of course, the creatures themselves: dwarves, elves, trolls, animal servants, helpful birds and, the most frequently recurring of all folk adversaries, the treasure-guarding dragon. There are magic objects in abundance: a ring of invisibility, secret entrances into the underworld, magic swords, and doors into mountains. Dreams foretell and taboos admonish, the violation of which could bring dire results.

There are tasks to be performed, riddles to solve, and foes to be outwitted or outfought. Folk motifs form the very warp and woof in the texture of this tale, which is not surprising since Tolkien, as a medievalist, is immersed in folk tradition, a tradition that gives substance not only to the best known epics but to most medieval narratives and to "fairy tales."

In fact, it is probably its resemblance to what today's readers see as the nursery tale that has resulted in *The Hobbit* being relegated to elementary school shelves. The fat, comfort-loving Bilbo can easily remind a reader of Winnie-the-Pooh, who had to have his "little something" at eleven o'clock or of another epicurean, Peter Rabbit, who risked all for a feast in Farmer McGregor's garden. Bilbo's home-loving nature can also call to mind the domestic Water Rat and Mole of Kenneth Grahame's *Wind in the Willows*, for Bilbo found the sound of a kettle singing out to announce the hour for tea the most heartening in the world. And Bilbo's descent into the depths of the mountain where he loses track of time and finds himself confronted by menacing and riddling adversaries certainly bears a resemblance to *Alice's Adventures in Wonderland*. Bilbo also can be seen as similar to such diminutive heroes of international fairy tales as the master of "Puss-in-Boots," "Jack in the Beanstalk," and the endless stream of youngest of three sons who, through no outstanding qualities of their own, are propelled to riches and renown through the aid of magic objects or supernatural helpers.

INSIGHTS INTO THE HUMAN PSYCHE

But even if *The Hobbit* is only a children's story, it should be analyzed more closely for deeper levels of meaning, for it is the kind of story that has provided the most profound insights into the human psyche.

Both Freud's and Jung's studies of folk materials supported the theory that the unconscious expresses itself through such channels as dreams and fantasy. The protagonist in so many of these tales encounters his greatest obstacles alone, as a dreamer. Even in large-scale epics the hero fights single-handedly although the stakes are much higher than in fairy tales. Beowulf confronts both Grendel and Grendel's mother alone, and [King] Arthur and Modred, as the only survivors on a corpse-strewn battlefield, decide the future of the kingdom through man-to-man struggle. It is also suggestive that the descents in so many of these stories have a universal appeal. Trips into the underworld abound in Greek hero tales and myths as well as in Germanic lore. Just as Orpheus seeks Eurydice, just as Beowulf goes down into the sea to fight Grendel's mother in her lair, just as Alice falls into an underground realm, so Bilbo descends into the heart of the mountain to encounter Gollum and, later, Smaug. Freudian symbolism might also explain the prominence given in well-known tales to the nicknames of swords such as *The Hobbit*'s Orcrist (the Biter) and Glamdring the Foe-Hammer (the Beater), the acquisition of which is an important event in the life of the hero. Some of the most memorable episodes in the Arthurian tales are those describing Arthur's passing the test devised to identify the rightful king by miraculously freeing the sword from the stone, and his receiving the gem-encrusted Excalibur from the lady of the Lake. If Freud's view of the sword as a phallic symbol is correct, then it does not seem farfetched to view these scenes as vestiges of the coming-into-manhood ritual. Surely Freudian sex symbols are found with startling frequency in these stories. Recall, for instance, the prominence of keys, locks, caves, chalices, and cups in these works. . . .

BILBO'S POTENTIAL

When we are first introduced to Bilbo, he is far from being a boy hobbit in terms of years, but his maturity is questionable. His primary concerns, like those of any child, are with physical comforts. Eating is probably his favorite activity. He seldom ventures from his hobbit hole, a dwelling interestingly womblike in its isolation from the shocks of the world. Bilbo is noticeably annoyed when Gandalf arrives with the dwarf visitors since he would prefer to live what appears to be a somewhat withdrawn, self-centered life.

Early in the story it is clear, however, that Bilbo has much more in him than he is giving expression to. The potential for tension lies between the Baggins and the Took sides of his nature; through his mother, Belladonna Took, he is related to an adventurous family and has inherited aggressive tendencies. However, he has evidently repressed this more spirited side of his personality in favor of the Baggins impulses, which tend to be rather fuddy-duddy and more than a little feminine. Bilbo is much more interested, for instance, in keeping a tidy house, cooking a tempting meal, and keeping himself in pocket handkerchiefs than he is in venturing boldly into the world to find what life may have in store for him.

In other words, at the beginning of the tale, Bilbo's personality is out of balance and far from integrated. His masculinity, or one may say his Tookish aggressiveness, is being repressed so that he is clinging rather immaturely to a childish way of life. He has not even begun to realize his full potential. The womblike peace and security of his home is disturbed with the arrival of Gandalf, who may be seen as a projection of the Jungian archetype of the "wise old man" since he resembles the magic helper of countless stories: Merlin of the Arthurian cycle, Odin of Norse legend, or the helpful old person of the fairy tale, to name but a few. Like his prototypes, Gandalf sounds the call to adventure and motivates the reluctant hobbit to leave his home, helps him in the early stages of his venture into perilous realms, and then leaves him when he can stand alone.

At the outset of their adventure, Bilbo, like a typical young adolescent, is uncertain of his role, or "persona," to use a Jungian term. The dwarves quickly reinforce his insecurity; Gandalf asked him to join the group to be a burglar, but the dwarves carp that he acts more like a grocer than a burglar.

He fears that he cannot live up to Gandalf's expectations, and during the early conflicts with the trolls and goblins, Bilbo is completely dependent upon the wizard for help. The most prominent force in these early events is luck, or chance. It is only through chance that the key to the trolls' cave is found, thus providing unearned access to the magic swords so necessary for later trials. If the sword is seen as a phallic symbol, its miraculous appearance at the beginning of the journey supports the ritualistic pattern of maturation in Bilbo's adventures.

THE DECISION TO FACE LIFE

One of the most crucial incidents of the story takes place when Bilbo finds himself unconscious and separated from the dwarves within the mountain domain of the goblins. In this underground scene he must face an important trial; he must make a decision whose outcome will be a measure of his maturity. After accidentally finding the ring, Bilbo wonders whether or not he should summon up the courage to face whatever dangers await him. Unlike the unsure, regressive hobbit he was, Bilbo suddenly exclaims: "Go Back? No good at all! Go sideways? Impossible! Go Forward? Only thing to do!" For the first time Bilbo finds within himself a strength he didn't know he possessed. With unprecedented courage he decides to face life rather than to withdraw from it. This decision marks an important step in his psychological journey.

The danger he decides to face at this time, of course, is Gollum, the vaguely sensed but monstrous inhabitant of the underground lake. The association of this adversary with water and the attention given to his long grasping fingers and voracious appetite suggest a similarity to Jung's Devouring-Mother archetype, that predatory monster which must be faced and slain by every individual in the depths of his unconscious if he is to develop as a self-reliant individual. The fact that the talisman is a ring is even more suggestive of Jungian symbology since the circle is a Jungian archetype of the *self*—the indicator of possible psychic wholeness. The psychological importance of this confrontation is further supported by the imagery of the womb and of rebirth which marks the details of Bilbo's escape.

Wearing the ring of invisibility, Bilbo finally makes his way to the exit from the subterranean realm of darkness only to find a menacing figure humped against the opening. The gleaming, cold green eyes tell him it is Gollum.

> Bilbo almost stopped breathing, and went stiff himself. He was desperate. He must get away, out of this horrible darkness, while he had any strength left. He must fight. . . . And he was miserable, alone, lost . . . thoughts passed in a flash of a second. He trembled. And then quite suddenly in another flash, as if lifted by a new strength and resolve, he leaped . . . a leap in the dark . . . he only missed cracking his skull on the low arch of the passage.

Narrowly missed by Gollum's desperate effort to grab him, Bilbo begins falling and lands in a new tunnel. The text continues:

> Soon the passage that had been sloping down began to go up again, and after a while it climbed steeply. That slowed Bilbo down. But at last the slope stopped, the passage turned a corner and dipped down again, and there at the bottom of a short incline, he saw, filtering round another corner—a glimpse of light. Not red light, as of fire or lantern, but a pale out-of-doors sort of light.

REBIRTH

But Bilbo is no sooner out of the reach of Gollum when he is confronted by new dangers from the goblins. Here again the ring helps him in his escape, which is described in terms highly suggestive of the traumatic natal experience:

> "I must get to the door, I must get to the door!" he kept saying to himself, but it was a long time before he ventured to try. Then it was like a horrible game of blindman's bluff. The place was full of goblins running about, and the poor little hobbit dodged this way and that, was knocked over by a goblin who could not make out what he had bumped into, scrambled away on all fours, slipped between the legs of the captain just in time, got up and ran for the door.

> It was still ajar. . . . Bilbo struggled but he could not move it. He tried to squeeze through the crack. He squeezed and squeezed, and he stuck! It was awful. . . . He could see outside into the open air: . . . but he could not get through. . . .

> Bilbo's heart jumped into his mouth. He gave a terrific squirm. Buttons burst off in all directions. He was through.

The suggestion of rebirth symbolically expressed in these passages is consistently carried out in the episodes that follow, and they clearly demonstrate that a metamorphosis has indeed taken place. When Bilbo rejoins his friends, he is unquestionably changed. The dwarves begin to notice a difference when, through the aid of his ring, Bilbo is able to appear suddenly in their midst without detection, a feat much more befitting a burglar than a grocer. The delight and astonishment experienced by the dwarves is felt even more deeply by Gandalf, who is "probably more pleased than all the others."

> It is a fact that Bilbo's reputation went up a very great deal with the dwarves after this. If they had still doubted that he was really a first-class burglar, in spite of Gandalf's words, they doubted no longer.

The new respect which Bilbo has earned from his companions in turn leads to increased self-confidence; he is becoming a very different kind of hobbit. His decision to face danger has profoundly changed him.

STABILIZING THE NEWLY BALANCED PERSONALITY

The Tookish and Baggins sides of his personality have been brought into a new harmony. His Baggins impulses are beginning to be counter-balanced, thus bringing about a desirable psychic tension, which can result only when a balance of opposites exists. This is not the end of the journey, however, for the sudden change must be stabilized through reinforcing experiences. In fact, Gandalf remains with the party to see them through the adventure with the wargs and the goblins. It is during this episode that Gandalf summons help from the eagles, an act with possible symbolic significance since, according to Jung, the bird archetype is a powerful transforming agent. Similarly Beorn, with his interesting man-beast metamorphic possibilities, fits surprisingly well into Jung's conjectures regarding the archetypal figures of the unconscious.

The topography of the journey also has possible metaphoric significance. It is within a mountain reached through an underground descent that Bilbo finds the ring and passes his first trial. It is now within a wood, Mirkwood, that Gandalf puts Bilbo in charge of the group. Woods have long been recognized as an archetype for danger, so Mirkwood is the appropriate setting for Bilbo to demonstrate his self-reliance. The wizard leaves his charge alone at the edge of the forest to face this next important test of manhood in the woods, and the spider finds Bilbo worthy of Gandalf's trust. He not only finds the courage to confront his adversary; he actually distinguishes himself by his valor. The monstrous enemy that threatens to hold and enmesh the hero in its web is a common metaphor for the paralysis of the victim, symbolically in a state of psychic fixation.

Whether the spider with whom Bilbo battles is interpreted as a Jungian shadow figure, embodying evil, or as the Devouring-Mother facet of the anima is immaterial. The symbolism is clear without specific terms: a lone protagonist must free himself from a menacing opponent that has the power to cripple him forever. With the aid of a miraculously acquired sword and a magic talisman, he is able to face the danger and overcome it. . . .

From this point on, Bilbo has the self-esteem needed to fulfill his responsibilities as a mature and trustworthy leader. It is through his ingenuity that they escape from the dungeon prisons in the subterranean halls of the wood-elves. This last episode also reveals telling symbolic details in that the imprisonment is underground and the escape through a narrow outlet into the water is yet another birth image.

FINAL STAGES OF THE QUEST OF MATURATION

The climactic adventures of Bilbo are of course the episodes with Smaug, who, like the traditional dragon of folklore, has laid waste the land and is guarding a treasure. If viewed in the light of Jungian symbology, the contested treasure can be seen as the archetype of the self, of psychic wholeness. Thus this last series of events marks the final stages of Bilbo's quest of maturation.

When the group arrives at the Lonely Mountain (another site aptly symbolic), it is noteworthy that it is Bilbo who prods the dwarves into beginning the dangerous search for the secret door. The helpful bird motif is again instrumental; this time, in accordance with the message read by Elrond from the moon letters on the map, the tapping of a thrush alerts Bilbo to look for the keyhole which is suddenly visible in the rays of the setting sun. The discovery of the door, swinging open with the turn of the key, presents the hobbit with his greatest challenge so far. Knowing that the dwarves expect him to be the one to explore the secret passage, Bilbo is ready with a response, even before he is asked:

> ... I have got you out of two messes already, which were hardly in the original bargain, so that I am, I think, already owed some reward. But third time pays for all as my father used to say, and somehow I don't think I shall refuse. Perhaps I have begun to trust my luck more than I used to in the old days.

Although his request for company on this dangerous mission is turned down, Bilbo nonetheless courageously enters through the enchanted door, steals into the mountain, puts on his ring, and creeps noiselessly "down, down, down into the dark. He was trembling with fear, but his little face was set and grim. Already he was a very different hobbit from the one that had run out without a pocket-handkerchief from Bag-End long ago. He had not had a pocket-handkerchief for ages. He loosened his dagger in its sheath, tightened his belt, and went on."

And so with this description, Tolkien makes it clear that Bilbo is facing his most demanding trial of physical courage by daring to descend alone into the dragon's lair. With every step, Bilbo feels internal conflict:

> "Now you are in for it at last, Bilbo Baggins," he said to himself. "You went and put your foot right in it that night of the party, and now you have got to pull it out and pay for it! Dear me, what a fool I was and am!" said the least Tookish part of him. "I have absolutely no use for dragon-guarded treasures, and the whole lot could stay here forever, if only I would wake up and find this beastly tunnel was my own front-hall at home."

If he is ever to turn back, the time for it comes when his senses are assailed by the heat, the red light burning even brighter, and the terrifying sounds of bubbling and rumbling coming from the dragon hole. Tolkien describes this climactic moment:

> It was at this point that Bilbo stopped. Going on from there was the bravest thing he ever did. The tremendous things that happened afterwards were as nothing compared to it. He fought the real battle in the tunnel alone, before he ever saw the vast danger that lay in wait.

From this point on, Bilbo's physical courage is unquestioned. It is true that his reputation flags a little when his first descent into the dragon's den touches off a devastating rampage, but he reasserts his leadership during the second descent by learning of the dragon's one vulnerable spot, the piece of information so vital in finally ridding the land of its menace. In the last descent Bilbo acquires the Arkenstone, the gem so important to both the elves and the dwarves. Again, it is significant to note that the incident incorporates Jungian symbols, for the problem presented by the Arkenstone results in a different kind of test for Bilbo. To solve it he needs moral rather than physical courage.

BILBO AS ANTI-HERO

A truly critical question arises in considering this incident and the remainder of the story. I have taught this work many times and am constantly hearing complaints of dissatisfaction from students who feel that the last part of the book is both puzzling and anticlimactic. Many report that they felt a real loss of interest while reading the final chapters. Why does Bilbo keep the Arkenstone without telling the dwarves and then use it as a pawn in dealing with their enemies? Why, they ask, did Tolkien have a rather uninteresting character, rather than Bilbo, kill Smaug? Why is Bilbo, the previous center of interest, knocked unconscious so that he is useless during the last Battle of Five Armies? Isn't it a fault in artistic structure to allow the protagonist to fade from the picture during episodes when the normal expectation would be to have him demonstrate even more impressive heroism?

Answers to these questions are clear if the story is interpreted as the psychological journey of Bilbo Baggins. It stands to reason that Tolkien does not have Bilbo kill the dragon because that would be more the deed of a savior or culture hero, such as St. George, or the Red Cross Knight, or Beowulf. The significance of this tale lies in fact in the very obviously anti-heroic manner in which Tolkien chooses to bring Bilbo's adventures to a conclusion. As a result, Bilbo emerges as a symbol of a very average individual, not as a figure of epic proportions. Bilbo has not found eternal glory, but, rather, the self-knowledge that a willingness to meet challenge is not necessarily incompatible with a love of home. By giving expression to his Tookishness, he has found a new harmony and balance. And in realizing his full potential, Bilbo demonstrates that even his Baggins side provides him with values that are not without importance. Thorin recognizes this special worth in his final tribute to the hobbit:

> There is more in you of good than you know, child of the friendly west. Some courage and some wisdom, blended in measure. If more of us valued food and cheer and song above hoarded gold, it would be a merrier world.

Thus, at the conclusion of his adventures Bilbo finds the greatest prize of all: a knowledge of his own identity. In maturing psychologically, he has learned to think for himself and to have the courage to follow a course he knows to be right—in spite of possible repercussions. This maturity is demonstrated in the Arkenstone episode. His decision to use the gem as a means of negotiating with the opposition is made with the knowledge that it might mean the sacrifice of his friendship with Thorin and the dwarves. But Bilbo makes that choice. Like the hero in a medieval romance, he is confronted with a dilemma. Like Gawain, he has to face moral as well as physical trials. Bilbo makes the decision independently, trusting his own judgment and being willing to face censure and, if necessary, isolation. Bilbo's solution to his ethical problem satisfied Gandalf. The initiate has survived all ordeals successfully. In achieving self-reliance and self-knowledge, he had indeed found the Jungian jewel hard to attain. And furthermore, Bilbo knows the role he was created to fill, for when Gandalf tells him: "You're a very fine person . . . but you are only a little fellow in a wide world, after all," the hobbit answers simply, "Thank goodness."

A Jungian Interpretation

Timothy R. O'Neill

Timothy R. O'Neill is the author of *The Individuated Hobbit: Jung, Tolkien, and the Archetypes of Middle-earth*, from which this viewpoint is excerpted. In it, O'Neill relates Carl Jung's psychology of self-realization to Bilbo's growth throughout *The Hobbit*. Ego, shadow, libido, the unconscious—all are given potent images in this tale of the hobbit who refuses treasures of wealth in favor of the treasure of the Self.

Bilbo Baggins of Bag End was as conventional a hobbit as any other—despite the influence of his scandalous mother—and, like his conservative associates, eschewed adventure in all its distasteful forms. The most dangerous adventure of all, of course, is the journey into one's own psyche; and it is just that adventure that Bilbo undertakes in the fiftieth year of his life.

Nor is he really dragged kicking and screaming by the wizard and thirteen Dwarves. As they sang of the silence and majesty, the gleaming crystal columns and torchlit halls of the Lonely Mountain, Bilbo felt a stirring in his heart:

> Then something Tookish woke up inside him, and he wished to go and see the great mountains, and hear the pine-trees and the waterfalls, and explore the caves, and wear a sword instead of a walking stick.[1]

But this glimpse of the shadow world, the sudden revealing of a forgotten strain of Tookishness, is too much for this watchful, timid hobbit consciousness:

> Suddenly in the wood beyond The Water a flame leapt up— probably somebody lighting a wood fire—and he thought of plundering dragons settling on his quiet Hill and kindling it all to flames. He shuddered; and very quickly he was plain Mr. Baggins of Bag End, Under-Hill, again.[2]

1. J.R.R. Tolkien, *The Hobbit* (New York: Ballantine Books, 1966), p. 28. 2. Ibid.

The potency of these newly awakened symbols is so compelling that Bilbo must suppress the strange and disquieting feelings they evoke, unbidden, from the depths of what serves a hobbit for an unconscious. The Tookishness subsides.

This "Tookishness" is explicitly personified as the "fabulous Belladonna Took," Bilbo's mother. It is a female figure; a magical, potent figure out of Faërie, and the author and manipulator of his urges to climb above his humdrum hobbit existence. It is also his link with the collective past—the narrator speculates that some hobbit in the Took genealogy must have taken a fairy (Elvish) wife, another reference to the mystical and reverential, dimensions quite foreign to hobbit affairs. This is the first inkling that Bilbo is about to break out of his one-sided life, and it frightens him. Well it might, for even in the brave departure from the Shire, "running as fast as his furry feet could carry him,"[3] he could not have guessed what horrors lay ahead. How many hobbits of his generation had been obliged to deal with trolls, or seen trolls, or even believed in them? Only Bilbo, one presumes.

A WORLD OF SYMBOLS

And fearsome trolls they are. Bilbo's world is a dream world, a Faërie world; and in the world of dreams, of the psyche, the aggressive animal may symbolize unrestrained libido.[4] The trolls, although nominally anthropomorphic, seem to fall into this functional category—if there was ever inarticulate, unrestrained libido in action, it is the trio of Bert, Bill, and Tom. This may be regarded as the first sign of the power, the numinous potency, of the complexes that reside in Bilbo's unconscious. . . .

The travelers' brief respite in Rivendell allows the interpretation of Thorin's map, and the secrets hidden in it by magic are revealed by Elrond. Elrond is a symbol of the union of opposites (Elf and Man); it is only logical that he should be the one to find the key to the map—the moon-letters, runes that are revealed only by moonlight. He brings forth the hidden instructions ("stand by the grey stone when the thrush knocks") from the depths of the unconscious, the clue which will unlock the secrets of the hidden psyche. The moon is often connected, at least in the male psyche, with

3. Ibid., p. 41. 4. Carl G. Jung, *The Collected Works of Carl G. Jung*, vol. 5, *Symbols of Transformation* (New York: Pantheon, 1967), p. 328.

the unconscious, as the sun may symbolize in men's dreams and imagination the conscious.

After their departure from Rivendell, wizard, Dwarves, and hobbit are confronted by a mountain storm; the sudden fury and flashes of lightning portend symbolically the approach of a sudden psychic change, and the change which is about to occur is the most dramatic and significant of all.

Bilbo's progress thus far has only hinted at the coming crisis, the first stirrings of a change that may express the symptoms of neurosis; but this is not the real psyche, only a dream psyche. The appearance of certain portents, numinous images charged with inflated power that surge from the depths of the unconscious, serve as warnings—warnings that invariably make Bilbo long for the solid comfort of his hobbit-hole. The last thing Mr. Baggins wants to undertake at this point is a journey Under Hill into the depths of his forgotten mind and a confrontation with the unlovely demons of the imagination that lurk there. Attention is reversed now, from an outward to an inward perspective, and the frightful fiend is thus ahead rather than behind. But with thirteen Dwarves pulling him on and a wizard standing rear guard to head off any thoughts of malingering, Bilbo must march on.

Descent may symbolize the direction of attention and energy into the unconscious, and this is where Bilbo is dumped unceremoniously during the party's headlong flight from the pursuing mountain goblins. Lost and alone, he stumbles exhausted, and his hand finds—by chance?—the Ring. . . .

DESCENT INTO THE UNCONSCIOUS

"Deep down here by the dark water lived old Gollum, a small slimy creature."[5] . . . Gollum paddles about his little cold pool of water deep at the mountain's roots. The deep water is associated symbolically with the unconscious, with depth and knowledge and wisdom. Bilbo's progress has thus been *descent* into the *unconscious,* in the first timid search for enlightenment. But true wisdom for Bilbo must be shunted aside—the first order of business is to get out of that mountain as soon as possible. The revelations of the unconscious are really too much! The key to escape is slimy old Gollum, repulsive though he may be. Their riddle game is a

5. Tolkien, *The Hobbit,* p. 79.

duel of conscious and unconscious preoccupations. Bilbo marshals images of an egg (symbolizing the eye of the conscious), eating (material world), sun on the daisies (*sol* as representation of the conscious); Gollum relies upon contrasting pictures: wind, darkness, the roots of mountains, fish. But Bilbo is careless and fated to be anything but rid of Gollum, whatever the outcome of the riddle game. He gives Gollum his *name*—an important piece of information not to be blurted heedlessly to anyone, much less a mildewy green-eyed figure of shadow who lives in a cave, eats raw goblins caught unawares, and talks to himself. And Bilbo, above all, has the Ring, in whose shining symmetry is encased Gollum's dark soul. . . .

EGO AND SHADOW

Bilbo is clearly the ego, as the focal personality thus far in the story. More than this, Bilbo is the reader's ego. Bilbo's adventure has become the reader's dream, his creative, vicarious inner experience. The ego has courageously (more or less) entered the forbidden recesses of the unconscious and collided unexpectedly with its dark mirror image. The collision is brief and incomplete—the two are now for the first time fully aware of each other's existence, and their fates are inseparably bound. The only possible end of this dream lies many years and many miles ahead, at the Cracks of Doom.

Ego and shadow face each other at the twilit border of dark and light, and they are tied together by a precious ring, the One Ring, the "One Ring to find them/One Ring to bring them all and in the darkness bind them." This is the ruling Ring, for it rules both their fates; and these fates are bound, as is foretold, "in the Land of Mordor where the Shadows lie."[6] . . .

The Ring is the focal point of the *symbolic* story, and as such subtly overwhelms the overt plot like the latent content of a dream that belies the manifest experience. To say that either *The Hobbit* or *The Lord of the Rings* is a tale of there and back again is to suggest that [Dante's] *Divine Comedy* is a book about cave exploring. Tolkien's faërie world is a world of light and dark, a realm with very few softer tones (and whenever a character seems to assume a mantle of grey ambivalence, the cause is invariably the Ring). At the

6. J.R.R. Tolkien, *The Lord of the Rings* (New York: Ballantine Books, 1970), I:81.

border is the twilight, the furthest marches of the conscious, where things are not as they seem; and binding these realms together is the precious Ring.

The Ring is perfect in form, and stands for the Self. . . . The Ring's symmetry is perfectly balanced, a graceful circle, distilling the concepts of balance and perfection and the union of all opposites that will characterize the Self after its realization. Its material is gold, because of its incorruptible nature as in the philosophy of alchemy. Jung was fascinated by the complex and powerful imagery of medieval alchemy. . . . In any case, the form and function of the Ring are not left in doubt. The Ring's fate is etched inside and out in fiery letters:

> *One Ring to rule them all, One Ring to find them.*
> *One Ring to bring them all and in the darkness bind them.*[7]

The Ring is the Self, the potential force that promises finally to make whole both hobbit and Middle-earth.

But Bilbo is not through spelunking—ahead lie the Lonely Mountain and a far more formidable foe than wretched Gollum. Bilbo must now earn his title of burglar—or "expert treasure-hunter," as he would doubtless prefer to be called—by dickering with [the dragon] Smaug the Mighty, "greatest and chiefest of catastrophes." . . .

COMMITTED TO SELF-REALIZATION

Bilbo is terrified. Sting [his sword] and Ring are hardly more than lucky charms in the great treasure cave, not proof against the fearful flamethrower. Smaug is what we of Othello's trade [soldiers] call an area weapon: precise location of the target is not required, nor is fastidious marksmanship necessary for good terminal effect. But Bilbo has guts that belie his species' reputation. None of the Dwarves, not even the venerable, much-decorated Thorin Oakenshield, who proved his mettle in the Goblin Wars, has volunteered to help him burgle treasure with the dragon so near. As he treads the tunnel coming ever nearer to the uninviting red glow the "least Tookish part of him" wavers, wishing yet again for the comfy hole at Bag End.

This is the persona (the "good decent hobbit") railing impotently at the anima (the Tookish part, personified as the great Belladonna, from whom he has surely inherited the

---

7. Tolkien, *Lord of the Rings*, I: 81.

propensity for disturbing sleeping dragons); but the objections are too little and much too late. He is committed to the path of Self-realization, like it or not. In fact, the controlled social mask is already slipping away, no longer supported by the need to maintain a reputation for the neighbors.

The nature of Bilbo's journey across the landscape of the psyche is revealed by his reply to Smaug's inquiry: "Who are you and where do you come from, if I may ask?"

> "You may indeed! I come from under the hill, and under the hills and over the hills my paths led. And through the air. I am he that walks unseen."

Over hill and under hill, indeed; Bilbo is too modest (if that is possible). "I am the friend of bears and the guest of eagles. I am Ringwinner and Luckwearer." . .[8]

This is a complex and pregnant sort of name. It traces his path through conscious and unconscious (over hill and under hill) that has led him this far; establishes his foundation in both worlds ("friend of bears"—i.e., chthonic, earthy, bound to the animal shadow, the instinctive foundation of the psyche; and "guest of eagles"—one who may also soar at will in the light of consciousness). He glories in his new position as pivotal figure in the drama, the link between worlds (Ringwinner) and the key to fortune (Luckwearer) by possession of the magical transcending treasure.

POWERFUL LIBIDO

But Bilbo succumbs to a near fatal weakness at this critical point. He has in the euphoria of the moment reveled too thoughtlessly in Belladonna's triumph, ignored the conscious part of him, which would have been more cautious and circumspect in talking to dragons. Smaug is sure-footed in the dark world, he has dwelt there long; Bilbo is a stranger in the perilous realm, and he has barely stepped into it before the incautious foot is thrust in his mouth, tipping off the worm to dangerous details of the plan. "*Thief* in the *Shadows!*" [O'Neill's italics] snarls the beast, "my armour is like tenfold shields, my teeth are swords, my claws spears, the shock of my tail a thunderbolt, my wings a hurricane, and my breath death!"[9]

This uncouth outburst is one that reveals the volume and fury of the long-repressed libido, the surging, powerful en-

8. Tolkien, *The Hobbit*, p. 213. 9. Ibid., p. 216.

ergy that has for so long been denied conscious symboliza-
tion. Smaug has for the moment ceased to be a transcen-
dental, transforming symbol and become pure animal
power, untamed psychic drive. But transforming symbol is
his major role still, the winged serpent, and like St. George,
Bilbo must slay or outwit the beast to pave the way for the
Self's advent. He has already done this, though he has no
way of knowing it with his careless clues—Smaug is soon up
and around for the first time in years, and Bilbo has provided the clue through the help of the magic thrush that allows Bard the Bowman to finish the monster and quench his
flames. The black arrow pierces the gap in Smaug's armor,
and the treasure is now lying unguarded in the darkness under the mountain.

Now, as Bilbo and the Dwarves begin their greedy inven-
tory of the reclaimed wealth, there is a significant discovery.
Bilbo, unknown to Thorin and company, has found the
Arkenstone, Heart of the Mountain. "Indeed there could not
be two such gems, even in so marvellous a hoard, even in all
the world."[10] It is a perfect crystalline gem, a sparkling pale
globe of light, the most cherished heirloom of the Dwarves
of Erebor.

It is related in symbolism to the *lapis philosophorum*, the
Philosopher's Stone of alchemy, which contains within its
perfect symmetry the means of unifying the opposites, and
means of transforming base metals into gold (also a union of
opposites). In Jungian terms, it is a symbolic realization of
the Self through individuation:

> The goal of individuation, as pictured in unconscious images,
> represents a kind of mid-point or center in which the
> supreme value and the greatest life-intensity are concen-
> trated. It cannot be distinguished from images of the supreme
> values of the various religions. It appears as naturally in the
> individuation process as it does in the religions ... a four-
> square city or garden ... as the *imago Dei* in the soul, as the
> "circle whose periphery is nowhere and whose center is
> everywhere," as a crystal, a stone, a tree, a vessel or a cosmic
> order. ...[11]

Certainly its location, deep in the treasure cave at the
mountain's roots, suggests its abode in the unconscious.
Now it is more than a potential: it, like the Ring, is in Bilbo's
"pocketses."

10. Ibid., p. 225. 11. M.L. von Franz, *C.G. Jung, His Myth in Our Time* (Boston: Little
Brown, 1975), pp. 73–74.

It does not remain there long, of course, and Bilbo uses this barter to resolve the political impasse between the Elves and Lakemen on one side and the Dwarves, "under bewilderment of the treasure," on the other. The Arkenstone is both symbol and instrument of his new-found Self; he blends now the pragmatic hobbit of the Shire with the courage and vision of the Tookish adventurer.

Indeed, the little burglar has retrieved more from the dragon's hoard than golden chalices and glittering jewels; his treasure is the treasure of the Self, beside which the wealth of the King under the Mountain, the splendor and worldly pomp and lucre are small change. At the last he has no use for more of this gold than his small measure—enough to be a well-to-do hobbit and live out his life in comfort and contemplation at Bag End (or so he believes). Bilbo Baggins will never be the same. The prosaic gentlehobbit is now poetic as well, his stuffy constricting persona shed (and Old Belladonna silenced), and the realization of his full potential within reach.

"My dear Bilbo!" observes Gandalf. "Something is the matter with you! You are not the hobbit that you were."[12]

12. Tolkien, *The Hobbit*, p. 284.

CHAPTER 2

Meaning in *The Lord of the Rings*

READINGS ON
J.R.R. TOLKIEN

Modern Ideas of Heroism Are a Cornerstone of *The Lord of the Rings*

Roger Sale

Roger Sale examined the portrayal of modern heroism in his book *Modern Heroism: Essays on D.H. Lawrence, William Empson, and J.R.R. Tolkien.* In the following essay, a precursor of that book, Sale argues that despite Tolkien's distaste for his own times, his hero is very much a product of the twentieth century. The portrait of the lonely, scared, but compassionate hero who binds himself to others may partake of all the heroes of the past, but his response is a reaction to the modern world.

In any study of modern heroism, if J.R.R. Tolkien's *The Lord of the Rings* did not exist it would have to be invented. For at one place or another in this massive trilogy all the heroic issues of the western world, from *Beowulf* to D.H. Lawrence, are enacted. . . .

In Tolkien's Middle-earth lie the riders of Rohan, Beowulf-like in their love of lore, their simple and great strength, and their belief that brave men die well in defense of their lord and their honor; Aragorn, half-elven figure of romance, the wandering ranger who becomes King Elessar of Gondor; gigantic Wordsworthian tree-like Ents who swoop down in revenge on the man who treated them wantonly; Sam Gamgee, the namesake of Pickwick's servant, staunch in his servility and love of domesticity; Sam's master, Frodo Baggins, the real hero in this book where all must be heroic, who acts like any modern alienated man but who also is Tolkien's affirmation of possibility in a world where all old and other heroic types are by themselves inadequate. It is, thus, epic and romance and novel by turns, held together by a central myth that manages to partake of all the myths of all the heroes of the past without ever ceasing to be a myth of Tolkien's own devising. . . .

TOLKIEN COULD NOT ESCAPE HIS TIME

For it is Tolkien's lot, just as it has been that of all great writers, to be an historian of his own imagination and to describe the history of his world as he traced his imaginative boundaries. His world, furthermore, is not entirely his own but belongs to us as well, not just because we read him but because we are of his time and his century. Personally perhaps Tolkien would have wished it differently for in much he has written is a great sense of distaste for his own times, and when he has spoken in his own voice (and not as an historian) he can be very harsh:

> Not long ago—incredible though it may seem—I heard a clerk of Oxenford declare that he 'welcomed' the proximity of mass-production robot factories, and the roar of self-obstructive mechanical traffic, because it brought his university into 'contact with real life.' He may have meant that the way men were living and working in the twentieth century was increasing in barbarity at an alarming rate, and that the loud demonstrations of this in the streets of Oxford might serve as a warning that it is not possible to preserve for long an oasis of sanity in a desert of unreason by mere fences, without actual offensive action (practical and intellectual). I fear he did not. In any case the expression 'real life' in this context seems to fall short of academic standards. The notion that motor-cars are more 'alive' than, say, centaurs or dragons is curious; that they are more 'real' than, say, horses is pathetically absurd. ("On Fairy-Stories," in *Essays Presented to Charles Williams* [London, 1947], p. 77)

But fortunately we need not trust the artist when we have such a magnificent tale to trust instead. For Tolkien is not of Middle-earth any more than he is of the germanic dark ages that are his special area of scholastic competence. Willy nilly he belongs to our time, and the more he attempts to ignore or escape this fact the worse he becomes as a writer.

A VERY MODERN HEROISM

William Empson finishes his *Some Versions of Pastoral* with the statement that virtue, intelligence, and good manners are alike lonely and absurd confessions of human limitations. They are, he adds, all the more necessary in our world. That is the idea of modern heroism perhaps most congenial to the liberal spirit, for it accepts the facts of modern life at something like Tolkien's private evaluation of them, and then simply refuses to knuckle under. Empson is a cheerful man, however, and a consistently graceful one, and Tolkien is neither. He is a Christian, not a skeptic, and he believes that the taproot to the past is not yet dried or withered. It would be difficult, therefore, to expect that Tolkien would warm to the idea that his imagination is vastly superior to his theology and that his imagination is of his own time. There are many heroisms in *The Lord of the Rings*, and some are staunch in their commitment to what Empson and many others would consider laughably out of date. Tolkien knows how he wants to reply to their derision, and his defense of his view of the world is careful and polished. But it is, finally, worth rather little because the heroism he writes of best is very modern and even very Empsonian; imagination betrays belief here, as it does so often, yet opens us onto larger worlds too.

For Frodo must try to survive and to win by surviving, and in that case not only valor and physical prowess but the very idea of battles against enemies is not particularly germane. Tolkien has arranged his story so that Sauron cannot openly affect Frodo at all. He binds Frodo only as Frodo binds himself, and Frodo is heroic because he recognizes there is something more important than the question of whether or not he is bound. The landscape of Frodo's great deeds is Sauron's weapon, and for that reason one can call the book Christian and Frodo a pilgrim. But it is a landscape fashioned by the imagination of this century; the wasteland, the valley of ashes, the nightmare cities of [Lawrence's] Rupert Birkin and [Kafka's] Joseph K. What these other authors have tended to think of as the human condition Tolkien finds the grounds for heroic quest, but the circumstances and the atmosphere are the same. He differs from the others primarily because he believes and shows that loneliness, though necessary and unavoidable, is partly a chosen state, the result as much of despair as of the facts of life.

SAM AND SMÉAGOL

It is for this reason that Sam and Sméagol are so important. In their different ways they are better equipped than Frodo

to carry the Ring to Mordor. But they are antagonists because imaginatively they are Frodo's inferiors; they cannot
trust or sympathize with each other and they cannot understand Frodo's trust and sympathy for them both. Sam feels
the power of the Ring only momentarily, and childishly even
then, while Sméagol has been totally corrupted by it, and in
each case they are protected in a way Frodo cannot be. Sam
serves Frodo and Sméagol serves the Ring, but only Frodo
serves the heroic idea of the Ring's destruction. If neither is
of anything like Frodo's stature, however, he is lost without
them. But Frodo knows this and because he knows it can
"find" himself in his love for Sam and his compassion for
Sméagol and his dependence on them. As long as he is thus
dependent, and willingly so, the urge to possessiveness that
lies at the heart of the Ring's power to destroy can be com-
batted. Frodo's virtue lies in his good manners, and his good

"MY COMMENT ON THE WORLD"

*When asked to participate in a symposium on children's
books to be published in the* New Statesman, *Tolkien
drafted a long letter in April 1959 explaining why he was declin-
ing. He eventually sent only a one-paragraph note of refusal; the
following is from the unmailed draft.*

I am not specially interested in children, and certainly not in
writing for them: i.e. in addressing directly and expressly those
who cannot understand adult language.

I write things that might be classified as fairy-stories not because I wish to address children (who qua children I do not believe to be specially interested in this kind of fiction) but because I wish to write this kind of story and no other.

I do this because if I do not apply too grandiloquent a title to
it I find that my comment on the world is most easily and naturally expressed in this way. . . .

I hope 'comment on the world' does not sound too solemn. I
have no didactic purpose, and no allegorical intent. (I do not
like allegory (properly so called: most readers appear to confuse it with significance or applicability) but that is a matter too
long to deal with here.) But long narratives cannot be made out
of nothing; and one cannot rearrange the primary matter in
secondary patterns without indicating feelings and opinions
about one's material.

Humphrey Carpenter, ed., *The Letters of J.R.R. Tolkien*. Boston: Houghton Mifflin,
1981.

manners are his recognition of the blessed and cursed otherness of his servant and his wretched guide.

In a moment of respite on the stairs of Cirith Ungol, before Sméagol takes them to Shelob, Frodo and Sam have a conversation about the songs that will be sung of them after this is all over. Sam does most of the talking, but Frodo makes the key points: 1) "You may know, or guess, what kind of tale it is, happy-ending or sad-ending, but the people in it don't know. And you don't want them to." 2) "No, they never end as tales. . . but the people in them come, and go, when their parts ended." 3) "Why Sam, to hear you somehow makes me as merry as if the story was already written. But you've left out one of the chief characters: Samwise the stouthearted . . . and Frodo wouldn't have got far without Sam, would he. . . ." 4) "It's not good to worry about him [Sméagol] now. We couldn't have gotten so far, not even within sight of the pass, without him, and so we'll have to put up with his ways. If he's false, he's false" (II, 321–322).[1] Sam can begin to understand what Frodo is saying, but he cannot by himself rise to the grim and yet almost sublime equipoise of Frodo's weary generosity. But he knows that quality is there in Frodo, as indeed, for a moment, does the Gollum. For after this conversation Frodo and Sam fall asleep and Sméagol discovers them thus, peaceful in each other's arms:

> A strange expression passed over his lean hungry face. The gleam faded from his eyes, and they went dim and grey, old and tired. A spasm of pain seemed to twist him, and he turned away, peering back up towards the pass, shaking his head, as if engaged in some interior debate. Then he came back, and slowly putting out a trembling hand, very cautiously he touched Frodo's knee—but almost the touch was a caress. For a fleeting moment, could one of the sleepers have seen him, they would have thought that they beheld an old weary hobbit, shrunken by the years that carried him far beyond his time, beyond friends and kin, and the fields and streams of youth, an old starved pitiable thing. (II, 324)

This is Sméagol's finest moment, and so, by implication, it is Frodo's finest moment too. Beyond friends and kin, old and tired, Sméagol loves the specialness that is Frodo's care of him. The love is almost without parallel in our modern literature, because it is neither filial nor sexual but the tentative unbelieving response to a caring so unlikely it seems

1. Quotations from *The Lord of the Rings* are taken from the revised edition (Boston: Houghton Mifflin, 1967).

heroic even to the Gollum. Whatever might have come afterwards because of this moment is destroyed when Sam wakes up first. He accuses Gollum of being a sneak, and by the time Frodo wakes Sméagol is back to his old whining and sniveling self, ready to lead the hobbits to Shelob.

THE CORNERSTONE OF THE TRILOGY'S GREATNESS

So in a book about hobbits and their return to a world made new, Frodo is the one who can be returned to himself as he sees the light shine in others. Perhaps in Tolkien's official scheme of things this need not seem as important as the original turning out from self to see the world as it is meant to be seen. But still, Frodo finds in this turning out a means to self-knowledge, and in his scarred and beautiful relationship with Sméagol he finds himself and lives by the light of the self he finds. He is saved from the worst ravages of the Ring because he binds himself to others rather than to love of power, and that is his heroism. That is what most profoundly arouses Tolkien's imagination and sympathy too—it may not be what *The Lord of the Rings* is all about and it certainly is not all that it is good for, but it is the cornerstone of its greatness. Over and over in the trilogy we are told of the prices that must be paid when one is called upon to pay them, and with Gandalf, Aragorn, Merry, Pippin, Faramir, the faded elven Kings, and many others we see that such prices are being demanded and paid. But these are ancient heroisms, ancient prices and payments, known and felt to be old and therefore always a trifle artificial, derived, and decorative.

THE HEROISM OF OUR TIME

But this very artificiality is our guide to the genuineness of Frodo's heroism and to our understanding that Tolkien is an historian of heroic acts. For in his Middle-earth, as all the other "great deeds" are chronicled, we respond to that which is most like ourselves because our author so responds too. We see, without in the least needing to make the seeing into a formulation, what the heroism of our time is and can be: lonely, lost, scared, loving, willing, and compassionate—to bind oneself to the otherness of others by recognizing our common livingness. History may create the conditions of chaos, but man's nature is to reply to history as well as to acknowledge it.

Christian Morality in *The Lord of the Rings*

Richard Purtill

The roots of morality and thus of heroism in *The Lord of the Rings* trilogy are deeply planted in Christian tradition, argues Richard Purtill. Critics who miss the Christian basis of Tolkien's writing, says Purtill, misunderstand both Christianity and Tolkien. Purtill is the author of *J.R.R. Tolkien: Myth, Morality, and Religion* as well as *Lord of the Elves and Eldils*, from which this essay is excerpted.

Both C.S. Lewis and J.R.R. Tolkien . . . are Christians, and their morality is essentially Christian morality. . . .

Let me now briefly describe Tolkien's world, as many hints, indirect references, and direct statements give it to us. Just as in Lewis's space trilogy the state of Earth is supposed to be the state it is in, and Lewis's secondary world "starts," so to speak, at the orbit of the moon, so for Tolkien recorded history is supposed to be much as it actually is, and Tolkien's secondary world "starts" before history begins. In both cases there is some "interpenetration." In [Lewis's *That Hideous*] *Strength* the Arthurian legend becomes history, and in Tolkien it is suggested that elves, hobbits, and other creatures linger on into recorded history. But before recorded history there are certain events which Tolkien, as a Christian, holds to have actually occurred—for instance, the fall of man. Thus, since there are men in Tolkien's story, they must be fallen men; the Fall is in the *past* of Tolkien's world. And, of course, the men in the story of the Ring are obviously fallen men.

What about the other races? Not being "sons of Adam," they are not necessarily fallen; they may be like Lewis's Malacandrans or Perelandrans. And, in fact, there are some analogies between Lewis's "races" and Tolkien's. Let me first give a table of my proposed correspondences, and then defend it.

Excerpted from *Lord of the Elves and Eldils: Fantasy and Philosophy in C.S. Lewis and J.R.R. Tolkien,* by Richard Purtill (Grand Rapids, MI: Zondervan, 1974). Reprinted by permission of the author. (Footnotes in the original have been adapted in this reprint.)

Tolkien's	correspond to	Lewis's
Elves (wizards)	"	Good eldils (Oyarses)
Dwarves (ents?)	"	Malacandrans
Orcs, trolls (Sauron)	"	"Bent" eldils (The "Bent One")

Elves and orcs are unlike eldils in that eldils are purely spiritual beings. (But the function of elves in Tolkien's story is like that of eldils in Lewis's trilogy as, for example, Tom Bombadil's function is rather like Merlin's in *Strength.*) Elves are like eldils in being confirmed in goodness or badness; there is no such thing as an evil elf of a good orc in Tolkien. Ents are evidently not confirmed in goodness like elves. Treebeard says of his people,

> "I do not understand all that goes on myself, so I cannot explain it to you. Some of us are still true Ents, and lively enough in our fashion, but many are growing sleepy, going treeish, as you might say. Most of the trees are just trees, of course; but many are half awake. Some are quite wide awake, and a few are, well, ah, well getting *Entish.* That is going on all the time.

> "When that happens to a tree, you find that some have *bad* hearts. Nothing to do with their wood: I do not mean that. Why, I knew some good old willows down the Entwash, gone long ago, alas! They were quite hollow, indeed they were falling all to pieces, but as quiet and sweet-spoken as a young leaf. And then there are some trees in the valleys under the mountains, sound as a bell, and bad right through. That sort of thing seems to spread. There used to be some very dangerous parts in this country. There are still some very black patches."

However, the ents have an "anti-race," like the elves. Treebeard says, "Maybe you have heard of Trolls? They are mighty strong. But Trolls are only counterfeits, made by the Enemy in the Great Darkness in mockery of Ents, as Orcs were of Elves." This may suggest that trolls and orcs are actually *created* by the Enemy, but elsewhere Gandalf denies that the Enemy can create; he can only spoil and corrupt. In fact, "Nothing is evil in the beginning. Even Sauron was not so," which suggests that he is, like Satan, a fallen being of great power.

Dwarves, like the Malacandrans, seem to be basically good, but there seems to be a possibility of individual falls; an evil dwarf is not an impossibility. And Gimli the dwarf in some way rises above his dwarvish destiny, becoming a sort of adopted elf.

Hobbits pose a special problem, and here I indulge in a bit of speculation which might have been entirely rejected by Tolkien himself. All that he himself says is that

> it is plain indeed that Hobbits are relatives of ours: far nearer to us than Elves, or even than Dwarves. Of old they spoke the languages of Men, after their own fashion, and liked and disliked much the same things as Men did. But what exactly our relationship is can no longer be discovered.

However, the hobbits are continually referred to as "halflings," a term Tolkien explains as "half the size of a grown man." Can there also be some suggestion here of half-*breeds?* Can the hobbits in fact be the offspring of an interbreeding of two other races? If so, which two? Not elves and men. The offspring of such unions appear in the story in the persons of Elrond and Aragorn, and they are quite unlike hobbits. I once thought hobbits might be the offspring of an elf-dwarf cross and connected in some way with the "old quarrel" between elves and dwarves. Gimli falls in love with Galadriel (in a remote and chivalric way, it is true, yet she is a sort of elvish saint or superwoman and he is not correspondingly great). What if some dwarvish king or warrior had fallen in love with a more eccessible elf-maiden and carried her off? Might this not have led to a spreading quarrel (Helen of Troy long before Troy), and might not the offspring of such a union, perhaps intermarrying with other dwarves, have founded a new race who found it best to vanish quietly into a remote corner of the world?

I still think this possible, from what Tolkien tells us of his world, but I am now inclined to think that a mixed dwarf-human ancestry is more plausible in view of the part hobbits play in the story. For, if hobbits are partly human, much is explained: the fact that they have no language of their own but speak that of men; their resemblances to both men and dwarves in certain respects; and, above all, the vital role they play in the process in which the Third Age—the age of many "speaking races"—comes to an end, and the Fourth Age—the age of man—begins.

A CONSTANT MORAL STRUGGLE

Be this as it may, the real moral focus of Tolkien's story is on the two races, hobbits and men. They can sink to complete damnation, as the Ringwraiths have done, and as Bilbo or Frodo might have. But they can rise to something like sanctity, as Frodo does. We have detailed pictures of moral struggle in men (Boromir, Théoden, Denethor), in most of the hobbit characters (especially Frodo, Sam, and Bilbo, but also Merry and Pippin), and in the wizard Saruman who is at least ostensibly a man or elf-man.

The constant temptation of all the characters is to give in, give up the struggle and cooperate with the Dark Lord. Against this the virtues characteristic of the heroes of the story are courage, will and endurance, and loyalty and love. We see the first sketch of this in Bilbo, hero of *The Hobbit.* At the beginning of the story he is seemingly a fussy, self-important little man (not middle-aged; that is a mistake which arises from applying human time-scales to longer-lived creatures). Partly by clever pressure from Gandalf, partly from injured vanity, he commits himself to an adventure with Thorin and his dwarves. As the dangers start, he begins to find his courage, first trying to pick a troll's pocket (with disastrous results), then giving the alarm during the capture by the goblins. Lost in the flight from the goblins after Gandalf rescues the troop, Bilbo meets Gollum and outwits him in the dark, finds his magic ring and begins to use it. In the forest he saves the dwarves from the giant spiders, aided by a magic ring and an elvish blade, but showing a great deal of courage and resourcefulness. He rescues the dwarves from the Elven-king's dungeons, but the real test of his courage is when he twice faces Smaug, the great dragon, gaining the knowledge that enables Bard, the hero, to kill the villain.

At the end of the tale, however, Bilbo shows his real stature. Faced with the refusal of the dwarves to share their wealth with the townsfolk against whom they aroused the dragon, and whose captain slew the dragon, Bilbo determines to see justice done. He gives the Arkenstone to the Elf-king and Bard to bargain with, then goes back to face the wrath of the dwarves. Love of justice and love of peace here raise Bilbo to a height not far below Frodo, the Ring-bearer.

FRODO ACTS FOR THE SAKE OF OTHERS

Frodo rises to greater heights because from the beginning he accepts the burden of the Ring purely for the sake of others. It is no mere adventure that sends Frodo riding out of the Shire, but a willingness to suffer so that others may be saved—a willingness which is tested to the last grim degree on the black plains of Mordor. Frodo is not Christ, the Ring is not the Cross, and the salvation his sacrifice wins is a purely secular salvation. But there are obviously echoes of these greater realities in the fictional "Passion" of Frodo. "Greater love has no man than this, that a man lay down his life for his friends," says Christ, and Frodo's journey is at least an illustration of this.

The growth of Frodo in courage and loyalty is clear enough as the story develops. At the first real test, in the den of the Barrow-wight, he is tempted to use the Ring to save himself.

> A wild thought of escape came to him. He wondered if he put on the Ring whether the Barrow-wight would miss him, and he might find some way out. He thought of himself running free over the grass, grieving for Merry, Sam, and Pippin, but free and alive himself.[1]

He rejects the temptation and begins to grow toward his final stature. There are other crises, and the Ring itself betrays him several times. But he is able to resist the call of the Ringwraiths to surrender on Weathertop and at the Ford of Bruinen, and to make up his own mind when assailed by the enemy on Amon Hen.

> ... suddenly he felt the Eye. There was an eye in the Dark Tower that did not sleep. He knew that it had become aware of his gaze. A fierce eager will was there. It leaped towards him; almost like a finger he felt it, searching for him. Very soon it would nail him down, know just exactly where he was. Amon Lhaw it touched. It glanced upon Tol Brandir—he threw himself from the seat, crouching, covering his head with his grey hood.
>
> He heard himself crying out: *Never, never!* Or was it: *Verily I come, I come to you?* He could not tell. Then as a flash from some other point of power there came to his mind another thought: *Take it off! Take it off! Fool, take it off! Take off the Ring!*
>
> The two powers strove in him. For a moment, perfectly balanced between their piercing points, he writhed, tormented. Suddenly he was aware of himself again. Frodo, neither the Voice nor the Eye: free to choose, and with one remaining instant in which to do so. He took the Ring off his finger. He was kneeling in clear sunlight before the high seat. A black shadow seemed to pass like an arm above him; it missed Amon Hen and groped out west, and faded. Then all the sky was clean and blue and birds sang in every tree.[2]

Frodo grows even greater as he journeys on with Sam and Gollum. His gentleness to Gollum almost conquers the crea-

---

1. J.R.R. Tolkien, *The Fellowship of the Ring*, rev. ed. (New York: Ballantine Books, 1969), p. 195. 2. Ibid., p. 519.

ture's withered heart, and his steady endurance of his burden as it grows almost overwhelming contains a moving echo of the Way of the Cross. Indeed, his nightmare journey across the blasted plains of Mordor with Sam and Gollum tends sometimes to dominate our memory of the book, so that it is easy to forget how much laughter and enchantment and delight the story contains. . . .

THE RING HAS SATANIC POWER

It may be well here to clear up a minor misunderstanding about the Ring itself. It has been blithely identified with Power by both friendly and unfriendly critics. Mary Ellman accused Tolkien's characters of being afraid of power, and even some of his admirers talk merely about the "dangers of power." But, of course, the Ring has not merely neutral power, but satanic power: the Dark Lord "has put a great part of his own power into it," and this is why its destruction does more than deprive Sauron of *more* power—it destroys him. When Gandalf and Galadriel refuse the Ring, it is not because "power corrupts"; they are, apart from Sauron, the most powerful persons in the story. Rather, they rejected it because using the Ring to do good would be attempting to use Satan's power to do good, and this will inevitably defeat the good purpose and turn it to evil.

Saruman tries to tempt Gandalf with the power of the Ring and the plea that the end justifies the means.

> ". . . listen, Gandalf, my old friend and helper!" he said, coming near and speaking now in a softer voice. "I said *we*, for *we* it may be, if you will join with me. A new Power is rising. Against it the old allies and policies will not avail us at all. There is no hope left in Elves or dying Numenor. This then is once choice before you, before us. We may join with that Power. It would be wise, Gandalf. There is hope that way. Its victory is at hand; and there will be rich reward for those that aided it. As the Power grows, its proved friends will also grow; and the Wise, such as you and I, may with patience come at last to direct its courses, to control it. We can bide our time, we can keep our thoughts in our hearts, deploring maybe evils done by the way, but approving the high and ultimate purpose: Knowledge, Rule, Order; all the things that we have so far striven in vain to accomplish, hindered rather than helped by our weak or idle friends. There need not be, there would not be any real change in our designs, only in our means."[3]

Both in the case of Saruman and in the case of Gollum,

---

3. Ibid., p. 340.

there is a sense that there may be a real possibility of their redemption. When Gandalf pleads with Saruman after his defeat, Saruman wavers for a moment. Just before Gollum betrays Frodo, he almost gives in to love for him. Each being in the story is good or evil by his own choice, and that choice is a genuinely free one, though powerful forces from inside and out attempt to influence it. As Gandalf says of Gollum:

> "Even Gollum was not wholly ruined. He had proved tougher than even one of the Wise would have guessed—as a hobbit might. There was a little corner of his mind that was still his own, and light came through it, as through a chink in the dark: light out of the past. It was actually pleasant, I think, to hear a kindly voice again, bringing up memories of wind, and trees, and sun on the grass, and such forgotten things.

> "But that, of course, would only make the evil part of him angrier in the end—unless it could be conquered. Unless it could be cured." Gandalf sighed "Alas! there is little hope of that for him. Yet not no hope. No, not though he possessed the Ring so long, almost as far back as he can remember. For it was long since he had worn it much: in the black darkness it was seldom needed. Certainly he had never 'faded.' He is thin and tough still. But the thing was eating up his mind, of course, and the torment had become almost unbearable."[4]

. . . The responsibility of each person to do God's work, the danger of using evil means—this is Tolkien's message.

4. Ibid., pp. 86–87.

A Grand Adventure but a Dangerous Blueprint for Human Affairs

Kenneth McLeish

Scholars debate the source of the morality in *The Lord of the Rings*, but generally suggest that, whatever its basis, if humans would return to the hierarchical rural decency Tolkien depicts, all would once again be right with the world, charges Kenneth McLeish. McLeish examines the influences of popular culture and mass fiction of Tolkien's time and concludes that *The Lord of the Rings* is permeated with a dangerously shallow view of human affairs and a disturbing attachment to the values of the Victorian era. Read the trilogy for great entertainment, he urges, but not for a blueprint for society. McLeish is author or editor of several dozen books, including one on the complete myths and legends of the Greeks, *Children of the Gods*.

YIN AND YANG

A clue to the essential nature of *The Lord of the Rings* is the almost total absence of femininity. I don't just mean that we hear nothing of Mrs. Gandalf, Merry's girl-friends (he surely wasn't a Brandybuck for nothing) or the home life of our own dear Wormtongue (was Mrs. Gríma a shrew—or nagged to shreds?). I don't mean that the few female characters we *do* hear about are cardboard figures from Welsh legend (like the ineffable Arwen, who was, if you'll pardon Tolkien's prose, 'so like in form of womanhood to Elrond that Frodo guessed she was one of his close kindred') or knockabout comediennes from the Victorian stage (*The Wooing of Sam and Rosie Gamgee* would surely have rolled 'em

Excerpted from Kenneth McLeish, "The Rippingest Yarn of All," in *J.R.R. Tolkien: This Far Land*, edited by Robert Giddings. Copyright © 1983 Vision Press Ltd. Reprinted by permission of A.P. Watt Ltd. on behalf of Valerie McLeish.

in the aisles. . . .) By absence of femininity I meant the lack of any true gentleness, grace or what the Oxford dictionary calls 'passivity' in the characters, of any vision of behavior beyond gruff comradeship (or its mirror sycophancy), bully-boy rant (or its mirror fortitude) and, to remind us now and then that our heroes are really just like us, the brushing away of a furtive but manly tear. . . .

Homer's *Iliad*, an epic which *does* include the feminine, hinges on the quarrel between Agamemnon (the masculine principle in nature, or *yang*, personified) and Achilles (the feminine principle, or *yin*) over a captured princess; its climactic battle (between Achilles and another yangy male, Hector) is not only preceded by one of the most moving 'feminine' scenes in literature, the farewell between Hector, Andromache and their baby son (who is terrified by his father's overshadowing helmet-plumes), but is followed by another, in which Priam pitifully pleads with the Greeks for Hector's corpse. Homer's *Odyssey*, the 'quest' narrative to end them all, charts Odysseus' growth not only as he comes to terms with every conceivable variety of female (calculating Calypso, nymphet Nausicaa, Marlene-Dietrich Circe), but more importantly as he realizes that the gentle and pliable qualities in his own nature are strength, not weakness, and as he persuades first his wife Penelope and then his people that because he has changed, has united the warring aspects in his own nature, he is worthy at last to be Penelope's husband and his people's king.

Where is this kind of profundity in *The Lord of the Rings*? Do its characters grow, in yin-and-yang harmonization or in any other way? Boromir, to be sure, learns that he is as greedy for the Ring as anyone else, that he is not the gentil parfit knight he thought himself; Frodo is revealed more and more as 'the outsider' (Camus, and Sartrean existentialism, were much in the air as Tolkien wrote); Gandalf turns from grey to white convincingly enough to pass the strictest window-test. But this is declaration of character, not growth: in each case it reveals only what was latent from the start. Like a preacher, Tolkien first tells us what his moral lessons are going to be, then goes through them painstakingly one by one. The dwarves become more dwarfish, the elves more elvish, the orcs more orc-like, even the hobbits more hobbity. The underlying moral messages are 'Discover your true self, and be true to it', and—less creditably—'Be wary of anyone Not Like

Us.' I think only the kindly old Ents avoid such pragmatic chauvinism—and all even they ever want is to be left alone.

Comparing Tolkien with Homer—as Tolkien would have been the first to point out—is pompous and silly. All he claimed to be doing was producing 'mythologies', extending his plunderings of the Red Book, already used in *The Hobbit* (his masterpiece, because it never aspires to allegorical significance, and is therefore superbly self-consistent); he nevertheless pointed out that

> since my children and others of their age, who first heard of the finding of the Ring, have grown older with the years, this book speaks more plainly of those darker things which lurked only on the borders of the earlier tale, but which troubled Middle-Earth in all its history.

It speaks of them all, that is, except—as J. W. Lambert pointed out when he first reviewed the book—except for God and sex. Leaving God aside for the moment, let's consider sex. Is there, somewhere in the morass of material which might have constituted *Silmarillion II* (and still might: *there's* a thought) Tolkien's *Tristan and Isolde*, his solution to the problems of uniting yin and yang? Or was *The Lord of the Rings* intended from the start as no more than an adult *Hobbit*, a fairy-tale for grown-up people?—in which case, like all half way decent tale-tellers (Bilbo himself states as much), if a particular aspect of experience didn't suit Tolkien's story, he left it out. Fair enough. But for those who claim higher status for *The Lord of the Rings* than that of a simple tale, the absence of sex—to say nothing of its benign transfiguration, love—is a matter to be reckoned with.

UPMARKET AND DOWN

Grown-ups, writing tales for children (and for other grown-ups): those are the key factors. What other tales might Tolkien himself, or his children, have experienced? What was a chap (or a chap's friend) likely to be reading in the 1900s, or in the 1930s (when Tolkien himself started publishing children's books, and presumably sniffed out the market first)? On what well-established foundations, in short, on what familiar ground, was the edifice of his life's work laid down?

I stress that I'm not talking about things like *Beowulf,* the *Kalevala* or the *Mabinogion,* the material Tolkien and his friends loved reading aloud to each other over mugs of ale. This kind of source-material is well documented elsewhere (and the documents should be known to every self-respecting Tolkien enthusiast. *A propos*, has anyone noticed the links between his work and Hermann Hesse's *Narcissus and Gold-mund* or *The Glass Bead Game*? Worth looking up.) I'm talking about popular literature, mass fiction, the furniture of the growing mind which we all take for granted as we grow, which helps our growing and which we generally put aside as soon as we've grown.

Curiously, this brings us straight back to God, to that other element crucial to literary stature which is missing from *The Lord of the Rings* (because it consistently confuses the metaphysical with the supernatural). The first inkling comes from the writings of Tolkien's donnish colleague and friend C. S. Lewis. Lewis was much concerned with metaphysics, with the Problem of Good and Evil (the capitals—and the simplification of the issue—are his), and produced a clutch of books (notably *The Screwtape Letters*) depicting the quest of and for the human soul in the form of a kind of Shavian fishing-manual, full of urbane jokes and shallow-profound metaphorical advice—'Whatever you do, don't cast where God is, or you'll foul your line.' He also wrote a legend-cycle for children, the *Narnia* books, which Tolkien heartily disliked and in which Good heroically and interminably battles Bad. But the clue lies less in any of these works than in his three remarkable science-fiction novels for adults, the first of which, *Out of the Silent Planet*, was published in 1938, just before *The Hobbit*. (Like Tolkien, Lewis went on in subsequent books, *Perelandra* and *That Hideous Strength*, to darken and broaden an originally simple theme.)

Out of the Silent Planet starts with a lone walker in a leafy, placid Shire, who can't find a pub and calls instead at a lonely house. Here he meets someone, a 'slender man' (the adjective is fanged) who claims to be a fellow spirit ('"By Jove," said the slender man, "Not Ransome who used to be at Wedenshaw?"'), and takes him for a ride and on a quest on which ultimately the whole future of the race depends. Like Bilbo in *The Hobbit*, Lewis's nudgingly-named Ransome travels with strange companions to very strange places; like Bilbo, he triumphs in the end over terrible evil by a mixture of ruefulness, determination and muddling through; like Bilbo, he is forever changed by his experience.

The difference is that Lewis's hero journeys not overland to Misty Mountains and beyond, but through space to Mars. *Out of the Silent Planet*, for all its overtones of Christian redemption and of decency and honesty fighting the fascist beast—overtones which Lewis, like Tolkien later with *The Lord of the Rings*, strenuously and disingenuously disclaimed—is an H. G. Wells science-fiction tale made over for a darker age. The traveller is a middle-class 'loner'; his 'slender' companion is at his least trustworthy when he smiles; mysterious, attractive beings are met *en route*, and reluctantly abandoned; there is an all-important battle and a sad aftermath. This is *Hobbit* country, but it is also the well-charted territory favoured by the literate Edwardian middle class.

Lewis is a far worse writer than Tolkien, chiefly because he lets his moral messages overburden his prose. But whatever its quality, *Out of the Silent Planet* reminds us how much *The Lord of the Rings* also owes to H.G. Wells. One example, in particular, leaps out of Tolkien's narrative. When Frodo, Sam and Gollum finally begin struggling up Mount Doom, the landscape, in its mixture of desolation, devastation and threat, seems uncannily familiar. It's not the Brecon Beacons, the Peak District or the Scottish Highlands (much too sinister); it's not even modelled on those shattered, barren vistas we all known as a fall-out from twentieth-century war. The impression that you've been there before arises because you *have*, in Wells's *The War of the Worlds*, first published in 1898, and a best-seller for ten years (i.e. all through Tolkien's adolescence). In this book, Martians and earthmen face each other for the final battle on just such scorched, bleak and above all menacing terrain. Wells could have been in the back of Tolkien's mind as he wrote *The Hobbit*, too: the terrifying film of *Things to Come* was issued in 1936, and its reputation would have reached even the most kinematophobic Oxford don, as it occasioned Questions in the House [British Parliament] and even Letters to *The Times* [of London]. There was a fine film of *The War of the Worlds* in 1953, two years before the publication of *The Return of the King*. Still another Wells story, *The Island of Doctor Moreau* (again hugely popular during Tolkien's adolescence) is about ugly, satanic and pitiable creatures, animal/human hybrids produced by vivisection and genetic manipulation. One of the most striking of them all (the puma-creature) has large, pale eyes, grasping bony hands and hissing speech. . . .

We shall never know if Tolkien consciously imitated (or even remembered) Wells; but clearly the man was around at the crucial time to strike sparks in Tolkien's adolescent mind. So was the masterpiece of another fine writer, Kenneth Grahame, whose *The Wind in the Willows* (first published in 1908, when Tolkien was 16) could be found on every middle-class child's bookshelf for three generations, a superb (if daunting) model for any aspiring writer of children's fantasy. There's no need to rehearse the similarities in detail—the description of Mole's house at the beginning, the gargantuan meals, Toad's Sackville-Bagginsy social pretension, Badger's twinkly-eyed crustiness (so like Gandalf's)—but two sections in particular are close to Tolkien in both spirit and style. The chapter at the end, in which all the nasty creatures from the Wild Wood are routed, is described with the same panache as Tolkien uses for Merry's or Pippin's adventures with the orcs ... ; and the chapter in *The Wind in the Willows* which I always found baffling as a child, in which the animals hear distant pan-pipes and are transported into a kind of rural trance, an ecstatic revelling in the sounds, smells, feel and psychic peacefulness of nature, is remarkably like what happens to Frodo and his friends when they stay with the Elves, and is told in that archly suggestive, Dante-Gabriel-Rossetti style—writing about magic trances was once as embarrassing to English authors as discussing sex or metaphysics—which is the hallmark of all Edwardian writing involving nature-mysticism, from the twee mythological rehashings of Andrew Lang to the poems of Walter de la Mare and the plays of Barrie (about whose *Peter Pan* Tolkien wrote in his 1910 diary 'indescribable, but shall never forget it as long as I live').

Wells, Grahame and Barrie: for many of those of us who passed our childhood and adolescence in the 1930s and 1940s, those are potent names. We learned from them that there was a world outside our own, much less comfortable and inhabited by unpredictable and often monstrous mutations of our own kind; we learned that our own world was safe and desirable, and could, if we used ingenuity and courage, be saved from outside threat. (It needs no palantír to see more anti-fascist implications here.) We're not quite in Tolkien territory—dignity and elevation of style are missing—but we're getting close.

OUR SORT

The over-simplification of moral issues in Wells, Grahame or Barrie was self-declaring and harmless, and made their work a wholesome tonic for the growing mind: silly enough to see through, but serious enough at least to raise the problems that perplex the young. A far more insidious, and far more sinister, influence comes in another type of children's literature, embodied in Tolkien's boyhood by the public-school sagas of Talbot Baines Reed and the adventure stories of Captain Marryat or G.A. Henty, and in his children's childhood by the messing-about-in-boats yarns of Arthur Ransome on the one hand, and on the other the 'he smiled grimly as the Boche spun out of control to his well-earned doom' tales of Percy F. Westerman and the unspeakable (but readable) Captain W.E. Johns. For adults, exactly the same philosophies were persuasively peddled in the 1910s and 1920s by Sapper, Edgar Wallace, Dornford Yates and their ilk, and in the 1930s and 1940s by what Colin Watson memorably christened the 'snobbery with violence' school of detective fiction whose joint headmistresses were Agatha Christie and the learned but muddle-headed Dorothy L. Sayers.

This literature is dangerous because it takes all ethical or moral problems for granted, as part of a desirable *status quo* which the villains constantly challenge and the heroes constantly reaffirm. Without exception, it hymns the British Imperial certainties of Tolkien's youth, a time when no one except foreigners like Freud and Marx—seriously 'got in the way of things'. Society, by and large, worked well—and it was sturdily structured on the premise that everyone knew his place. Women's place, for example, was firmly at home, queening it at tea beside the buddleia or scrubbing and scrimping behind the scenes; the few eccentrics who chained themselves to railings or chaired Fabian Society meetings were regarded by everyone else (including the majority of their own sex) as 'unladylike', 'beyond the pale'. The Lower Orders were servile or perky to a man—and the extent of their servility or perkiness depended on their employers' whim. Even within the ruling class there were Those who Decided and Those who Agreed: in real life, the Cabinet formulated policy and the Whips ensured that the House of Commons enacted it; in popular literature every Raffles, Berry or Holmes had a devoted but flea-brained sidekick, and Wimsey, Poirot and their rivals delighted in outsmarting everyone in sight; even in the public-school dorms and studies of *Stalky and Co.* or on Ballantyne's notorious *Coral Island* there were patrol-leader types and the

Good Scouts they led.

Outside this charmed circle, as everyone knew . . . , but as only troublemakers like Wells and Shaw kept pointing out, there was a vast, inarticulate army who maintained the edifice: the factory-workers, labourers, salesmen and shopgirls of country towns. They surfaced every five years (males over 21, at least) to vote at elections; but Parliament was reliably a talking-shop, and real government was carried on discreetly and imperturbably by a civil service as silkily irreplaceable as a first-class family retainer, and by the occasional, essential derring-do of aristocratic loners. It was Ruritania, happy and glorious; it was Tolkien's Shire. Only when the inarticulate army of the suburbs became the all-too-visible (and embarrassingly dead) army of the War to End Wars [World War I] was the Edwardian British twilight seen at last for what it was, the genteel decadence of a once thriving and invincible force.

It is my view that the books of Yates, Sayers and their like—favourite reading, we are assured, of the governing class—dangerously carried this shallow view of affairs, this smug or brainless clinging to the ethical verities of a vanished Victorian era, into the wholly alien decades of the first world war, the Depression and the General Strike   and that *The Lord of the Rings* still perpetuates them in an (even less appropriate) era of mass democracy on the one hand and the imminent possibility of a nuclear apocalypse on the other. The view—which had once been true—that 'all that sort of thing can be left to Our Betters' or to 'Those Who Know about Such Things' underlies every page of *The Lord of the Rings*, an indication of how far in the establishment past its author's view of affairs was formed, and of how little it had been shaken by Mosley, the Spanish Civil War, the abdication, Chamberlain, by the aristocratic oafs who generalled and air-marshalled Britain through the Phoney War (till Churchill, that visionary ostracized for a dozen years by his own caste, was plummeted into power), and by Dachau, Hiroshima and the closing of the Iron Curtain (all events predating *The Lord of the Rings*, and proving that the world was a bigger and far more dangerous place than placid Oxfordshire, and could never be so scaled-down again).

There are those who claim that all this turmoil *is* reflected in *The Lord of the Rings*, that the message underlying it is that if only humanity would return to a species of hierarchical rural decency (but never religious—God is, as I have said, rigorously excluded from Tolkien's cosmology), all might again be well. There are, Tolkien says somewhere, many people who know nothing of Frodo's and Sam's adventure, but who are able to sleep more easily in their beds because it has taken place. I would suggest two things: first, that carrying a Ring to dump into a volcano against all odds, helped by a representative of every species (a League of Nations with a constitution borrowed from the Icelandic sagas), and rescued at crisis-points by coincidence (Gwaihir the Windlord, yet!), by magic or by blundering-through (the climax on Mount Doom is a glorious, shambolic *mess*, one of the very few places in the whole epic where Tolkien contrives even a twitch of irony at his characters' expense)—I would suggest that this is a very poor allegory for how we should run our century, and second, that it was precisely this Edwardianly cosy view of human affairs in real life that cost Britain its Empire, cost Europe millions upon millions of its young men, and, unless we abandon it right now, will quite possibly cost us this planet and everything on it.

THE QUALITY OF TOLKIEN

... For the reasons outlined above (among others) I don't think Tolkien is an epic writer to compare with Homer, and I find his mythopoeic view of life too restricted, too simplistic, to stand up against the moral truths, meticulous observation and metaphysical profundity of the finest novelists (e.g. Balzac, Mann or Proust). The cult that has mushroomed round his imagined world is as dottily devoted, and ultimately as frivolous (because remote from reality) as those endless genealogies of invented races and grammars of made-up languages that stuffed Tolkien's own mind and plump up even his minor work. I think that the vision of society put forward in *The Lord of the Rings* is old-fashioned, wrong-headed and a lethal model for late twentieth-century living, as likely to succeed as the wooden rifles and bean-poles with which Dad's Army once hoped to keep the invading Hun at bay. To put it bluntly, we live in a nasty, dangerous and brutal world, and dressing up in elven-cloaks, baking lembas and writing poems in Entish, though a commendable and delightful game, is a way of avoiding, not finding, the truth of life.

So where does that leave Tolkien? If those of his cultists who take him seriously are dangerously deluded, does that

necessarily make him a fool as well? Of course not. The time
has come to lay my cards on the table and say that I think
Tolkien was one of the finest writers of escapist fantasy in
any language and of any time. (Homer, Tolstoy, Dickens,
aren't in competition. Their subject was reality.) His verse
may be appalling, his prose convoluted and often arch, and
his inspiration a magpie's nest of half-remembered instances from every piece of literature he ever read, from
King Lear to *Noddy in Toyland*. But he hooks you from the
first sentence, and drags you gasping and sighing through
every spiral of his narrative, leaving you always hungry, always wanting more. The Quest is one of the surest of all fictional plots. It has a clearly marked start and a clearly de-
fined end—and this clarity allows for all manner of
diversions, twists and turns *en route*. In Tolkien's landscape
every stone and tree has a part to play and a story to tell—indeed trees come to life and *tell* their stories. His world is full
of wonders; magic is not special, but particular to everyone.
Any author who invents Moria, Rivendell, the Ringwraiths,
my own favourites the Ents, Gandalf and Saruman, is a storyteller to reckon with—and when he goes on to detail his
fantasy with whole cycles of history, whole geographies,
whole languages, how can we not be charmed? Tolkien's
world, unlike the real world of infinite possibility in which
we live, offers the attractions of completeness: he has anticipated every question and found an answer before you asked.

If your work is a magpie's hoard, what matters for greatness is the use you make of the glittering jewels you find—
and this, I suggest, is the main facet of Tolkien's genius. He
keeps reminding us of other things, stirring our memory of
books, images and ideas we'd long forgotten; but he gives
each memory, each allusion, a new twist and so redoubles
its power. (Well, not always. The whole Theoden episode is
a very faint echo of the hero-sagas from which it derives: try
Beowulf, or consider what Wagner—whom Tolkien so
heartily despised—did with Nordic mythology in *his The
Ring.*) The underground sequences are brilliantly brought
off, the finest portions of the book; the Balrog, Shelob and
above all Gollum are both persuasive delineations of evil
and creepily credible as characters; the Ents (though their
origin could be unkindly traced to Enid Blyton's *The Faraway Tree* and their siege of Isengard, as recounted by
Merry . . . , to Hesiod's version of the Earthborn Giants' at-

tack on the Olympian gods) are a spectacular creation, as convincing a metaphor for the force and dignity of nature as Bombadil is a plastic one. And, most striking of all, Tolkien's careful blend of tones of voice—he moves in a paragraph from the down-to-earthness of the Hobbits (all grumbling bellies and hamster-like alarm) to the 'Lo! how brave the banners blew' alliterative-epic nonsense of the Rohirrim, the stabbing gutturals of the orcs, the hooming and hom-ming of the Ents and the hissing duplicity of Gríma and Sméagol—all this gives the story forward movement, pace, and that essential ingredient of all good yarns, unexpected-ness: you *have* to turn each page to see what horrors or de-lights are lurking there.

So, from the great cycles of saga and from the far less el-evated but no less evocative tales that helped to form his and our youth, Tolkien assembles a hundred ideas, a thousand strands of narrative, and weaves them into a single, glowing tapestry, a work which reveals not only the capacious liter-ary ragbag that was his mind, but also his genius for orga-nization and redeployment. He is like a museum curator, with exhibits from all the world's cultures arranged to give maximum delight. And if—as I have suggested—a major part of his collection consists of pages torn from the chil-dren's or grown-ups' escapist adventure-stories of the twen-tieth century, what he has written beggars all his sources, and—providing we never take it as any kind of answer to the world's problems—is stunningly readable, breathtakingly exciting and morally unambiguous: in short, the ripping yarn to end them all.

Charges of Racism in *The Lord of the Rings* Are Mistaken

Patrick Curry

Tolkien has been accused of being an English chauvinist, of trying to perpetuate divisions between classes, even of being a racist, reports Patrick Curry. While the hobbits are to a large degree a self-portrait of the English, readers will connect them with rustic peoples anywhere in the world. As to charges against Tolkien of bias and bigotry, Curry points out that class awareness in the trilogy merely reflects modern reality; moreover, "interracial" marriage and friendships between members of different races assert "the wonder of multicultural difference" rather than any sort of apartheid. Curry is the author of *Defending Middle-Earth: Tolkien, Myth and Modernity*, from which this essay is excerpted.

It is as neighbours, full of ineradicable prejudices, that we must love each other, and not as fortuitously 'separated brethren.'[1]

Hobbits, according to Tolkien, were more frequent 'long ago in the quiet of the world. . . .' They 'love peace and quiet and good tilled earth: a well-ordered and well-farmed countryside was their favourite haunt. They do not and did not understand or like machines more complicated than a forge-bellows, a water-mill, or a hand-loom. . . . Their faces were as a rule good-natured rather than beautiful, broad, bright-eyed, red-cheeked, with mouths apt to laughter, and to eating and drinking.' They thought of themselves as 'plain quiet folk' with 'no use for adventures. Nasty disturbing uncomfortable things! Make you late for dinner!' 'Nonetheless,' their chronicler notes, 'ease and peace had left this people

Excerpted from *Defending Middle-Earth: Tolkien, Myth and Modernity*, by Patrick Curry. Copyright © 1997 by Patrick Curry. Reprinted with permission from St. Martin's Press, Inc.

still curiously tough. They were, if it came to it, difficult to daunt or to kill. . . .' In other words, they manifested 'the notorious Anglo-hobbitic inability to know when they're beaten.'[2]

Hobbits were also inclined 'to joke about serious things,' and 'say less than they mean.' Indeed, they 'will sit on the edge of ruin and discuss the pleasures of the table, or the small doings of their fathers, grandfathers, and great-grandfathers, and remoter cousins to the ninth degree, if you encourage them with undue patience.' Similarly, they preferred speeches that were 'short and obvious,' and 'liked to have books filled with things that they already knew, set out fair and square with no contradictions.' They were 'a bit suspicious . . . of anything out of the way—uncanny, if you understand me.'[3] It wasn't difficult to acquire a reputation for peculiarity in the Shire.

But as Tolkien notes, in addition to their wealth 'Bilbo and Frodo Baggins were as bachelors very exceptional, as they were also in many other ways, such as their friendship with Elves.' The nephew of 'mad Baggins,' as he eventually became known, Frodo was something of an aesthete and intellectual, who, 'to the amazement of sensible folk . . . was sometimes seen far from home walking in the hills and woods under the starlight.'[4] None of this was usual among their peers, and Sam the gardener, although recently and exceptionally lettered, was a more typical hobbit than his fellow Companions—or as Tolkien put it, 'the genuine hobbit.'

Like some readers, Tolkien himself sometimes found Sam, as he wrote:

> very 'trying.' He is a more representative hobbit than any others that we have to see much of; and he has consequently a stronger ingredient of that quality which even some hobbits found at times hard to bear: a vulgarity—by which I do not mean a mere 'down-to-earthiness'—a mental myopia which is proud of itself, a smugness (in varying degrees) and cocksureness, and a readiness to measure and sum up all things from a limited experience, largely enshrined in sententious traditional 'wisdom.' . . . Imagine Sam without his education by Bilbo and his fascination with things Elvish![5]

Even with this kind of conservative peer pressure, however, your behaviour had to be extreme to land you in any real trouble, for the Shire at this time had hardly any government: 'Families for the most part managed their own affairs. . . . The only real official in the Shire at this date was the Mayor of Michel Delving,' and 'almost his only duty was to preside at banquets. . . .' Otherwise there were only hereditary heads of clans, plus a Postmaster and First Shirriff—the latter less for Inside Work than 'to see that Outsiders of any kind, great or small, did not make themselves a nuisance.'[6]

ENGLISHNESS

Now it doesn't take any great perceptiveness to see in 'these charming, absurd, helpless' (and not-so-helpless) hobbits a self-portrait of the English, something which Tolkien admitted: '"The Shire" is based on rural England and not any other country in the world,' and more specifically the West Midlands: Hobbiton 'is in fact more or less a Warwickshire village of about the period of the Diamond Jubilee' (i.e. 1897).[7]

Compare the portrait by George Orwell writing in 1940, and one still instantly recognizable, albeit sadly altered in some respects, of a conservative people neither artistically nor intellectually inclined, though with 'a certain power of acting without thought'; taciturn, preferring tacit understandings to formal explication; endowed with a love of flowers and animals, valuing privateness and the liberty of the individual, and respecting constitutionalism and legality; not puritanical and without definite religious belief, but strangely gentle (and this has changed most, especially during the 1980s), with a hatred of war and militarism that coexists with a strong unconscious patriotism. Orwell summed up English society as 'a strange mixture of reality and illusion, democracy and privilege, humbug and decency.'[8]

True, these attributes are inextricably mingled with ones that the English have wanted to find in the mirror; nor are they eternal and immutable. Because this image partakes of a national pastoral fantasy, however, it does not follow that it has no reality. A social or literary criticism that is afraid to admit the relative truth of clichés and stereotypes is hamstrung from the start. Also, it is worth noting that Tolkien's portrait is not altogether a flattering one; it includes greed, small-minded parochialism and philistinism, at least—even in Frodo, Sam and the other hobbits of his story were able to rise above these regrettable characteristics of the English bourgeoisie.

However, although Tolkien drew on the tiny corner of the world that is the West Midlands of England, readers from virtually everywhere else in the world connect the hobbits with a rustic people of their own, relatively untouched by modernity—if not still actually existing, then from the alternative reality of folk- and fairy-tale. Doubtless this has been made possible by setting his books in a place that, while it feels like N.W. Europe, is made strange and wonderful by its imaginary time. Otherwise, I have no doubt, they would have suffered from the same limitations of time and place as Kipling's *Puck of Pook's Hill* and G.K. Chesterton's poems, however wonderful these otherwise may be. Tolkien's tale, in contrast, has probably achieved as close to universality as is given to art.

COUNTRY FOLK

The hobbits are recognizably modern in important respects, especially in their bourgeois and anti-heroic tenor. Thus, one famous hobbit, when asked by a large eagle, 'What is finer than flying?,' only allowed his native tact, and caution, to overrule suggesting 'A warm bath and late breakfast on the lawn afterwards.'[9] As several commentators have noticed, it is crucial that Bilbo and Frodo *be* modern, in order to 'accommodate modernity without surrendering to it,'[10] by mediating between ourselves and the ancient and foreign world they inhabit. But in other ways, the hobbits have much older roots. They remind us of 'the archetypal pre-Industrial Revolution English yeoman with simple needs, simple goals, and a common-sense approach to life,'[11] and also of the English before their defeat in 1066, when the 'Norman Yoke' imposed centralized autocratic government, a foreign language and an alien cultural tradition.

The bucolic hobbits also clearly fall within the long tradition in English letters of nostalgic pastoralism, celebrating a time 'when there was less noise and more green.'[12] As Martin J. Weiner notes, 'Idealization of the countryside has a long history in Britain.' It extends from Tennyson's mid-Victorian *English Idylls* and William Morris's 'fair green garden of Northern Europe,' through the rural essays of Richard Jefferies and the Poet Laureate Alfred Austin's *Haunts of Ancient Peace* (1902)—which could easily be the title of a song by Van Morrison today—to Kipling's 'Our England is a garden,' and George Sturt listening to his gardener (note), 'in whose quiet voice,' he felt, 'I am privileged to hear the natural fluent, unconscious talk, as it goes on over the face of the

country, of the English race.' In short, a deep cultural gulf
had opened between England's southern and rural 'green
and pleasant land' and her northern and industrial 'dark satanic mills'; or as Weiner puts it, with unintentional aptness,
'The power of the machine was invading and blighting the
Shire.'[13]

The irony is, of course, that since 1851 over half the pop-
ulation on this island has lived in towns, and by then England was already the world's first urban nation. Thus, as
Weiner writes, 'The less practically important rural England
became, the more easily could it come to stand simply for an
alternative and complementary set of values, a psychic balance wheel.'[14] But few things are that simple, and when applied to Tolkien, such glib simplification has led to a great
deal of misunderstanding. The related charges commonly
laid at Tolkien's door are several, and severe. They are also
almost entirely mistaken, so I shall use them to arrive at the
truth of the matter.

NATION AND CLASS

One of the first critics to attack Tolkien was Catharine
Stimpson, in 1969. 'An incorrigible nationalist,' she wrote,
Tolkien 'celebrates the English bourgeois pastoral idyll. Its
characters, tranquil and well fed, live best in placid, philis-
tine, provincial rural cosiness.'[15]

Now it is true that the hobbits (excepting Bilbo and Frodo,
and perhaps Sam . . . and Merry and Pippin) would indeed
have preferred to live quiet rural lives, if they could have.
Unfortunately for them, and Stimpson's point, there is much
more to Middle-earth than the Shire. By the same token, any
degree of English nationalism that the hobbits represent is
highly qualified. Tolkien himself pointed out that 'hobbits
are not a Utopian vision, or recommended as an ideal in
their own or any age. They, as all peoples and their situations, are an historical accident—as the Elves point out to
Frodo—and an impermanent one in the long view.'[16] It is
also possible, as Jonathan Bate suggests, to draw a distinction between love of the local land, on the one hand, and pa-
triotic love of the fatherland on the other. In *The Lord of the
Rings*, the lovingly detailed specificities of the natural
world—which include but far outrun those of the Shire—far
exceed any kind of abstract nationalism.[17]

Stimpson also accuses Tolkien of 'class snobbery'[18]—that

is, the lord of the manor's disdain for commoners, and, by extension, the working class. Well, in *The Hobbit*, perhaps; but only zealous detectors of orcism and trollism would ignore its other virtues, such as any quality as a story. And its hero, if no peasant, is plainly no lord. But with *The Lord of the Rings*—if this charge means anything worse than a sort of chivalrous paternalism, appropriate to someone growing up at the turn of this century, which now looks dated—then it fails.

There is certainly class awareness. But the idioms of Tolkien's various hobbits only correspond to their social classes in the same way as do those of contemporary humans. The accent and idiom of Sam (arguably the real hero of the book) and most other hobbits are those of a rural peasantry, while those of Frodo, Bilbo and their close friends range through the middle classes. Or take Orcs; their distinguishing characteristics are a love of machines and loud noises (especially explosions), waste, vandalism and destruction for its own sake; also, they alone torture and kill for fun. Their language, accordingly, is 'at all times full of hate and anger,' and composed of 'brutal jargons, scarcely sufficient even for their own needs, unless it were for curses and abuse.' In the Third Age, 'Orcs and Trolls spoke as they would, without love of words or things; and their language was actually more degraded and filthy,' writes Tolkien, 'than I have shown it.' As he adds, too truly, 'Much the same sort of talk can still be heard among the orc-minded; dreary and repetitive with hatred and contempt. . . .'[19]

But Orc speech is not all the same; there are at least three kinds, and none are necessarily 'working-class.'[20] And it can be found today among members of any social class; nor is money a bar. In fact, virtually all of Tolkien's major villains— Smaug, Saruman, the Lord of the Nazgûl, and presumably Sauron too—speak in unmistakably posh tones.[21] After all, the orc-minded are mere servants of Mordor; its contemporary masters (or rather, master-servants) much more resemble the Nazgûl, although today they probably wear expensive suits and ride private jets rather than quasi-pterodactyls. And although many fewer than Orcs (who knows? perhaps there are exactly nine[22]), they are infinitely more powerful, and to be feared.

There is also the obvious and fundamental fact of *The Lord of the Rings* as a tale of 'the hour of the Shire-folk, when they arise from their quiet fields to shake the towers and counsels of the Great.'[23] Nonetheless, the charge of pandering to social hierarchy has proved durable. Another unpleasant and related accusation sometimes made is racism.[24] Now it is true that Tolkien's evil creatures are frequently 'swart, slant-eyed,' and tend to come from the south ('the cruel Haradrim') and east ('the wild Easterlings')[25]—both threatening directions in Tolkien's 'moral cartography.'[26] It is also true that black—as in Breath, Riders, Hand, Years, Land, Speech—is often a terrible colour, especially when contrasted with Gandalf the White, the White Rider, and so on. But the primary association of black here is with night and darkness, not race. And there are counter-examples: Saruman's sign is a white hand; Aragorn's standard is mostly black; the Black Riders were not actually black, except their outer robes; and the Black Stone of Erech is connected with Aragorn's forebear, Isildur.[27]

Overall, Tolkien is drawing on centuries of such moral valuation, not unrelated to historical experience attached to his chosen setting in order to convey something immediately recognizable in the context of his story. As Kathleen Herbert noticed, Orcs sound very like the first horrified reports in Europe of the invading Huns in the fourth and fifth centuries: 'broad-shouldered, bow-legged, devilishly effective fighters, moving fast, talking a language that sounds like no human speech (probably Turkic) and practising ghastly tortures with great relish.'[28] (Théoden may well have been modelled on Theodoric I, the aged Visigothic king who died leading his warriors in a charge against Attila's Huns in the Battle of Chalons.)

Perhaps the worst you could say is that Tolkien doesn't actually go out of his way to forestall the possibility of a racist interpretation. (I say 'possibility' because it is ridiculous to assume that readers automatically transfer their feelings about Orcs to all the swart or slant-eyed people they encounter in the street.) But as Virginia Luling has pointed out, the appearance of racism is deceptive, 'not only because Tolkien in his non-fictional writing several times repudiated racist ideas, but because . . . in his sub-creation the whole intellectual underpinning of racism is absent.'[29] In any case, such an interpretation as the story in *The Lord of the Rings* proceeds, that would get increasingly harder to maintain— and this relates to another common criticism, also voiced by

Stimpson, that Tolkien's characters divide neatly into 'good and evil, nice and nasty.'[30] But as anyone who has really read it could tell you, the initial semi-tribal apportioning of moral probity increasingly breaks down, as evil emerges 'among the kingly Gondorians, the blond Riders of Rohan, the seemingly incorruptible wizards, and even the thoroughly English hobbit-folk of the Shire.'[31] (Incidentally, hobbits appear to be brown-skinned, not white.[32]) By the same token, Frodo, Gollum, Boromir and Denethor all experience intense inner struggles over what the right thing to do is, with widely varying outcomes; and as Le Guin has noted, several major characters have a 'shadow.'[33] In Frodo's case, there are arguably two: Sam and Gollum, who is himself doubled as Gollum/Stinker and Sméagol/Slinker, as Sam calls him.

'If you want to write a tale of this sort,' Tolkien once wrote, 'you must consult your roots, and a man of the Northwest of the Old World will set his heart and the action of his tale in an imaginary world of that air, and that situation: with the Shoreless Sea of his innumerable ancestors to the West, and the endless lands (out of which enemies mostly come) to the East.'[34]

Thus, as Clyde Kilby recounts, when Tolkien was asked what lay east and south of Middle-earth, he replied: '"Rhûn is the Elvish word for east. Asia, China, Japan, and all the things which people in the West regard as far away. And south of Harad is Africa, the hot countries." Then Mr. Resnick asked, "That makes Middle-earth Europe, doesn't it?" To which Tolkien replied, "Yes, of course—Northwestern Europe . . . where my imagination comes from".' (In which case, as Tolkien also agreed, Mordor 'would be roughly in the Balkans.')[35]

He reacted sharply to reading a description of Middle-earth as 'Nordic,' however: 'Not *Nordic*, please! A word I personally dislike; it is associated, though of French origin, with racialist theories. . . .' He also contested Auden's assertion that for him 'the North is a sacred direction': 'That is not true. The North-west of Europe, where I (and most of my ancestors) have lived, has my affection, as a man's home should. I love its atmosphere, and know more of its histories and languages than I do of other parts; but it is not "sacred," nor does it exhaust my affections.'[36]

It is also striking that the races in Middle-earth are most striking in their variety and autonomy. I suppose that this *could* be seen as an unhealthy emphasis on 'race'; it seems to me rather an assertion of the wonder of multicultural difference. And given that most of Middle-earth's peoples are closely tried to a particular geography and ecology, and manage to live there without exploiting it to the point of destruction, isn't this what is nowadays called bioregionalism? But no kind of apartheid is involved: one of the subplots of *The Lord of the Rings* concerns an enduring friendship between members of races traditionally estranged (Gimli and Legolas), and the most important union in the book, between Aragorn and Arwen, is an 'interracial' marriage. As usual, the picture is a great deal more complex than the critics, although not necessarily the public, seem to see.

NOTES

1. Hubert Butler, *Escape from the Anthill* (Mullingar: The Lilliput Press, 1986), 95.
2. J.R.R. Tolkien, *The Hobbit* (London: Grafton Books, 1991), 15. (Henceforth *Hobbit;* all page numbers are from this edition.) J.R.R. Tolkien, *The Lord of the Rings* (London: Grafton Books, 1991), I, 17, 18. (Henceforth *LoR;* all page numers are from this edition.) *Hobbit,* 16; *LoR,* I, 23. 'Anglo hobbitic': T.A. Shippey, *The Road to Middle Earth* (London: George Allen & Unwin, 1992 [1982]), 91.
3. Hobbits: *LoR,* I, 59; III, 173; II, 202; I, 50, 26, 219.
4. Frodo: *LoR,* I, 25, 67.
5. Sam: Humphrey Carpenter (ed.), *The Letters of J.R.R. Tolkien* (London: George Allen & Unwin, 1981), 105, 329 (on Sam). (Henceforth *Letters,* with page rather than letter numbers given.)
6. Shire: *LoR,* I, 28, 29, 75.
7. Shire/rural England: *Letters,* 250, 230; and see Clyde Kilby, *Tolkien and the Silmarillion* (Berkhamsted: Lion Publishing, 1977), 51. The hobbits' obsession with family genealogy is an Icelandic touch, however.
8. George Orwell, 'The Lion and the Unicorn: Socialism and the English Genius,' 527–64 in *Collected Essays, Journalism and Letters* (London: Secker and Warburg, 1968).
9. Warm bath: *Hobbit,* 113.
10. 'Accommodate modernity': Hugh Brogan, 'Tolkien's Great War,' in Gillian Avery and Julia Briggs (eds.), *Children and Thier Books* (Oxford, Eng.: Clarendon, 1989), 360. *Cf.* Shippey, *Road,* 55.

11. 'English yeoman': David Harvey, *The Song of Middle-Earth: J.R.R. Tolkien's Themes, Symbols and Myths* (London: George Allen & Unwin, 1985), 114.
12. Less noise: *Hobbit*, 15.
13. Martin J. Weiner, *English Culture and the Decline of the Industrial Spirit 1850–1980* (London: Penguin, 1985), 47, 61 (Sturt), 81, and Chapter 4 generally. See also Alun Howkins, 'The Discovery of Rural England,' 62–88 in Robert Coll and Philip Dodd (eds.), *Englishness. Politics and Culture 1880–1920* (London: Croon Helm, 1986).
14. Weiner, *English Culture*, 47, 49.
15. Catharine R. Stimpson, *J.R.R. Tolkien* (New York: Columbia University Press, 1969) (Columbia Essays on Modern Writers No. 41), 8, 13. See Hal Colebatch's critique of Stimpson in his *Return of the Heroes: The Lord of the Rings, Star Wars and Contemporary Culture* (Perth: Australian Institute for Public Policy, 1990), 61–66.
16. Historical accident: *Letters*, 197.
17. Land/fatherland: Jonathan Bate, *Romantic Ecology: Wordsworth and the Environmental Tradition* (London: Routledge, 1991), 11.
18. Stimpson, *Tolkien*, 13.
19. Orcs: *LoR*, II, 54; III, 520, 524.
20. 'Working-class': Brian Rosebury, *Tolkien: A Critical Assessment* (London: St. Martin's, 1992), 75–76.
21. Posh Tones: the last point is made by Colebatch, *Return*, 64.
22. Exactly nine modern Ringwraiths: joke.
23. Hour of the Shire-folk: *LoR*, I, 354.
24. Accusation: for a recent and typically thoughtless repetition, see Roz Kaveney, 'The Ring recycled,' *New Statesman & Society* (20/27.12.91) 47, who also associates Tolkien with 'a broadside attack on modernism and even on realism' (is *nothing* sacred?), and anachronistically blames him for current 'American commercial fantasy and science fiction.'
25. Evil creatures: *LoR*, II, 14, 357.
26. 'Moral cartography': Walter Scheps, 'The Fairy-tale Morality of *The Lord of the Rings*,' in Jared Lobdell (ed.), *A Tolkien Compass* (La Salle, IL: Open Court, 1975), 44–45; also 46, for discussion of the instances of blackness.
27. Counter-examples: see Rosebury, *Tolkien*, 79.

28. Kathleen Herbert, *Spellcraft: Old English Heroic Legends* (Hockwold-cum-Wilton, Norfolk: Anglo-Saxon Books, 1993) 271, 225.
29. Virginia Luling, 'An Anthropologist in Middle-Earth,' in Patricia Reynolds and Glen H. GoodKnight (eds.), *Proceedings of the J.R.R. Tolkien Centenary Conference* (Milton Keynes: The Tolkien Society, and Altadena, CA: Mythopoeic Press, 1995). However, as she adds, the Orcs—as distinct from the Haradrim, Variags and Easterlings—'are a separate problem, and one that Tolkien himself never really solved' (p. 56); see J.R.R. Tolkien, *Morgoth's Ring*, ed. Christopher Tolkien (London: HarperCollins, 1994), for his efforts to do so.
30. Stimpson, *Tolkien*, 18.
31. 'Kingly Gondorians': Brian Attebery, *Strategies of Fantasy* (Bloomington: University of Indiana, 1992), 33.
32. Brown-skinned: *LoR*, III, 229.
33. Ursula K. Le Guin, *The Language of the Night; Essays on Fantasy and Science Fiction*, ed. Susan Wood (London: The Women's Press, 1989), 57–58; and see Attebery, *Strategies*, 33, and Rosebury, *Tolkien*, 75–76. (This is simplistic?)
34. A tale of this sort: *Letters*, 212,
35. Kilby, *Tolkien*, 51–52.
36. North-west Europe: *Letters*, 375–76.

Care for the Earth and for Each Other

Robley Evans

Tolkien argues that there is much of value in Western society that should be saved, writes Robley Evans. In presenting a mythic story that invites readers to learn to respect all living things, Tolkien gives emotional and spiritual meaning to the "facts" of the Primary World—the physical world that often seems bleak. Evans is author of the *Writers for the Seventies* book on Tolkien, from which this essay is excerpted.

If we compare Tolkien to other contemporary writers, we see major differences. Unlike such writers of fantasy as Kurt Vonnegut, Tolkien is never crudely satiric; gentleness and love pervade his work and soften the criticism of modern society implicit in it. Where other authors present a bleak picture of the wasteland in which the soul struggles to survive alone, Tolkien gives us the Fellowship of the Ring as a happier alternative, a small society of loving creatures who are not alone in the universe. Tolkien argues that there is much of value in Western culture which should be saved, which *will* be saved, by the imaginative beings who have power to believe in themselves. Tolkien is a conservative in this sense; for all the elements of the fantastic in his work, the preservation of traditional values is most important to him. The fantastic affirms those values rather than attempting to substitute something else for them. Tolkien's writing style, too, is not meant to surprise or shock us; it is always subordinate to the story being told. It is his retelling of our most deeply believed myths about ourselves that makes *The Lord of the Rings* so moving.

WORDS SHARE THE REALITY OF THE PRIMARY WORLD

Tolkien is read because he tells a good story; his power to command Secondary Belief in his readers is real. History comes

Excerpted from *J.R.R. Tolkien*, by Robley Evans (New York: Crowell, 1972). Copyright © 1972 by Warner Books, Inc. Reprinted with the permission of Warner Books, Inc.

alive in the characters and events of *The Lord of the Rings* because Tolkien creates speeches and actions which have the "inner consistency of reality" and are not absolutely and destructively rooted in the "observed fact" of the Primary World. He has chosen to tell a story, rather, than write a philosophic discourse, and this decision was important because a narrative presents "inner" reality in a way a discursive essay does not: imagined beings who take their life from the hands of their creator touch our emotions, our imaginations, our religious sense of wonder, in ways words addressed to the intellect alone cannot. As William Blake wrote long ago, we cannot really imagine God as a cloud; we must imagine Him in the form most meaningful to us, that of a man. Men, or created beings of other races, act enough like men in Tolkien's fantasies, to remind us that we, too, progress through time toward death; that we, too, love life and fear evil. And in this way the fantastic in its narrative form comes closer to representing that total body of knowledge and being which is ourself more than many other literary kinds. In order to make this happen, the fantasist gives us actions and shapes which seem familiar; but he also frees us from dependency upon "observed fact" so that the imagination can work and our vision of the unknown world can show us new things in ourselves.

Behind Tolkien's choice of form lies an assumption about the nature of man which shines through his work: that men can love, admire good deeds, can seek truth because it is good. They are not "bad"; they are imperceptive, they are weak insofar as excessive self-pride makes them misuse their particular powers; they are available, however, to correction, to change, to the Power, used only for good, of the Enchanter. Words and literary forms are not things apart from human beings. They come up from the body and the feelings attached to the Primary World, as they are, and they share in that reality. And much more. The "Joy" of which Tolkien writes in "On Fairy-Stories" is "heavenly" all right, but it underlies the events in *The Lord of the Rings*, too, in the "turn" of the happy ending, and in the life of the narration itself.

A MYTHIC STORY IN WHICH ALL CAN SHARE

This is important because we also read Tolkien for other reasons which come through to us because of his way of presenting them. Tolkien has gone against the present style of literary fashion; he does not give us the private rhetoric of the symbolist or the inner-directed world of the despairing self-analyst whose psychological conflicts spin out a novel's length. Rather than make a meaningful world out of an individual's isolated and particular nature, he returns to the myths of the past and to the mythic story of the Quest in which all men can share. This argues for the universal significance of experience and so for the pervasive moral effects of the imagination. Individual suffering and bewilderment reveal valuable meaning in a mythic context; nor is suffering exceptional and meaningful only to the individual. If as Mark Schorer says, myths are images "that give philosophical meaning to the facts of ordinary life," then a writer of myth writes for his whole society as well as every individual who suffers and imagines in it. Fantasy is not escape in the sense of flight from reality, Tolkien reminds us, but an affirmation of man's ability to order reality, a schema for handling the problems which power creates, for "realizing imagined wonder." His success at reconstituting the fairy-story for the twentieth century lies in part in his sense of our moral necessities.

Another reason for reading Tolkien is his assertion that the Imagination has value in the Primary World. For many people, growing up in a culture which seems to emphasize the uniformity of lives on the assembly line or in split-level suburbs, works of fantasy must be suspect because they represent imagined existence and exceptional beings. Tolkien shows throughout *The Hobbit* and *The Lord of the Rings* that we can be surprised by our fellows: the hobbits of the Shire perform heroic feats we would never have expected. But it is this unexpected quality of the imagination, popping up when least expected, that readers must find attractive, especially since this power for good solves problems, directs actions, opens up possibilities in Tolkien's fantasies. And for readers who resist the homogeneity and conformity of contemporary life, there is appeal in the variety of imagined beings—elves, dwarves, ents, hobbits— who appear in the hills and valleys of Middle-earth. Not only the profusion of races, but the respect which they can show to each other must be important for Americans perplexed by racial segregation, sexual discrimination, xenophobia and their divisive, hate-engendering effects. In *The Lord of the Rings*, we find a Fellowship, a United Nations, based upon common needs and shared affection, even between the most disparate peoples. The fight against "possessiveness," the possibilities of "Recovery," are happy alternatives in a possessive society.

RESPECT FOR ALL LIVING THINGS

In Tolkien's world, respect is paid not only to other "races" but to living things generally. Perhaps the most important problem in the latter half of the twentieth century is presented by the natural environment, ravaged by possessive men in search of wealth and power. In the Trilogy, the evil beings are connected with such desecration; Saruman and Sauron both attack the natural organic world, leveling forests, covering vegetation with ash-piles, factories and their waste, the "produce" of slave-worked mines. But those who fight against evil respect the natural world, as guardians of all created beings. The ents care for their trees, the dwarves for their gleaming minerals. Aragorn finds help for wounds in the *athelas*, a wild herb. Sam grows an elven tree, the *Mallorn*, far from its home in Lorien. The imagination requires that even plants be permitted their own natures, and shown care rather than possessiveness. This general respect for all created life in *The Lord of the Rings* speaks to those among us who fear the disappearance of redwoods and whales, mountain wilderness and hidden seashores to serve society's destructive needs. If we try to turn every mountain valley into a national park with camping areas, general stores and play grounds, we have remade it in our image, and so extended a step further "the drab blur of triteness or familiarity" which must ultimately threaten our own necessary sense of wonder at other forms of life. And under our heavy hand, such unique life can be extinguished. *Care for the world* might be the theme of Tolkien's Trilogy.

Nor does the Imagination deny the existence of evil. Our society can be accused of hiding reality under its images: the glossy prints of the large-circulation magazines or the smiling caricatures of housewives discovering a new soap in television commercials. Distress is smoothed away, and suffering denied not only existence but value. People hurt, however; they suffer from poverty, hunger, loneliness, fear and a long list of human symptoms which no soap product or movie star can cure. They also suffer from the absence of great causes for which to suffer, paradoxical as that may seem. In Tolkien's fantasy, we do not escape from evil: there is no running away from the Shadow of Sauron. The ways in which created beings respond to the challenge such power presents distinguish them; make them more complex in nature than we think at first; make them moral. For a reader tired of seeing human beings as only partial figures caught in the conventions of social life and prescribed rituals, the revelation of hidden natures available for good or evil is valuable.

AN EMPHASIS ON FEELING, RATHER THAN REASON

And, finally, beyond it social implications, the imagination in its guise of the fantastic, separate from "observed fact," gives life to the world in a way the sciences, the academic disciplines which emphasize reason or mathematical formulae, do not. As man begins to discover more and more about the laws which govern life, and seems to be reducing life to equations tested in a laboratory, our human response is to seek the unreasonable, the irrational, feelings and visions which may be condemned by the scientist because they cannot be analyzed or represented statistically. Love, responsibility, and will power cannot be computed, yet they exist, and seem to have much more to do with human conduct than laws and figures. The appeal of fantasy implies instinctive rejection of what seems impersonal, unfeeling, insensitive to our human desires, in the century of nuclear bombs, germ warfare, and government policy beyond the power of any individual to influence.

In fact, Tolkien emphasizes feeling in *The Lord of the Rings.* Characters not only develop love for one another, they express it in companionship, in sacrifice, in loyalty. They show it by kissing and holding hands. They respond to their feelings by expressing anger or love. They have strong responses to events, and make decisions based on such feelings. Suffering, looked upon as an evil in a society which does not have a religious context in which to understand and accept it, is feeling which draws characters together in Tolkien and alters their vision of the world and of themselves. To confront anguish or pain in life—rather than repressing it and denying its existence—is a step toward reality.

THE INDIVIDUAL'S ABILITY TO MAKE THINGS HAPPEN

But the value of strong feeling as a causal element speaks to another point in Tolkien's work: the emphasis upon the individual and his ability to *do* something, to make things happen, even against what seem enormous odds. Part of the boredom which men experience in modern society comes from feeling that there is nothing worthwhile they can do to express themselves as individuals. After a day at the office, shuffling papers, we turn to expensive cars, drink or casual sex to give us a sense of purpose and value which the ordinary round of life does not provide. But these interests are not enough to really satisfy that wish to be "meaningful" which commitment to a larger social or spiritual purpose can give. In Tolkien's fantasy, we can see that under imaginative direction, action is possible. Men and hobbits make decisions and then take steps to fulfill them. Feeling and ideas are not bottled up and finally reduced to dreams, but lead to changes, realizations of vision, which imaginative created beings may direct. The quests of Frodo and Aragorn are a series of events in which the Hero chooses and performs.

Not that all actions have to be glorious. Part of the sympathy we feel for Frodo and Sam, who "act" heroically in their journey through Mordor, may come from our sense that to endure and be patient is all we can do. Frodo's heroism does not lie in his warrior's abilities (which are small) or his command of men. It lies in his commitment to a greater vision of life than himself, and it is his dogged plodding through the dispiriting wastes that makes him so significant. The justification for his heroism lies in the larger purposes he fulfills as Ring-bearer. We sympathize with his loneliness, his desperation, but we see he completes the designs of a universal plan, indeed, is the most important element in that plan. We may feel no such plan exists for us, but neither was Frodo very sure; his persistence in his quest is made in spite of, perhaps because of, this uncertainty, a willed affirmation of his own value. Frodo *puts* value in the universe, through his own efforts, and it is in this heroic act that we may find the positive analogy for our lives in the Primary World.

SOCIETY IS WORTH SAVING

We should also remember that Frodo's self-sacrifice is not only for the defeat of evil; it is also for the good of society, for the whole Community of created beings. This suggests, in turn, that in the mind of the fantasist, society is worth saving. It is not a mechanical horror designed to grind the individual down. Instead, personal commitment—*service*—is honored by the citizens of Middle-earth. The individual finds a responsible place for himself in his society; those who live outside society are identified with tyranny and self-destruction. A major reason for Tolkien's popularity among students and the "rebellious young" may be his classic insistence that the individual finds true freedom in the service of good, and that good can be social, providing security and purpose for others without being destructive of singularity and wilfullness.

Behind Tolkien's work, in other words, we can find a deeply religious commitment to Western culture and its values, ragged and unsatisfactory as they may seem to some of us. But Tolkien's use, in his major work, of our most pervasive myths—the Quest, the sacrifice of the god for the renewal of life, the battle of good and evil—suggests that he does not feel we have come so far from our origins that art and life, fantasy and human needs, are far apart. That he chose to cast his story in the Middle-earth of an earlier age, with a set of characters whom we may or may not have met before, argues for his faith in our imagination and our ability to believe. We must be able to want to realize "imagined wonder" in spite of the Primary World in which we also live. That we read *The Lord of the Rings* with tears and love argues for his success: we are willing to believe in this form of the myth of our life. Like the Christian myth which underlies Tolkien's view of experience in the twentieth century, the myth of the War of the Ring gives emotional and spiritual meaning to much of what we know. It, too, affirms the grandest moral purposes of the universe, and asserts that there are ultimate values in which we may believe. As Thomas Carlyle put it almost one hundred and fifty years ago, in a century when values seemed as problematic as in this one: "The Universe is not dead and demoniacal, a charnel-house with spectres; but godlike, and my Father's!"[1] Belief is not just faith in a church doctrine; it is a commitment to a meaningful reality and to our ability to believe in ourself. For *The Lord of the Rings* is a "joyful" book; and its happy ending is not the only source of that knowledge. We read it with delight because it makes us feel that pleasure, and thus it tells us not only that the universe is godlike but that we are, too. Tolkien can be accused of sentimentality, but this is not always a pejorative epithet. Feeling which reunites lovers, discovers lost children or parents, returns the wanderer to his long-abandoned home—feeling has an honorable place in the structure of the imagination, and our response to Tolkien's myth is an honest guide to our own—and society's—reality.

1. Thomas Carlyle, "The Everlasting Yea," *Sartor Resartus* (New York: Doubleday, Doran & Co., 1937), p. 188.

CHAPTER 3

The Writer's Art: Style and Sources in *The Lord of the Rings*

READINGS ON
J.R.R. TOLKIEN

The Lord of the Rings Succeeds on a Mythic Scale

W.H. Auden

Renowned poet and author W.H. Auden celebrated the publication of the third volume of *The Lord of the Rings* trilogy with the following essay. Auden writes that it is difficult to present a clear-cut conflict between Good and Evil and a story of a heroic Quest in a way that seems relevant to real life: an impersonal narrative seems just a document, while a subjective tale about a hero's quest seems to have little to do with the lives of whose who cannot take such journeys. Tolkien has managed to combine quest and conflict, says Auden, while maintaining a sense of historical and social reality with an attention to detail matched by no previous writer.

In *The Return of the King*, Frodo Baggins fulfills his Quest, the realm of Sauron is ended forever, the Third Age is over and J.R.R. Tolkien's trilogy *The Lord of the Rings* complete. I rarely remember a book about which I have had such violent arguments. Nobody *seems* to have a moderate opinion: either, like myself, people find it a masterpiece of its genre or they cannot abide it, and among the hostile there are some, I must confess, for whose literary judgment I have great respect. A few of these may have been put off by the first forty pages of the first chapter of the first volume in which the daily life of the hobbits is described; this is light comedy and light comedy is not Mr. Tolkien's forte. In most cases, however, the objection must go far deeper. I can only suppose that some people object to Heroic Quests and Imaginary Worlds on principle; such, they feel, cannot be anything but light "escapist" reading. That a man like Mr.

Reprinted from W.H. Auden, "At the End of the Quest, Victory," *The New York Times*, January 22, 1956, by permission. Copyright © 1956 by The New York Times.

Tolkien, the English philologist who teaches at Oxford, should lavish such incredible pains upon a genre which is, for them, trifling by definition, is, therefore, very shocking.

The difficulty of presenting a complete picture of reality lies in the gulf between the subjectively real, a man's experience of his own existence, and the objectively real, his experience of the lives of others and the world about him. Life, as I experience it in my own person, is primarily a continuous succession of choices between alternatives, made for a short-term or long-term purpose; the actions I take, that is to say, are less significant to me than the conflicts of motives, temptations, doubts in which they originate. Further, my subjective experience of time is not of a cyclical motion outside myself but of an irreversible history of unique moments which are made by my decisions.

FALSE IMAGE VS. IMPERSONAL DOCUMENT

For objectifying this experience, the natural image is that of a journey with a purpose, beset by dangerous hazards and obstacles, some merely difficult, others actively hostile. But when I observe my fellow men, such an image seems false. I can see, for example, that only the rich and those on vacation can take journeys; most men, most of the time must work in one place.

I cannot observe them making choices, only the actions they take and, if I know someone well, I can usually predict correctly how he will act in a given situation. I observe, all too often, men in conflict with each other, wars and hatreds, but seldom, if ever, a clear-cut issue between Good on the one side and Evil on the other, though I also observe that both sides usually describe it as such. If, then, I try to describe what I see as if I were an impersonal camera, I shall produce, not a Quest, but a "naturalistic" document.

Both extremes, of course, falsify life. There are medieval Quests which deserve the criticism made by Erich Auerbach in his book *Mimesis:*

> The world of knightly proving is a world of adventure. It not only contains a practically uninterrupted series of adventures; more specifically, it contains nothing but the requisites of adventure * * * Except feats of arms and love, nothing occurs in the courtly world—and even these two are of a special sort: they are not occurrences or emotions which can be absent for a time; they are permanently connected with the person of the perfect knight, they are part of his definition, so

that he cannot for one moment be without adventure in arms nor for one moment without amorous entanglement * * * His exploits are feats of arms, not 'war,' for they are feats accomplished at random which do not fit into any politically purposive pattern.

And there are contemporary "thrillers" in which the identification of hero and villain with contemporary politics is depressingly obvious. On the other hand, there are naturalistic novels in which the characters are the mere puppets of Fate, or rather of the author, who, from some mysterious point of freedom, contemplates the workings of Fate.

TOLKIEN COMBINES THE HEROIC QUEST WITH A SENSE OF REALITY

If, as I believe, Mr. Tolkien has succeeded more completely than any previous writer in this genre in using the traditional properties of the Quest, the heroic journey, the Numinous Object, the conflict between Good and Evil while at the same time satisfying our sense of historical and social reality, it should be possible to show how he has succeeded. To begin with, no previous writer has, to my knowledge, created an imaginary world and a feigned history in such detail. By the time the reader has finished the trilogy, including the appendices to this last volume, he knows as much about Mr. Tolkien's Middle-earth, its landscape, its fauna and flora, its peoples, their languages, their history, their cultural habits, as, outside his special field, he knows about the actual world.

Mr. Tolkien's world may not be the same as our own: it includes, for example, elves, beings who know good and evil but have not fallen, and, though not physically indestructible, do not suffer natural death. It is afflicted by Sauron, an incarnation of absolute evil, and creatures like Shelob, the monster spider, or the orcs who are corrupt past hope of redemption. But it is a world of intelligible law, not mere wish; the reader's sense of the credible is never violated.

Even the One Ring, the absolute physical and psychological weapon which must corrupt any who dares to use it, is a perfectly plausible hypothesis from which the political duty to destroy it which motivates Frodo's Quest logically follows.

A TICKLISH BUSINESS

To present the conflict between Good and Evil as a war in which the good side is ultimately victorious is a ticklish

ELEMENTS OF A QUEST STORY
In an essay on "The Quest Hero," W.H. Auden spells out six essential elements of a typical Quest tale.

1) A precious Object and/or Person to be found and possessed or married.

2) A long journey to find it, for its whereabouts are not originally known to the seekers.

3) A hero. The precious Object cannot be found by anybody, but only by the one person who possesses the right qualities of breeding or character.

4) A test or series of Tests by which the unworthy are screened out, and the hero revealed.

5) The Guardians of the Object who must be overcome before it can be won. They may be simply a further test of the hero's *arete*, or they may be malignant in themselves.

6) The Helpers who with their knowledge and magical powers assist the hero and but for whom he would never succeed. They may appear in human or in animal form.

W.H. Auden, "The Quest Hero," *Texas Quarterly* IV (1962). Reprinted in Neil D. Isaacs and Rose A. Zimbardo, eds., *Tolkien and the Critics: Essays on J.R.R. Tolkien's* The Lord of the Rings. Notre Dame, IN: University of Notre Dame, 1968.

business. Our historical experience tells us that physical power and, to a large extent, mental power are morally neutral and effectively real: wars are won by the stronger side, just or unjust. At the same time most of us believe that the essence of the Good is love and freedom so that Good cannot impose itself by force without ceasing to be good.

The battles in the Apocalypse and *Paradise Lost*, for example, are hard to stomach because of the conjunction of two incompatible notions of Deity, of a God of Love who creates free beings who can reject his love and of a God of absolute Power whom none can withstand. Mr. Tolkien is not as great a writer as Milton, but in this matter he has succeeded where Milton failed. As readers of the preceding volumes will remember, the situation in the War of the Ring is as follows: Chance, or Providence, has put the Ring in the hands of the representatives of Good, Elrond, Gandalf, Aragorn. By using it they could destroy Sauron, the incarnation of Evil, but at the cost of becoming his successor. If Sauron recovers the Ring, his victory will be immediate and complete, but even without it his power is greater than any his enemies can bring against him, so that, unless Frodo succeeds in destroying the Ring, Sauron must win.

A PLAUSIBLE REASON FOR EVIL TO LOSE THE WAR

Evil, that is, has every advantage but one—it is inferior in imagination. Good can imagine the possibility of becoming evil—hence the refusal of Gandalf and Aragorn to use the Ring—but Evil, defiantly chosen, can no longer imagine anything but itself. Sauron cannot imagine any motives except lust for dominion and fear so that, when he has learned that his enemies have the Ring, the thought that they might try to destroy it never enters his head, and his eye is kept turned toward Gondor and away from Mordor and the Mount of Doom.

Further, his worship of power is accompanied, as it must be, by anger and a lust for cruelty: learning of Saruman's attempt to steal the Ring for himself, Sauron is so preoccupied with wrath that for two crucial days he pays no attention to a report of spies on the stairs of Cirith Ungol, and when Pippin is foolish enough to look in the palantir of Orthanc, Sauron could have learned all about Frodo's Quest. His wish to capture Pippin and torture the truth from him makes him miss his precious opportunity.

Sauron is not overthrown, however, before many brave men have died and much damage has been done and even his defeat involves loss—the three Elven Rings lose their power and the Elves must leave Middle-earth. Nor is the victory of Good over Evil final: there was Morgoth before Sauron and no one knows what dread successor may afflict the world in ages to come.

The demands made on the writer's powers in an epic as long as *The Lord of the Rings* are enormous and increase as the tale proceeds—the battles have to get more spectacular, the situations more critical, the adventures more thrilling—but I can only say that Mr. Tolkien has proved equal to them. Readers of the previous volumes may be interested to know that Gandalf's hunch about Gollum was right—but for Gollum, the Quest would have failed at the last moment.

From the appendices they will get tantalizing glimpses of the First and Second Ages. The legends of these are, I understand, already written and I hope that, as soon as the publishers have seen *The Lord of the Rings* into a paperback edition, they will not keep Mr. Tolkien's growing army of fans waiting too long.

The Lord of the Rings Is Greatly Overrated

Edmund Wilson

Well-known critic Edmund Wilson chronicled and commented on much of the literature of the twentieth century. He writes that he has read the entire *Lord of the Rings* trilogy to his seven-year-old daughter, a *Hobbit* fan, and does not consider the books to be very well done. Far from being a book for adults, Wilson says, *The Lord of the Rings* is a children's book that got out of hand.

In 1937, Dr. J.R.R. Tolkien, an Oxford don, published a children's book called *The Hobbit*, which had an immense success. The hobbits are a not quite human race who inhabit an imaginary country called the Shire and who combine the characteristics of certain English animals—they live in burrows like rabbits and badgers—with the traits of English country-dwellers, ranging from rustic to tweedy. (The name seems a telescoping of rabbit and Hobbs.) They have elves, trolls and dwarfs as neighbors, and they are associated with a magician called Gandalph and a slimy water-creature called Gollum. Dr. Tolkien became interested in his fairy-tale country and has gone on from this little story to elaborate a long romance, which has appeared, under the general title *The Lord of the Rings*, in three volumes: *The Fellowship of the Ring*, *The Two Towers* and *The Return of the King*. All volumes are accompanied with maps, and Dr. Tolkien, who is a philologist, professor at Merton College of English Language and Literature, has equipped the last volume with a scholarly apparatus of appendices, explaining the alphabets and grammars of the various tongues spoken by his characters, and giving full genealogies and tables of historical chronology.

Dr. Tolkien has announced that this series—the hypertrophic sequel to *The Hobbit*—is intended for adults rather than chil-

Excerpted from Edmund Wilson, "Oo, Those Awful Orcs," *The Nation*, April 15, 1956. Reprinted with permission.

dren, and it has had a resounding reception at the hands of a number of critics who are certainly grown-up in years. Mr. Richard Hughes, for example, has written of it that nothing of the kind on such a scale has been attempted since *The Faerie Queen*, and that "for width of imagination it almost beggars parallel.". . .

A CHILDREN'S BOOK THAT GOT OUT OF HAND

But if one goes from these eulogies to the book itself, one is likely to be let down, astonished, baffled. The reviewer has just read the whole thing aloud to his seven-year-old daughter, who has been through *The Hobbit* countless times, beginning it again the moment she has finished, and whose interest has been held by its more prolix successors. One is puzzled to know why the author should have supposed he was writing for adults. There are, to be sure, some details that are a little unpleasant for a children's book, but except when he is being pedantic and also boring the adult reader, there is little in *The Lord of the Rings* over the head of a seven-year-old child. It is essentially a children's book—a children's book which has somehow got out of hand, since, instead of directing it at the "juvenile" market, the author has indulged himself in developing the fantasy for its own sake; and it ought to be said at this point, before emphasizing its inadequacies as literature, that Dr. Tolkien makes few claims for his fairy romance. In a statement prepared for his publishers, he has explained that he began it to amuse himself, as a philological game: "The invention of languages is the foundation. The 'stories' were made rather to provide a world for the languages than the reverse. I should have preferred to write in 'Elvish.'" He has omitted, he says, in the printed book, a good deal of the philological part; "but there is a great deal of linguistic matter . . . included or mythologically expressed in the book. It is to me, anyway, largely an essay in 'linguistic esthetic,' as I sometimes say to people who ask me 'what it is all about.' . . . It is not 'about' anything but itself. Certainly it has *no* allegorical intentions, general, particular or topical, moral, religious or political." An overgrown fairy story, a philological curiosity—that is, then, what *The Lord of the Rings* really is. The pretentiousness is all on the part of Dr. Tolkien's infatuated admirers, and it is these pretensions that I would here assail. . . .

BOTH PROSE AND VERSE ARE AMATEURISH

The Lord of the Rings . . . is indeed the tale of a Quest, but, to the reviewer, an extremely unrewarding one. The hero has no serious temptations; is lured by no insidious enchantments, perplexed by few problems. What we get is a simple confrontation —in more or less the traditional terms of British melodrama— of the Forces of Evil with the Forces of Good, the remote and alien villain with the plucky little home-grown hero. There are streaks of imagination: the ancient tree-spirits, the Ents, with their deep eyes, twiggy beards, rumbly voices; the Elves, whose nobility and beauty is elusive and not quite human. But even these are rather clumsily handled. There is never much development in the episodes; you simply go on getting more of the same thing. Dr. Tolkien has little skill at narrative and no instinct for literary form. The characters talk a story-book language that might have come out of [children's author] Howard Pyle, and as personalities they do not impose themselves. At the end of this long romance, I had still no conception of the wizard Gandalph, who is a cardinal figure, had never been able to visualize him at all. For the most part such characterizations as Dr. Tolkien is able to contrive are perfectly stereotyped: Frodo the good little Englishman, Samwise, his doglike servant, who talks lowerclass and respectful, and never deserts his master. These characters who are no characters are involved in interminable adventures the poverty of invention displayed in which is, it seems to me, almost pathetic. On the country in which the Hobbits, the Elves, the Ents and the other Good People live, the Forces of Evil are closing in, and they have to band together to save it. The hero is the Hobbit called Frodo who has become possessed of a ring that Sauron, the King of the Enemy, wants (that learned reptilian suggestion—doesn't it give you a goosefleshy feeling?). In spite of the author's disclaimer, the struggle for the ring does seem to have some larger significance. This ring, if one continues to carry it, confers upon one special powers, but it is felt to become heavier and heavier; it exerts on one a sinister influence that one has to brace oneself to resist. The problem is for Frodo to get rid of it before he can succumb to this influence.

DISAPPOINTINGLY INEFFECTUAL "HORRORS" LEAD TO A FLAT CLIMAX

Now, this situation does create interest; it does seem to have possibilities. One looks forward to a queer dilemma, a new kind of hair-breadth escape, in which Frodo, in the Enemy's kingdom, will find himself half-seduced into taking over the enemy's point of view, so that the realm of shadows and horrors will come to seem to him, once he is in it, once he is strong in the power of the ring, a plausible and pleasant place, and he will narrowly escape the danger of becoming a monster himself. But these bugaboos are not magnetic; they are feeble and rather blank; one does not feel they have any real power. The Good People simply say "Boo" to them. There are Black Riders, of whom everyone is terrified but who never seem anything but specters. There are dreadful hovering birds—think of it, horrible birds of prey! There are ogreish disgusting Orcs, who, however, rarely get to the point of committing any overt acts. There is a giant female spider—a dreadful creepy-crawly spider!—who lives in a dark cave and eats people. What one misses in all these terrors is any trace of concrete reality. The preternatural, to be effective, should be given some sort of solidity, a real presence, recognizable features—like Gulliver, like Gogol, like Poe; not like those phantom horrors of Algernon Blackwood which prove so disappointing after the travel-book substantiality of the landscapes in which he evokes them. Tolkien's horrors resemble these in their lack of real contact with their victims, who dispose of them as we do of the horrors in dreams by simply pushing them or puffing them away. As for Sauron, the ruler of Mordor (doesn't the very name have a shuddery sound?) who concentrates in his person everything that is threatening the Shire, the build-up for him goes on through three volumes. He makes his first, rather promising, appearance as a terrible fire-rimmed yellow eye seen in a water-mirror. But this is as far as we ever get. Once Sauron's realm is invaded, we think we are going to meet him; but he still remains nothing but a burning eye scrutinizing all that occurs from the window of a remote dark tower. This might, of course, be made effective; but actually it is not; we never feel Sauron's power. And the climax, to which we have been working up through exactly nine hundred and ninety-nine large close-printed pages, when it comes, proves extremely flat. The ring is at last got rid of by being dropped into a fiery crater, and the kingdom of Sauron "topples" in a brief and banal earthquake that sets fire to everything and burns it up, and so releases the author from the necessity of telling the reader what exactly was so terrible there. Frodo has come to the end of his Quest, but the reader has remained untouched by the wounds and fatigues of his journey. An impotence of imagination seems to me to sap the whole story. The wars are never dynamic; the or-

NOT "RABBIT" AND "HOBBS"

Tolkien biographer Daniel Grotta reports on the origin of the word "hobbit."

Tolkien was never certain how he came to invent the word "hobbit." It was more spontaneous generation than calculation; certainly, not the combination of "rabbit" and (Thomas) "Hobbes," as the eminent American critic Edmund Wilson speculated. "I don't know where the word came from," admitted Tolkien. "You can't catch your mind out. It might have been associated with Sinclair Lewis' *Babbit.* Certainly not rabbit, as some people think. Babbit has the same bourgeois smugness that hobbits do. His world is the same limited place." Another theory on the origin of the word hobbit is advanced by Paul Kocher, author of *Master of Middle Earth.* According to Kocher, the Oxford English Dictionary defines the Middle English word "hob" (or "hobbe") as a rustic or a clown, a sort of Robin Good-fellow (the English equivalent of the "little people" of Celtic mythology). Since hobbits seem to display many of the characteristics of hobs—small size, simple nature, love of countryside,—then perhaps Tolkien unconsciously transformed a word with which he was undoubtedly familiar into a new creature. In any event, the word "hobbit" is uniquely Tolkien's invention, like "pandemonium" in Milton's *Paradise Lost* and "chortle" in Carroll's *Alice in Wonderland.*

Daniel Grotta, *The Biography of J.R.R. Tolkien: Architect of Middle-Earth*, second edition. Philadelphia: Running Press, 1978.

deals give no sense of strain; the fair ladies would not stir a heartbeat; the horrors would not hurt a fly.

AN APPETITE FOR JUVENILE TRASH

Now, how is it that these long-winded volumes of what looks to this reviewer like balderdash have elicited such tributes as those above? The answer is, I believe, that certain people—especially, perhaps, in Britain—have a lifelong appetite for juvenile trash. They would not accept adult trash, but, confronted with the pre-teen-age article, they revert to the mental phase which delighted in *Elsie Dinsmore* and *Little Lord Fauntleroy* and which seems to have made of Billy Bunter, in England, almost a national figure. You can see it in the tone they fall into when they talk about Tolkien in print: they bubble, they squeal, they coo; they go on about Malory and Spenser—both of whom have a charm and a distinction that Tolkien has never touched.

As for me, if we must read about imaginary kingdoms, give me James Branch Cabell's Poictesme. He at least writes for grown-up people, and he does not present the drama of life as a showdown between Good People and Goblins. He can cover more ground in an episode that lasts only three pages than Tolkien is able to in one of his twenty-page chapters and he can create a more disquieting impression by a reference to something that is never described than Tolkien through his whole demonology.

Tolkien's Understanding and Use of Mythology Create a Profound Effect

Ruth S. Noel

Tolkien made a lifetime study of the world's mythologies, writes Ruth S. Noel. His works were an attempt to revive interest in mythology, and in this he was eminently successful. Noel is the author of *The Mythology of Middle-Earth*, from which this essay is excerpted.

There is something in Professor John Ronald Reuel Tolkien's works that lies deeper than fantasy or escape. This quality is the same as that found in authentic myths and folk tales, a sense generated by the nearly forgotten but potent beliefs and traditions that form the skeleton of old lore. Researchers such as Sir James Frazer have compared and explicated some of these sources, tracing great epics and bedtime stories alike back to the first human struggles to bring order to the world. The sense of depth in Tolkien's works has its source in the author's understanding and selective use of the ancient themes from mythology.

This [essay] discusses some of the purposes of myth, the effect of myth on the development of Middle-earth, and Tolkien's philosophies on myth.

Although primarily a philologist, Tolkien studied mythology for most of his life. He was one of the world's greatest authorities on the Old English and Middle English languages, and was a specialist in Old English and related Teutonic and Celtic lore. With his works he made an eminently successful effort to revive the decreasing interest in mythology. The Teutonic and Celtic mythologies that most interested Tolkien had never been given the emphasis that had been placed upon classical Greek and Roman mythology; Tolkien's works have helped to arouse interest in these areas. This can be seen in the number of recent works based on these myths.

To thoroughly appreciate Tolkien's works, it is necessary to have an understanding of mythology. Unfortunately, the study of mythology itself is a very uncertain one, and it is seldom possible to reconstruct a single clear-cut version of a myth with its sources and purposes neatly set out. Contemporary records of pre-Christian myths are often contradictory or confused. Later accounts of these myths are more coherent, but both the conversion to Christianity and the effort of organizing the material have often biased the telling of ancient lore. So much has been lost from Celtic and Teutonic mythology that it is doubtful that a single, fundamental, and coherent interpretation will ever be made of what remains. Trends in interpretation change, new material is discovered, and, on occasion, old material is found to be unreliable. Only rarely does a comprehensive, scientific inquiry, such as that of Jakob and Wilhelm Grimm into Teutonic mythology, or a dedicated, gifted retelling of the myths, like that of the twelfth-century Icelandic writer Snorri Sturluson, bring mythology alive to the reader.

UNDERSTANDING THE PURPOSES OF MYTHOLOGY

The understanding of mythology requires the understanding of its purposes. The purposes of mythology are to glorify history with supernatural events, to explain the unknown, and to hallow tradition. First, historical myths augment history with supernatural events and divine beings, suggesting that the civilization concerned has been singled out for divine guidance. Second, myths that explain the unknown attempt to bring order to a chaotic conception of the world and to provide formal answers to questions that cannot be answered practically. Third, myths that hallow tradition describe the supernatural circumstances in which the traditions came about, glorifying the traditions in order to perpetuate them. Comparable mythologies have evolved in virtually every culture because man universally faces the same challenges, asks the same questions, and lives in awe of the same forces.

There are two levels of myth in *The Lord of the Rings*. Not only is it written as an epic myth itself, but it also presents the internal mythologies of the peoples of Middle-earth. The three basic purposes of myth are served in these internal mythologies. The histories are peopled with divine and immortal beings, questions about the unknown are given answers, and traditions, are hallowed and maintained.

Tolkien was aware of mythology's purposes and used it meaningfully. His fidelity to the purposes of myth produces a coherent internal mythology for the epic of Middle-earth and provides significant depth for the characterization of both individuals and nations.

THE EFFECTIVENESS OF TOLKIEN'S USE OF MYTH

Tolkien's adaptation of mythology to his works has a profound effect on the reader. This effectiveness is not accidental. Mythic themes deal with basic challenges that face man universally and eternally, such as love, fate, and death. Mythic thought is traceable to the very emergence of human imagination. Such symbolism can be seen in Paleolithic art with its records of ceremonial events and its expressionistic depiction of nature. Even earlier symbolism can be seen in Neanderthal burials, in which the manner of burial was determined by some dawning concept of an afterlife, or imaginative attempt at restoration of life to the dead.

Mythological themes are vastly ancient and are a basic part of the subconscious working of the mind. Thus they have the power to thrill or terrify in the same way that dreams do. In fact, the symbols common in mythology sometimes arise spontaneously in dreams. The study of psychology is doing much to explain the motivation of mythic themes.

Because of the powerful connotation of myth, Tolkien considered mythic themes the most effective way to glorify or debase his characters. An independent author, seldom influenced by his contemporaries, Tolkien must have used his own reactions as a basis for choosing his mythological themes. Sometimes his selections are questionable, such as the apparent death of nearly every important character. Other themes, however, produce a stifling, nightmare horror or a spiritual sense of exultation. The considerable popularity of Tolkien's works attests to the appeal of his selections.

Although the sources of many of Tolkien's themes are to be found in mythology, specific influences are sometimes difficult to trace. Sometimes the theme's source . . . can be located with certainty. Sometimes the theme, such as that of Sauron's powerful, lost Ring, is ubiquitous so that it is difficult to determine a particular source. Sometimes the ideas, such as those concerning the nature of the Elves and Dwarves, are so general that they do not seem to have come from a single source, but rather to have been absorbed through a sort of literary osmosis. In cases of the latter kind, . . . [it] is not intended that all the references should be taken as direct influences on Tolkien's writing. On the other hand, it is more than likely that Tolkien was familiar with all of them.

TOLKIEN'S WORKS FORM THEIR OWN GENRE

Tolkien's works form a continuation of the mythic tradition into modern literature. For this reason they form a genre by themselves. In no other literary work has such a careful balance of mythic tradition and individual imagination been maintained. Authors who have been compared with Tolkien emphasize either the mythic or the imaginative side of their works to the detriment of the other. Tolkien, however, maintains a consistent homogeneity.

Throughout the works, the fiction is maintained that the prehistoric chronology of the Third Age of Middle-earth is the source of the mythologies we know. Tolkien excuses his use of names and themes from historic mythology on the basis that *The Lord of the Rings* tells the true story, imperfectly remembered in our historic lore. Bilbo's song, "There is an inn," sung by Frodo, is a good example: Tolkien presents what he pretends is the original form of the nursery rhyme "Hey diddle diddle," where the cow jumps over the moon.

The adaptation of mythological themes to imaginative fiction is a difficult challenge. Mythology is a conservative medium: myths are always repeated in a traditional way, rather than being casually left to the teller's whim. However, the constant retelling of myths over hundreds, even thousands, of years wears them smooth, concentrates them, until everything superfluous is worn away. In contrast, modern literature is dependent on innovation and creativity for its success. In combining the two literary philosophies, Tolkien produced a myth that is coherent and readable from the modern point of view, and a work of imaginative fiction made concrete by its basis in the ancient and universal language of myth. The result of the combination is sometimes self-conscious, forced, and unwieldy, but much of it is re-markably vivid, dimensional, and evocative.

THE QUALITIES OF MIDDLE-EARTH

The success of Tolkien's works is based on the vividness, di-mensionality, and evocative qualities of Middle-earth. To say Middle-earth was created by Tolkien would be an oversim-plification. Instead, Middle-earth exists on three levels. First, it is the actual continent of Europe, with landscapes, vegeta-tion, animal life, and some of man's ancient works, taken from reality. Second, Middle-earth is the product of the po-etic imagination of the early Europeans, who peopled the mountains, forest, and sea with divine, semidivine, and de-monic beings. Finally, Tolkien superimposed his imagina-tion on the lands and their natural and supernatural inhabi-tants, enhancing the mood of the landscape and deepening the character of its peoples.

Whatever Middle-earth is, it is not Faerie. It is not, as Faerie is said to be, a remote, inviolable land of indescrib-able beauty. There are isolated fragments of Faerie, or rather reconstructions of it, in Tolkien's Middle-earth, in such places as Lórien. On the whole, however, there is very little of the supernatural in the geography of Middle-earth.

Nevertheless, there is a curiously timeless quality about Middle-earth. Its history spans thousands of years, and the time of the War of the Ring is apparently both prehistoric and pagan, although the primary culture is feudal and such anachronisms as coffee and potatoes have intruded. This sense of mingled time-frames is reminiscent of that of Mal-ory's *Le Morte Darthur*, a resemblance that may not be acci-dental. In *Le Morte Darthur*, myths about Celtic gods are at-tributed to the approximately fifth-century King Arthur, but are set in the culture and language of medieval chivalry. The result in both Malory's and Tolkien's works is a curiously opposite suspension of time. *The Lord of the Rings* appears to have the timelessness the hobbits ascribed to Lórien: "as if inside a song a medieval song sung to a pagan tune.

TOLKIEN'S ESSAY "ON FAIRY-STORIES"

The best available guide to what Tolkien felt about the mythology that inspired his works is found in his essay "On Fairy-Stories." Tolkien wrote this essay at the time he was beginning *The Lord of the Rings*, and it later appeared in the book *Tree and Leaf.* In view of the way *The Lord of the Rings* finally developed, the essay's insights on magic, *eucatastrophe*, and justice are particularly valuable.

The magic Tolkien admired was magic devoid of sleight-of-hand fakery, mystery uncontaminated by cloak-and-dagger sensationalism, and miracle unconfined to orthodox religion. The purpose of this magic is to exercise the sense of wonder and to fulfill wish. Magic is the process which produces eucatastrophe.

Eucatastrophe is Tolkien's word for the anti-catastrophic "turn" (*strophe* in Greek) that characterizes fairy stories. This turning occurs when imminent evil is unexpectedly averted and great good succeeds. To Tolkien, tragedy was the purest form of drama, while eucatastrophe, the antithesis of tragedy, was the purest form of the fairy story. In "On Fairy-Stories," Tolkien gives the purpose and effect of eucatastrophe: "It does not deny the existence . . . of sorrow and failure . . . it denies universal final defeat . . . giving a fleeting glimpse of Joy, Joy beyond the walls of the world, poignant as grief."

To Tolkien, the most satisfying form of eucatastrophe, and that which he developed to the greatest extent in his works, was denial of death. This concept is basic to Christianity, but also plays an important part in pagan myth. The desire for eternal life runs deep in the human imagination—burial practices of even some Neanderthal peoples reflect a hope of life beyond the grave. Sometimes, as in Scandinavian mythology, the afterlife was visualized as a continuation of earthly life: in Odin's hall, warriors fought and feasted until the end of the world. The fighting and feasting were an important part of the Celtic afterlife as well, but the Celts added a significant element in their lyrical descriptions of the unearthly beauty and joy of the otherworld. However, it is not the physical aspect of the afterworld, or the events that take place there, that are important. (Tolkien wisely gave only the most sparse account of the Blessed Realm.) The need is to believe, even briefly or metaphorically, that death can be denied, even with the recognition of the necessary departure from the living world. This is the eucatastrophe from old lore which Tolkien has striven to supply.

Another theme that Tolkien found in fairy stories was justice. In his own works, it is unfailingly meted out, although he sparingly doles out the deepest doom, death, never giving it to any character introduced by name except as punishment for inexpiable sins or as a victorious resolution of all life's conflicts.

Tolkien's adherence to justice and mercy is his greatest concession to the Christian philosophy. For a dedicatedly Christian author, Tolkien wrote an unusually sympathetic account of a pagan world. The combination is again reminiscent of Malory's *Le Morte Darthur*, where pagan themes, motives, and moods are interspersed with Christian ideals.

REALISM VS. JUSTICE AND MERCY

Despite Tolkien's statement to the contrary, justice is not inherent in fairy stories. For example, he said that "The Frog Prince" is about the importance of keeping promises. In the version collected by Jakob and Wilhelm Grimm, the princess indeed promised the frog a place by her dish and on her pillow if he recovered her golden ball. But when he came for his reward, she angrily dashed him against the wall. He became a prince thereupon, and married the disloyal and undeserving princess. This sort of caprice of fate is as common in folk tales as is justice.

The emphasis on fate rather than on justice is as much the hallmark of modernism in literature as it was of pre-Christian myth. It is no longer necessary for a work of fiction to come to a conclusion that satisfies the desire for justice or mercy. It is not even necessary to reach any resolution. The same effect occurs in myth when the favor of the gods is bestowed or withdrawn arbitrarily. This point of view is one of realism: justice and mercy are less facts than spiritual ideals.

Tolkien demonstrated this in his overall view of the quest, where he showed justice to be a goal—unrealized but attainable. He gave two roles to justice in view of his combination of pagan fatalism and Judeo-Christian ethics. In the pagan sense, justice is to be striven for so that one may meet fate honorably. In the Judeo-Christian sense, it is sought in order that one may reject evil. Appropriately to these two roles, Tolkien resolved the story in two directions, with the idealist, Frodo, departing to eternal life beyond the world, and the realist, Samwise, returning to the center of the world's life, the hearth of home.

Tolkien Fails to Achieve His Artistic Goals in *The Lord of the Rings*

C.N. Manlove

In his essay "On Fairy-Stories," Tolkien spelled out his conception of "Recovery," the necessity for a writer to produce a new perception in his work. C.N. Manlove examines Tolkien's concept of "Recovery" and concludes that while the author is moderately successful in parts of *The Lord of the Rings* his flat descriptions and poor characterizations reveal a general failure to achieve his artistic aims. Manlove is a lecturer in English literature at the University of Edinburgh, Scotland.

Tolkien's stylistic aims are associated with his conception of 'Recovery': the writer is to generalize and depersonalize his descriptions (though not emasculate them) to make them universally available. The reader will hopefully come thereby to a fresh view of objects he has long taken for granted, and through that to a recovery of what are for him their archetypes. Sensibility is thus not to be extended so much as reminded:

> However good in themselves, illustrations do little good to fairy-stories. The radical distinction between all art (including drama) that offers a *visible* presentation and true literature is that it imposes one visible form. Literature works from mind to mind and thus is more progenitive. It is at once more universal and more poignantly particular. If it speaks of *bread* or *wine* or *stone* or *tree*, it appeals to the whole of these things, to their ideas; yet each hearer will give to them a peculiar personal embodiment in his imagination. Should the story say 'he ate bread', the dramatic producer or painter can only show 'a piece of bread' according to his taste or fancy, but the hearer of the story will think of bread in general and picture it in some form of his own. If a story says, "he climbed a hill

Excerpted from *Modern Fantasy: Five Studies*, by C.N. Manlove (New York: Cambridge University Press, 1975). Reprinted by permission of the author.

and saw a river in the valley below', the illustrator may catch, or nearly catch, his own vision of such a scene; but every hearer of the words will have his own picture, and it will be made out of all the hills and rivers and dales he has ever seen, but specially out of The Hill, The River, The Valley which were for him the first embodiment of the word. (*TL*, p. 67)[1]

The method can be seen best in the description of Lothlórien (without doubt the finest set-piece in the book).[2] When Frodo arrives at Cerin Amroth, he sees

> a great mound, covered with a sward of grass as green as Spring-time in the Elder days. Upon it, as a double crown, grew two circles of trees: the outer had bark of snowy white, and were leafless but beautiful in their shapely nakedness; the inner were mallorn-trees of great height, still arrayed in pale gold. High amid the branches of a towering tree that stood in the centre of all there gleamed a white flet. At the feet of the trees, and all about the green hillsides the grass was studded with small golden flowers shaped like stars. Among them, nodding on slender stalks, were other flowers, white and palest green: they glimmered as a mist amid the rich hue of the grass. Over all the sky was blue, and the sun of afternoon glowed upon the hill and cast long green shadows beneath the trees. (*LR*, I, 364–5)[3]

... Our subconscious has been here before, and Tolkien has only to beckon it in. Hence the vagueness of the account. First the mound seems to be wholly covered with the grass, and then we are told it was crowned with trees: this begins the blurring. Then the grass was 'as green as Spring-time in the Elder days'. Its green colour becomes conceptualized: spring is only metaphorically green. As for the Elder days, we know nothing of spring then, but we are being asked to imagine. The trees seem more specific, but the two circles evoke the archetype of the secret centre, and the white circle about the gold seems as 'right' as the yolk of an egg surrounded by the white.[4] Then, with the towering tree, we reach, as we desire, the hub; to return outwards to the flowers which we see as a mass. We do not see the white trees: they are 'beautiful in their shapely nakedness', but what that means, our subconscious must tell us. The flowers are described as 'golden flowers shaped like stars', 'white and palest green', but they are so much anyone's 'idea' of a flower that they do not stand out; so too with the blue sky, the sun, and the long green shadows. It is finely done. Tolkien indicates the desired response in Frobo's 'He saw no colour but those he knew, gold and white and blue and green, but they were fresh and poignant, as if he had at that moment first perceived them and made for them names new and wonderful' (*LR*, I, 365).

The stylistic aim of 'Recovery' may also explain why the landscapes of *The Lord of the Rings* are both elemental and repetitive. There are three main mountain ranges, the Misty Mountains, the Emyn Muil and the Mountains of Mordor, all of them barriers to progress, all similar in height and all young, jagged and rocky. There are three main towers (the White Tower of Minas Tirith, Orthanc and Barad-dûr); two rather similarly constructed cities (though one is of living wood and the other of stone)—the City of the Galadrim and Minas Tirith; three tunnels through mountains, each fraught with horror (that through Moria, the Paths of the Dead and the Pass of Cirith Ungol); three plains (the Brown Lands, the grasslands of Rohan and the plain of Gorgoroth); and three forests (the Old Forest, Lothlórien and Fangorn). Through our experience of these, Tolkien would presumably hope that our archetypal images of The Hill, The Mountain, The Forest, The Plain and The Tower will be more surely brought to life in our minds.

The usually absolute distinctions between good and evil[5] may also be a function of this technique: to come at the 'this-ness' of a thing, it must be presented pure. Thus for example every detail about the orcs—their squat appearance (*LR*, II, 50, 138), crooked legs (II, 50), hairy arms (II, 58), swart or sallow faces (I, 339; II, 171), bad breath (II, 58), loathsome foods (II, 54; III, 190), hideous dialects (II, 48), even their harsh medicine (II, 51, 52)—points in one direction, and is aimed at producing one response: loathing. The same method to reverse effect is seen with the good. This polariz-ation may well be intended to make it easier for the reader to grasp essences. Those like Edmund Wilson who complain that Tolkien has nothing new to say about good and evil[6] would then have missed the point.

It is possible, again, that the style required for 'Recovery' explains the use of simile (which leaves the terms discrete) rather than metaphor in *The Lord of the Rings*. The 'stock' nature, too, of such similes may be part of this style. Bilbo leaves his home at Bag End 'like a rustle of wind in the grass' (*LR*, I, 44); the piled spears of the Rohirrim, the warriors of Rohan, bristle 'like thickets of new-planted trees' (III, 67; see also II, 129); the Ents, in Isengard, 'went striding and storming like a howling gale, breaking pillars . . . tossing up huge slabs of stone into the air like leaves' (II, 173); when Aragorn dismisses the Host of the Dead, they 'vanished like a mist that is driven back by a sudden wind' (III, 153); as Frodo and Sam approach Mount Doom, Barad-dûr grows nearer 'like the oncoming of a wall of night at the last end of the world' (III, 212).

Some similes are, however, constantly repeated, so frequently that not even a ritualistic function seems adequate to account for them. The Elves are invariably associated with starlight (*LR*, I, 221, 369, 380; II, 339), particularly their eyes (I, 239; III, 310); mountain ranges and standing-stones always look like teeth (I, 141, 416; III, 68); the orcs and Gollum appear as insects, especially spiders (I, 416; II, 147, 220, 244, 253; III, 227); whenever a battle-onslaught is described, the analogy of a wave is used (II, 138, 140, 142; III, 112, 119, 226). One feels here in fact that Tolkien could have found some different terms for his figures instead of wearing the same trope to a shadow.

All the features of the book that we have examined may fit in with Tolkien's stylistic intentions,[7] but the question of whether they come over powerfully is another matter. To write a generalized style is not to escape having to write well: Lothlórien succeeds as a picture not because it is non-specific, but because it is done with skill. An 'archetypal' aesthetic is no excuse for an anaemic performance. It is in this light that we must now consider Tolkien's method.

REPETITIVE AND AMBIGUOUS DESCRIPTIONS OF CHARACTERS

This is the picture he offers us of Celeborn and Galadriel, the Lord and Lady of Lothlórien,

> Very tall they were, and the Lady no less tall than the Lord; and they were grave and beautiful. They were clad wholly in white; and the hair of the Lady was of deep gold, and the hair of the Lord Celeborn was of silver long and bright; but no sign of age was upon them, unless it were in the depths of their eyes; for these were keen as lances in the starlight, and yet profound, the wells of deep memory. (*LR*, I, 369)

We are not told how tall they were, nor is there any detail about their clothing apart from its whiteness which would help us to see it. The contrasting colours of their hair only brings us to the verge of seeing the Rich, Full Woman and the Grave, Elderly Man—a verge from which we are thrust

"RECOVERY"

Tolkien expresses his desire to see things as they should be seen in this excerpt from his essay "On Fairy-Stories."

We should look at green again, and be startled anew (but not blinded) by blue and yellow and red. We should meet the centaur and the dragon, and then perhaps suddenly behold, like the ancient shepherds, sheep, and dogs, and horses—and wolves. This recovery fairy-stories help us to make. In that sense only a taste for them may make us, or keep us, childish.

Recovery (which includes return and renewal of health) is a re-gaining—regaining of a clear view. I do not say "seeing things as they are" and involve myself with the philosophers, though I might venture to say "seeing things as we are (or were) meant to see them"—as things apart from ourselves. We need, in any case, to clean our windows; so that the things seen clearly may be freed from the drab blur of triteness or familiarity—from possessiveness.

J.R.R. Tolkien, "On Fairy-Stories," *Tree and Leaf*. London: Allen & Unwin, 1964.

back, because though Tolkien seems at first to have mentioned the silver hair as a sign of age, he in fact goes on to deny this, 'no sign of age was upon them'. The method here seems almost one of shifting us away from any certainty in the portrayal. Tolkien tells us that they did not look old, unless one looked at the depths of their eyes, but then deals with the surface of the eyes first, going on, '*for* these were keen as lances', before returning us to his original point. Yet at the same time he is asking us to accept a quite complex situation: that their eyes were both extroverted and introverted. His generalized style is of little use in making us feel complex effects like this. Nor, morever, is it good enough even by the standards of the 'Stock Response'. Granted an 'archetypal' method, the archetypes still have to be vividly realized and felt. Yet the portrait of Galadriel and Celeborn lacks wholeness and power, is without the certainty and vigour with which any art worth its salt must be informed.

Hair, eyes and dress—these are the features Tolkien fixes on continually in his portrayals; and in most of them he repeats the idea of eyes being both sharp and profound. Thus Arwen, daughter of Elrond the Elf-King,

Young she was and yet not so. The braids of her dark hair were touched by no frost, her white arms and clear face were flawless and smooth, and the light of stars was in her bright eyes, grey as a cloudless night; yet queenly she looked, and thought and knowledge were in her glance, as of one who has known many things that the years bring. Above her brow her head was covered with a cap of silver lace netted with small gems, glittering white; but her soft grey raiment had no ornament save a girdle of leaves wrought in silver. (*LR*, I, 239)

And of Éowyn, Théoden's niece,

Grave and thoughtful was her glance.... Very fair was her face, and her long hair was like a river of gold. Slender and tall she was in her white robe girt with silver; but strong she seemed and stern as steel, a daughter of kings ... fair and cold, like a morning of pale spring that is not yet come to womanhood. (*LR*, II, 119)

The picture of Arwen has little to offer that that of Galadriel does not give us. We start with the concept of the 'old-young woman': though this is better done than before, in that the contrast is not left to the eyes to make themselves, but is between them and her whole physical appearance, it is still a repetition. Moreover, words are not really working: to say her white arms and clear face were flawless and smooth is to say something twice. And are cloudless nights grey? As for the analogies between human figures and nature—'frost', 'light of stars', 'cloudless night', 'hair like a river', 'fair and cold, like a morning of pale spring'—these are no doubt functions of a general pattern of imagery in the trilogy, but here the piling of them seems only the result of an inability to concentrate on the human figure alone and to see it vividly; indeed Tolkien seems to have lost track of what he is supposed to be describing when he talks of 'pale spring that is not yet come to womanhood'. Further, the hair 'touched by frost' comes over not so much 'nature imagery' as awkwardly precious.

With many of the characters the descriptions we have are often perfunctory: so much so that in fact there is very little to differentiate them. Boromir, we are told, is 'a tall man with a fair and noble face, dark-haired and grey-eyed, proud and stern of glance' (*LR*, I, 253); Aragorn, slightly taller and of slimmer build (I, 305), is otherwise a man with 'a shaggy head of dark hair flecked with grey, and in a pale stern face a pair of keen grey eyes' (I, 169); and the men of Gondor, Mablung and Damrod, are 'goodly men, pale-skinned, dark of hair, with grey eyes and faces sad and proud' (II, 267). With the dwarf Gimli and the Elf Legolas we have not even this: Legolas is introduced to us as 'a strange Elf clad in green and brown' (I, 253); and Gimli is 'a younger dwarf at Glóin's side—his son Gimli' (ib.). Possibly, though, Tolkien intends the names to be suggestive here: Legolas perhaps conveys the slender and vigorous, and Gimli the short and determined (bradawl overtones!); or else he hopes that the words 'Elf' or 'dwarf' will do their work unaided. Yet he could have done much more. One is not asking for a particular Elf, or even one that can be seen: only for a sense of Elfishness, or any sense at all that the creation has been left.

It may be that Tolkien was aiming at a kind of moral characterization which precludes any physical description, but he does not seem to have felt the morality very powerfully either. Glorfindel the Elf-lord is thus described, 'Glorfindel was tall and straight; his hair was of shining gold, his face fair and young and fearless and full of joy; his eyes were bright and keen, and his voice like music; on his brow sat wisdom, and in his hand was strength' (*LR*, I, 239). The account becomes directly conceptual: all the items are functions of a moral portrayal; to say his hair was of shining gold is not so much to say anything about his hair as to comment on what he stands for. But each item appears in a dead list: one feels not that Tolkien is inside the character working out, but outside it, trying, though not very strenuously, to get in.

SELF-CONSCIOUS WRITING DISTANCES THE READER

Unfortunately, and in a strange way, even when Tolkien really does try to get in, the result is embarrassing. He has a romantic longing to be a part of what he sees as the heroism and beauty of the world of his fantasy, but in fact these are no real part of his experience. The result can be seen in this typical instance taken from the charge of the horsemen of Rohan in defence of beleaguered Minas Tirith,

> Suddenly the king cried to Snowmane and the horse sprang away. Behind him his banner blew in the wind, white horse upon a field of green, but he outpaced it. After him thundered the knights of his house, but he was ever before them. Éomer rode there, the white horsetail on his helm floating in his speed, and the front of the first *éored* roared like a breaker foaming to the shore, but Théoden could not be overtaken. Fey he seemed, or the battle-fury of his fathers ran like new fire in his veins, and he was borne up on Snowmane like a god of old, even as Oromë the Great in the battle of the Valar when the world was young. His golden shield was uncovered, and lo! it shone like an image of the Sun, and the grass flamed into green about the white feet of his steed. For morn-

ing came, morning and a wind from the sea; and darkness was removed, and the hosts of Mordor wailed, and terror took them, and they fled, and died, and the hoofs of wrath rode over them. And then all the host of Rohan burst into song, and they sang as they slew, for the joy of battle was on them, and the sound of their singing that was fair and terrible came even to the City. (*LR*, III, 112–13)

Every word and cadence carries a gush of *voulu* emotion and hits a false note; this 'joy of battle' is the joy of someone who has never been in this kind of battle. A few pages later we find an image, dear to romantic hearts, of Taillefer (the Norman supposed to have walked at the head of William's army at Hastings, singing and throwing a jewelled axe in the air), when Éomer sees the rescuing fleet, 'And then wonder took him, and a great joy; and he cast his sword up in the sunlight and sang as he caught it' (*LR*, III, 123). It is self-conscious: there is a self to be conscious that it is not a part of it. And it is, incidentally, an obstruction to the reader's response. Tolkien so gets in the way with these excited cries that he becomes the sole audience of what he describes;[8] once more, and in a different way, the reader loses touch with the characters and the material of the fantasy.

ACTION IS RARELY USED TO DEFINE OR DIFFERENTIATE CHARACTERS

Nor do we get much sense of character through the action of the book. The best we are given for the Fellowship as a whole is the description of the different sounds of their footsteps as they journey in the darkness of Moria, 'the dull stump of Gimli's dwarf-boots; the heavy tread of Boromir; the light step of Legolas; the soft, scarce-heard patter of hobbit-feet; and in the rear the slow firm footfalls of Aragorn with his long stride' (*LR*, I, 325). And behind that Frodo thinks he hears 'the faint fall of soft bare feet'. But elsewhere there is nothing that any of them do which is the peculiar result of being a hobbit or a dwarf or a Gondor man. Frodo succeeds by virtue both of the smallness and the stubborn courage which hobbits have, but this is not what one means by racial peculiarity nor, given Gimli's nature, are hobbits the only people to show these features. As if aware of this, Tolkien sometimes tries to impose characteristics on to the people of his fantasy. When the hobbits Pippin and Merry are found by Gandalf and the others sitting in the ruins of Isengard smoking their pipes, and Théoden says he did not know hobbits smoked, Merry launches forth on a history of how the custom grew up in the Shire; upon which,

> 'You do not know your danger, Théoden,' interrupted Gandalf. 'These hobbits will sit on the edge of ruin and discuss the pleasures of the table, or the small doings of their fathers, grandfathers, and great-grandfathers, and remoter cousins to the ninth degree, if you encourage them with undue patience. Some other time.' (*LR*, ɪɪ, 163–4; see also ɪɪɪ, 146–7)

But the attempt to make the hobbits into quaint and endearing characters is too isolated to succeed; we would not need this account if we had been given any real sense of hobbit peculiarities before. One feels a bit awkward: it is not surprising Tolkien rushes on. The badinage between Gimli, Legolas and the hobbits on the same occasion is similarly sudden and nervous. Gimli's love of mines and stone is more consistently presented: his lament over Durin in the mines of the dwarves at Khazad-dûm and his pleasure in the hard rock of the Hornburg are fine (*LR*, ɪ, 329–30; ɪɪ, 137). But these special features are pinned on without ever being expressed in action, and invariably occur in fleeting interludes. Since they have no links with the surrounding material to direct them, they often become overpitched, as in Gimli's paean to Legolas on the caverns of Helm's Deep (ɪɪ, 152–3), or his too-violent worship of Galadriel (ɪɪ, 35, 118; ɪɪɪ, 253). The appendices to *The Lord of the Rings* on the lore, genealogies and languages of the various races of Middle-earth are partly an attempt at the imposition of character by scholarship.[9]

A WEAK VISION DOES NOT "RECOVER" FRESHNESS

The weakness of the characterization in Tolkien's fantasy frustrates one of his primary aims. For he set out to recover for us in his book a freshness of vision which we are without; and if there is no vision, there can be no freshness. The way the characters tend to run together into a nondescript soup is also precisely counter to the moral polarity he has set up within his fantasy. His picture of the alliance of the peoples of Middle-earth against Sauron is one of a cooperative effort by different races, each with a separate identity, in which the author at least goes through the motions of taking a delight. It is precisely that they retain their generic individualities in coming together that should define the good; and under Sauron and the power of the Ring that identity should fade (*LR*, ɪ, 56). . . .

THE FORCES OF DARKNESS MEAN MORE TO TOLKIEN

As far as Tolkien's descriptions of the 'good' characters in his book are concerned: one gets the impression that he has not really experienced what he is describing, or else that it does not really matter to him. With the evil figures and landscapes of his fantasy it is different. In the portrait of Shelob, for example, there is a marked increase of pressure,

> [Sam] saw suddenly, issuing from a black hole of shadow under the cliff, the most loathly shape that he had ever beheld, horrible beyond the horror of an evil dream. Most like a spider she was, but huger than the great hunting beasts, and more terrible than they because of the evil purpose in her remorseless eyes. Those same eyes that he had thought daunted and defeated, there they were lit with a fell light again, clustering in her out-thrust head. Great horns she had, and behind her short stalk-like neck was her huge swollen body, a vast bloated bag, swaying and sagging between her legs; its great bulk was black, blotched with livid marks, but the belly underneath was pale and luminous and gave forth a stench. Her legs were bent, with great knobbed joints high above her back, and hairs that stuck out like steel spines, and at each leg's end there was a claw.
>
> As soon as she had squeezed her soft squelching body and its folded limbs out of the upper exit from her lair, she moved with a horrible speed, now running on her creaking legs, now making a sudden bound. (II, 334) [10]

Here all the details are fused in one intense reaction, horror and loathing. It is not, by the way, that we the readers respond more easily to evil than to good, but the fact that Tolkien has done so first that is the case here. This is not so with *all* the evil characters: the orcs are not very well realized; but on the whole it can be said that the forces of darkness mean more to Tolkien than those of light. For all the destruction of the Dark Lord and his powers, the vision of *The Lord of the Rings* remains peculiarly Manichaean....

There are further drawbacks to *The Lord of the Rings*, not the least of which, given the flabbiness of material, and allowing for the sense of scale demanded by epic, is its length. The epithet 'endless worm' coined by one critic seems only too apt.[11] Doubtless there is such a thing as the sheer number of pages the reader has had to turn that can add poignancy to the story—one almost feels this is the case as we come to the great close of Malory's epic. But not with Tolkien's book, for we have never been very much involved anyway. Perhaps also the length of the story and the time he took to write it go some way towards explaining his failure of detachment: his involvement in Middle-earth may well have increased in direct proportion to the time and space at his disposal. Certainly he manages to avoid this fault in his short stories. . . .

It would be easy to conclude that all this results from Tolkien's having been sentimental, evasive and morally uncertain as a man and inadequate as an artist. Yet the weakness of *The Lord of the Rings* may equally come from the fact that he did not express himself fully. The book was largely born out of a reaction against the modern world in which he lived: nostalgia and wish-fulfilment, which were only one part of Tolkien the man, are its essence. That there was more to the author than the work shows can be argued from its very poverty of realization: Tolkien may have found that the good, the beautiful and the age-old did not excite him so much or so plainly as he liked to believe. It is possible that his work becomes facile and weak because of an oversimple judgement on the modern world which is its source and end. *The Lord of the Rings* would thus be a picture rather of Tolkien's uncertainty than of Tolkien himself.

NOTES

1. *TL.* J.R.R. Tolkien, *Tree and Leaf* (Allen & Unwin, 1964).
2. Possibly it owes much to Milton's description of Paradise, or alternatively even to C.S. Lewis' account of Milton's technique in his *A Preface to 'Paradise Lost'* (1942), pp. 46–50.
3. *LR.* J.R.R. Tolkien, *The Lord of the Rings*, 3 vols., 2nd ed. (Allen & Unwin, 1966).
4. On the mandala archetype suggested here, see C.G. Jung, 'Concerning Mandala Symbolism', and 'Mandalas', *The Archetypes and the Collective Unconscious*, in *The Collected Works of C.G. Jung*, trans. R.F.C. Hull, 2nd ed. (Routledge & Kegan Paul, 1969), IX, i, 355–90.
5. There are exceptions among the secondary characters— Boromir, Théoden (at first), Denethor, Saruman and Gollum—and it will be noticed that all of these are killed off.
6. 'Oo, Those Awful Orcs!'; repr. in Edmund Wilson, *The Bit Between My Teeth* (W.H. Allen, N.Y., 1966), pp. 326–32.
7. In a sense even the derivative character of the book, its roots in earlier literature, could be seen as part of 'Recovery': the familiar is being made new.

8. In his 'The Homecoming of Beorhtnoth Beorhthelm's Son', *Essays and Studies*, n.s. VI (1953), 1–18, Tolkien partly condemns this ignorant romantic enthusiasm: we are shown how the young man Torhthelm, who glories in heroism however rash, and indulges in heady sentiments, has lost touch with the real world of suffering and struggle that the older Tídwald knows. Heroism has a place, Tolkien says, only when it has a firm grip on the real world. The imbalance in *The Lord of the Rings* invites parody—and has received it in the *Harvard Lampoon* (by Henry N. Beard and Douglas C. Kenney) *Bored of the Rings* (Signet Books, N.Y., 1969).

9. Cf. Spacks, in N.D. Isaacs and R.A. Zimbardo, eds., *Tolkien and the Critics, Essays on J.R.R. Tolkien's* The Lord of the Rings (Notre Dame, Indiana, 1969), p. 98, 'rhetoric and . . . references seem automatic. . . . All too often, Tolkien asserts rather than demonstrates character'; and Roger Sale, 'Tolkien and Frodo Baggins', *Tolkien and the Critics*, pp. 266–8, 269–70.

10. On spiders, see Tolkien in Charlotte and Denis Plimmer, 'The Man who understands Hobbits', *Daily Telegraph Magazine* (22 March 1968), p. 31: '"Spiders . . . are the particular terror of northern imaginations"; '"The female monster is certainly no deadlier than the male, but she is different. She is a sucking, strangling, trapping creature.'" See also J.R.R. Tolkien, *The Hobbit*, 2nd ed. (Allen & Unwin, 1951), ch. viii. One critic has seen the portrayal of Shelob, who is, she says, impaled by Sam's knife 'somewhere in the region of the womb', as a picture of Tolkien's 'subtle contempt and hostility towards women' (Catherine R. Stimpson, *J.R.R. Tolkien*, Columbia Essays on Modern Writers, no. 41 (Columbia Univ. Press, N.Y., 1969, 19).

11. Maurice Richardson, 'New Novels', *New Statesman and Nation* (18 Dec. 1954), p. 836, 'My first impression is that it [*The Two Towers*] is all far too long and blown up. What began as a charming children's book has proliferated into an endless worm.' See also Mark Roberts, 'Adventure in English', *Essays in Criticism*, VI (1956), p. 459. Tolkien, however, thought that the great defect of his epic was that it was too short (*LR*, I, 6).

Tolkien's Sources: The True Tradition

T.A. Shippey

Although Tolkien disapproved of academics' tracing the literary influences on particular works, T.A. Shippey argues that a familiarity with the literature Tolkien drew on in writing *The Lord of the Rings* can only enhance the reader's understanding and enjoyment. Shippey identifies sources from ancient writings such as *Beowulf* through modern authors. This essay is an appendix in Shippey's book *The Road to Middle-Earth*.

Tolkien himself did not approve of the academic search for 'sources'. He thought it tended to distract attention from the work of art itself, and to undervalue the artist by the suggestion that he had 'got it all' from somewhere else. This [essay] accordingly does not attempt to match 'source' to 'passage' in Tolkien. It does however offer a brief guide to the works which nourished Tolkien's imagination and to which he returned again and again; since many of them are not well known, this may give many people who have enjoyed Tolkien something else to enjoy. Whether that changes their reading of *The Lord of the Rings* or *The Silmarillion* is less important: though in fact comparison with 'the sources', in my experience, almost always brings out Tolkien's extremely keen eye for the vital detail.

He was also very quick to detect the bogus and the anachronistic, which is why I use the phrase '*true* tradition'. Tolkien was irritated all his life by modern attempts to rewrite or interpret old material, almost all of which he thought led to failures of tone and spirit. Wagner is the most obvious example. People were always connecting *The Lord of the Rings* with *Der Ring des Nibelungen*, and Tolkien did not like it. 'Both rings were round', he snarled, 'and there the resemblance ceases' (*Letters*, p. 306). This is not entirely true. The motifs of the riddle-contest, the cleansing fire, the broken weapon preserved for an heir, all occur in both works, as of course does the theme of 'the lord of the Ring as the slave of the Ring', *des Ringes Herr als des Ringes Knecht.* But what upset Tolkien was the fact that Wagner was working, at second-hand, from material which *he* knew at first-hand, primarily the heroic poems of the *Elder Edda* and the later Middle High German *Nibelungenlied.* Once again he saw difference where other people saw similarity. Wagner was one of several authors with whom Tolkien had a relationship of intimate dislike: Shakespeare, Spenser, George MacDonald, Hans Christian Andersen. All, he thought, had got something very important not quite right. It is especially necessary, then, for followers of Tolkien to pick out the true from the heretical, and to avoid snatching at surface similarities.

OLD ENGLISH SOURCES

The single work which influenced Tolkien most was obviously the Old English poem *Beowulf*, written in Tolkien's opinion somewhere round the year 700. The best edition of this is by F. Klaeber (1950). There are many translations of it, including the one by J.R. Clark Hall and C.L. Wrenn to which Tolkien wrote the 'Preface' in 1940. The reasons for its appeal to him, however, seem to me to be expressed best in R.W. Chambers, *Beowulf: an Introduction* (1959). The first two chapters of this show with particular force and charm the way in which history and fairy-tale are in *Beowulf* intertwined. Other Old English poems which Tolkien used include *The Ruin, The Wanderer* and *The Battle of Maldon,* all conveniently edited and translated in Richard Hamer's *A Choice of Anglo-Saxon Verse* (1970), and the 'Treebeard-style' gnomic poems *Maxims I* and *II*, edited and translated, along with *Solomon and Saturn II,* in my *Poems of Wisdom and Learning in Old English* (1976). Tolkien's own edition and translation of the poem *Exodus*, prepared for publication by Joan Turville-Petre, [was] published by Oxford University Press in 1981. Significantly enough, Tolkien valued the work as an example of Christian material treated in an old-fashioned or heroic style; his own fiction, one might argue, was a similar mixture but the other way round.

OLD NORSE SOURCES

The poem of *Solomon and Saturn* just referred to centres on a riddle-contest, a form with two other prominent examples, both in Old Norse. One is the *Vafo#rúonismál*, one of twenty-nine poems in the *Elder* or *Poetic Edda*, a collection made in Iceland perhaps about AD 1200. Tolkien knew this well, drawing on the poem *Völuspá* for the names of the dwarves in *The Hobbit*, on the *Fáfnismál* for the conversation with Smaug, and on the *Skírnismál* for the 'tribes of orcs' and the 'Misty Mountains'. More generally the whole collection gives a sharper edge than *Beowulf* to the ideal of heroism, and a stronger sense of a tumultuous history filtering down to echo and hearsay. Both points are well brought out in the old, now-superseded edition of the *Corpus Poeticum Boreale*, by Gudbrand Vigfusson and F. York Powell (1883), as also in Ursula Dronke's much later edition of four poems, *The Poetic Edda, Volume I: Heroic Poems* (1969). There is an old-fashioned translation of the whole of *The Poetic Edda* by Lee M. Hollander (1962); a much better one has recently appeared, *Norse Poems*, by Paul B. Taylor and W.H. Auden (1981). An earlier version of this last was dedicated to Tolkien.

The other major riddle-contest in Old Norse appears in *The Saga of King Heidrek the Wise*, edited and translated by Christopher Tolkien (1960). The relevance of this to all Tolkien's work, including *The Silmarillion*, should be obvious; the combination of pride, ferocity and sadness in the older poem of 'The Battle of the Goths and Huns' which has found its way into the saga seems to be the note that Tolkien often aimed at, and as often disapproved. Another *fornaldarsaga* or 'saga of old times' of much interest to Tolkien readers is the *Völsunga Saga*; William Morris's translation of it in 1870 was reprinted with an introduction by Robert W. Putnam (1962) and it has also been edited and translated by R.G. Finch in the same series as Christopher Tolkien's *Heidrek* (1965). Meanwhile the other great work of Old Norse mythology, later and more 'novelistic' in tone than the poems, is the *Prose Edda* of Snorri Sturluson, written in Iceland between 1225 and 1241. This too is a work of 'mediation', like Tolkien's; Snorri was a Christian trying to preserve pagan material for his countrymen and for the cause of poetry. In several ways, especially its combination of respect for antiquity with a certain detached humour, Snorri prefigures Tolkien. One of the 'lost' poems known only by its quotations was a model for 'Aldarion and Erendis'; . . . another poem added to a manuscript of Snorri's *Edda* by some well-wisher is the *Rígsthula*. . . . There is a good translation of most of Snorri's work in *The Prose Edda*, trans. Jean I. Young (1966).

NINETEENTH-CENTURY FAIRY-TALE COLLECTIONS

It is a jump of many centuries to the great 'fairy-tale' collections of the nineteenth, but . . . Jacob Grimm at least thought the similarity between German fairy-tale and Scandinavian 'Edda' striking enough to prove that both were the debris of a greater unity. Whether this is so or not, the folk-tales of North-West Europe affected Tolkien profoundly. The three major collections (from his point of view) were probably those by the brothers Grimm, printed first in 1812, but expanded, revised and translated ever since: I have used *The Complete Grimm's Fairy Tales*, no translator named, published in London by Routledge and Kegan Paul in 1975, but Tolkien certainly read them in German––he relished the dialect forms of 'Von dem Machandelboom', quoting it in the original in 'On Fairy-Stories' (*TL*, p. 32). Another work he refers to is *Popular Tales from the Norse*, collected by P.C. Asbjörnsen and J.I. Moe and translated by Sir George Dasent, published first in English in Edinburgh, 1859, but reprinted in London by The Bodley Head, 1969. In the same modern series (1968) is *English Fairy Tales* by Joseph Jacobs, a reprint from 1890; No. 21, 'Childe Rowland' is a 'Dark Tower' story. . . . Tolkien also quoted from J.F. Campbell's *Popular Tales of the Western Highlands* (1890–3).

BALLADS

Parallel to the fairy-tale tradition collected by the Grimms and others is the ballad tradition, also preserved by collectors of the nineteenth century and containing much similar, and similarly archaic material. The greatest collection of these is certainly F.J. Child's *The English and Scottish Popular Ballads*, first published in five volumes by Houghton Mifflin, Boston, 1882–98, and reprinted by Dover Publications, New York, 1965. Particularly vital to this are the philological introductions to each ballad, see especially no. 19, 'King Orfeo', no. 60, 'King Estmere', and others; while Tolkien also almost certainly read Lowry C. Wimberly's commentary *Folklore in the English and Scottish Ballads* (1928). Tolkien probably also knew the Danish collection begun by Svend Grundtvig, *Danmarks gamle Folkeviser*, out in 12 volumes from 1853 onwards, and partly available to English readers in *A Book of Danish Ballads*, ed. Axel Olrik, trans. E.M. Smith-Dampier (1939). The collection includes several elf-and-mortal or mermaid-and-mortal ballads like Tolkien's own poems. . . . The collector's father, Nicolai Grundtvig, was in my opinion the 'Beowulfian' whom Tolkien most respected—he appears, in 'Monsters' as one of the 'very old voices' calling ' "it is a mythical allegory" . . . generally shouted down, but not so far out as some of the newer cries'. Grundtvig senior was also remarkable for his efforts to reconcile his studies in pagan antiquity with his position as evangelistic reformer and 'apostle of the North', arguing for Óthinn as a 'forerunner', Earendel-like, of the Messiah, both 'sons of the Universal Father'.

AMERICAN TRADITIONS

But Tolkien was also interested in later traditions, and even in American traditions: anyone who reads the 'Introduction' to *English Folk-Songs from the Southern Appalachians* (1917) will be struck by the strange resemblance of the mountain country of North Carolina before the First World War to 'the Shire' as Tolkien described it. Nor is this accident. A piece by Mr Guy Davenport in the *New York Times* (23 February 1979) records Tolkien grilling an American classmate of his for 'tales of Kentucky folk . . . family names like Barefoot and Boffin and Baggins and good country names like that'. *Old* country names, one might add: in Kentucky and its neighbours, Tolkien obviously thought, there had for a time been a place where English people and English traditions could flourish by themselves free of the chronic imperialism of Latin, Celtic and French. In the same way Fenimore Cooper's hero Natty Bumppo prides himself on being 'a man whose blood is without a cross'; and Tolkien recorded an early devotion to Red Indians, bows and arrows and forests ('OFS' in *TL*, p. 39). The journey of the Fellowship from Lórien to Tol Brandir, with its canoes and portages, often recalls *The Last of the Mohicans*, and as the travellers move from forest to prairie, like the American pioneers, Aragorn and Éomer for a moment preserve faint traces of 'the Deerslayer' and the Sioux. . . . The complaint in one of the sillier reviews of *The Lord of the Rings*, that none of its characters (except Gimli) had 'an even faintly American temperament', is as imperceptive as irrelevant. . . .

MEDIEVAL INFLUENCES

The medieval or middle period between the high vernacular culture of North-West Europe and the collecting or 'reconstructing' era of Child and the Grimms was in several ways a disappointment to Tolkien, though of course he found much in its more traditional poems such as *Pearl, Sir Gawain* and *Sir Orfeo*. His translations of these must be recommended (see 'Abbreviations' under *SGPO*), as also the edition of *Sir Gawain* by himself and E.V. Gordon (*SGGK*), and of *Pearl* by E.V. Gordon alone (1953). Tolkien's assistance to the latter is acknowledged. Tolkien also lived for many years with the *Ancrene Riwle*, or *Ancrene Wisse*, and those concerned to seek out an influence on him might read *The Ancrene Riwle*, translated by Mary Salu, a pupil of his (1955). That work was written *c.* 1225, in Herefordshire. Close in both place and time was the *Brut*, an Arthurian Chronicle-epic by one Layamon. Tolkien certainly valued this as a repository of past tradition, borrowing from it, for instance, Éowyn's word 'dwimmerlaik'. At some stage he must also have noted that the stream by which the poet lived—it is a tributary of the Severn—was the River Gladdon. Part of the poem can be found in *Selections from Layamon's Brut*, ed. G.L. Brook with preface by C.S. Lewis (1963). I am also persuaded that Tolkien found stimulus in the slightly later legends of St Michael and St Brendan in *The Early South English Legendary*, edited by C. Horstmann for the Early English Text Society (1887).

Two other clear medieval English influences on Tolkien are *Mandeville's Travels*, written about 1375, and available in a modern translation by M.C. Seymour (1968); and the *Lais* of Marie de France, also available in translation by Eugene Mason (1911). The latter is a clear source for 'Aotrou and Itroun', the former perhaps the best guide to Tolkien's notions of the trees of Sun and Moon, the *Paradis terrestre*, and the road to it encumbered by enchantments like those of the Dead Marshes. Many phrases from this book seem to have stayed in Tolkien's mind. One should add that for all their names and preferred languages, both 'Sir John Mandeville' and Marie de France were certainly English by nationality.

Dealing with Tolkien's knowledge of other languages could protract this essay interminably, but a source of the highest importance was clearly the Finnish epic *Kalevala*, which Tolkien knew in the translation of W.F. Kirby (1907).... Also recommendable is the Irish *imram, The Voyage of Bran Son of Febal*, ed. Kuno, Meyer (1895–7). Tolkien's wanderings in German romance, though probably considerable, . . . are too complex for me to trace. Some guides through the wilderness of heroic legend can be found, however, in the philologists: and when it comes to it these were the men whom Tolkien probably followed with the keenest and most professional interest. Three major works may be cited, though they give the interested reader no more than a taste: *Grimm's Teutonic Mythology*, trans. J.S. Stallybrass (1882–8); R.W. Chambers, *Widsith, a Study in Old English Heroic Legend* (1912); and R.M. Wilson, *The Lost Literature of Medieval England* (1952). It should be noted that a vital part of this latter came out as early as 1941, in plenty of time for Tolkien to recall it in *The Lord of the Rings. . . .*

HISTORIES AND CHRONICLES

The last major 'old' source for Tolkien which need be mentioned lies in history and chronicle. Gibbon's *Decline and Fall of the Roman Empire* certainly stayed in Tolkien's mind, though probably in the same compartment as Wagner; 'Radagaisus' may be found in its 'Index', if not 'Radagast', as also 'Fredegarius', though not 'Frodo'. Of the Latin histories which Gibbon used the most interesting for Tolkien were probably Saxo Grammaticus's *History of the Danes*, of which Books 1–9 were translated by Oliver Elton, with an introduction by F. York Powell (1894); and *The Gothic History of Jordanes* translated by C.C. Mierow (1915). One has to add that Mr Mierow's grasp of Gothic, unlike his Latin, is feeble. The true opinions of Jordanes lie buried in Karl Müllenhoff's notes to Mommsen's edition of 1882. A final note on the Germanic tribes as they appealed to Tolkien's imagination may be found in Sir Charles Oman's classic, *A History of the Art of War in the Middle Ages* (1898). Its description on pp. 48–51 of the Lombards, that other Germanic 'horse-folk' *par excellence*, strongly recalls the Riders of the Mark.

MODERN WRITERS

When it comes to modern writers, Tolkien was notoriously beyond influence (though reports of his skimpy reading have been much exaggerated. . .). Three authors of his youth must remain prominent in any account. One is George MacDonald, whose influence Tolkien both admitted and minimised, see references in the 'Index' to *Letters:* besides *The Princess and the Goblin* of 1872 and *The Princess and Curdie* ten years later one should note especially *Phantastes* (1858) and *Lilith* (1895). Tolkien also read William Morris, probably with more appreciation: Morris after all knew a good deal of Icelandic and had been stirred by heroic story, trying to reproduce its effects in three of the romances of his last years, *The House of the Wolfings* (1888), *The Roots of the Mountains* (1889) and *The Glittering Plain* (1891). The first is clearly about Goths; the second gave a hint for Gollum, as for Brodda the Easterling in *The Silmarillion*; the last is about a quest for the Undying Lands. In my introduction to the World's Classics 1980 reprint of Morris's *The Wood at the World's End* (1894) I suggest a slight connection between that and the bewilderments of Fangorn Forest. Finally—though Tolkien never mentions him in a letter—I cannot help thinking that Tolkien knew Kipling's stories well, especially the collections *Puck of Pook's Hill* (1906) and *Rewards and Fairies* (1910). In both the theme of an unchanging Englishness is strong, as is that of smithcraft; and Puck's dislike for the word 'fairies' and the 'sugar-and-shake-your-head' Victorian concepts attached is exactly that of Tolkien (see especially the story 'Weland's Sword').

A RETURN TO ENGLISH TRADITIONS

I do not think Tolkien would have had much time for Kipling's 'Indian' works. The centre of all that has been mentioned in this essay is English tradition, though Tolkien was prepared to accept connections by blood with Iceland or Saxony or America, and (in a more gingerly way) by old proximity with the Irish or even the Finns. However he was in some ways what would now be called an 'ethnic' writer, though the rule for 'ethnicity' seems to be that anyone can have it *except Anglo-Saxons* (Tolkien was not quite a WASP). Largely this restriction is a penalty of success; since English is international the language naturally ceases to carry strong national sentiment. Behind that success, though, Tolkien was conscious of many centuries of discouragement which had suppressed native tradition in England more quickly, perhaps, than in any other European country. He valued what was left the more highly. In much of what he wrote and read one can see him trying to return to the time before confusion set in, when the traditions of the Shire and the Mark were uncorrupted.

ABBREVIATIONS

Letters	*Letters of J.R.R. Tolkien*, edited by Humphrey Carpenter with the assistance of Christopher Tolkien (London: George Allen & Unwin, 1981).

'OFS'   'On Fairy-Stories', see *TL* below.

'Preface'   Preface to *Beowulf and the Finnesburg Fragment: a Translation into Modern English* by J.R. Clark Hall, revised by C.L. Wrenn (London: George Allen & Unwin, 1940).

SGGK   *Sir Gawain and the Green Knight,* edited by J.R.R. Tokien and E.V. Gordon (Oxford: Clarendon Press, 1925).

SGPO   *Sir Gawain and the Green Knight, Pearl and Sir Orfeo,* translated by J.R.R. Tolkien, edited and with a preface by Christopher Tolkien (London: George Allen & Unwin, 1975).

TL   *Tree and Leaf* (London: George Allen & Unwin, 1964). This contains both 'Leaf by Niggle' and 'On Fairy-Stories', first published in 1945 and 1947 respectively. References to both are by page in this volume.

Chronology

1892

John Ronald Reuel Tolkien, called Ronald, is born January 3, in Bloemfontein, the capital of Orange Free State, South Africa.

1894

Hilary Tolkien is born February 17.

1895

Mabel Suffield Tolkien, Ronald's mother, returns to England with her sons to visit her family.

1896

Arthur Reuel Tolkien, Ronald's father, dies in South Africa on February 15.

1899

The Boers (Dutch settlers; the word is Dutch for "farmer") of South Africa declare war on the British.

1900

Mabel Tolkien, along with her sons, converts to Roman Catholicism. Ronald enters King Edward VI School. Britain annexes the Boer Republic of South Africa, renaming it the Transvaal Colony; a guerrilla war will drag on for two years.

1902

The Boers of South Africa surrender unconditionally to the British, bringing the Boer War to an end; the Boers are made citizens of the British Empire.

1903

A scholarship student at King Edward VI School, Tolkien studies Middle English and Greek.

1904

Mabel Tolkien dies in England from complications of diabetes. Father Francis Morgan, their parish priest, becomes guardian of Ronald and Hilary.

1905

Ronald and his brother move in with their Aunt Beatrice.

1908

Unhappy at their aunt's, Ronald and Hilary move to Mrs. Faulkner's boardinghouse; Ronald meets Edith Bratt.

1910

Tolkien publishes several editorials, reports, articles (including at least one in Latin), and a poem in the King Edward VI School *Chronicle* from November 1910 through July 1911. He becomes a debater—in Anglo-Saxon, Greek, and Gothic—while also studying Old Norse and Spanish.

1911

With friends Christopher Wiseman, R.Q. Wilson, and later Geoffrey B. Smith, Tolkien creates the "T.C.B.S." (Tea Club and Barrovian Society). He enters Exeter College at Oxford University on a scholarship to study classics, but eventually specializes in comparative philology.

1915

After he takes a First Class degree in English from Oxford (specializing in Old and Middle English), he enters the British army. Commissioned a second lieutenant in the Lancashire Fusiliers, he begins training.

1916

Tolkien marries Edith Bratt. After serving in the Battle of the Somme (as batallion signalling officer), he is invalided out of the fray in November with an intractable case of trench fever (a disease carried by lice, characterized by a high fever). His friends R.Q. Wilson and Geoffrey Smith die in the war.

1917

While convalescing (he spends much of this year in the hospital), Tolkien begins to write *The Book of Lost Tales*, which will eventually become *The Silmarillion*. His first son, John, is born.

1918

Now a full lieutenant, Tolkien receives postings within England. After the armistice in November, he returns to Oxford and begins work as a junior staff member on the *Oxford New English Dictionary*.

1920

Tolkien is appointed reader in English language (a teaching position) at Leeds University. His second son, Michael, is born.

1922

Publishes *A Middle English Vocabulary.* Two Britons, Howard Carter and Lord Carnarvon, discover the relatively untouched tomb of Tutankhamen in Egypt's Valley of the Kings. James Joyce's *Ulysses* is published in France. T.S. Eliot publishes *The Waste Land;* Herman Hesse publishes *Siddhartha.*

1924

Tolkien is made professor of English language at Leeds (the youngest person to have held this position). His third son, Christopher, is born.

1925

Publishes *Sir Gawain and the Green Knight,* which he co-edited with E.V. Gordon. Moves from Leeds to Oxford when he is named Rawlinson and Bosworth Professor of Anglo-Saxon at Oxford University.

1926

Becomes friends with C.S. Lewis, who joins the Oxford faculty. Lewis and other friends (all Oxford dons) join an informal reading club, the Coalbiters, formed by Tolkien. A.A. Milne publishes *Winnie the Pooh.*

1929

His daughter, Priscilla, is born.

1930

Begins writing *The Hobbit.*

1931

The Inklings literary society is founded by an Oxford undergraduate, Tangye Lean, for the purpose of reading unpublished works; Tolkien and Lewis are among those who attend and read their works in progress. The British government's severe economic measures cause rioting in the streets of London and Glasgow. Great Britain abandons the gold standard, which erodes confidence in the banking system.

1932

The Protective Tariffs Acts end free trade, helping restore economic stability in Great Britain. Aldous Huxley publishes *Brave New World.*

1933

As Adolf Hitler gains power in Germany, the Oxford Union, the university's debating society, debates this proposition:

"That this House will in no circumstances fight for its King and Country." The pacifist position wins 275 to 153.

1936

Tolkien delivers his lecture *"Beowulf:* The Monsters and the Critics," to the British Academy. Included in *Proceedings of the British Academy* for 1936, it will also be published separately the following year.

1937

Publishes *The Hobbit, or There and Back Again.* At the suggestion of his publisher, Allen and Unwin, Tolkien begins work on a sequel, which will become *The Lord of the Rings.* Neville Chamberlain becomes prime minister, announcing as his goal the achievement of peace in Europe, which he will pursue by offering concessions to Germany and Italy.

1938

The *New York Herald Tribune* awards the American edition of *The Hobbit* its prize as best juvenile book of the year.

1939

Tolkien delivers the 1939 Andrew Lang Lecture, "On Fairy Stories." Germany begins annexing smaller European countries; in August it signs a nonaggression pact with Russia, and on September 1 invades Poland. On September 3, Great Britain and France declare war on Germany; World War II has begun. The United States declares neutrality, but will enter the war in 1941.

1940

Germany launches the Battle of Britain in August, intended to destroy the Royal Air Force in preparation for the invasion of England. Germany defeats France, invades Norway, and overruns Denmark, Luxembourg, Belgium, and the Netherlands. Winston Churchill becomes prime minister.

1945

Tolkien is named Merton Professor of English Language and Literature at Oxford University. Germany surrenders May 7. The United States drops the world's first atomic bombs on the Japanese cities of Hiroshima (August 6) and Nagasaki (August 9); Japan surrenders August 14.

1947

"On Fairy-Stories" is published in *Essays Presented to Charles Williams,* along with contributions from Dorothy L. Sayers, C.S. Lewis, A.O. Barfield, Gervase Mathew, and W. H. Lewis.

1949

Tolkien publishes *Farmer Giles of Ham.*

1950

Tolkien offers *The Lord of the Rings* to Collins publishers. They will decline to publish it and return it in 1952.

1951

Publishes a revised edition of *The Hobbit, or There and Back Again.*

1954

Publishes *The Fellowship of the Ring: Being the First Part of The Lord of the Rings* and *The Two Towers: Being the Second Part of The Lord of the Rings.*

1955

Publishes *The Return of the King: Being the Third Part of The Lord of the Rings.*

1959

Retires from Oxford University.

1962

Publishes *Ancrene Wisse: The English Text of the Ancrene Riwle* and *The Adventures of Tom Bombadil and Other Verses from The Red Book.*

1964

Publishes *Tree and Leaf.*

1965

Ace Books publishes an unauthorized American edition of *The Lord of the Rings,* without offering royalties to the author. After Tolkien spreads the word about the unauthorized edition and readers reject the Ace edition in favor of the more expensive authorized version, Ace agrees to pay royalties on all the books it has sold. Meanwhile, helped by Ace's promotion of the book, a "campus cult" has formed around the books. American enthusiasm for Tolkien spreads to other countries, and "suddenly," several years after original publication, the books become tremendous best-sellers (selling around 3 million copies around the world by the end of 1968).

1966

Publishes third edition of *The Hobbit, or There and Back Again* (he will continue to make corrections in subsequent editions).

1967

Publishes *Smith of Wootton Major.*

1968

Ronald and Edith Tolkien move to Lakeside, Pool (near Bournemouth, England).

1971

Edith Tolkien dies.

1972

Tolkien returns to Oxford to live. He is awarded the C.B.E. (Commander of the Order of the British Empire), and Oxford University confers on him an honorary doctorate of letters.

1973

While visiting friends in Bournemouth, Tolkien falls ill. He dies September 2.

1975

Tolkien's translation of *Sir Gawain and the Green Knight, Pearl, and Sir Orfeo*, edited by Christopher Tolkien, is published.

1976

The Father Christmas Letters is published, edited by Baillie Tolkien (Christopher's wife). (This edition contains more of the letters and text than are found in subsequent editions.)

1977

The Silmarillion, edited by Christopher Tolkien, is published.

1979

Pictures by J.R.R. Tolkien, with foreword and notes by Christopher Tolkien, is published; a revised edition will be published in 1992.

1981

Letters of J.R.R. Tolkien: A Selection, edited by Humphrey Carpenter, with the assistance of Christopher Tolkien, is published. *The Old English Exodus*, with text, translation, and commentary by J.R.R. Tolkien, edited by Joan Turville-Petre, is published.

1983–1996

Twelve volumes in *The History of Middle-earth* series (edited by Christopher Tolkien) are published. They are greatly anticipated by fans still fascinated by Tolkien's original saga.

1998

Roverandom, a children's book by Tolkien, edited by Christina Scull and Wayne G. Hammond, is published.

FOR FURTHER RESEARCH

Alida Becker, ed., *The Tolkien Scrapbook*. New York: Grosset & Dunlap, 1978.

Humphrey Carpenter, *The Inklings*. Boston: Houghton Mifflin, 1979.

——, *Tolkien: A Biography*. Boston: Houghton Mifflin, 1977.

Lin Carter, *Tolkien: A Look Behind* The Lord of the Rings. New York: Ballantine, 1969.

Jane Chance, *The Lord of the Rings: The Mythology of Power*. New York: Twayne, 1992.

Katharyn F. Crabbe, *J.R.R. Tolkien*. New York: Frederick Ungar, 1981.

Robley Evans, *J.R.R. Tolkien*. Writers for the 70s series. New York: Crowell, 1972.

Verlyn Flieger, *A Question of Time: J.R.R. Tolkien's Road to Faerie*. Kent, OH: Kent State University Press, 1997.

Robert Foster, *A Guide to Middle-earth*. New York: Ballantine, 1971. (New edition published 1978. See also the entry for the 1990 edition below, under "Interesting and Helpful Editions.")

Robert Giddings, ed., *J.R.R. Tolkien: This Far Land*. Totowa, NJ: Barnes & Noble, 1984.

David Harvey, *The Song of Middle-earth: J.R.R. Tolkien's Themes, Symbols and Myths*. London: Allen & Unwin, 1985.

Randel Helms, *Tolkien's World*. Boston: Houghton Mifflin, 1974.

Mark Robert Hillegas, ed., *Shadows of Imagination: The Fantasies of C.S. Lewis, J.R.R. Tolkien, and Charles Williams*. Crosscurrents/Modern Techniques series. With an afterword on J.R.R. Tolkien's *The Silmarillion* by Peter Kreeft. Carbondale: Southern Illinois University Press, 1979.

Neil D. Isaacs and Rose A. Zimbardo, eds., *Tolkien and the*

Critics. Notre Dame, IN: University of Notre Dame Press, 1968.

———, *Tolkien: New Critical Perspectives.* Lexington: University Press of Kentucky, 1981.

Clyde S. Kilby, *Tolkien and the Silmarillion.* Wheaton, IL: Harold Shaw, 1976.

Paul H. Kocher, *Master of Middle-earth: The Fiction of J.R.R. Tolkien.* Boston: Houghton Mifflin, 1972.

Jared Lobdell, ed., *A Tolkien Compass: Including J.R.R. Tolkien's Guide to the Names in* The Lord of the Rings. LaSalle, IL: Open Court, 1975.

Richard Mathews, *Lightning from a Clear Sky: Tolkien, the Trilogy, and the Silmarillion.* Milford Popular Writers of Today series. San Bernardino, CA: Borgo Press, 1978.

Stephen O. Miller, *Middle Earth: A World in Conflict.* Baltimore: T-K Graphics, 1975.

Charles W.R.D. Moseley, *J.R.R. Tolkien.* Writers and Their Work series. Plymouth, UK: Northcote House, in association with the British Council, 1997.

Jane Chance Nitzsche, *Tolkien's Art: A "Mythology for England."* New York: St. Martin's Press, 1979.

Ruth S. Noel, *The Languages of Middle-earth.* Boston: Houghton Mifflin, 1980.

———, *The Mythology of Middle-earth.* Boston: Houghton Mifflin, 1977.

Timothy R. O'Neill, *The Individuated Hobbit: Jung, Tolkien, and the Archetypes of Middle-earth.* Boston: Houghton Mifflin, 1979.

Anne C. Petty, *One Ring to Bind Them All: Tolkien's Mythology.* University: University of Alabama Press, 1979.

Richard L. Purtill, *J.R.R. Tolkien: Myth, Morality, and Religion.* San Francisco: Harper & Row, 1984.

———, *Lord of the Elves and Eldils: Fantasy and Philosophy in C.S. Lewis and J.R.R. Tolkien.* Grand Rapids, MI: Zondervan, 1974.

Roger Sale, *Modern Heroism: Essays on D.H. Lawrence, William Empson, and J.R.R. Tolkien.* Berkeley and Los Angeles: University of California Press, 1973.

Mary Salu and Robert T. Farrell, eds., *J.R.R. Tolkien, Scholar and Storyteller: Essays in Memoriam.* Ithaca, NY: Cornell University Press, 1979.

T.A. Shippey, *The Road to Middle-earth.* Boston: Houghton Mifflin, 1983.

J.E.A. Tyler, *The New Tolkien Companion.* New York: St. Martin's Press, 1979. Supersedes Tyler's *The Tolkien Companion* of 1976 by the same publisher.

Richard C. West, *Tolkien Criticism: An Annotated Checklist.* Kent, OH: Kent State University Press, 1970. Revised edition, 1981.

INTERESTING AND HELPFUL EDITIONS

J.R.R. Tolkien, *The Annotated Hobbit.* Introduction and notes by Douglas A. Anderson. Boston: Houghton Mifflin, 1988.

———, *The Peoples of Middle-earth.* Ed. Christopher Tolkien. London: HarperCollins, 1996. (*The History of Middle-earth* 12) This final volume in the series includes a history of the Appendices to *The Lord of the Rings.*

———, "Guide to the names in *The Lord of the Rings,*" in *A Tolkien Compass*, ed. Jared Lobdell. LaSalle, IL: Open Court, 1975.

J.R.R. Tolkien and Robert Foster, *The Complete Guide to Middle-earth: From* The Hobbit *to* The Silmarillion. 1971. Reprint, New York: Ballantine, July 1990.

Revised editions of *The Lord of the Rings* trilogy were published by Ballantine (New York) in 1965. A further revised edition was published by Allen and Unwin (London) in 1966, and further corrections were made in later British editions. Houghton Mifflin's 1987 edition (Boston) attempted to include all the changes from the British editions as well as some corrections that appeared only in the Ballantine edition. HarperCollins (London) published the Houghton Mifflin version with further corrections in 1994.

TOLKIEN ON THE INTERNET

Many websites focus on various aspects of Tolkien and his work, including such specialized interests as linguistics, Tolkien's art and maps, character histories and genealogies, and biographical material. A good place to start is the Tolkien Network, with links to many Tolkien sites: www.tolkien.nu. Some sites feature audio downloads, which allow you to hear the author's voice; one such site offers both a ten-minute BBC interview with the author from 1971 and a written transcript of the interview: http://village.vossnet.co.uk/h/hpttrsn/jrrt_int.htm.

INDEX

Also by Philippa Carr

The Miracle at St. Bruno's
The Lion Triumphant
The Witch from the Sea
Saraband for Two Sisters
Lament for a Lost Lover
The Love Child
The Song of the Siren
Will You Love Me in September
The Adultress

KNAVE OF HEARTS

KNAVE OF
HEARTS

PHILIPPA CARR

G. P. Putnam's Sons
New York

Library of Congress Cataloging in Publication Data

Knave of hearts.
I. Title.
PR6015.I3K6   1983   823'.914   82-21406
ISBN 0-399-12810-7

PRINTED IN THE UNITED STATES OF AMERICA

Fic.

Contents

—————•—————

THE FAMILY TREE

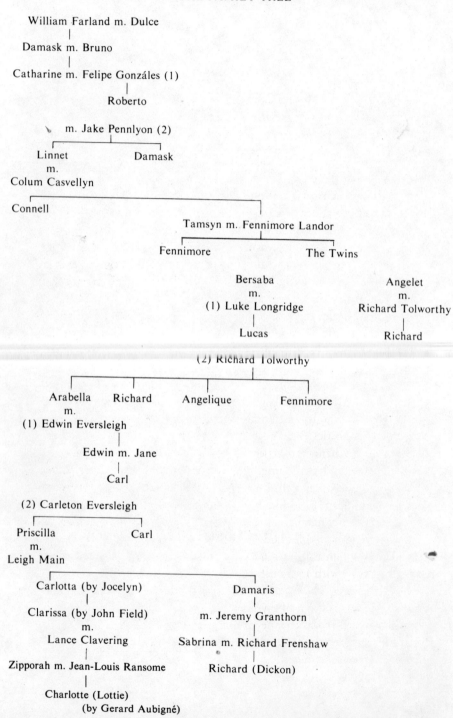

William Farland m. Dulce

Damask m. Bruno

Catharine m. Felipe Gonzáles (1)

Roberto

m. Jake Pennlyon (2)

Linnet   Damask
m.
Colum Casvellyn

Connell

Tamsyn m. Fennimore Landor

Fennimore   The Twins

Bersaba   Angelet
m.   m.
(1) Luke Longridge   Richard Tolworthy

Lucas   Richard

(2) Richard Tolworthy

Arabella   Richard   Angelique   Fennimore
m.
(1) Edwin Eversleigh

Edwin m. Jane

Carl

(2) Carleton Eversleigh

Priscilla   Carl
m.
Leigh Main

Carlotta (by Jocelyn)   Damaris

Clarissa (by John Field)   m. Jeremy Granthorn
m.
Lance Clavering   Sabrina m. Richard Frenshaw

Zipporah m. Jean-Louis Ransome   Richard (Dickon)

Charlotte (Lottie)
(by Gerard Aubigné)

The Rejected

On the day when the Comte d'Aubigné arrived at Eversleigh I had
been out riding and when I came into the hall he was there in close
conversation with my mother. I was aware at once that we had a very
distinguished visitor. He was not young—about my mother's age,
perhaps a few years older—and he was most elegantly dressed in a
manner not quite English; his frogged coat of dark green velvet was a
little more fancy than I was accustomed to seeing, the fringed waist-
coat more delicate, the striped breeches fuller, and the buckled shoes
more shining. He wore a white wig which called attention to his
flashing dark eyes. He was one of the most handsome gentlemen I had
ever seen.

"Oh, there you are, Lottie," said my mother. "I want you to meet
the Comte d'Aubigné. He is going to stay with us for a few days." She
put her arm through mine and thus presented me to him. "This," she
went on, "is Lottie."

He took my hand and kissed it. I was aware that this was no ordinary meeting and that something very important was taking place.
Knowing my mother well, I guessed that she was very anxious for us
to like each other. I did like him immediately, mainly because of the
way he kissed my hand and made me feel grown-up, which was just as
I wanted to feel at this time for the fact that I was not quite twelve
years old was a great irritation to me. If I had been older I should have
eloped by now with Dickon Frenshaw, who occupied my thoughts almost exclusively. There was a family connection between Dickon and
myself. He was the son of my grandmother's cousin and I had known
him all my life. It was true he was about eleven years older than I, but
that had not prevented my falling in love with him, and I was sure he
felt the same about me.

7

Now there was a lilt in my mother's voice. She was looking at me earnestly as though to discover what I thought of our guest. He was watching me intently.

The first words I heard him say, and he spoke in English with a strong foreign accent, were: "Why, she is beautiful."

I smiled at him. I was not given to false modesty and I knew that I had inherited the good looks of some long dead ancestress whose beauty was notorious in the family. I had seen a portrait of her and the likeness was uncanny. We had the same raven black hair, and deep-set dark blue eyes, which were almost violet; my nose might have been a fraction shorter than hers, my mouth a little wider, but the resemblance was striking. She had been the beauty of the family. Her name had been Carlotta, and it added to the mystique that before this likeness was apparent, I should have been christened Charlotte, which was so similar.

"Let us go into the winter parlor," said my mother. "I have sent for some refreshment for our guest."

So we did and wine was brought, over which he talked in a way which I found both exciting and amusing. He seemed determined to charm us and it was clear that he knew how to do that very well. He told us a great deal about himself in a short space of time and I felt he was presenting himself to me, even more than to my mother, and wished to make a good impression. He need not have had any doubt about that. He was a spellbinding talker and seemed to have led a varied and most vivid life.

The time sped by and we parted to change for dinner. I had certainly not been so amused and interested since I had last seen Dickon.

During the next few days I spent a great deal of time in his company. Often I rode with him, for he said he was eager for me to show him the countryside.

He talked to me about life in France where he was attached to the Court as some sort of diplomat, I gathered. He had a château in the country and a house in Paris, but he was often at Versailles at the Court, for, he told me, the King rarely ever went to Paris . . . journeying there only when it was impossible for him to avoid going.

"He is very unpopular because of the life he leads," said the Comte; and told me about King Louis XV and his mistresses, and how heartbroken he had been on the death of Madame de Pompadour, who had not only been his mistress but the ruler of France in all but name.

These glimpses of life in France fascinated me and I was delighted that the Comte talked openly to me as though he were unaware of my youth, a state which my mother constantly stressed ever since my feelings for Dickon became apparent.

The Comte described the fantastic entertainments which were given at Versailles and which he was expected to attend. He talked so vividly that he made me see the exquisite gentlemen and beautiful ladies as clearly as I could the life in the country to which he escaped now and then.

"I hope," he said, "that one day you will do me the honor of visiting me."

"I should like that," I replied enthusiastically, and that pleased him very much.

It must have been about three days after his arrival. I was in my bedroom getting dressed for dinner when there was a gentle tap on the door.

"Come in," I called, and to my surprise my mother entered.

There was a glow about her which I had noticed lately. I guessed she was pleased to have a visitor, and I was glad, because we had had enough tragedy lately. She had been so unhappy since my father's death. Following that, she had lost a very dear friend in the doctor who had attended my father. He had suffered a horrible death in a fire at his hospital. That had been a terrible time, for my governess was burned to death in the fire also. Such events had had a sobering effect on us all, but most of all on my mother. Then, of course, there was the matter of Dickon, about which she was very upset, and this worried me a great deal, for as much as I should like to comfort her, I could not, because doing so meant promising to give up Dickon. So I was very relieved that she was lifted out of her depression, if only temporarily.

"Lottie," she said, "I want to talk to you."

"Yes, Mother," I replied, smiling at her.

"What do you think of the Comte?" she asked.

"Very grand," I answered. "Very elegant. Very amusing. In fact, a very fine gentleman. I wonder why he called on us. I think he must have been here sometime. I get the impression that the place is not quite strange to him."

"Yes, that's true."

"Was he a friend of Uncle Carl's?"

"A friend of mine," she said.

She was really behaving rather oddly, fumbling for words. She was usually so direct.

"So," she went on, "you do ... like him?"

"Of course. Who could help it? He is most interesting. All that talk about the French Court and the château. All those grand people. He must be very important."

"He is a diplomat and works in Court circles. Lottie, you do ... er ... *like* him?"

"Mother," I said, "are you trying to *tell* me something?"

She was silent for a few seconds. Then she said quickly: "It was long ago ... before you were born. ... It had to be before you were born. I was very fond of Jean-Louis."

I was astonished. It seemed strange that she should call my father Jean-Louis. Why did she not say "your father"? In any case, she did not have to tell me how fond she had been of him. I had seen her nurse him through his illnesses and witnessed her grief at his death. I knew more than anyone what a loving and devoted wife she had been.

So I said: "Of course!" a little impatiently.

"And he loved you. You were so important to him. He often said what joy you had brought into his life. He said that when you came into it you made up for his affliction."

She was staring ahead of her; her eyes were bright, and I thought that at any moment she would start to cry.

I took her hand and kissed it. "Tell me what you want to, Mother," I said.

"It was thirteen years ago when I came back to Eversleigh after all those years. My ... I call him uncle but the relationship was more involved than that. Uncle Carl was very old and he knew he had not long to live. He wanted to leave Eversleigh in the family. It seemed that I was the next of kin."

"Yes, I know that."

"Your father was unable to come. He had had that accident which ruined his health ... so I came alone. The Comte was staying at En-

derby and we met. I don't know how to tell you this, Lottie. We met
... and became ... lovers."

I looked at her in amazement. My mother ... with a lover in Eversleigh while my father was lying sick at Clavering Hall! I was overwhelmed by the realization of how little we knew about other people.
I had always thought of her as strictly moral, unswerving in her adherence to convention ... and she had taken a lover!

She was gripping my hands. "Please try to understand."

I did understand, in spite of my youth, far better than she realized. I
loved Dickon and I could understand how easy it was to be carried
away by one's emotions.

"The fact is, Lottie, there was a child. *You* were that child."

Now the confession had taken on a fantastic aspect. I was not the
daughter of the man whom I had always believed to be my father but
of the fantastic Comte. I was incredulous.

"I know what you are thinking of me, Lottie," my mother rushed
on. "You are despising me. You are too young to understand. The ...
temptation overwhelmed me. And afterwards your father ... I mean
Jean-Louis ... was so happy. I could not have told him. I couldn't
have confessed my guilt. It would have wounded him mortally. He
had suffered so much. He was so happy when you were born and you
know how it was between you. You were also so good to him ... so
sweet, so gentle, so considerate ... and that meant a great deal to him.
He had always wanted children ... but apparently he could not have
them. I could, as I proved, and so, Lottie, now you know. The Comte
is your father."

"Does he know this?"

"Yes, he knows. That is why he has come here ... to see you. Why
don't you say something?"

"I ... can't think what to say."

"You are shocked?"

"I don't know."

"My darling Lottie, I have broken the news too abruptly. He wants
you to know. He has become so fond of you in a short time. Lottie,
why don't you say something?"

I just looked at her. Then she took me into her arms and held me
tightly.

"Lottie ... you don't despise me...."

11

I kissed her. "No . . . no. . . . Dear Mother, I just don't know what to say . . . what to think. I want to be by myself. I want to think about it all."

"Tell me this first," she said. "It makes no difference to your love for me."

I shook my head. "Of course not. How could it?"

I kissed her fondly and she seemed like a different person from the one I had known all my life.

———

My feelings were so mixed that I could not sort them out. It was a startling revelation. I suppose everyone receives some sort of shock sometime, but to discover that a man you have believed all your life to be your father is not and to have another introduced into that role was, to say the least, bewildering.

The Comte was such a dazzling figure that I felt proud, as surely anyone would have to be, to acknowledge him as a father. That emotion was immediately followed by shame when I thought of poor Jean-Louis, so kind, gentle, and self-sacrificing. He had cared so deeply for me and it was not in my nature to be indifferent to such devotion. His eyes used to light up when I appeared and when I sat beside him his eyes would glow with a tenderness which warmed me. I had made a great show of looking after him just to see his pleasure in my presence. One cannot lightly dismiss such a father and rejoice in his replacement. When he had died I had been desolate—so had my mother, for that matter. She had loved him too. People's emotions were too deeply involved for me at my age to understand then, but try as I might I could not suppress the excitement my mother's revelation had aroused in me.

Strangely enough I did not connect the Comte's fortuitous reappearance with my involvement with Dickon. If I had thought about it, I would have accepted the fact that he had not come to England by chance after all those years.

When I went down to dinner I was composed. My mother watched me anxiously and there was a constrained atmosphere throughout the meal which the Comte did his best to disperse entertaining us with amusing stories of life in the infamous Court of France.

When we rose from the table my mother pressed my hand and

looked appealingly at me. I smiled at her, kissed her hand and nodded. She understood. I accepted my new father.

We went into the punch room to drink some after-dinner wine and my mother said: "I have told her, Gerard."

He swept aside all embarrassment and, coming to me, took me into his arms; then he held me away from him.

"My daughter," he said. "I am so proud. This is one of the happiest moments of my life."

And after that all the embarrassments were gone.

———

I spent a great deal of time in my father's company. My mother arranged it, I believe. Very often she left us alone together. She seemed anxious that we should get to know each other. He talked constantly about my visiting France and said he would not be content until he had shown me his château, and I said I should not be content until I had seen it.

I was fascinated by him—everything about him pleased me: his easy manners, his gallantry, even what we in England might call his dandyism. It enchanted me. But most of all I was delighted by the fact that he treated me as a grown-up, and because of this it was not long before I was telling him about Dickon.

I loved Dickon. I was going to marry Dickon. Dickon was the most handsome man I had ever seen.

"I think," I said, "that you must have been rather like him . . . once."

"Ah," he replied laughing, "you see what the years do. I am no longer handsome like Dickon. My only consolation is that Dickon will come to this pass one day."

"What nonsense!" I cried. "You are as fascinating in your way. Dickon is just younger . . . although he is a lot older than I. About eleven years older."

My father put his head on one side and said: "Poor old man."

I knew that I could talk to him about Dickon as I never could to my mother.

"You see," I explained, "she hates him. It has something to do with tricks he played when he was a boy. He was very mischievous, as most boys are. I am sure *you* were just as bad."

13

"I dare say," he agreed.

"So it is rather silly to have prejudices about people. . . ."

"Tell me about Dickon?" he said.

So I tried to describe Dickon, which wasn't easy. "He has beautiful blond hair which curls about his head. I think it is what is called hyacinthine. I have always liked hyacinths for that reason. His eyes are blue . . . not dark blue like mine, but lighter. His features look as though they have been sculpted by a great artist."

"Apollo has returned to Earth," said the Comte lightly.

"He is very charming."

"So I gathered."

"In an unusual way," I said. "He never seems to take things seriously . . . except us. I think he takes that seriously. He has a quick wit which can be cruel sometimes . . . though never to me. Somehow that makes me love him more. He would be too perfect without it."

"A little imperfection makes the charm irresistible," said the Comte. "I understand."

"If I tell you something, you won't tell my mother, will you?"

"I promise."

"I think she is a little jealous of him."

"Really?"

"Well, you see, it is due to her mother . . . my dear grandmother, Clarissa. She is a darling. Long before she married my mother's father, she had a romance—very brief but very memorable—with a young boy. It was very—"

"Innocent?"

"Yes. He was transported because of the 'Fifteen Rebellion. Then she married my grandfather and my mother was born. The young man returned years later after my grandfather was dead, but instead of marrying my mother he married her cousin Sabrina, then he was killed at Culloden. Sabrina had his child and that was Dickon. He was brought up by my grandmother and by Sabrina and they both doted on him. They still do. I have always thought that my mother believed her mother loved Dickon more than she did her . . . her own child. It's a bit complicated, but do you see?"

"I do."

"Therefore she hated Dickon."

14

"Isn't there a stronger reason than that?"

"Oh, reasons build up, don't they? You only have to start by disliking people and then you can find all sorts of reasons why you should."

"I see you are something of a philosopher."

"You are laughing at me."

"On the contrary, I am overcome with admiration. If I smile it is because I am so happy that you should confide in me."

"I thought perhaps you might influence my mother."

"Tell me more."

"Dickon and I are in love."

"He is many years older than you."

"Only eleven. And people grow up."

"An indisputable fact."

"And when I am forty he will be fifty-one. We shall both be old then . . . so what does it matter?"

"True, the gap lessens with the passing of the years, but alas, it is the present that we must consider. I think he has been a little premature with his proposal of marriage."

"Well, I don't. Queens are betrothed in their cradles."

"True again, but often those betrothals come to nothing. In life one often has to wait and see. What do you want to do? Marry Dickon now . . . at your age!"

"I suppose everyone would say I'm not old enough. But I would wait until I am fourteen say."

"Still very young, and what is it . . . two or more years away?"

I sighed. "We shall have to wait till then, and when I am fourteen nothing . . . just nothing . . . is going to stop me."

"Perhaps then, no one will want to."

"Oh, yes, my mother will. I tell you she hates Dickon. She says he wants Eversleigh not me. Oh, you don't know. But Eversleigh belongs to my mother. It was left to her, you see, and I am her only child, therefore presumably it would come to me in time. That's why, she says, Dickon wants to marry me."

"And you, what do you think?"

"I know he wants Eversleigh. He is managing Clavering at the moment, but it is not nearly as big as this place. He says that when we are married he will come to Eversleigh. It is all very natural, isn't it? He's ambitious. I shouldn't want him to be otherwise."

"And your mother thinks that, but for Eversleigh, he would not wish to marry you."

"That's what she says."

"And," he added, looking at me quizzically, "there is no way of finding out."

"I don't want to find out. Why shouldn't he want Eversleigh? I know it has a part to play in his wanting me. How could it be otherwise? To like someone because they own a house is no different from liking someone because they have pretty hair or eyes."

"I think it might be considered rather different. The eyes and hair are part of a person . . . a house is not."

"Well, never mind about that. I am going to marry Dickon."

"And I can see that you are a young lady of great determination."

"I wish you could persuade my mother. After all . . . you are a member of the family now, aren't you? As my father, you should have a say in the matter, though I warn you nobody's say is going to have any effect on me."

"I can well believe that, and as an only recently recognized member of the family circle and one whose right to his daughter's regard is as yet fragile, I would not venture to attempt to persuade her. I could only offer advice, and advice, as we know, even if we listen to it, is something we only take when it agrees with what we intend to do. So I will only say to you what I would to anyone with a problem and that is: wait and see what happens."

"How long?"

"Until you are of an age to marry."

"And if it is really Eversleigh he wants?"

"You have said that you know he does."

"But more than me, I mean."

"The only way to find out is for your mother to leave Eversleigh to someone else and then see if he wants you."

"She would have to leave it in the family."

"No doubt some long-lost relative will appear."

"Dickon is a member of the family. My Uncle Carl wouldn't leave it to him because his father was what he called 'a damned Jacobite.' Uncle was a trifle illogical because my mother's grandfather was one too. But perhaps he felt that wasn't so bad being a generation earlier."

"It brings us all back to the golden rule. Wait and see. And after all, my dearest Lottie, when you consider the facts there is little else you can do."

"You don't think I'm too young to know my own mind ... which is what my mother says."

"I think you are mature enough to know exactly what you want from life. I'll tell you another golden rule. Take it, if you must, but when the reckoning comes, pay up cheerfully. It's the only way to live."

I looked at him steadily and said: "I'm glad you came back. I'm glad to know the truth. I'm glad you're my father."

A smile of satisfaction spread across his face. There was nothing sentimental about my new father. Jean-Louis's eyes would have filled with tears if I had said something like that to him.

My father said: "This is the time to offer my invitation. I shall have to leave shortly. Will you come back with me ... for a little visit? I should love to show you something of my country."

———

I was proud to travel with him and revel in that special treatment he received wherever he went. He was rich and powerful in his own country, of course, but he had a natural air of distinction which was not lost on those whom we encountered. He commanded the best service naturally, as though it were his right, and people presumed it was and gave it to him unquestioningly.

A new world was opening to me and I realized how quietly we had lived in the country. True, there had been the occasional visits to London, but they had been few and I had never been to Court, though I believed our Court presided over by good, but homely, King George and his plain consort Queen Charlotte was very different from that of the profligate Louis XV of France. It was a cynical commentary on life that the virtuous—and none could deny our King and Queen were that—should be jeered at while the immoral—and Louis XV's Court was undoubtedly that—should be admired. Well, perhaps not exactly admired, but considered interesting, and a position there was certainly enviable.

My new father was determined to enchant me, to lure me, as I see now, to an appreciation of his country and his way of life. And I was willing enough to be charmed.

We took the journey to Aubigné fairly slowly, breaking our journey at night in delightful inns. The Comte proudly called me his daughter and I shone in reflected glory.

"We shall visit Paris and perhaps Versailles later," he said. "I shall not let you go until you have seen a great deal of my country."

I smiled happily. None could have been more eager to see than I.

He was delighted with my prowess on horseback for he said it was a more interesting way of traveling than by coach. They were golden days, riding side by side with him, still marveling at the fact that he was my father, still feeling twinges of remorse that I should be so pleased about it, chattering away blithely with less restraint than I showed towards my own mother or ever had to Jean-Louis. The reason was, I suppose, that the Comte was a man of the world and his attitude towards me was that I was aware of the basic facts of life. He implied that he saw no reason to protect me from what a person of my intelligence must already know. It made it easy for me to talk to him about Dickon. He seemed to understand my feelings and never insulted me by suggesting that I could not feel as deeply as I said I did because I was too young. I felt no longer a child in his company and that was one of the reasons why I enjoyed being with him so much.

It was not until we were in France that he told me of his family and whom I should meet. Strangely enough, until that time I had not thought of his having a family. He had talked so much about his life at Court that I could not imagine him in the heart of domesticity.

He began: "My daughter Sophie would be a year or so older than you. I hope you will be friends."

"Your daughter!" I cried as the realization dawned upon me. "Why ... she is my sister."

"Half sister," he corrected. "Her mother died five years ago. She is a good girl. She will become your friend, I am sure. In fact I shall insist that she does."

"A sister ..." I murmured. "I do hope she likes me. All your insistence won't be able to make her if she doesn't."

"She has been brought up to obey ... a little more strictly, I imagine, than you have been."

"Sophie," I murmured. "How interesting. Oh, I do look forward to seeing her."

"I want you to be prepared for our household. I also have a son,

18

Armand, Vicomte de Graffont. Graffont is a small estate we have in the Dordogne district. Armand will, of course, have my title when I die. He is five years older than Sophie."

"So . . . I have a brother, too. How exciting! I wonder how many people have families they don't know about."

"Thousands. Life is not always lived to a regular pattern, you know. I suppose almost everyone has a secret tucked away somewhere."

"It is fascinating. Oh, I do so long to meet them. Will they be at the château or in Paris?"

"Sophie will be at the château with her governess. I cannot speak for Armand. He leads his own life."

"It sounds so interesting."

"I trust you will find it so."

"I am so excited. It grows more fascinating every minute. First a new father . . . and now a sister and brother. Are there any more relations?"

"Distant ones who won't concern you. That is all my immediate family circle."

I was so excited I scarcely noticed the countryside. We had come to France by way of Le Havre and traveled to Elboeuf and then spent a night at Evreux, the capital of Eure, in which province the château d'Aubigné was situated.

When we reached Evreux, the Comte sent two of the grooms on to the château to warn them of our coming, and very soon we were making our way southwards, for, said the Comte, now that he was so near home he had an irresistible urge to be there.

As we approached, I had my first glimpse of the castle, which was set on a slight incline; built of gray stone it was overpoweringly intimidating with its buttresses and corbelled watch towers. I gazed in wonder at the imposing edifice with its pepperpotlike roofs on either side of the gatehouse.

The Comte saw how impressed I was and said: "I am gratified. I think you like my château. Of course, it is no longer as it was originally. Once it was just a fortress. What you see now is as it became in the sixteenth century, which was when French architecture was at its best."

Dusk was falling and in the half-light the château looked mysterious, almost forbidding, and excited as I was when I rode into the courtyard I felt a sudden shiver of apprehension as though I was being warned of a certain menace.

"In the morning I will show you the inside of the château myself," said the Comte. "I am afraid you will find me rather boastful and overproud."

"Anyone would be," I told him.

"Well, it is your family now, Lottie," he replied.

I stood in the hall with the Comte beside me, his hand on my shoulder while he watched me closely to see the effect his home was having on me. Needless to say, I was overcome with mixed emotions. It was so grand, so redolent of the past; I could believe that I had stepped into another century; there was a pride in my knowledge that I belonged to the people who had lived here for centuries, and after what had happened to me I was prepared for anything. But there was that faint feeling of unease which persisted and which I could not understand.

I looked at the ancient walls hung with tapestries depicting what appeared to be scenes of battle, and where there was not tapestry there were gleaming weapons; several suits of armor stood in darkened corners like watching sentinels and I could easily have convinced myself that they moved and that there was something here in this hall which was assessing me in the same way as I was this house. On the long oak table were two candelabra—one at each end—and the candles threw flickering light on the vaulted ceiling.

A man came hurrying into the hall; he looked very important in his blue-and-green livery with heavy brass buttons. He greeted the Comte obsequiously.

"Everything is prepared, Monsieur le Comte," he said.

"Good," said my father. "Does the Vicomte know I have returned?"

"Monsieur le Vicomte was out hunting when your messengers arrived. He has not yet returned."

The Comte nodded. "Mademoiselle Sophie. . . ?"

"I will send someone to her apartment, Monsieur le Comte."

"Do so, with all speed."

The man disappeared and the Comte turned to me.

"It is best for you to meet Sophie first. She can make sure that everything is all right."

"What will they say when they know?"

He looked at me questioningly and I went on: "When they know who I am . . . our relationship."

He smiled blandly. "My dear child, it is not for anyone to question my actions."

At that moment I had my first glimpse of Sophie.

She was coming down the beautiful staircase which was at the end of the hall. I studied her eagerly. There was no physical resemblance between us whatsoever. She was short in stature with dark brown hair and olive skin. She was certainly not very pretty—in fact she was what kindly people call homely and those less kind call plain. She was over-weight and too dumpy to be attractive, and her blue gown with its tightly laced bodice and large hooped skirt, which stood out round her like a bell, did nothing for her.

"Sophie, my dear," said the Comte, "I want you to come here and meet Lottie."

She came forward hesitantly. I guessed she was greatly in awe of her father.

"I want to explain to you about Lottie. . . . She is going to stay with us for a visit and you are to make sure she is comfortable while she is with us. I have something very important to tell you about her. She is your sister."

Sophie's jaw dropped a little. She was astonished and that did not surprise me.

"We have just discovered each other. Now, Sophie, what have you got to say?"

Poor Sophie! She stammered and looked as though she were going to burst into tears.

I said: "*I* am very pleased to have a sister. I always wanted one. It's like a miracle to me."

"There, Sophie, listen to your sister," said the Comte. "I am sure you feel the same. You will get to know each other in the next few days. In the meantime, Lottie is tired. She wants to get out of her riding habit and wash, I daresay. Sophie, you know where she is sleeping. Take her there and make sure she has everything she wants."

21

"Yes, Papa," said Sophie.

"A room has been prepared for her?"

"Yes, Papa, the grooms said you were bringing a young lady."

"All is well then. Lottie, go up with Sophie. She will show you the way."

I felt sorry for Sophie. I said: "I shall have to learn to find my way about the château. It's vast, isn't it?"

"It is large," she agreed.

"Take her up then," said the Comte, "and when she is ready bring her down, and we will eat then. Journeys make one hungry."

"Yes, Papa," said Sophie quietly.

He laid his hand on my arm. "You and Sophie must be friends," he said. I glanced at Sophie and guessed that for her that was a command. I did not take such commands. But I did want to make the acquaintance of my sister. I wanted to be friends, but we should only be so if friendship came naturally; and at the moment I could not tell what she was thinking of me.

"Please come with me," said Sophie.

"Thank you," I replied and was glad that Jean-Louis had taught me French. His mother had been French, and although he was very young when she left him, he had a natural aptitude and had kept it by reading in that language; and he taught me to speak and write it. My mother had been eager for this. I saw now that it was because my real father was French. This now enabled me to converse easily with Sophie.

I followed her up the staircase and finally we came to my room. It was very grand with a four-poster bed, the curtains of which were moss green with a tracery of gold thread; they matched those at the windows, and the colors were brought out in the Aubusson carpets which added such luxury to the room.

"I hope you will be comfortable," said Sophie formally. "Here is the ruelle where you will make your toilette."

This was a curtained-off alcove in which was all that was needed for my comfort.

"The saddle horses had already come with your baggage. It has been put here."

I had an idea that she was trying to act as normally as possible to hide her astonishment at the revelation of our relationship.

I wanted to know how she felt and I couldn't resist asking: "What did you think when your father told you who I was?"

She lowered her eyes and fumbled for words, and I was suddenly sorry for her because she seemed afraid of life—something I promised myself I would never be—and she was also afraid of her father, with whom I had quickly become on easy terms.

I tried to help her. "It must have been a great shock to you."

"That you should exist?" she said. "Well ... no ... These things happen. That he should bring you to the castle and introduce you like that ... " She lifted her shoulders. "Well, yes. I was a little surprised, because ... "

"Because I have only come on a short visit?"

"That's what I mean. If you had been going to live here with us ... "

She paused. She had an irritating habit of not finishing her sentences; but perhaps that was due to the shock she had received. She was right. As I was merely a visitor I could have been introduced as such at first and then if the Comte wanted to break the news of our relationship he might have done so less abruptly.

"I find it all wonderfully exciting," I said. "To find I have a sister is so thrilling."

She looked at me rather bashfully and said, "Yes, I suppose it is."

At that moment the door opened and a face appeared.

"Oh, it's you, Lisette," said Sophie. "I might have guessed."

A girl came into the room. She could not have been much older than I—a year or two at the most. She was very pretty with fair curling hair and sparkling blue eyes.

"So she is here. . . ." Lisette tiptoed into the room and surveyed me.

"Oh," she said. "You're beautiful."

"Thank you," I replied. "I am delighted to be able to return the compliment."

"You speak ... prettily. Doesn't she, Sophie? Not quite French but none the worse for that. Is this your first visit to France?"

"Yes." I looked from her to Sophie. "Who are you?"

The girl answered: "Lisette. I live here. I am the niece of Madame la Gouvernante, the Femme de Charge. La Tante Berthe is a very important lady, is she not, Sophie?"

Sophie nodded.

"I have been here since I was six years old," went on Lisette. "I am now fourteen. The Comte is very fond of me. I take lessons with Sophie, and although I am merely the niece of La Gouvernante, I am an honored member of the household."

"I am delighted to meet you."

"You are very young to be a friend of the Comte's. But they say the King sets the fashion and we all know how it is at Versailles."

"Hush, Lisette," said Sophie flushing hotly. "I must tell you what Papa has just told me. Lottie is ... his daughter. She is my sister."

Lisette stared at me; the color flooded her cheeks and her eyes shone like sapphires.

"Oh no," she said. "I don't believe it."

"Whether you do or not, it makes no difference. He has told me and that is why she is here."

"And ... your mother?" Lisette was looking at me questioningly.

"My mother is in England," I told her. "I have just come for a visit."

Lisette continued to look at me as though she saw me in a new light.

"Did the Comte visit her often?"

I shook my head. "They hadn't seen each other for years. I only knew he was my father when he visited us a short time ago."

"It is all so odd," said Lisette. "I don't mean your being a bastard. Heaven knows there are plenty of them about. But not to see you all those years and then to bring you here and make no secret about it."

"My father feels he does not have to keep secrets," said Sophie.

"No," said Lisette quietly. "He acts as he wishes and everyone must accept that."

"Lottie wants to wash and change. I think we should leave her now."

With that she took Lisette's arm and led her out of the room, and Lisette seemed to have been so overcome by the news of my identity that she went docilely.

"Thank you, Sophie," I said.

I found a dress in my baggage—hardly suitable to the grandeur of the château, but it was of a deep blue shade which matched my eyes and I knew was becoming. In due course Sophie arrived to take me down. She had changed but her dress did no more for her than the one in which I had first seen her.

24

She said: "I don't know what you thought of Lisette. She had no right to come in as she did."

"I thought her interesting, and she is very pretty."

"Yes." Sophie looked rueful as though regretting her lack of claim to that asset. "But she does give herself airs. She is only the housekeeper's niece."

"I gather the housekeeper is a very important person in the château."

"Oh, yes. She looks after the domestic side . . . the kitchens and the maids and the running of the whole place. There is a good deal of rivalry between her and Jacques, who is the major domo. But my father has been very good to Lisette, having her educated here. I think it is part of the bargain he made when Tante Berthe came. I always call her Tante Berthe because Lisette does. Actually she is Madame Clavel. I don't think she is really Madame but she calls herself that because it is better for a position of authority than Mademoiselle. She is very stern and prim and no one could imagine her ever having a husband. Even Lisette is in awe of her."

"Lisette is not the least bit reserved."

"Indeed no. She pushes herself forward on every occasion. She would love to join us at table but Armand would never have that. He has strong ideas about the servants and that is all Lisette is . . . in a way. I think she has to do quite a lot of things for Tante Berthe. But it was just like her . . . pushing in as she did. She was astounded to hear who you were."

"Yes, I gathered that. But I suppose a great many people would be."

Sophie was thoughtful. "My father does exactly what he wants, and quite clearly he is proud of you and wants everyone to know he is your father. You are a beauty."

"Thank you."

"I don't need thanks for saying it. I always notice people's looks. I suppose it is because I am so plain myself."

"But indeed you are not," I lied.

But she just smiled at me. "We should go down," she said.

The first meal in the château was a rather ceremonious occasion. I don't remember what we ate. I was too excited to notice. The candles on the table gave a touch of mystery to the room—tapestried like the hall—and I had an eerie feeling that I was being watched by ghosts who would appear at any moment. Everything was so elegant—cutlery, silver goblets, and silent-footed servants in their blue and green livery gliding back and forth whisking away dishes and replacing them with a speed which was like magic. What a contrast to Eversleigh with the servants trudging in and out with their tureens of soup and platters of beef and mutton and pies!

But it was, naturally, the company which demanded my attention. I was presented to my brother, Armand, a very worldly young man about eighteen years old, I imagined, who appeared to be greatly amused to discover who I was.

He was very handsome and very like the Comte in appearance though lacking that firmness of jaw which perhaps comes later in life, for I was sure Armand would be just as intent on having his own way as his father was, but perhaps had not yet mastered the technique. At least that was my impression of him. He was fastidious, that much was obvious; his dandyism was more pronounced than that of his father. I sensed this by the manner in which he lightly adjusted his cravat and touched the silver buttons on his jacket. His expression was one of haughtiness and his manner was intended to remind everyone that he was an aristocrat. His eyes rested on me with some approval and I felt a glow of pleasure; the striking looks which I had inherited from my ancestress Carlotta were a passport to approval wherever I went.

The Comte sat at the head of the table and Sophie at the extreme end. She seemed pleased because of the distance between them. I was on the Comte's right and Armand was immediately opposite me, but it was such a large table that we all seemed a long way apart.

Armand asked me a great many questions about Eversleigh. I explained how my mother had recently inherited the grand house and that I had spent the greater part of my life at Clavering in another part of the country.

Sophie was silent and everyone seemed to forget that she was there, but I was drawn continually into the conversation, able to hold my own until they turned to Court matters about which I listened rapt with fascination.

Armand had returned from Paris in the last few days and he said that the attitude of the city's people was changing.

"It is always in the capital that such changes are first visible," said

26

the Comte, "though Paris has hated the King for a long time now. The days are well past when he was known as the Well Beloved."

"It is the Well Hated now," added Armand. "He refuses to go to his capital unless it is absolutely necessary."

"He should never have built that road from Versailles to Compiègne. He should never have lost the regard of the people of Paris. It is downright dangerous. If only he would change his way of life there might be time yet. . . ."

"He never would," cried Armand. "And who are we to blame him?" Armand's eyes slid round to me rather maliciously, I thought. I knew what he meant. He was accusing my father of resembling the King in his morals. It wasn't fair. I felt a great urge to defend my newly found father against his cynical son. "But," went on Armand, "I believe the Parc aux Cerfs is scarcely in use now."

"It is because he grows old. However, I think the situation is becoming more and more dangerous."

"Louis is the King, remember. No one can change that."

"Let us hope no one tries to."

"The people will always be dissatisfied," said Armand. "There is nothing unusual about that."

"There have been riots in England," I put in. "It is said to be because of the high cost of food. They brought in the soldiers and several people were killed."

"That's the only thing to do," said Armand. "Bring in the military."

"We should make the economy stronger," said the Comte. "Then we should not have these areas of poverty. The people, when roused, can be a formidable force."

"Not while we have the army to keep them in check," said Armand.

"The people may try to raise their voices one day," the Comte went on.

"They'll never dare," retorted Armand lightly. "And we are boring our new sister Lottie with this dreary talk." He spoke my name with the emphasis on the last syllable which made it sound different and rather charming.

I smiled at him. "No, I am not in the least bored. I am finding everything too exciting for that and I like to know what is going on."

"You and I will ride together tomorrow," said Armand. "I will show you the countryside, little sister. And, Papa, I suppose you are proposing to show Lottie Paris?"

"Very soon," said the Comte. "I have promised myself a jaunt to town."

The meal seemed to go on for a long time and in due course it was over and we went into a little room where we drank wine. Even excited as I was, I was so tired that I found it difficult to keep my eyes open. The Comte noticed this and told Sophie to take me to my room.

———

The days were full of new impressions, and yet how quickly they slipped past! I was enchanted by the château itself; a magnificent piece of architecture which was the more fascinating because it bore the mark of several centuries. It was necessary to be some distance from it to see it in all its glory, and during those first days it was a delight to ride away from it and then halt to look back at the steep pitched roofs, the ancient battlements, the pepperpot towers, the corbeled parapet supported by more than two hundred machicolations, the cylindrical keep overlooking the drawbridge and to marvel at its sheer strength and apparent impregnability.

I felt moved to think that this was the home of my ancestors and then again I was aware of that twinge of remorse because I had been so happy in dear, comfortable Clavering with my mother and Jean-Louis, which was all I asked for them.

But how could anyone help being proud of being connected with the Château d'Aubigné!

At first I believed that I should never learn the geography of the inside of the château. In those early days I was continually getting lost and discovering new parts. There was the very ancient section with its short spiral staircases; in this were the dungeons and there was a distinct chill in that part of the building. It was very eerie and I should have hated to be there alone. I knew that fearful things had happened there, for there the family's enemies had been imprisoned. I could guess at the dark deeds which had been perpetrated in those gloomy dungeons. The Comte himself showed them to me . . . little dark cells with great rings attached to the walls to which prisoners had been manacled. When I shivered, he put his arm round me and said: "Perhaps I should not have brought you here. Will it make you like the château less? But, Lottie, my dear, if you are going to live life to the full, you must not shut your eyes to certain features of it."

After that he took me to those apartments where, in the past, he and his ancestors had entertained kings when they traveled in the district. In these rooms with their elegant furnishings, I was shown a different aspect of the château.

From the battlements one looked for miles over beautiful country to the town some way off with its shuttered houses and narrow streets. There were so many impressions to absorb in a short time and I often thought: I will tell Dickon about this when we meet. He would be most interested and I was sure he would be in his element looking after an estate like this one.

But it was the people around me who interested me more than anything.

I was frequently with the Comte, for it seemed as though he could not have enough of my company, which, considering the way in which he ignored Sophie, was remarkable. I had obviously made a great impression on him, or it may have been that he had really loved my mother and I reminded him of that long-ago romance. I wondered. She must have been very different from the people he would have known. I had seen a portrait of his wife and she was just like Sophie, timid and nervous looking. She had been very young, obviously, when the portrait had been painted.

Sometimes Sophie would come to my room and Lisette would join us. I often felt that Sophie wanted to forbid the girl's intrusion, but she seemed afraid of her—as she was of so much.

I myself was rather pleased when Lisette came, for her conversation was lively, and in spite of the fact that I was growing fond of Sophie, I did not find her company very enlivening.

I had caught a glimpse of the formidable Tante Berthe, a big woman with a stern face and tight lips which looked as though they would find it very difficult to smile. I had heard that she was very pious and kept the serving girls in order, which, Lisette told me, was quite a task as the men were always trying to seduce the girls.

"You know what men are," said Lisette laughing at me. "They are torn between their desire for the girls and their fear of Tante Berthe. If

29

any of them were caught in what they call *flagrante delicto*, which means caught in the act, she would insist on their being dismissed."

"Surely the Comte would not allow that to happen."

"You mean in view of his own inclinations." Lisette continued to laugh. She did not seem to care what she said about anyone and I was sure she would never restrict her own behavior. It was true that she had the redoubtable Tante Berthe behind her, and that lady would surely not allow her own niece to be turned away.

Lisette liked to talk about lovers and I thought she did it to tease Sophie. I quickly came to the conclusion that she very much enjoyed showing her superiority in wit and looks over poor Sophie.

"One day a husband will be found for me," she said, "just as yours will be, Sophie." Her mouth hardened. "The difference will be that yours will be a nobleman and mine a good solid member of the bourgeoisie who finds favor with Tante Berthe."

Sophie looked apprehensive, as she always did at the mention of marriage.

"It might be very pleasant," I told her.

"I know it will be awful," she replied.

I told them about Dickon and they listened avidly, especially Lisette.

"Trust you," said Lisette, who enjoyed treating me with a mingling of familiarity and camaraderie, as though we were two of a kind.

"It can't be long now," said Sophie mournfully. "I shall be taken to Court. Papa thinks I shall be perfectly safe there. The King likes young girls but he won't look at me."

"I sometimes think," said Lisette, "that I should like to be selected by the King's pander to minister to His Majesty's delight."

"Lisette!"

"Well, it would be better than being pushed off to some boring old gentleman who has a little money, but not too much, for being the niece of a housekeeper—even such a housekeeper—does not warrant too much."

"You mean you would like to go to the Parc aux Cerfs?" asked Sophie incredulously.

"They say it is most luxurious and when the King grows tired of the girls they are given a good dowry and can marry, which they do,

30

the dowry making them very desirable. Those dowries, they say, are more than an average husband can earn in a very long time. So those girls . . . and their husbands . . . are lucky. Don't you think so, Lottie?"

I pondered it. "I believe a lot of people starve here and in England," I said. "But from what I hear, it is worse in France. If those girls please the King in that way of their own free will and are paid for it, it may be it is better than living in dire poverty all their lives."

"You talk like Armand," said Sophie. "He is very loyal to the King and would like to live just as he does. He loathes the complaining poor—especially when they riot. He says they will never be content, whatever they have, so why bother to make conditions better for them."

"It is hard to pass an opinion on those girls." I temporized. "One would have to experience the sort of places they come from. Perhaps we are complacent . . . and lucky never to have known hardship."

Lisette was studying us thoughtfully, but she did not speak, which was unusual for her.

"At least," said Sophie, "they can choose their own husbands."

Poor Sophie, she was always uneasy when marriage was talked of.

I had been at the château a week when the Comte announced that he was going to take me to Paris and perhaps, if possible, give me a glimpse of the Court at Versailles.

I was greatly excited, but when he said that Sophie should accompany us she was thrown into a state of apprehension because she was afraid a husband would be found for her.

A few days later we were in Paris. I was so fascinated by this great and enchanting city that I did not think of Dickon for two whole days. When I realized the omission I reproached myself for it.

We went first to the Comte's magnificent town house—one of the mansions situated in the Rue Saint Germain which were called *hôtels* and belonged to the country's most wealthy noblemen. With their emblazoned pediments these tall buildings were very grand and impressive. The house was as luxuriously furnished as some parts of the château but in the style which had become so popular during the reign of Louis XV—a combination of classic severity and the rococo. I knew little of such things then and I learned later. All I was aware of at that time was that the exquisite beauty overwhelmed me, and it

31

gave me infinite pleasure merely to look at the handsome chairs upholstered in Gobelin tapestry and the unusual sofas called sultanes, the carved cabinets and the inlaid tables. The rugs and carpets were of delicate coloring and complemented beautifully the paintings which adorned the walls. The Comte pointed out with pride his Boucher and Fragonard—two painters who had just been making their way when he had bought their pictures and were now Court painters for the King, a monarch who might be profligate and given more to erotic pursuits than matters of state, certainly had an appreciation of art. This had been encouraged by Madame de Pompadour when she had been alive and ruled the country through her lover.

I was enchanted by the mansion and even more so by its exquisite furnishings and priceless art.

Then there was Paris itself—city of charm, noise, gaiety, mud, and ... contrasts. Perhaps it was the last of these which struck me more than anything else, when I come to look back—those few glimpses I had of the squalor and horror which existed side by side with the utmost elegance and richness.

The Comte was determined that I should love Paris. I was to discover later that there was a motive in this and that he and my mother were planning to divert my thoughts from Dickon. At that time I put it down to an intense national pride. And indeed he had much to be proud of in that respect.

So he was determined to show me everything, but first he took us to a fashionable dressmaker that Sophie and I might have dresses made for a presentation at Versailles.

"I want you to be acknowledged by the King," he told me, "because without that you cannot go to Court. It may be that you won't be. We have to wait and hope that he will appear. All you have to do is curtsey lower than you ever have done before and if he addresses you, answer him clearly. It would be a brief encounter and if he should speak to you I will make it known that you are on a brief visit to France in case he should ask someone to make plans for you. There will be others present, all hoping for the honor of being addressed—however briefly—by the King, and he will be passing through the anteroom on his way to some engagement."

"And for this we must have new dresses?"

"You must do me credit," said the Comte.

"It seems a great deal of formality."

"That," said the Comte, "is France."

So we went to the dressmaker—a very soignée woman—who seemed very old and was so patched and powdered that her face was scarcely visible. It was as though she were wearing a mask. She brought out bales of material which she caressed with long white fingers as though they were loved ones; she summoned her assistants and they turned me about, unpinning my hair and treating me as they might have done a bundle of merchandise; and all the time the dressmaker's piercing eyes studied me. They glinted as she said: "She is a child ... as yet ... but we will do something."

And to me: "When you are older ... when you have become a woman eh? ... then it will be a joy to dress you."

They decided on rich peacock blue silk for me. "Very simple," she cried. "We show the child ... but the woman to come."

She spent a lot of time with me, less with Sophie. It was blue for her too, a light turquoise shade.

I laughed when we came out. "She takes her dresses very seriously," I said.

"She is one of the greatest dressmakers in Paris," Sophie told me. "She once dressed Madame de Pompadour."

I was impressed, but more interested in the sights of Paris than the forthcoming visit to Versailles which was the reason for so much planning.

The Comte and I were often alone. He seemed to want that, and poor Sophie was often excluded from our expeditions. We did not always use his coach but for fun would take the little carriages which were called *pots de chambre* because of their shape, and although they exposed us to the weather we did not mind that in the least. In these we would ride round Paris. Whenever I hear the *clip-clop* of horses' hooves on a road, I can be transported to those days which seemed to hold a special magic for me.

The Comte wanted me to understand the life of Paris. He wanted me to hear the people coming in through the barriers from the country in the early morning bringing the produce they sold in the markets. It was a city which awoke early, and at seven o'clock, although there were no carriages on the roads, people began to stir and go to their business. I was most amused when the waiters from the lemonade shops came running to the various apartment houses with their trays of coffee and rolls for the *petit déjeuner* of the people who lived there. The various trades seemed to have their special times for making themselves seen and heard. At ten o'clock the legal practitioners went to the Chatelet, and wigged and gowned, they made an extraordinary spectacle, while those whose cases they were going to try ran along beside them. At midday it was the stockbrokers. But at two o'clock all was quiet. That was the dinner hour and it was not until five that the city became lively again. Then it was at its most noisy, for the streets were blocked with carriages and pedestrians.

"The most dangerous time is when it begins to get dark," said the Comte. "No lady must ever be out alone at that time. Thieves abound ... and worse. The Watch is not yet on duty and no one is safe. Later on, when the streets become full of people, it is not so bad."

The play started at nine, and after that the streets quietened down a little until round about midnight when carriages carrying people from supper and gambling parties would go rumbling through the streets.

I loved it all. I wanted to get up early to see the peasants arrive with their fruit, flowers, and provisions of all sorts as they made their way to Les Halles. I wanted to see the bakers of Gonesse bringing in their bread. I wanted to buy coffee from the coffee women who stood on the street corners with their tin urns on their backs; it was two sous a cup and served in earthenware vessels but it tasted like nectar to me. I loved the street singers, some of them singing sacred hymns and others specializing in obscenity.

I think the Comte enjoyed those days, too, and perhaps he saw Paris more intimately than he ever had before. He would dress very simply when he took me walking and he always held my arm firmly. I was touched by the way he always protected me from the splashing of carriages, for the Paris mud was notorious and contained an element of sulphur in it which would burn holes in one's clothes if not removed at once. He took me to Notre Dame, that great landmark of a great city. How it inspired me with its grandeur, but most of all by its antiquity. We went inside, and when he had shown me the glorious wheel window in the north transcept and the rose window over the organ and we had climbed the three hundred and ninety-seven spiral steps of the turret to look at Paris from the top of the cathedral, we sat inside in the gloom and the Comte told me of some of the events which had taken place in the history of Notre Dame. Later, as we looked at the gargoyles which decorated the walls of the cathedral, my mood changed. They were such strange faces . . . so wicked . . . so cunning.

"Why did they put them there?" I demanded. "They have spoiled its beauty."

All the same, I could not stop looking at those hideous faces . . . saturnine . . . evil, but what struck me most was that they seemed to be leering, revelling.

"In what are they revelling?" I asked.

"The follies of human nature, I always thought," answered the Comte.

Though my dismayed reaction was not lost on him, he was still determined to show me all sides of this magnificent city of contrasts. Our rides took us past various prisons. Two stand out in my memory—the Conciergerie on the Quai de l'Horloge, whose circular towers could be seen from the bridges and bank of the river; and the Bastille at the Porte St. Antoine with its grim bastions and towers. I shuddered at the sight of the gallery from which cannon projected.

"They are not all criminals who are imprisoned there," the Comte explained. "Some are victims of their enemies . . . men whose politics have betrayed them . . . or perhaps they have become too dangerous through Court intrigue."

He then told me of the infamous *lettres de cachet*, which were warrants of imprisonment issued by the kings of France. Although they were countersigned by a minister, they had to be signed by the King. "There is no redress," said the Comte. "Any man can receive his *lettre de cachet* and never discover the reason why, for once he is incarcerated in the Bastille, he has little hope of ever getting out."

Looking up at those grim walls I wondered about the people who were living behind them. "But it is so unfair . . . so unjust!" I cried.

"Life often is," said the Comte. "One has to be always wary to make sure one does not take a false step which could end in disaster."

"How can you be sure of that?"

"One can't. One has to walk carefully and one does learn as one gets older. In one's youth one can be rash."

He did not want me to be too depressed; that evening we went to a play. How I loved to see the audience, elegantly clothed and magnificently coiffed, all laughing and calling to one another.

Sophie was with us. She obviously enjoyed the theater and when we returned to the *hôtel* I stayed in her room for a while and we discussed the play and laughed over the evening's entertainment. I did believe I was getting to know Sophie better and beginning to understand that she had been rather lonely, that she wanted to confide and was really rather glad that she had found a sister.

We shall be great friends, I told myself. But then I remembered that I should shortly be returning to England and wondered when we should meet again. When she married, I promised myself, I shall visit her; and she will visit me.

Finally came the great thrill of our visit to Versailles. Oddly enough, after the exploration of Paris, it did not impress me as greatly. Perhaps I had become satiated by so much splendor and luxurious extravagance. Of course I found it magnificent; the Le Notre gardens were superb, the terraces and the statues, the bronze groups and ornamental basins from which the fountains rose and fell—they were like fairyland; the orangery had been built by Mansard, the Comte told me, and was reckoned to be the finest piece of architecture in the whole of Versailles, and I could well believe that; and it was impossible not to be impressed by the great central terrace and stretch of grass called the *tapis vert*. But what I remember most about Versailles was that crowded antechamber, named the *oeil de boeuf* because of its oval window, in which I, with Sophie and the Comte, waited for the King to appear from his apartments.

Everyone was very elaborately dressed, and the Comte, I supposed because he was an important person at Court, stood in a prominent position near the door with me on one side and Sophie on the other.

There was an air of suppressed tension in that room and such eagerness on the faces of everyone. They were all so anxious that the King should notice them on his passage through the room. I kept thinking of those people in the Bastille who had been despatched there for something of which they might well be unaware, and just because they had displeased someone who had the power to put them there. But hadn't the Comte said the *lettres de cachet* had to be signed by the King?

36

There was a sudden hush, for a man had come into the room. The King of France! He was followed by several men but I had eyes only for the King. I think I should have known him for the King anywhere. He had an air of great distinction, and carried himself in a way I can only describe as aloof. It was a handsome face, certainly marked by debauchery, but the good looks remained. He moved with grace and was most exquisitely dressed; diamonds glittered discreetly on his person. I could not take my eyes from him.

He was close to us now and the Comte had caught his eye. I felt myself propelled forward and curtsied as low as I could. Sophie did the same and the Comte bowed low.

"Ah, Aubigné," said the King; his voice was deep and musical.

"I would present my daughters, Sire," said the Comte.

I could feel those weary looking eyes on me. A very charming smile appeared on the King's face and for a few seconds he looked straight at me.

"You have a very pretty daughter, Comte," he said.

"On a visit from England, Sire. She returns there soon to her mother."

"I hope we shall see her at Court before she goes."

The King had passed on. Someone else was bowing with the utmost servility.

The Comte was delighted. As we rode back to Paris in the carriage he said: "It was a great success. The King actually spoke of you. That's why I told him you were here only on a visit. He liked you. That was clear. Aren't you flattered?"

"I have heard that he likes all young girls."

"Not all," said the Comte with a laugh, and I noticed that Sophie shrank into a corner of the carriage. I felt sorry for her because the King had scarcely glanced at her.

When we reached Paris the Comte said that he wanted to speak to me and asked me to join him in the *petit salon* where he would join me shortly.

I changed into a simpler dress and went down to the room where he was waiting for me.

"Ah, Lottie," he said, "flushed with success, I see."

"It was a very brief glory," I reminded him.

"What did you expect? An invitation to sup with him? God forbid. I should not have taken you if that had been possible."

"I didn't expect anything. I was just surprised that he looked at me what was it for . . . two seconds?"

"You are a beautiful girl, Lottie. You stand out in a crowd. It means that now the King has spoken to you . . . or been aware of you . . . you could go to Court if the occasion arose. It is always well to be in a position to go."

"Well, I shall be on my way home soon. I suppose I should be thinking of my return now. I only came for a short visit, didn't I?"

"And you have enjoyed that visit?"

"It has been wonderfully exciting and different from anything I have ever known before."

"I don't intend to lose you now that I have found you, you know."

"I hope you won't."

He looked at me steadily. "I think, Lottie, that you and I understand each other well. We stepped easily into the roles of father and daughter."

"I suppose we did."

"I am going to tell you something. I have written to your mother asking her to marry me and she has consented."

I stared at him in amazement. "But . . . " I stammered. "Her . . . her home is at Eversleigh."

"When a woman marries she leaves her home and goes to that of her husband."

"You mean she will come to live here?"

He nodded. "And it is your home too," he added.

This was bewildering. First a father appearing, then the scenes I had witnessed during the last weeks and now . . . my mother was going to marry the Comte.

"But . . . " I said because I had to go on talking in the hope of collecting my wits meanwhile. "You . . . er . . . you haven't seen each other . . . for years before you came to England."

"We loved each other long ago."

"And then . . . nothing happened."

"Nothing happened! *You* happened. Moreover we are both free now. Neither of us was then."

"It seems to me so very sudden."

"Sometimes one knows these things at once. We did. You don't seem very pleased. Are you wondering about yourself? Lottie, it is my earnest wish and that of your mother that you will be with us. This is your home now."

"No. . . . My home is in England. You know about Dickon."

"My dear, you are so young. You know there can be no thought of a marriage yet."

"But I do know I love Dickon and he loves me."

"Well, you have to grow up a little, don't you? Why shouldn't you do that growing up here?"

I could not think of anything to say. I wanted to be alone to ponder this new turn in affairs and to ask myself what effect it was going to have on my life.

The Comte was saying: "Your mother is making arrangements to come to France."

"She can't leave Eversleigh."

"Arrangements will have to be made. In fact she has been making them for some time. We agreed to this two weeks ago. We both decided that having found each other we were not going to risk losing each other again. Lottie, I can never explain what a joy it has been to find you . . . and your mother. I thought of her over the years and it seems she did of me. What is between us is something which rarely comes."

I nodded and he smiled at me fondly, realizing that I was thinking of Dickon; and although he believed that I could not possibly understand, he did not say so.

"Now we have a chance to regain what we have lost. We both realize that. Nothing is going to stand in our way. Your mother will be coming here soon. We shall be married then. I wanted you to hear it first from me. When your mother comes she will tell you what arrangements have been made. In the meantime we must prepare for the wedding."

He put his arms about me and drawing me to him, kissed me. I clung to him. I was very fond of him and proud that he was my father. But when I tried to look into the future, it seemed very misty to me.

The news that my father was to be married was received in his household with some consternation, I think, although no one said very much to me. Armand shrugged his shoulders and seemed cynically amused because the bride was to be my mother, and the romantic plans were clearly the outcome of an old love affair.

"So we have a sister and *belle mère* at one stroke," he said, and I was sure he went off to laugh about it with his cronies—worldly young gentlemen like himself.

Sophie was inclined to be pleased. "He will be so taken up with his own marriage that he won't think about arranging one for me," she confided to me.

I replied: "You worry too much. If you don't want to marry the man they choose for you, just say so. Be firm. They can't drag you screaming to the altar."

She laughed with me and it occurred to me that we were beginning to get on very well.

Lisette talked excitedly of the marriage.

"He must be deeply enamored," she said, "for there is no need to get heirs."

"Surely that is not the only reason for marrying," I said.

"It usually is the main one in France. Otherwise men would never marry. They like a variety of mistresses."

"How cynical you all are! Don't you believe in love?"

"Love is very fine when there are advantages to let it flourish in comfort. I think that is the view of most people. I have learned to stare cold hard facts in the face and it seems to me that on this occasion your father must be truly in love."

"And that amazes you?"

"I suppose such things can happen to anyone—even to men like the Comte."

She shrugged her shoulders and laughed at me.

I was delighted to see my mother when she arrived. She seemed to have cast off years. I felt very tender towards her because I realized that her life had not been easy. True, she had loved the Comte and betrayed her husband, but that was one of the reasons for her years of contrition, and being the woman she was, she suffered very deeply through

40

what she would call her sin. Now she blossomed; her eyes shone and there was a faint flush on her cheeks. She looked years younger. Like Pilgrim, I thought, when the burden fell from his shoulders. She was like a young girl in love.

The Comte had changed too. I was amazed that two elderly people—at least they seemed elderly to me—could behave like two young people in love. For indeed, they were in love, and love appeared to have the same effect on people in their forties as it did on those in their teens.

She embraced me; and the Comte embraced me; and we all embraced each other. All the retainers came into the hall to greet her. They bowed low and were all smiling and chattering and the Comte stood by, like a benign god, smiling on the happiness he had created.

Armand and Sophie greeted her with their own special brand of behavior: Armand, smiling rather condescendingly as though he were confronting two children who were having a special treat, and Sophie nervously, certain that her new stepmother would find faults in her, in spite of the fact that I had assured her my mother was the easiest person in the world to get along with.

They were to be married the following week and the ceremony would take place in the castle chapel. I was all eagerness to ask questions about what was happening at Eversleigh but I did not get a chance to talk to my mother alone until much later in the evening.

We had eaten in the dining room and I saw how impressed and enchanted she was by the château—just as I had been; and when we arose from the table she asked me to take her to the room which had been prepared for her.

"We have hardly had a word alone since I arrived," she said.

When we were in her room she shut the door and as she looked at me some of the happiness faded from her face, and I felt misgivings that all was not as well as it had seemed.

I said: "There is so much I want to know. What about Eversleigh? What are you going to do about everything there?"

"That is what I want to explain to you. It is taken care of. . . ."

Still she hesitated.

"Is something wrong?" I asked.

41

"N—no. It has all worked out very well. Lottie, I have made Eversleigh over to Dickon."

"Oh!" I smiled. "It is what he wanted, and of course, it is the solution."

"Yes," she repeated. "It is what he wanted and it is the solution."

"So . . . he'll have Eversleigh . . . and Clavering. I suppose he'll be at Eversleigh most of the time. He loves that place and of course he *is* one of the family. If Uncle Carl had not been so eccentric it would have gone to him."

"Well, he has it now, and I have a letter for you, Lottie."

"A letter?"

She was a long time producing it and when she did she held it as though it were some dangerous weapon.

"It's from Dickon!" I said.

"Yes," she answered. "It will explain."

I threw my arms about her and kissed her. I was longing to read the letter but did not want to do so until I was alone, and as she had asked me to talk to her I did not feel that I could leave her immediately.

"It's wonderful," I cried. "Everyone gets what they want! And you are happy, aren't you, Mother? You truly love him, don't you?"

"I have always loved Gerard."

"It's so romantic . . . one of those 'and they lived happily ever after' endings. It's nice to know they do occur sometimes."

"We intend to be happy . . . after all these years. And, Lottie, this will be your home, you know."

I frowned. "Well, I suppose so really. But I shall visit my relations in England. I suppose my grandmother will be at Eversleigh with Dickon's mother."

"They will not be able to tear themselves away from him, and Eversleigh is a big house. They need not get in his way."

I was smiling. It was all working out so happily. I would go to Eversleigh and he would be there. I was clutching his letter in my hand and it was difficult to stop myself tearing it open.

Perhaps she understood my impatience for she said: "Well, that is what I wanted to tell you."

"Dear Mother," I replied, "it is lovely to see you here. It is the most exciting and beautiful place you could imagine. I love it. And it is wonderful that you and the Comte are going to be so happy."

"He is so fond of you. He was delighted with you as soon as he saw you."

"I like him, too. Good night, Mother. I'll see you in the morning. There is so much to talk about."

"Good night, my child," she said, "and always remember that everything I have ever done has been for your good."

"I know that. Good night. Sleep well."

Then I was gone.

As soon as I was in my room I slit the envelope and read his letter.

> Dearest little Lottie,
>
> When you read this Eversleigh will be mine. It was like a miracle. Prince Charming appears out of the blue and whisks your mother off to his romantic castle and she leaves Eversleigh to me.
>
> Isn't that exciting? I often think of you and our little romance. It did amuse you, didn't it? Our little game of pretense? We tried to forget that you were only a child and I must admit that at times you did not seem so. But facts are facts. You are going to live in France now. You will meet interesting people, for I believe Monsieur le Comte leads a very colorful life. I am so pleased that you will have such a wonderful time.
>
> I shall soon be installed in Eversleigh with my mother and your grandmother. It is a family house, isn't it? Generations of the Eversleigh clan have lived here . . . so even when I marry they won't be moving out. I daresay that will be fairly soon. I am really so much older than you, Lottie, and it is time I was settled—especially now that I have Eversleigh and new responsibilities.
>
> My blessings on you, dear Lottie. I hope you won't forget the pleasant times we had together.
>
> > Dickon

I read it through again. What did he mean? There were three facts which kept going round in my head. Eversleigh was now his. I was a child. He was going to marry soon.

It was all over then. Dickon no longer loved me, no longer wanted me. He wrote as though what had been between us had been some game of make-believe.

I began to see it all very clearly. It *had* been Eversleigh he had wanted. And now that he had it I had no place in his picture of the future.

I had never felt so miserable in the whole of my life. I threw myself onto the bed and stared up at the tester.

It was over. There was no need now for Dickon to marry me to get what he wanted.

So . . . he had jilted me.

The Procuress

There was great excitement throughout the capital and indeed throughout the entire country because of the royal wedding. The people seemed to have forgotten their grievances and were growing excited at the prospect of all the fêtes and entertainments which would be planned to celebrate the great occasion. The weather was beautiful, the may was in blossom; and it was a time for rejoicing.

It was three years since my mother had married my father and it amazed me to see how happy they were together. I think I had grown a little cynical. Dickon's defection had made me grow up over night. I still thought of him; he was enshrined in my heart as the perfect lover, and no matter what I heard of him, nothing could change that. I used to talk about him to Lisette and Sophie, building up romantic dreams, in which there was always the same terrible mistake; he had not written that letter jilting me; he had not married and all this time he had been pining for me, for he had received a false letter from me.

It eased me, that dream, ridiculous as it was, for there were letters from my grandmother and Sabrina telling us how wonderful Dickon was and how happy with his dear wife, Isabel, who had brought him a fortune and new interests in life.

My mother always gave me the letters to read with a certain embarrassment and apprehension, but I had learned to hide my feelings; I would read them avidly and then go away and tell myself I didn't believe a word of them.

"Dickon's father-in-law is a very influential man," wrote Sabrina. "He is a banker and some high official at Court. It is all rather secret and we are not sure what he does there. He has his finger in many pies . . . and that means Dickon has too. You may be sure he makes the most of everything that comes his way. . . ."

Once my grandmother and Sabrina came to visit us. They wanted to assure themselves that my mother and I were really happy.

Dickon did not come with them. "I suppose he can't get his fingers out of all those pies," I said maliciously.

They laughed and replied that Dickon was indeed busy. He was in London a great deal and there was Eversleigh to run. He surrounded himself with good men . . . the right people.

"He talks of you often, Lottie," said my grandmother. "He was so sweet to you when you came to stay, wasn't he? Not many young men would have taken so much notice of a little girl."

My mother put in rather tartly: "He took a lot of notice of Eversleigh and that included Lottie at that time."

My grandmother ignored that and insisted: "It was a charming gesture to take so much interest in a little girl and he used to do everything to make Lottie happy."

Yes, I thought. He kissed me in such a way that I find hard to forget. He talked to me of marriage . . . and how happy we should be together. He persuaded me to love him. He tricked me, and when he got Eversleigh he jilted me.

I knew now that my mother had contrived it. She had sent for my father, who had come and changed everything. Then she had given up Eversleigh because she thought that when Dickon had it he would cease to want me.

And how right she had been! I suppose I should have been grateful to her, but I wasn't. I wouldn't have cared for what reason Dickon wanted me. Perhaps I refused to let myself forget him; perhaps the idea of lost love pleased me, made me feel that my life, though tragic, was full of interest. That may well have been the case, but the fact remained that Dickon was always ready to come into my thoughts, and with the memory would come that frustrated longing.

"There is only one fly in the ointment," said Sabrina; "they can't have children."

"Poor Isabel, she does so long for a healthy child," added my grandmother. "There have been two miscarriages already. It seems as though she is ill fated. Dickon is most disappointed."

"It is the only thing he cannot win for himself," I commented.

My grandmother and Sabrina never recognized irony when it was directed against Dickon. "Alas, that is so, my dear," said Sabrina sadly.

So there I was at the time of the royal wedding. The little Austrian girl, who was about my age, was coming to France to marry the Dauphin, who himself was not much older. The Comte would be at Court and I supposed we should all go to some of the entertainments. There would be balls and ballets and we should be able to catch a glimpse of the notorious woman, Madame du Barry, who was causing such a scandal at Court. She was vulgar and breathtakingly beautiful, I believed, and the King doted on her. Many had tried to remove her from her position, but the King remained enslaved.

There was always some intrigue in progress; life was rich, colorful, and uncertain—the more so because on occasions we heard of the rumblings of discontent throughout the country. News would reach us of riots in a small town, a farmer's haystacks being burned down, a baker's shop raided.... Small outbreaks in remote places. We took little notice of them. Certainly not during those golden days before the wedding.

The château had become my home by now but I never really got used to it. It could never be home to me as Clavering and Eversleigh had been. There I had been in the houses of my ancestors—of course, in a way, the castle was that too; yet there was something alien about it. It seemed full of echoes from the past and I could never quite forget those dungeons which the Comte had shown me soon after my arrival.

My mother had settled in with ease and had taken on the role of Madame la Comtesse without any apparent effort. I supposed that was because she was happy. I marveled that she, who had lived rather quietly, could suddenly become a figure of society, although throughout it all she preserved a certain air of innocence which was very attractive. There was mystery about her. She had a virginal air and yet it was well known that she had borne the Comte's child—myself—all those years before when she had been the wife of another man, and the Comte had had his own wife and family. As for the Comte, he had become a doting and faithful husband, which I was sure was something society had never expected of him. It was a miracle. The miracle of true love. That, I would say to myself, is how Dickon and I would have been had we been allowed to marry.

I was educated with Sophie according to French custom, which meant that there was an emphasis on what was considered gracious living rather than academic achievement. Literature was important as was an appreciation of art in any form, and fluency of language and the ability to converse with wit and charm; we must be skilled in courtly arts such as dancing, singing, and playing a musical instrument; and we had special teachers for these subjects. I found them very interesting—far more so than the tuition I had received from my English governesses. Lisette shared our lessons.

Lisette was very bright and learned with a feverish application as though she were determined to excel, which she did. Sophie lagged behind. I often tried to point out to her that it was not so much that she was slower to comprehend as that she believed herself to be, and so willed it.

She would always shake her head and Lisette said that she would never grow out of it until she married and found a husband and children who adored her. "And that," added Lisette, with one of her looks of wisdom, "will never come about because she will not believe it even if it were actually the case."

Lisette and I were high spirited. If something was forbidden we were always seized with the urge to have it. We broke the rules set down by our teachers and once, when we were in Paris, we slipped out after dark and walked through the streets, which was a very daring thing to do. We were accosted by two gallants and were really frightened when they took our arms and would not let us go. Lisette screamed and attracted the attention of some people who were passing. Fortunately they stopped and Lisette cried out that we were being held against our will. The gallants released us and we ran with all the speed we could muster, and so reached the *hôtel* in safety. We did not try that again, but it had been a great adventure and, as Lisette said, it was experience.

Sophie was quite different, timid and subdued; and we always had great difficulty in persuading her to do anything which was forbidden.

47

So Lisette and I became the friends, whereas Sophie always remained something of an outsider.

"It's as though *we* are the sisters," said Lisette smiling fondly at me.

There was one person of whom Lisette was afraid and that was Tante Berthe. But then the entire household was in awe of that formidable lady.

Sophie's continual fear was that a husband would be found for her; she dreaded that and had already made up her mind that whoever was chosen for her would dislike her for being expected to marry her.

Lisette said: "There is one consolation in being the niece of the housekeeper. One will very likely have the privilege of choosing one's own husband."

"I should not be surprised if Tante Berthe chose one for you," I commented.

"My dear Lottie," she retorted, "no one . . . not even Tante Berthe would make me marry if I did not want to."

"Nor I," I added.

Sophie listened to us round-eyed and disbelieving.

"What would you do?" she demanded.

"Run away," I boasted.

Lisette lifted her shoulders, which meant: Where to?

But I had an idea that if I were desperately determined my mother would not want me to be forced and she would persuade the Comte not to do so . . . so I felt safe enough.

This was the state of affairs when one day—it must have been about six weeks before the wedding—my mother told me that she and the Comte were going to visit some friends north of Angoulême and they were taking Sophie with them.

This threw Sophie into a state of trepidation for it could mean only one thing. It must be something to do with betrothal, because the Comte was not very fond of Sophie's company, and I was sure that if it had been a matter of pleasure only they would have taken me with them.

When we heard that they were visiting the Château de Tourville, the home of the Tourville family, and that there was an unmarried son of the family who was some twenty years old, it seemed as though Sophie's fears were justified.

I said good-bye to my parents and a despairing Sophie and then rushed back to Lisette and the two of us went to the top of one of the towers to watch the cavalcade until it was out of sight.

"Poor Sophie," said Lisette. "Charles de Tourville is a bit of a rake."

"How do you know?"

"One of the advantages of being the housekeeper's niece is that one has an ear—a foot rather—in both camps. Servants know a great deal about the families they serve and there is communication between them. Mind you, they are a bit suspicious of me in the servants' quarters. An educated young lady who is on terms of familiarity with the daughters of the house! Mind you, that doesn't go for much. Sophie is so mild and you, after all, dear Lottie, are a bastard sprig and a belated rush into respectability by your parents doesn't alter that."

Lisette always amused me with her banter. Sometimes she seemed to despise the nobility but she studied so hard at lessons because she was so anxious to be regarded as a member of it. If I had my dreams about Dickon's one day returning to me with explanations and reconciliations, she had her dreams of marrying a duke and going to Court and perhaps catching the King's eye and becoming as great an influence there as Madame du Barry.

We often lay on the grass overlooking the moat weaving rosy dreams of the future. Sophie used to be quite baffled by the outrageous situations we conjured up; they were so fantastic and alike in one respect. Lisette and I were always the glorious heroines in the center of our romantic adventures.

During the time Sophie was away—it was fourteen days and much of that was spent in traveling—we did spare a thought for her and wondered whether she would come back betrothed to Charles de Tourville. We made plans to comfort her and to keep her mind from the horror marriage would mean to her.

Our amazement was great when she did come. She was a different Sophie. She had become almost pretty. Even her lank hair had a special sheen to it; and the expression on her face was almost rapt.

Lisette and I exchanged glances, determined to find out what had happened to change her.

We might have guessed. Sophie was in love.

She even talked about it.

49

"From the moment I saw Charles ... I knew ... and so did he. I couldn't believe it. How could *he* feel like that ... ?"

"Like what?" demanded Lisette.

"In ... love," murmured Sophie. "With me."

I was delighted for her and so was Lisette. We were very fond of her and were always trying to help her when we were not endeavoring to make her join in some mischief. She talked of nothing else but Charles de Tourville ... how handsome he was, how charming, how brilliant. They had ridden together—not alone, of course, but in a party; but Charles had always contrived to be beside Sophie. Her father and Charles's father had become great friends; and my mother and Charles's mother had found so much to talk about.

The visit had been a great success and nothing would ever be the same again.

Sophie had found her true self. She had been brought face to face with the fact that her lack of beauty had been largely due to herself. She was still reserved—one did not change one's entire character overnight—but Charles had done a great deal for her and even before I met him I liked him for doing that.

Lisette said to me when we were alone: "Do you think he really fell in love with her or is it because he wants the marriage? An alliance with Aubigné would be very desirable for a family like the Tourvilles."

I looked rather apprehensively at the knowledgeable Lisette with her ears in two camps and who was in possession of all the gossip from servants who had got it from servants in other households. The thought had occurred to me too, but I would not allow myself to believe it. I wanted so much for Sophie to cast off her shyness and self-deprecation. I wanted her to be happy.

I asked my mother about it. She said: "It worked so well. It was just as we hoped. Charles is very charming and of course the Tourvilles were very anxious for the match. Your father is delighted. We were all rather surprised that Sophie was such a success. Charles seemed to work some magic on her."

"The magic of love," I said dramatically.

"Yes," agreed my mother, looking back I was sure to those long-ago days when my father had come into her life and shown her that

50

she was not the sort of person she had hitherto believed herself to be. Just as Charles de Tourville had done for Sophie.

———

So Sophie was to be married. The wedding would not take place for some months, for the whole Court and my parents' circle of friends would be taken up with the royal wedding in May. But the preparations would go on for some time, for, besides the making of the trousseau, there were marriage settlements which needed a great deal of negotiations where such families as the Aubignés and Tourvilles were concerned.

Sophie was the most important member of the household now. She was given her own maid—Jeanne Fougère, a girl a few years older than herself who had been one of the serving girls and was delighted to become a lady's maid. She took her duties seriously, and because Sophie was so pleased to have her and she so happy to be there, an immediate bond sprang up between them.

It was pleasant to watch Sophie's progress but Lisette was growing restless. She had been educated as we were and yet was never really allowed to cross the social barrier; she did not sit at table with us but ate her meals with Tante Berthe and Jacques, the major domo, in a special small dining room where, Lisette told me, formality was at its greatest. But being Lisette she found some amusement in the procedure, and as both Tante Berthe and Jacques were prodigiously interested in food, what was served in their dining room could be compared very favorably with that eaten in the great hall or the family *salle à manger*. Lisette was grateful to have the education of a daughter of a nobleman but at times I fancied I caught a glimmer of resentment in her eyes.

It was typical of her that, with Sophie so much in demand and being constantly whisked away from us, she should think of our doing something which would amuse us and show Sophie, when we had the opportunity of telling her, that we too could live excitingly.

One of the servant girls had told her about Madame Rougemont, the great clairvoyant, who could see into the future and could give the most glowing accounts of what was to come.

The serving girl had herself been to Madame Rougemont. It had been the most exciting adventure. She had sat in a room and Madame Rougemont had read her palm and looked into the crystal ball.

51

"I see a tall dark gentleman," she had told the girl. "You are going to meet him soon and he will fall in love with you."

"And," said Lisette, "no sooner did she step outside Madame Rougemont's salon than there he was. She said it was wonderful and she is going to meet him again. But wasn't that strange? She had said a tall dark gentleman . . . and there he was."

The more Lisette thought about it the more determined she became that we ourselves must pay a visit to Madame Rougemont. We had reason for trepidation. Our previous foray into the streets had not been very successful, in fact we had had a real scare. I reminded Lisette of this and she said: "Well, you know why. We did not have the right clothes. We must get some."

I suppose we could have borrowed some from the servants with whom Lisette was on such good terms, but she had heard that second-hand clothes were sold in the Place de Grève on Mondays and decided that it would add spice to the adventure if we purchased them ourselves.

How we laughed! It was necessary to slip out of the house in the morning, which was not easy, for we had to elude our governess and tutors. We chose a time when we had no lessons and went into the streets in our morning gowns which were the plainest we had.

What fun it was to walk through Paris! I would never lose the exhilaration I felt in those streets. Walking was different from riding; one saw more; one became more a part of the scene.

There were people everywhere and no one took much notice of us except the occasional man who threw us a speculative glance.

Lisette, who had more freedom than I, was more familiar with the streets. She was allowed occasionally to go on some errand for Tante Berthe in the company of one of the servants. She reveled in her knowledge. She showed me the shops as we passed.

"There," she said, "is the grocer-druggist. You can buy lots of things there . . . brandy, paint, sugar, lemonade, and confiture of all kinds with arsenic and *aqua fortis*. So if you want to poison someone you will know where to come."

"Do people really . . ."

"Of course they do. Have you never heard of the Marchioness de Brinvilliers, who, a hundred years ago, poisoned people who were in her way? She used to try her poisons out on the hospital patients and went visiting the sick and taking little goodies for them. Then she would come and see what effect they had had and whether it was safe to use them."

"How diabolical."

"People are like that sometimes," said Lisette blithely.

She pointed out the narrow winding streets through which we must not venture, and even she had no desire to do so. She also identified an old *marcheuse*, a fearful little creature who scuttled past; her face was scarred with the ravages of some terrible disease.

"Once," said Lisette, "she was a beautiful woman. But a life of sin made her diseased and now she is fit only to run errands for the lowest type of prostitute. A lesson to us all," she added piously. "It just shows what terrible things can happen to women."

She was sad for a moment. Lisette's moods did change rather rapidly; and then she brightened.

"Here is the Place de Grève. No executions here today because it is a Monday . . . but secondhand clothes instead."

I couldn't help crying out with pleasure, for ahead of us was a noisy crowd of people—mostly women—parading before the onlookers in all sorts of garments. Some wore hats with feathers; others had pulled gowns over their own. They screamed and laughed and chattered; and the vendors at the stalls looked on, crying out: "What a miracle!" "The fit is perfect!" "It becomes you, madame. You are a lady in that garment."

"Come on," said Lisette, and we were part of the crowd.

Lisette found a brown gaberdine dress—somber in hue but which somehow set off her beautiful blonde hair. I found a dark purple which was plain, the sort which might have been worn by a shopkeeper's wife.

Gleefully we made our purchases and no one took any special notice of us as we scuttled away through the streets back to the *hôtel*. We went up to my room and there tried on the dresses and rolled about in mirth as we assured ourselves that in them no one would have the slightest notion where we came from.

We could scarcely wait to set out on the real adventure. Lisette knew exactly where to go. The serving girl who had told her about the fortune teller had walked past the place with her only the day before.

On the way we passed the Bastille and I shivered as I always did and wondered how many of the people who were incarcerated there were innocent of any crime.

I tried to interest Lisette in the subject. She would surely know something about the *lettres de cachet*, but she was not interested in anything but the fortune which lay in store for her.

We found the house. It was in a narrow street of tall houses. We mounted the steps and found the heavy door was open. We stepped into a hall. There a concierge sat in a boxlike room with glass panes through which he could see who came in.

"Up the stairs," he said.

We went up. It was different from what I had expected. There was a carpet on the stairs of a rich red and a certain air of brash luxury about the place.

A girl in a low-cut blue dress came out of a room at the top of the first flight of stairs. She studied us very closely and smiled.

"I know," she said. "You have come to have your fortunes told."

"Yes," said Lisette.

"Come this way."

She took us into a little room and told us to sit down, which we did. Lisette giggled. I think now she was a little nervous. I certainly was and I had a feeling that we were being watched and began to wonder whether we had been unwise to come. My anxiety increased as I remembered that other ill-fated exploration we had taken and the young men who had come along and seized us. I started to wonder what would have happened if that crowd of people had not come along precisely at the right moment.

I looked at Lisette. Her eyes were brilliant—they always were when she was excited.

"Why are we waiting here?" I whispered.

"Perhaps Madame Rougemont has another client."

The girl who had shown us in appeared.

"Madame Rougemont will see you now," she said.

We rose and the girl signed to us to follow her. We did so and were ushered into a room with a large window looking down on the street.

Madame Rougemont's face was painted and patched to such an extent that it was difficult to know how much of what we saw was really

54

her. She wore a red velvet gown the color of her curtains, and her hair was most elaborately dressed and I guessed that a great deal of it was not hers either. Her plump hands were loaded with rings; she looked rich and vulgar and she frightened me. If I had been alone I should have been tempted to turn and run out of the house.

"Ah, my dears," she said, smiling falsely at us, "so you want to look into the future?"

Lisette said: "Yes, that is so."

"Why else should you come to Madame Rougemont, eh? Well, sit down."

She peered at us. "Two very pretty young ladies. There is nothing I like better than finding a happy future for pretty ladies. Have you the money for the sitting?"

Lisette reached into her pocket and found it.

Madame Rougemont took it and put it into a little drawer. She looked intently at Lisette, and then at me.

"Come and sit at this table, dears. I'll tell you together, shall I? First one . . . then the other . . . unless, of course, there are secrets. Those I shall tell you when we are alone . . . if that is necessary. But first let me see if they are there. You are very young, aren't you? Tell me your ages, my dears. It helps a little."

Lisette said she was seventeen. I exaggerated a little and said I was sixteen.

"And you live here . . . in Paris?"

"Some of the time," I told her.

"Not always. You are with one of the rich families, eh?"

"Yes," I said quickly. "Yes."

"I thought so. Give me your hands."

She took mine first. "A pretty little hand," she said. "So white and clean. How do you manage to keep them so white . . . a lady's hands. That's what they are."

Her fingers gripped my hand tightly and the look of speculation in her eyes alarmed me. I knew we shouldn't have come. I glanced at Lisette. She was still enjoying the adventure.

Now Madame Rougemont had taken one of her hands so that she held us both.

"Another pretty little hand," she said. "Oh, I see great things here.

Rich husbands for you both. . . . Long journeys and excitement . . . plenty of it. You are very soon going to meet a lover. Oh, I envy you. You are going to be so happy."

I heard myself say: "Is it the same for both of us then?"

"There are variations, of course, but you are both lucky young ladies. You are going to meet your fate . . . one of you will meet it today."

"Which one?" asked Lisette.

Madame Rougemont put her hand to her head and closed her eyes.

"I think," she said, "that we should look into the crystal ball. First the fair lady."

She drew the crystal towards her and closed her eyes. Then she began to speak in a dreamy voice. "I see him. He is tall, dark, and handsome. He is close . . . very close. . . . He will love you dearly. You will ride in carriages. Beware of hesitation. If you do not act promptly you will lose your good fortune, my dear." She turned to me. "And now you, little lady. Ah, here it is again. The finger of fate. Your future will be decided soon . . . and it is in your hands. When fate comes to you you must be ready to grasp it. Again hesitation could lose all. It may seem sudden but if you do not take advantage of what the gods offer you now you could regret it all your life. I see that your fate is entwined with that of the other lady and that is what makes it difficult for me to speak more openly. Don't despair. If your turn is not today, it will be tomorrow."

I stood up, for every moment I was growing more and more uneasy. There was an oppressiveness about the place which seemed to shut me in.

"We should be going," I said. "Thank you very much, Madame Rougemont."

Lisette stood beside me. I think she was beginning to catch my uneasiness.

Madame Rougemont said: "You would like some refreshment. I never send my clients away without a little hospitality. I have a salon just across the passage. Come on."

"No," I said. "We must go."

But she held us firmly by our arms.

"We serve wine here," she said. "A little wine bar. Ladies and gentlemen like to come in when they are thirsty."

The girl who had shown us in appeared again; she opened a door and we were more or less pushed into a room in which were little tables and red plush chairs.

A man was sitting in one of them. He looked as though he were tall and he was certainly dark and handsome.

"Ah, Monsieur St. Georges," said Madame Rougemont. "How nice to see you! I was just going to drink a glass of wine with these two young ladies. Please join us."

She made a sign and a waiter appeared. She nodded to him and he went away.

Monsieur St. Georges bowed, and taking Lisette's hand and then mine kissed them and said he was delighted to make our acquaintance.

We all sat down at the table. A good deal of my fear had disappeared. As for Lisette, she was undoubtedly enjoying the adventure.

"These young ladies are attached to one of the big houses," said Madame Rougemont. "That's so, is it not, my dears?"

"Tell me," said the young man. "Which one?"

Lisette and I exchanged quick glances. I felt myself flushing. There would be great trouble if it were known that we had come to the fortune teller. Tante Berthe was always warning Lisette of the dangers of life in Paris. It was the surest way to make Lisette want to sample it.

The silence went on for several seconds. Both of us were trying to think of the name of a rich family for whom we might be working.

Lisette was quicker than I. She said: "It is the Hôtel d'Argenson."

"That would be in ..." said Monsieur St. Georges.

Again that pause and Lisette said: "In Courcelles. ..."

"In Courcelles! Oh, you have come a long way."

"We are fond of walking," I said.

"I see."

He drank off his glass of wine and I saw him make some sort of sign to Madame Rougemont. She said: "I have an appointment with another client." She leaned towards Lisette and whispered something which Lisette told me afterwards was: "See, here is your dark handsome man."

He watched her disappear. Then he said sharply: "Who are you and what are you doing in a place like this?"

"What do you mean?" I cried. "A place like this. ..."

"Do you mean you don't know what sort of place it is? *Mon Dieu*, here we have the innocents in Paris. Tell me where your home is. The truth now. You are not serving girls. Where did you get those clothes?"

"At the Place de Grève," I answered.

I saw a smile touch his lips. "And you live . . . ?"

"In the Rue Saint Germain."

"And at which house?"

"Is that any concern of yours?" asked Lisette.

"Yes, young lady, it is, because I am going to take you back there."

I felt great relief and gratitude towards him, and I said before Lisette could answer: "It is the Hôtel d'Aubigné."

For a moment he was silent; then he seemed as though he were suppressing laughter.

"You are a pair of very adventurous young women," he said. "Come on. You are going home."

He led us to the door; as we reached it Madame Rougemont appeared. She was smiling blandly.

"Well, Monsieur St. Georges. You are pleased . . . ?"

He said in a low voice: "I am taking these ladies home. They belong to one of the great families in France. Good God, woman, have you no sense?"

He was clearly rather angry with her but when he turned to us he was all smiles.

"Now," he said, "I am going to take you out to the street. I am going to put you into a *pot de chambre* which will take you back to the *hôtel*. Go straight in at once and never be so foolish again."

"Why is it so foolish to have one's fortune told?" asked Lisette defiantly.

"Because frauds tell fortunes. That is not all. Fortune telling is not the main business of that woman. Something you are too young to understand, but never do it again. If you do, you deserve all you get. Now go back and don't be such silly little girls again."

We came out into the street; he hailed the carriage, paid the driver and told him where to take us. He stood back and bowed as we drove away.

We were subdued until we reached the *hôtel*. Then we went up to my room and took off our secondhand dresses. Mine had suddenly be-

58

come repulsive to me and I wondered who had worn it before.

"What a strange adventure!" I said. "What was it all about?"

Lisette looked wise. She had guessed, of course.

Madame Rougemont was what was known as a procuress. The fortune telling was a blind. She had her dark and handsome gentleman waiting and they plied the girls with wine to make them acquiescent.

"You're making it up."

"No. I see it all clearly now. That girl met her young man because he was waiting for her."

"Do you mean that Monsieur St. Georges was waiting for us?"

"He was a noble gentleman. Therefore there were two for him to choose from."

"But he didn't."

"Not when he realized who we were. Imagine the Comte's rage if anything had happened to you."

I stared at her in horror.

Lisette was thoughtful and then she said: "I wonder which one of us he would have chosen."

————

A grand ball to celebrate Sophie's betrothal was to be held in the *hôtel* and preparations went on for days. Sophie was in a twitter of excitement and it was wonderful to see her so happy. She was thrilled about the new ball dress which was being made for her. I was to have one too.

"You realize that this is a very special occasion," she said. "You will meet Charles and see for yourself how wonderful he is."

"I very much look forward to meeting him," I said. "I think he must be a bit of a miracle worker."

"He is different from everyone else," she cried ecstatically.

She and I paid several visits to the Paris dressmaker who was said to be the most fashionable in town. Sophie's dress was of pale blue with yards of shimmering chiffon in the skirt and a low-cut bodice which fitted her firmly and managed to make her look almost slender. Her dumpiness was less noticeable nowadays because of her radiant face. She was really becoming rather pretty. I was to have a similar dress in pink, which the dressmaker said would be a foil to my dark hair.

"It will be your turn next," she said, as she fitted the gown on me.

59

In spite of the excitement I did notice that Lisette was rather quiet, and I fancied she was getting more resentful than she used to be about not being quite one of us. I sympathized with her, for it did seem to be a little unkind to let her take lessons with us, ride with us, be our constant companion and then on social occasions make it clear that she did not belong.

She went off by herself a good deal and often I looked for her and could not find her. If I had not been so absorbed by the coming ball, I might have thought something odd was happening. She seemed secretive and sometimes appeared to be enjoying a private joke. Usually she would have shared amusing incidents. But, I told myself, perhaps I was imagining again as I often did.

I was with my mother more during those days for she had thrown herself wholeheartedly into the preparations.

"Your father is very pleased about this match," she said. "He will be glad to see Sophie settled."

"I suppose the Tourvilles are a very distinguished family?"

"They are not quite Aubigné," replied my mother with a certain pride, and I suddenly remembered the years she had spent as the wife of Jean-Louis, so far removed, it seemed to me, from the life she led as Madame la Comtesse.

"I think they are delighted to marry into the family," she went on. "And as I said, your father is very pleased."

"And Sophie is happy."

"That's the best of all and I am so happy about it. She is not an easy girl ... and so different from you, Lottie."

"I shall not be so easily disposed of."

She laughed at me. "Don't you think Sophie is very happy to be, as you say, disposed of?"

"Sophie is in love."

"So will you be one day."

She spoke earnestly because she knew I was thinking of Dickon and she hated anything to disturb the perfect life she had found with her Count.

"I will never be again."

She tried to laugh as though it were a joke; then she put her arms about me and held me against her.

60

"My dear, dear child, it is a long time ago. It would have been so wrong to have allowed that to go on. Why even now you are very young."

"The ball might have been for us both . . . Sophie and me . . . to celebrate our betrothals."

"You are living in a false dream. You would never have been happy with Dickon. It was so ridiculous. He was years older than you and because you were only a child it was easy for him to deceive you. He wanted Eversleigh and as soon as he got it he no longer thought of you."

"I think I should have been the best judge of that."

"A child . . . of what was it . . . twelve? Not quite that. It was preposterous. You should have seen his face when I offered him Eversleigh. He was quite cynical, Lottie."

"I knew he wanted Eversleigh."

"He wanted only Eversleigh."

"It is not true. He wanted me too."

"He would have taken you as part of the bargain. Oh, Lottie, it hurts you, but it is better to face facts. It is heartbreaking to discover that someone who professes to love you is lying. But you were only a child . . . and it is all finished now. You are not really grieving. I have seen you joyously happy. You are just trying to keep it all alive . . . when you remember to. But it is dead, Lottie; and you know it."

"No," I contradicted her. "What I felt for Dickon will never die."

But she did not really believe me. Her own experiences had taught her to expect a "happily ever after" ending.

At last the great day came. Lisette arrived in my room to see me when I was dressed.

"You look beautiful, Lottie," she told me. "You will overshadow the prospective bride."

"Oh, no. Sophie looks really pretty. Love has worked miracles."

She seemed rather thoughtful, but I confess I was so eager to meet Charles de Tourville that I was not thinking much about Lisette.

At the top of the staircase was the Comte, looking magnificent in his brocade coat, discreetly flashing a few diamonds, and his curled white wig setting off his fine features and his lively dark eyes; my mother, standing beside him in pale lavender, looked beautiful and very much the Comtesse. I marveled at her yet again, remembering the quiet lady of Clavering. And beside her was Sophie, radiant in pale turquoise blue and happiness.

I was in the charge of Madame de Grenoir, a distant cousin of the Comte's, who appeared at times like this when she was needed and was only too happy to act as chaperone. I was to sit quietly with her, as became my years, and when a gentleman asked me to dance, if he were suitable, I might accept. If he were not, Madame de Grenoir—who was adept at handling such situations, having had much experience of them—would make it clear that I was not available.

Once more I was handicapped by my youth. But at least I had been presented to the King and he had spoken to me, although that was a long time ago and the Comte had made sure that I did not come in the presence of the King again.

Many members of the nobility would be present tonight because they were in Paris for the royal wedding. It was the best possible time to give a ball.

I sat there watching the people arrive. One or two men glanced at me and hesitated, but Madame de Grenoir gave them such cold looks that they moved on. I felt again that frustration with my youth and promised myself that I would soon escape from it. In a year I should be considered quite grown up.

Madame de Grenoir was telling me about other balls she had attended and other girls whom she had chaperoned.

I said: "You really must be a very experienced practitioner. What an occupation! Chaperone for girls! Not exactly exciting."

Then it happened and found me quite unprepared.

Sophie was coming towards me and there was a man with her. He was tall and dark and I recognized him at once. I stood up uncertainly. Madame de Grenoir was beside me, laying a hand on my arm.

"Lottie," said Sophie, "I want you to meet Charles de Tourville. This is Lottie, Charles, of whom I have told you so much."

I felt the color rush into my face, for the man who was taking my hand was none other than Monsieur St. Georges, who had rescued Lisette and me from Madame Rougemont.

His lips were on my fingers and the eyes he raised to me held a hint of mischief.

"I have so longed to see you," he said. "It is true Sophie has told me so much about you."

Sophie was laughing. "You look alarmed, Lottie. I haven't told *all*. I have only told Charles the nice things."

"And," he added, "the more I heard the more eager I was to meet you."

Sophie was watching me intently, urging me to admire. I sought for words, but for once could not find anything to say.

"My father is going to open the ball with me in a moment," said Sophie. "I think the guests have all arrived now. If they are late they cannot expect to be received, can they?"

I stammered: "It ... it is a great pleasure to meet you."

"There will be many meetings," he answered, "when I am a member of the family."

"Charles," said Sophie. "You will have to dance with the Comtesse."

"It will be a pleasure," he answered. "And later I hope that Mademoiselle Lottie will honor me."

"Of course she will, won't you Lottie?"

"Thank you," I said.

Sophie looked over her shoulder at me as she laid her hand on his arm in a proprietary manner and they walked away.

I was too stunned to do anything but stare after them.

"It is so good when a marriage is a love match," Madame Grenoir was saying. "Those two ... so happy. I have seen some who are far from happy. This is quite different ... a very, very happy arrangement."

When the dance began I was immediately taken onto the floor. I had no lack of invitations to dance, and providing the men were suitable, I was allowed to accept them. Madame Grenoir kept her alert eyes on me as I danced and I was aware of her watching all the time. My partners were flirtatious, expressing ardent admiration, but I scarcely listened to them. I could not wait until the moment when Charles de Tourville came for me.

He was smiling in a manner which I can only call mischievous.

"I have been waiting for this moment," he said, as soon as we were out of earshot of Madame Grenoir.

"Oh?" I said. "Why?"

"You are not going to pretend that we have not met before, are you?"

"No," I replied.

"You were a very naughty little girl and I caught you, didn't I? Do you often have such adventures?"

"That was the only one of that kind."

"You learned your lesson, I hope."

"I suppose we were a little adventurous."

"Not a little. Very adventurous, I should say. However, as long as you learned that it is unwise for little girls to stray into the dubious haunts of the city, good can come of it. I must say I was delighted to meet you."

"It wasn't a surprise for you?"

"Of course not. I knew who you were as soon as I discovered where you lived. Don't forget, our families are to be united. We have to know about each other . . . not everything, of course. That would be asking too much. But we should know those little things which cannot be hidden. Like a beautiful daughter, for instance. There has to be some explanation. I know that there was a charming sequel to the Comte's English romance and that sequel so enchanted him that he kept her with him and married her mother."

"I think I would rather not discuss my family's affairs."

"Our family's. I shall be a member soon."

"Tell me about that woman . . . that fortune teller, Madame Rougemont."

"One of the most notorious brothel keepers in the town. Forgive me. You are an innocent young girl. Do you know what a brothel is?"

"Of course I do. I am not a child."

"Then you will not need me to explain. She has quite a fashionable apartment in another district but she does a little business in the quarters to which you went. I am surprised that a young lady in your position should have gone into such a house . . . in such a street."

"I told you it was an adventure."

"Is life in the Hôtel d'Aubigné so dull then?"

"I did not say it was dull, but we are kept under strict control."

"Not strict enough obviously."

"Well, we slipped out."

"You were fortunate that I was there."

"I have often wondered about that. What were you doing there?"

"What every man does there. Looking for pretty girls."

"You! You mean . . . ?"

"I mean exactly what you are thinking."

"But you are going to marry Sophie!"

"Well?"

"Why then . . . should you be looking for someone else?"

"That someone else would have nothing to do with my marriage."

I was horrified and desperately sorry for Sophie. Here was another of those blasé young men to whom marriage was a matter of convenience. Dickon was back in my thoughts. Oh, how could they behave in such a way!

"I see that you are getting ready to despise me."

"I think I already do. How much longer does this dance go on?"

"A little while yet, I hope. You are a very attractive young lady, Mademoiselle Lottie."

"I would rather not hear you talk to me like that."

"I was only telling the truth. When you grow up you are going to be irresistible, I know."

"I do hope Sophie is not going to be unhappy but I very much fear for her."

"I promise you that she is going to be the happiest bride in Paris."

"With you visiting Madame Rougemont? What will happen when she discovers?"

"She will never discover. I shall see to that, and it will be precisely because there will be some others to charm me and satisfy my baser instincts that I can be a figure of chivalric love to my bride."

"I think you are the most cynical man I ever met!"

"Call it realistic. I don't know why I am telling you the truth. It is not very flattering to me, is it? Oddly enough, I have to tell you. But then you found me out, didn't you? We found each other out. No use trying to cover up our sins after such blatant exposure. Still, I like you to know the truth about me. I have grown very fond of you, Lottie."

"When?"

"Well, it began when I looked through a peep hole and saw one of

65

the most beautiful girls I have ever seen gazing into a crystal ball. A tall dark handsome man, said Madame Rougemont. Well, she was right, wasn't she?"

"Are you trying to flirt with me?"

"You do invite it, you know."

"I think Sophie should be warned."

"Will you warn her? She won't believe you. Besides, who are you to talk? What if I told of my first meeting with you in Madame Rougemont's brothel? You would be in trouble then, wouldn't you?"

"And so would you. They would surely want to know how you happened to be there."

"So you see we are both caught in our particular web of intrigue. Dear Lottie, I do believe those wretched musicians are reaching their finale. I shall dance with you again this evening and then we will talk of more pleasant things. Alas . . . it is au revoir."

He released me and bowed; then he gave me his arm and took me back to Madame Grenoir.

I felt very disturbed and in a strange way excited. More than anyone else I had ever met he reminded me of Dickon.

Madame de Grenoir chattered about the Tourvilles, "A noble family . . . not like the Aubignés, of course . . . but wealthy enough. They have a château somewhere near Angoulême and a *hôtel* in Paris like most noble families. It is an excellent match, and he is a charming young man, is he not?"

I found it difficult to sit there and listen to her and was glad to be dancing again. I was looking out for him all the time and once or twice I saw him; then he gave me a smile and flashed a message at me with his eyes which I was sure meant that he would be with me as soon as he could.

The time came and there I was dancing with him again.

"This is the highlight of the evening for me," he said. "You don't look quite so angry as you did. Have you thought better of it?"

"I still think badly of you."

"And I still think you are enchanting. Do you know, I have come to the conclusion that sinners often are . . . more than saints, that is."

"I do hope Sophie is not going to be hurt. I am sure she doesn't know you at all."

"I promise to keep her in blissful ignorance."

"I suppose you have had lots of adventures . . . with women?"

"Right," he said.

"I won't call them love affairs. They are not that . . . just sordid little adventures."

"I suppose you could be right again, but the pleasant thing is that while they are happening they don't seem what you say they are."

"You have this modern French outlook."

"Oh, it is not modern. It has been like that for centuries. We make a success of living because we know how to set about it. Wisely we don't sigh for the unattainable. We take what is offered and learn to live with it without regrets. It is this realism, this acceptance of life as it is, which puts us at the peak of civilization. It is why we are such wonderful lovers, so amusing, so charming. It is a matter of experience. Oddly enough the best mistress I ever had—to date—was the one my father chose for me when I was sixteen years old. It's an old French custom, you know. The boy is growing up. He will get into mischief, so find a charming older woman who will initiate him. It is part of that sensible outlook on life which my countrymen have worked out to perfection."

"I really don't want to listen to your boasting of your prowess," I said.

"Well, let us leave something so obvious unsaid. Let's talk of other things. Lottie, I am delighted that you are to be my little sister. I hope we shall get to know each other very well indeed."

"I think it hardly likely."

"Oh, that's not very kind."

"People who are not kind themselves should not expect kindness in others."

"Are you worried about Sophie?"

"Yes . . . very."

"You have a sweet nature. Have you noticed that she has been less happy since she has known me?"

"You must know very well what a difference it has made to her. That's why . . ."

"You don't look deeply enough into life, dear Lottie. Sophie is happy. *I* have made her happy. Isn't that something to be proud of, to earn Sophie's gratitude and that of her family? I assure you I intend it to stay like that. Sophie and I will live amicably together with the children we shall have and when we are old and gray people will point to us as the ideal couple."

"And in the meantime you will continue with your secret adventures?"

"That is the key to all successful marriages—as every Frenchman knows."

"Does every Frenchwoman know it?"

"If she is wise, I think she does."

"It is not my idea of happiness and I am glad that I am not a Frenchwoman."

"There is something very English about you, Lottie."

"Of course there is. I *am* English. I was brought up in England. There is much I like about France but this ... profligacy ... I ... I loathe."

"You do not look like a puritan and that is what makes you so fascinating. You are warm ... you are passionate. You can't deceive a connoisseur such as I am. And yet you talk so primly."

He held me close to him suddenly, I felt quite excited and at the same time I wanted to tear myself away and run back to Madame Grenoir. I think I must have betrayed something for he was smiling in a complacent way.

"Lottie," he said, "we are going to meet ... often. I am going to make you like me ... yes, I think I can make you like me quite a lot."

"I never shall. I can only feel sorry for poor Sophie. Will this dance never end?"

"Alas, it ends too soon. But never fear, you and I are going to be good friends."

I wanted to get away.

"You look a little put out, dear," said Madame Grenoir. "Are you tired?"

"Yes," I answered. "I should like to go."

"I don't think you can do that until after midnight. Then perhaps ..."

I danced again. I hardly noticed with whom. I was upset. He had reminded me so much of Dickon. Dickon had talked like that. He

68

had never tried to make me like him because he was good; rather he had stressed his weaknesses. How this man had brought it all back!

I was glad when the ball was over. I went to my room and took off my gown. I was sitting in my petticoats brushing my hair when Sophie came in. She was radiant and did not look in the least tired.

She sat on my bed, her skirts billowing round her; she looked young, fresh, and . . . vulnerable.

"What a lovely ball! What did you think of Charles? Isn't he wonderful? He says such marvelous things. I never thought there could be anyone quite like him."

"He is very good looking," I said.

"I think he rather liked you."

"Oh . . . I didn't notice. What made you think that?"

"It was the way he looked when he was dancing with you."

"Oh, did you see us? Weren't you dancing?"

"Most of the time, yes. But the second time I was sitting with your mother and a few others. I watched you all the time." I felt my face turning pink. "What were you talking about?"

"Oh . . . I've forgotten. Nothing important."

"He was watching you all the time."

"People usually do when they are talking."

"Not so . . . intently. You know . . ."

"No, I'm afraid I don't. If it were important, I'd remember, wouldn't I? Sophie, you ought to go to bed. Aren't you tired?"

"No. I feel as though I could go on dancing all night."

"It would have to be with Charles."

"Oh, yes, with Charles."

"Good night, Sophie. Sleep well."

I almost pushed her out and she went away to dream of her incomparable Charles, whom she did not really know at all.

When she had gone I put on a wrap, for I felt a great urge to talk to Lisette. I wondered if I should tell her what had happened. She was very worldly. She would probably think nothing of it and say that what Sophie did not know could not grieve her.

I went along to her room and knocked gently. There was no answer.

I opened the door quietly and tiptoed in. I went to the edge of her bed and whispered: "Lisette. Are you asleep? Wake up. I want to talk."

My eyes had grown accustomed to the gloom and I saw that Lisette's bed was empty.

———

During the days which followed I saw a great deal of Charles de Tourville, for whenever possible he contrived to be at my side. I tried to keep up an air of frigid disapproval, for disapprove of him I most certainly did; but I found myself looking for him and being disappointed if he were not there. I could not understand myself but I enjoyed talking to him. I tried to insult him at every turn. I endeavored to convey to him how much I despised his way of life; but I could not hide from myself the fact that I enjoyed berating him—and he was shrewd enough to know it.

The fact was that I was bewildered. I was too young to realize what was happening. I was not afraid of life, as Sophie was; I was avid for it. I was ready to rush forward and savor it without wondering what the consequences would be. When I understood myself better I realized that my nature was by no means frigid. I wanted experience. Dickon had aroused me when I had been too young to realize that I was being physically stimulated and I had sublimated my feelings for him into a devotion and what I thought of as abiding love. Now Charles de Tourville came along and he reminded me so much of Dickon that I could not help being attracted by him.

I was young and ignorant, and although he was not old in years, he was in experience. I think he understood exactly what was happening to me and found it very diverting. Since he was the sort of man who would visit an establishment like that of Madame Rougemont, he was no doubt in search of fresh sensation, and a young girl such as I could provide just that. I gathered later that it was not such a coincidence as I had first thought that he should happen to be at Madame Rougemont's when Lisette and I called there. Up to that time he had been a frequent visitor there and had looked in almost regularly to see if there was anyone who could amuse him for a while.

Naturally the families met often, which meant that he was constantly in the house. The wedding was to take place in three weeks time when all the excitement over that of the Dauphin and Marie Antoinette had died down.

In the meantime, as the families were both in Paris, and my father would no doubt take part in some of the ceremonies of the royal marriage, we saw a great deal of each other.

The Tourvilles gave a ball and once more I danced with Charles, and this time I was conscious of Sophie as she watched us. She insisted that Charles seemed to like me very much and when I protested that I thought he had a very poor opinion of me, she assured me that this was not so.

"Oh," I said, "he is so much in love with you that he even likes your family."

And that seemed to please her.

When I saw Lisette next I told her who Charles de Tourville was, and what a shock I had had at the ball.

"Is it really so?" she cried; and she started to laugh. But when I talked of him she did not seem very interested.

"I only hope he doesn't tell about us," I said.

"How could he? He'd have to explain how he happened to be there."

"Lisette," I said, "I came to tell you about it when the ball was over, but you weren't in your bed."

She looked at me steadily and said: "Oh . . . you must have come when I was in one of the attics with the servants watching the guests depart. There is a good view up there."

And I forgot about that until much later.

———

It was the day of the Dauphin's wedding and my parents had gone to Versailles to attend the reception afterwards which was to be held in the Galerie des Glaces. I felt an uneasiness which I could not shake off. My thoughts were filled with Charles de Tourville and his coming marriage to Sophie. I fervently wished I could forget that man and not be so disturbed by his presence. It was not that I liked him . . . in fact I disliked all that he stood for; but, on the other hand, when he was not present, it seemed dull; and if he were to put in an unexpected appearance, I would feel an elation which, try as I might, I could neither suppress nor ignore.

There was to be a fireworks display in the evening and Charles and Armand were to conduct Sophie and me to the palace so that we could have a good view. However, during the afternoon the skies be-

71

came overcast, the rain pelted down and the thunder and lightning were really alarming.

Sophie was terrified, as she always had been of thunder, and Charles comforted her solicitously under my cynical eyes. He was clearly amused by my attitude.

"No trip to Versailles," announced Armand. "There'll be no fireworks tonight."

"The people will not be very pleased. A lot of them are trudging out to Versailles just to see them," said Charles.

"They can't blame the King for the storm," said Armand with a laugh. "Though I have no doubt some of them will."

"I daresay they will do the fireworks display on another occasion," added Charles. "Perhaps here in Paris, which would be sensible. It would save the trip to Versailles."

"What an end to the wedding day!" I murmured.

"People are going to say it is a bad omen," added Charles.

"Poor little bride," I couldn't help saying, looking straight at Charles. "I hope she will be happy."

"They say she looks like a girl who can take care of herself," Charles replied, gazing into my eyes. "There are some like that. Perhaps that sort need more of a man than our little Dauphin has so far proved himself to be."

"Hush!" said Armand in a mocking voice. "You speak treason."

That evening the four of us played a card game while we listened to the rain spluttering onto the windows of the *hôtel*. The streets were quiet; it was very different from what we had expected it to be and rather an anticlimax to all the fuss there had been about the royal wedding.

The next day my parents returned to the *hôtel*. My mother was ecstatic about the reception at Versailles. Sophie and I made her tell us all about it. It had taken place in the chapel of the palace and my parents had been very honored to be present. This was because some long way back my father had a blood connection with the royal family.

"Poor little Dauphin!" said my mother. "He looked most disconsolate in spite of his gold spangled net garments. Most unhappy and uncertain. *She* looked enchanting. She is a most attractive girl . . . so fair and dainty . . . and she was beautiful in a white brocade gown with panniers which made her look so graceful. We went through the Galerie des Glaces and the Grands Appartements to the chapel where the Swiss guards were assembled. Those dear children! They looked so young, they made me want to weep as they knelt before Monseigneur de la Roche-Aymon. I thought the Dauphin was going to drop the ring and the gold pieces he had to bestow on the bride."

"What about the fireworks display?" I asked.

"Oh, that is going to be later . . . in Paris. In a week or so, I imagine. There was so much disappointment about it. It has to take place or the people will feel they have been cheated. What do you think? The little Dauphiness made a blot on the marriage contract as she signed her name. The King seemed quite amused."

"They will be saying that is an omen," said Armand. "What with the storm and the blot . . . they'll really have something to work on. And wasn't there an earthquake somewhere on the day Marie Antoinette was born?"

"In Lisbon," said my father. "What has Lisbon to do with France? The people will like her. Oh, yes, they will cheer her, for she is very pretty."

"And that accounts for a great deal with the French," I put in, which made them all laugh.

Then my mother went on to describe the reception presided over by the King.

"How old he is getting!" She sighed. "It is a good thing that there is a Dauphin to follow on."

"A pity the boy is not older and more of a man," added the Comte.

"Boys grow up," my mother reminded him.

"Some take a long time doing it."

"Oh, it was so beautiful," went on my mother. "Although it was dark outside it was as light as day in the Galerie. I don't know how many candelabra there were and each had thirty candles. I counted them. The young people looked adorable stitting at the table which was covered with green velvet decorated with gold braid and beautifully fringed. You should have been there. As a matter of fact the people were so disappointed because of the cancellation of the fireworks display that they were determined to see something and broke into the palace. They stormed up to the Galerie and mingled with the

73

guests." She turned to my father. "Do you know, at one time, I felt rather frightened."

"No need to be on such an occasion," my father answered. "The people are pleased about the wedding. As a matter of fact they are quite fond of the Dauphin and are longing for the King to die so that his grandson can take his place. They long to turn du Barry out on the streets, and as soon as the King dies that is what they will do."

"I heard the Dauphiness made a little gaffe which is amusing the whole Court and beyond," said Armand. "When she saw the du Barry close to the King she was interested and asked what was the function of the beautiful lady. 'To amuse the King,' was the answer. 'Then,' said our little girl, so anxious to please her new papa, 'I shall be her rival.' "

Everyone laughed.

"There was a shocked silence," the Comte said. "But Louis knows exactly how to deal with such situations, in whatever else he fails, and all agree that he has the most gracious manners at Court. He patted the hand of the little Dauphiness and said he was delighted that she had become his little granddaughter, and poor Marie Antoinette was quite unaware of the social error she had committed."

"She won't be for long," said Armand.

"Well," added my mother, smiling at Sophie, "weddings are in the air. I wish the greatest happiness to the brides and their grooms."

———

The date of the fireworks display had now been announced. It was to take place in the Place Louis XV and already workmen were busy setting lamps along the Champs Élysées; and in the Place Louis XV itself, a Corinthian temple was being put up near the King's statue.

It was exciting to be in the streets during those May days. People who had goods to sell were making the most of the occasion. The well-known markets were busy and new ones had been set up wherever it was possible to do so. Salespeople were everywhere; medallions of the royal bride and groom were on sale with the flags of France and Austria; at every street corner there was a coffee woman and lemonade sellers, who seemed to be doing a good trade with the thirsty people of Paris as well as with those who had come into the city from the surrounding countryside.

It was impossible not to be caught up in the mood, and as the sun was shining after the great storm, it was good to be out.

Charles suggested that the four of us take a stroll down the Champs Élysées to see how the decorations were progressing. Then we could wander into the Place Louis XV to take a look at the much talked of Corinthian temple. The people would be amusing in any case.

So Charles, Armand, Sophie, and I set out that morning.

We were all full of high spirits. Armand was quite amusing in his cynical way, although he said he hated the people—"the unwashed" he called them. He said the smell of them offended him. He was a very fastidious gentleman.

Charles warned him. "Don't let them see your contempt, my dear fellow. Even on such a day as this, with all their loyalty to the crown, they could easily take offense."

Sophie was radiant, but my feelings were mixed. I was elated because I enjoyed Charles's company so much and I kept telling myself that when they were married they would go to his estates in the south and I should not see them very often. That would be good, because I did not really like the man.

But that morning I was determined to enjoy myself.

We strolled along. A band was playing somewhere. From a building fluttered the flags of France and Austria, reminding the people that the country now had a reliable ally through this marriage which would mean more to France than the happiness of two young people.

We strolled down the Champs Élysées. It was going to look beautiful tonight with all those lamps aglow. In the Place Louis XV figures of dolphins were being set up and there was the grand medallion of the Dauphin and his bride. I stood beneath the bronze statue of the King on horseback surrounded by figures representing Prudence, Justice, Force, and Peace.

Charles was beside me. "You look good there, sister Lottie," he said. "Tell me, are you prudent, just, forceful and peace-loving?"

"Perhaps I have not lived long enough to discover."

"A very wise answer," he commented. "It is not always easy to be prudent and just, and if you are going to show force can you be peaceful?"

"I suppose one must aim to have these qualities."

"As long as one tries perhaps that is good enough. It is not always possible to succeed, though, is it? You are looking at me severely, Lottie. I don't know why you do that so often, when you know you really like me very much."

Sophie was coming towards us and I saw the watchful look in her eye. There was a hint of the distrust she had always had of herself before the coming of Charles.

"We were talking about the statues," I said, "and Charles was saying how difficult it was to have the four qualities they represent."

Charles took her by the arm. "Come, Sophie," he said, "let us look at them more closely and you tell me what you think of the workmanship. It was Pigalle, I think . . . but I'm not sure."

He drew her away from me and was smiling into her face with such love that she was completely satisfied.

When we left the Place Louis XV we walked leisurely home and on the way we passed a stall on which several kinds of ornaments were displayed. Among them were some delicately fashioned flowers in silk. The colors were beautiful and Sophie gave a cry of admiration.

"Why," she said, "that is just the color of my lavender gown."

"I believe you really like it," said Charles. He picked it up and held it against her dress. "Enchanting," he went on, and kissed her lightly on the cheek. The saleswomen—there were two of them—applauded. Charles gave them one of his quick speculative glances, which I noticed he bestowed on women and these two were young and one quite pretty.

"My lady must have it, do you not think so?" he asked.

The two women laughed and said the lady had a very kind admirer.

Charles paid for the flower and handed it to Sophie. She looked so happy as she took it that I felt a little lump in my throat. I hoped fervently that she would always remain in blissful ignorance of the kind of man he was.

He had picked up another flower. It was a red peony—a most lovely shade of scarlet.

He held it against my hair.

"What do you think?" he asked the salesgirls.

"A beautiful flower for a beautiful young lady," said the elder of them.

"I agree," said Charles. "Don't you, Sophie?"

Sophie stammered: "Y—yes . . . yes . . ." But I saw the uneasy look in her eyes again and I wanted to say that I would not have the flower. But that would have made the whole matter too important, so I took the flower and thanked Charles.

Then we made our way home, but I felt a little of the joy had gone out of the morning for Sophie.

I wished I could warn her that she must not show jealousy, for Charles was the kind of man who would be irritated by it. Her only happiness lay in taking what came her way and being grateful for it, not to ask questions, not to probe, to shut her eyes to what was not meant for her to see. Then she would have a chance of being happy— and only then.

How could I tell her that? How could I tell her that I spoke from experience of what her fiancé was really like?

I did, however, try to show her that I did not treasure my flower as she did hers. I had an opportunity when Lisette came to my room, as she was in the habit of doing—although lately I had seen less of her.

Sophie was with me, wearing the flower pinned to her dress and Lisette noticed it at once.

"It's lovely," cried Lisette. "I believe artificial silk flowers are becoming very fashionable."

"Charles bought it for me," Sophie explained. "From a stall in the street."

"You're a lucky girl. He does dote on you, doesn't he?"

Sophie smiled happily. "We were walking along and came to this stall. Nothing else on it caught my fancy but the flowers . . . they were very pretty."

Lisette examined it. "It is so cleverly made," she said.

"He bought one for Lottie."

"He had to . . . because I was there with Armand," I explained quickly.

"Where is yours?"

"I put it somewhere. I forget where. . . . Wait a minute. I think it's here."

I wanted to convey to Sophie that it meant nothing to me that Charles had given it.

77

I brought out the flower.

"What a lovely rich color!" said Lisette.

"I don't think it will go with anything I wear."

"Nonsense. Red is one of your best colors. It makes you look darker and passionate."

"What rubbish."

I took the flower from her and threw it into a drawer.

Sophie looked relieved. She could never disguise her emotion. Dear Sophie, she was so easy to deceive. Surely that archdeceiver, whom she was to marry, would manage with the utmost ease.

All was well. Sophie had a good chance of achieving the happy marriage which was so necessary for her.

————

It was about two days after the incident of the flowers when Charles called at the *hôtel*. Sophie had gone with my mother to the dressmaker to discuss her trousseau, so when Charles called it aroused no comment that I should be the one to receive him.

He seized both my hands and kissed them.

"Lottie!" he cried. "How glad I am to find you alone!"

"Was it accident or design?"

"A bit of both," he admitted. "I believe Sophie is at the dressmaker with your mama."

"You are well informed."

"It's a good habit in life. Now I want to take you somewhere. I have something to show you and you will really want to see it."

"Where would you take me?"

"Only for a walk through the streets, I promise you."

"A walk? But why...?"

"You will see. Come, get your cloak. We haven't a great deal of time."

"Were you going to show this to Sophie?"

"Certainly not. There is no reason why she should be particularly interested."

"Then why...?"

"Curb your curiosity and hurry. I don't want us to be too late. I promise to have you back in the house within an hour."

He had succeeded in exciting me as he always did.

"All right," I agreed. "But it is only to walk in the streets."

"That is all . . . on my honor."

"I am glad to know that you possess some."

"I am always known to be a man of my word."

What harm was there? I was not allowed to go out alone but I would be under the protection of one who was soon to be a member of the family. He would not dare behave in any but a reputable way. He was considerably in awe of my father and it had become clear to me that the Tourvilles wanted this marriage very much. So I put on my cloak and we went into the streets.

I was unprepared for what he had brought me to see and when I heard the sound of drums I was surprised and interested because a crowd of people had gathered. They were laughing; some cheered, some jeered.

"It's a procession of some sort," I said.

"You wait," said Charles. "You'll see an old friend of yours."

He gripped me firmly by the arm, for the crowds were pressing round us, and when they were too close he put an arm about me to protect me. I could not protest because I could see that the gesture was necessary. But I did feel an intense excitement as I was held close to him.

Then I saw. First came the drummer and with him a sergeant who carried a pike. Following these two was a groom leading a donkey and seated on this donkey, her face turned towards its tail, a crown of plaited straw on her head, was Madame Rougemont. There was a large placard hanging round her neck and painted on it in startling red letters was the word PROCURESS.

She sat there impassive—her face that mask I had seen before—white lead and carmine. Her headdress had slipped a little but it had been elaborate. I did not understand half of what the crowd was yelling at her but it was mostly bawdy comment on her profession.

My eyes were fixed on Madame Rougemont, who sat the donkey with an air of unconcern, looking straight ahead of her with a certain dignity which I could not help admiring. I was expecting someone to pull her off the donkey at any moment, but no one did; and the crowd really was quite good humored. The drummer went on beating his drum and someone broke into a song which the rest of the crowd took up.

"I can't hear the words," I said to Charles.

"That is just as well," he answered with a grin.

Then he took me by the arm. "Come on," he said. "That is enough."

"You brought me here just to see that, didn't you?"

"I took you out because I enjoy your company and I know you do mine. That was an extra pleasure."

"Not much of a pleasure for Madame Rougemont."

"I think it happened to her once before."

"It did not make her give up her profession."

"Good Heavens, no! It would take a great deal more than that to make such a good businesswoman give up such a profitable profession."

"How shameful to be paraded through the streets like that . . . with everyone knowing."

"Save your sympathy. She'll be back at her work tomorrow."

"Not now that it is known . . . won't something be done about it?"

"I think that is hardly likely."

"But isn't what she is doing against the law?"

"I'll tell you something, Lottie. She has friends in high places. She runs a very fine establishment near the Cours de Reine and it is patronized by many powerful men. They would not want to see it disbanded, which I suppose it would have to be if she were convicted."

"I see. So if she were a poor procuress she would be a criminal?"

"It could be so. But what will happen is that she will dismount from her donkey and go back and carry on with her business."

"It is so . . . unjust."

"But prudent. And she is a forceful woman and no doubt peace-loving. You did admire those statues, didn't you, and you wanted an example of all qualities in action. My dear Lottie, our King had his own procurer until lately. Why Le Bel, his *valet de chambre,* was avid in his search for those charms which would appeal to Louis's jaded appetites. The secret room on the north wing of the palace was kept for them alone. It was called *Le Trébuchet,* the snare for birds; and there the young girls were kept that the King might visit them when it pleased him. That was before the Parc aux Cerfs was founded because it was considered better for Louis to have his girls outside the palace. The whole of France knew it. Such matters cannot be kept secret. So who is going to be unduly shocked by the activities of Madame Rougemont?"

"If the girls go willingly I suppose it is not the same as if they are taken by force."

"Force? That is not the gentleman's way. You can be sure that all those little girls in the *trébuchet* and the Parc aux Cerfs went willingly enough. A period of service . . . and then the rewards. It was irresistible."

"And those who were lured into the fortune teller's apartment?"

"Some might have had to be persuaded. But girls who consult fortune tellers are looking for adventures, would you not say?"

"I suppose I should be grateful to you for sending us home."

"You should indeed. How nice of you to remember. Perhaps the occasion will arise when you have the opportunity to show your gratitude."

"Let us confine it to words."

"For the moment," he said.

As we walked through the streets he said: "The wedding fever is still in the air. It won't die down until after the fireworks display."

"Shall we be able to see it from the *hôtel?*"

"Not very well. I think we might get out. All Paris will be out for the night. I know what we will do. We will make up our little foursome. Armand, you, Sophie, and myself. You would like that, would you not?"

I had to agree that I should.

I was sorry when we returned to the *hôtel* to find that Sophie was already back with my mother.

"We took a little walk," said Charles. "It is such a beautiful day."

Sophie was looking at me intently.

"I came to suggest that *we* take a walk," went on Charles, smiling at Sophie.

"Had you forgotten that I had told you I was going to the dressmaker?"

"I thought it was this afternoon."

He went over to her and laid his hand on her shoulder. "How pretty you look this morning," he said. "Are they making you some beautiful clothes?"

81

She smiled at him, her suspicions melting away.

What a liar he is! I thought. And what a good actor! Poor Sophie, I hope she is not going to be badly hurt.

Disaster in a Paris Square

It was the day of the fireworks and we were all eagerly waiting for dusk.

Armand had said we should try to get as near as possible to the Place Louis XV, and he and Charles debated whether it would be best to take a carriage.

"We shall never get through those little streets," said Armand. "The press of people will be too great."

"Well, let's go on foot if the ladies are willing."

Both Sophie and I said we should do that.

"Wear cloaks," advised Charles. "We don't want to look conspicuous. And watch, for there will be pickpockets abroad tonight. I'll swear that they are already swarming into Paris."

So it was agreed and we went. I was glad to see that Sophie had recovered her happiness and was as ready to enjoy the evening as any of us. But she was by nature timid and she was soon apprehensive of the crowds.

"Lottie," she whispered to me, "I don't like all these people. I wish we could go home."

"But we have come to see the fireworks."

"There are too many crowds."

"It's going to be fun," I assured her.

I thought of that often in the years to come. If only I had agreed with her and we had persuaded the men to take us back!

We were jostled. Charles caught my arm and held me against him. Sophie saw the gesture and a look of anguish appeared on her face.

"It's too crowded," she whispered.

"My dear, what did you expect?" asked Charles. "This show is for the whole of Paris, not just for us."

She didn't answer but turned slightly away. I was sure there were tears in her eyes.

Armand said: "They are going to start now."

A cry went up from the crowd as the fireworks exploded illuminating the sky.

More people were crowding into the square and it was difficult to keep one's balance. And then ... suddenly it happened. Something had gone wrong with the fireworks, which were shooting up into the sky. They were exploding with sharp retorts and were falling ... falling on the people in the square.

There was the briefest of silences followed by screaming voices. Then there was pandemonium. I felt myself caught up. It was Charles who picked me up and held me above the crowd.

"Sophie!" he screamed.

I could not see Sophie but I was aware of Armand, his eyes wide, bewildered and frantic.

Then I did see Sophie. I was seized with horror for some of the sparks from the fireworks had fallen on her hood, which was on fire.

Armand had seized her and was trying to smother the flames. I felt sick and faint. Charles was shouting: "Get her out. . . . We've all got to get out of here."

Sophie had fallen. I prayed swiftly: "Oh, God, please save her. She will be trampled to death."

In a few seconds I saw her again. Armand had picked her up and put her over his shoulder. She was limp but the fire was out.

Charles cried: "Follow me."

He had slung me over his shoulder as though I were a sack of coal. All around us were screaming people pushing in all directions in their efforts to get out of the square. I saw pushing hands and frantic faces and the noise was deafening.

Charles was forcing his way through the crowd. I could no longer see Armand and Sophie and I had a terrible fear that they had been trampled underfoot.

Perhaps people are blessed with superhuman strength when faced with certain situations. I really believed Charles possessed it on that night. It is difficult now to recall the stark horror of everything about us. Some people had brought their carriages into the square and were now trying to get out. The horses seemed to be maddened by the press of people and there was a further danger as carriages toppled over and the horses tried to break free. The noise was unearthly and terrible.

I was expecting to fall at any moment but Charles kept steadily forging his way through the crowd. There was a relentlessness about him, a ruthless determination to save us at any cost. He was the sort of man who was accustomed to getting what he wanted and now all his efforts were concentrated on getting us safely out of the square.

I looked about for Armand and Sophie but could not see them. I could see nothing but that seething mass of panicking, hysterical people.

I could not say how long it lasted. I was only aware of fear and anxiety not only for ourselves but for Sophie and Armand. A terrible premonition came to me that nothing was ever going to be the same after that night.

Some of the buildings were ablaze and that had started a fresh panic; fortunately for us it was on the far side of the square.

I can still hear the sounds of screams, the sobbing and anguished cries, when I recall that fearful night.

But Charles brought me safely through. I remember always his pale face grimy with smoke ... his clothes awry, his wig lost exposing his fine dark hair so that he seemed like a different man. I knew that if I survived that night I should have him to thank for it.

When we were apart from the crowd ... and safe ... Charles put me down. I had no idea where we were except that we had escaped from the Place Louis XV.

"Lottie," he said in a voice such as I had never heard him use before.

I looked at him and his arms were round me. We clung together. There were many people about. Some had come from the nightmare square; others were spectators who had come out to see what was happening. No one took any notice of us.

"Thank God," said Charles. "Are you ... are you all right?"

"I think so. And you ... you did it all."

There was a flicker of the old pleasantry but it did not seem quite natural. "I did it just to show that I am always at your service."

84

Then suddenly we were laughing and I think nearly crying at the same time.

Immediately we remembered Sophie and Armand. We looked back at the square. Smoke was rising to the sky and we could still hear the shouts and screams of people fighting to get free.

"Do you think. . . ?" I began.

"I don't know."

"The last I saw of Armand he was carrying her."

"Armand would get through," said Charles.

"Poor Sophie. I think she was badly hurt. Her hood was on fire for a time."

We were silent for a few seconds. Then Charles said: "There is nothing to do but get back quickly. We'll have to walk, I'm afraid. There is nothing to take us back."

So we began our walk to the *hôtel*.

———

My mother took me into her arms.

"Oh, Lottie . . . Lottie . . . thank God . . ."

I said: "Charles saved me. He carried me through."

"God bless him!" said my mother.

"Sophie and Armand . . ."

"They are here. Armand stopped a carriage and they were brought back. It was ten minutes ago. Your father has sent for the doctors. Armand is safe. Poor Sophie . . . But the doctors will be here at any moment. Oh, my dear, dear child."

I felt limp, dazed, exhausted, and unable to stand up.

As we went into the salon my father ran out. When he saw me he took me into his arms and held me tightly. He kept saying my name over and over again.

Armand came towards us.

"Armand!" I cried with joy.

"I got through," he said. "I was lucky. I brought Sophie out and there was a carriage. I made them bring us back here."

"Where is Sophie?" I asked.

"In her room," said my mother.

"She . . . ?"

My mother was silent and my father put an arm round me. "We

85

don't know yet," he said. "She has suffered some burns. The doctors must come soon."

I sat down on a couch with my mother beside me. She had her arm round me and held me as though she would never let me go.

I lost count of time. I could not shut out of my mind all that horror. I kept thinking of Sophie, and the waiting was almost as terrible as that nightmare journey through the crowd.

That was a night which none of us—including the entire French nation—was going to forget for a very long time. What had gone wrong with the fireworks no one knew, and had the people remained calm the damage would not have been great. But the panic of the crowd to get out of the square in frantic haste had resulted in many being trampled to death; one hundred and thirty-two people had been killed outright and two thousand badly injured on that terrible night.

Remembering the storm on the wedding day people began to ask themselves if God was displeased with this marriage. They were to remember what they called "these omens" later.

I had prayed fervently that Sophie should not die and I rejoiced when my prayers were answered; but I have sometimes wondered whether, had Sophie been given the choice, she would have chosen to live.

She kept to her bed for several weeks. The day which should have been her wedding day came and went. None of her bones had been broken—Armand had saved her from being trampled to death—but one side of her face had been so badly burned that the scars would be with her forever.

My mother nursed her and I wanted to help but whenever I went into the room Sophie was disturbed.

My mother said: "She does not want you to see her face."

So I stayed away, but I wanted to be with her, to talk to her, to comfort her if I could.

Even when she rose from her bed she would not leave her room and she did not want anyone to be with her except her maid Jeanne Fougère, who was devoted to her and of whom she had become very fond.

Jeanne spent her days in Sophie's apartments and both my father and mother were grateful to the girl, for she seemed able to comfort

Sophie as no one else could. I had hoped that I should be able to, but it was very clear that my half sister did not want that.

Jeanne was clever with her fingers and she devised a kind of hood of blue silk which covered half of Sophie's face. Fortunately the burns had not touched her eyes, although one side of her face was badly scorched and the hair would never grow again there; but it was the lower part of her jaw which had caught the full fury of the flames. The hood which Jeanne had made was, said my mother, very effective.

"She will emerge from her room in time," went on my mother. "And your father thinks that we should return to the country. Sophie will feel better there. The sooner she gets away from the place where it happened the better."

I said: "The wedding will have to be postponed for some time, I suppose."

My mother was thoughtful. "She won't see Charles," she said.

"I suppose she can't bear him to see . . ."

"Poor girl. It may be that now . . ."

"You mean he won't want to marry her?"

"I don't know. The Tourvilles are very eager for the marriage. A good deal is involved."

"Settlements? Money?"

"Yes, and your father would have liked an alliance with the Tourvilles. Sophie, however, has told Jeanne that she will never marry now."

"She may change her mind. She loved Charles very much."

"Well, you know she was always nervous . . . unsure of herself. The betrothal made such a difference to her. Now, of course, she just wants to hide herself away."

"I wish she would see me."

"I can't understand it. Perhaps it is because you are so very pretty. I think she has always been a little . . . well, not exactly jealous but aware that you are more attractive than she is."

"Oh . . . nonsense."

"Not nonsense at all. It is all very natural. She was never very attractive herself; although she did change after the engagement."

"Is Charles willing to go ahead?"

"Yes. As soon as it can be arranged."

"So it is just Sophie."

"No doubt she will change her mind. We must wait and see. And now your father thinks that the best thing we can do is return to the country."

So we did. Sophie sat in the carriage huddled in the corner, her face covered by Jeanne's hood and her cloak wrapped tightly round her.

I tried to talk to her but she clearly showed she did not want me to. I wished that Lisette was in our carriage but she did not, of course, travel with us. She had gone ahead to the château in the company of Tante Berthe.

It was a very gloomy journey.

———

Everything changed after the night of the fireworks. The château was different; it was as though the ghosts of so many who had suffered there had come out of their hiding places to remind us that life was cruel.

Poor Sophie! I suffered with her and I was bitterly hurt that the friendship she had felt for me no longer seemed to exist. She had her own rooms in the château; she had asked for this and nothing was denied her. My mother and my father—who, I suspect, had never been really fond of her—wanted to indulge all her wishes. So when she asked for this set of rooms in the turret she was given them, and with Jeanne she set up what was like a private home there. I realized why she had wanted those rooms. They were apart from the rest of the château and she could really feel shut off there. From the long narrow windows high in the tower she could look out on the surrounding country and see most of the arrivals and departures from the château.

She made it clear that she was happier alone and wanted to see no one. She had her needlework, at which she had been very good, and there were one or two card games which she and Jeanne played together. Jeanne had become quite an important person in the household because of the influence she had with Sophie and every one of us wanted to do all that was possible to make Sophie's life happier.

Lisette and I discussed Sophie. "It's strange," said Lisette, "that she doesn't want to see us. After all, we were her good friends before."

"I seem to be the one she has taken against," I said. "I don't think it is entirely due to her accident. Before that I noticed she seemed to be turning against me."

"I think she probably noticed that Charles de Tourville was aware of your charms."

"Oh, no. He was charming to her always and would marry her now."

"Of course. She is still the daughter—the *legitimate* daughter—of the Comte d'Aubigné." Lisette spoke rather tartly and I guessed she was still resentful because Sophie and I had been with her so rarely during our stay in Paris.

"Well, whatever the reason, he would go on with the marriage. She is the one who won't."

"Have you seen her face?"

"Not lately. I caught a glimpse at first. I know she is badly disfigured."

"She never really made the most of what she had when she had it," said Lisette.

"It's tragic. I wish I knew what I could do to help."

I had told Lisette about Madame Rougemont's ordeal, and she had listened intently.

"I have heard she is practicing just the same."

"Yes, I know. Charles de Tourville told me she is too useful to the nobility for them to allow her business to be closed."

"If she had been trading in poor prostitutes that would have been a different matter," said Lisette. Her mouth hardened. "You can scarcely call it fair."

"I never did. I consider it most unjust."

"Life often is," commented Lisette.

Charles came to the château.

"He has come to see Sophie," said my mother. "I think he hopes to persuade her to go on with the marriage."

"I am so pleased," I replied. "That will make her happy."

She did see him. He went alone to her turret rooms and only Jeanne was there with them. He said afterwards that she had kept Jeanne in the room all the time and she told him most emphatically that she was never going to marry.

He was very upset after the interview. He said to my mother: "She took off that hood thing she wears and showed me her face. I was horrified and I could not hide this, I'm afraid. But I told her it made

89

no difference. She wouldn't believe that. She said she intended to live the rest of her life in those turret rooms with Jeanne, who was the only one she wanted to see. She said she was sure of Jeanne's devotion. I told her she could be sure of mine but she said she did not think so, that she had given up all thought of marriage and her decision was irrevocable."

"It is early as yet," said my mother. "It was a terrible shock and she is still suffering from it. Charles, I am sure if you persist . . ."

He said he would. He stayed with us for three or four days and tried every one of those days to see Sophie, but she would not receive him.

I saw him often but never alone. There was always someone to chaperone me and I was not sorry. There were reasons why I did not want to be alone with him and I did not want to probe too deeply into them.

He went away eventually but in less than a month he came back again.

"He is very anxious to marry with Aubigné," said Lisette.

"I think he is really fond of Sophie," I replied.

Lisette looked at me scornfully. "Such a good family to be allied to," she said cynically.

But he had changed. He was quiet. I often saw his eyes on me broodingly and I thought a great deal about him; so that was one of the reasons why I did not want to be alone with him.

August had come and it was about this time that I began to notice the change in Lisette. There were times when she looked a little older and sometimes she seemed quite pale with little of that color which used to be so charmingly and delicately pink in her cheeks.

One day I said to her: "Lisette, are you well?"

"Why do you ask?" she demanded quickly.

"I thought you seemed a little pale . . . and somehow not quite yourself."

She looked quite alarmed. "Of course I'm all right," she said sharply.

But there was something wrong. I saw Tante Berthe watching Lisette closely and I thought, *Something is worrying her.* Once when I was going to see my mother I encountered Tante Berthe coming out of her room and she looked very stern and angry . . . more than that. I thought I detected anxiety and even fear.

My mother was very absentminded when I was with her. I asked if anything was wrong with Tante Berthe and she answered quickly: "Oh, no . . . no . . . nothing at all wrong with her."

Everybody was changing. Nothing had been the same since that fearful tragedy. What was happening to everyone? Even Lisette had ceased to be the vivacious companion she had once been.

Lisette herself came to my room one evening. She said with a grimace: "Tante Berthe is taking me with her to visit some relations."

"Relations! I didn't know you had any."

"Nor did I . . . till now. But they have appeared and they want us to go and see them. The Comtesse has given us permission to go."

"Oh, Lisette! How long are you going to be away?"

"Well, they are some distance from here . . . down in the south somewhere. So we can't go for just a week. I daresay it will be a month or two."

"Who is going to run the household?"

"Someone will take Tante Berthe's place."

"People have always said that nobody could. Oh, Lisette, I do wish you weren't going."

"So do I." She looked bleakly miserable for a few moments. "It's going to be such a *bore.*"

"Can't Tante Berthe go alone?"

"She is insisting that I go with her. You see, they know of my existence and want to see both their long-lost relations."

"Oh, dear. I'm not going to like it at all. It's so different here now. First Sophie . . . and now you."

I put my arms round her and hugged her. I have rarely seen her so moved. I thought she was going to cry and that was something I had never seen her do.

But she didn't. She withdrew herself and said: "I shall be back."

"I should hope so. And make it soon."

"As soon as I can. Rest assured of that. This" —she spread her arms— "is my home. That's how I always see it . . . in spite of not being one of you and only the niece of the housekeeper."

"Don't be silly, Lisette. You will always be one of us as far as I am concerned."

"I'll be back, Lottie. I'll be back."

"I know that. But I want it soon."

"Soon as I can," she said.

Before the month was out Lisette had left with Tante Berthe. I watched them from one of the towers and I wondered if Sophie was doing the same from hers.

I felt desolate.

————

Life had changed completely. I had lost both Sophie and Lisette and only now did I realize what parts they had played in my life.

I missed them terribly—Lisette understandably because she had always been amusing, vivacious, and lighthearted; but I missed Sophie's quiet presence too. It would have helped me if I could have gone to her room, tried to amuse her, talked to her. But she would not allow it, and although she did not shut me out completely, she implied that she liked to be left alone and on the rare occasions when I did climb the stairs to the turret, Sophie always contrived that Jeanne should be with her so that we could not talk intimately. My visits grew less and less and I guessed that that was what Sophie wanted.

Charles came often and everyone was amazed at his devotion, for the Tourville estates were a good distance from Aubigné and the journey long and tiresome; but he continued to come. On the last two visits he had not seen Sophie. She did not want to see him any more than she wanted to see me; and Jeanne had told my mother that Charles's visits upset Sophie so much that she would be affected by them for days afterwards.

My mother explained this to Charles and he listened attentively. "I think," she said, "seeing you—and Lottie and Armand too for that matter—brings back memories of that night. She may change . . ."

My mother looked sad, for she was beginning to believe that Sophie would never change.

"Leave her alone for a while," she added hopefully.

"I shall continue to come," said Charles; and when he said that I met his eyes and I knew that he did not come to see Sophie but me.

I wished that I could stop thinking of him, but I could not. I dreamed about him, yet the man in my dreams was half Dickon, half Charles. I was not sure which one it was and my feelings for Charles were beginning to be what they had been for Dickon.

I wished that Lisette was here. I could have talked to her and in her worldly way she would have given me advice.

I now clearly understood my feelings for Dickon. It had been innocent love, young love, "calf love" they call it; I saw no flaw in my idol; I had loved wholeheartedly. That was because I had been only a child with a child's idealistic dreams. I now knew that Dickon had wanted Eversleigh and that my mother had given it to him to show that when he had it, he was no longer eager for me. It had changed my feelings for him. I had heard that his wife had died giving birth to twins. So he had his heirs now. I knew he was an adventurer, an ambitious man with lusty appetites; and I knew, too, that I would have been disappointed in him, that I would have had to learn more of the ways of the world, that there would have been fierce battles between us. But I was still sure that some bond still held us together and that it was an attraction which would remain forever.

I had thought that Dickon would be the only one; but now there was Charles.

I had no illusions about Charles. He was worldly, amoral perhaps; he had his own code of behavior from which he would never swerve. He would never be faithful for long to any woman; he had been brought up with the philosophy of his ancestors—French ancestors at that. He would say they took a realistic view of life, which was that men were polygamous, and although they might love one woman more than others, that would not prevent their casting their eyes about and satisfying their sexual needs outside their marriages.

Now I was wiser. I was approaching seventeen and becoming knowledgeable of the world in which I lived. This was different from the world of my mother, Jean-Louis, my grandmother, and Sabrina. They had a different set of morals; they called them ideals. But this was France—a man's country, which most women accepted. I fancied I never would. So it was disturbing to realize that although Charles de Tourville came to Aubigné ostensibly to see Sophie, he did in fact come to see me.

The weeks passed. It was August when Lisette had gone away. It was now well into October ... a beautiful, colorful month with the copper beeches turning to orange and the oak trees to bronze. But how short-lived! Soon the wind would strip those beautiful leaves from the trees and the winter would be with us.

In the old days I had loved the winter. We would go out into the snow and come back and sit round the fire, talking ... Lisette, myself, and Sophie. We discussed people, life, any subject we could think of ... with Sophie contributing hardly anything and Lisette always one step ahead of me.

Now it would be different. I was going to find the long cold days monotonous. But perhaps Lisette would be back soon.

It was a great day when we heard that Tante Berthe had written that she would be returning to the château at the beginning of November.

"Thank heaven for that," said my mother. "Nothing runs as smoothly without Tante Berthe."

I was very excited at the prospect of having Lisette back with me. I imagined our conversations; we would work out a scheme for weaning Sophie from her solitude.

I remember the day well. It was the twelfth of November, a damp, misty, almost windless day—quite warm for the time of the year. I went to one of the turrets to watch for the arrival. I had been out the day before and had gathered green catkins from the hazel tree and a spray or two of gorse which I had found in a sheltered spot.

I planned to put them in Lisette's room to show her how pleased I was that she had returned.

It was almost dusk when I saw a party of horsemen in the distance; picking up my cloak I hurried down so that I should be in the courtyard to greet her.

I saw Tante Berthe—grim as ever—being helped out of her saddle by one of the grooms. But where was Lisette?

My mother had come out to greet Tante Berthe.

"Welcome back!" she cried. "We are so pleased to see you."

"Where is Lisette?" I asked.

Tante Berthe looked at me steadily.

"Lisette will not be coming back. She is married."

I was too choked to speak.

"Come along in," said my mother, speaking rather rapidly. "You must tell us all about it. I do hope Lisette is happy. I am sure she will be."

I followed them into the hall as though stunned.

Lisette ... married! Gone away to another life. Would I never see her again?

I felt bereft and rarely so wretched in the whole of my life.

94

Armand had been betrothed for some months to a young lady who was highly suitable, and everyone was very pleased about the proposed match. Marie Louise de Brammont was of the right family and upbringing and therefore an heiress to a considerable fortune. Marriage was so pleasant when everything was as it should be, particularly if the bride and groom had no particular aversion to each other.

Armand was like any other Frenchman. I was sure he had his amorous adventures but they were quite apart from marriage; and he was content with the match.

Both my father and mother realized that I was feeling the loss of Sophie's company and they knew too that Lisette and I had been special friends; they tried in every way to help me over this depressing period which the loss of my young companions had brought me to; they took me to Paris, but somehow the delights of that city did not stir me out of my melancholy; they only served to remind me of it more vividly. In the streets I kept remembering that walk down the Champs-Élysées where the lamps were being hung; and I could not bear to go near the Place Louis XV.

There was a great deal of gaiety but I could not feel part of it. I listened to Court gossip, but it was immaterial to me whether Marie Antoinette received Madame du Barry or not. If the King was bewitched by this woman from the gutters of Paris—where some people said she came from—let him be. I did not care that the Barriens—the party round Madame du Barry—had succeeded in getting Minister Choiseul dismissed, even though all this was of some importance to my father, who was deeply involved in Court intrigue. My mother used to be a little anxious about him because such activities could be dangerous. It was so easy to lose everything—one's life as well as one's estates. There were those dreaded *lettres de cachet* of which nobody spoke much because it was considered unlucky to do so.

But all the intrigue and gaiety of Paris could not lift me out of my gloom . . . until Charles came.

He must have known we were in Paris. I wondered afterwards whether my mother told him so. She knew that I was attracted by him and him by me; she still lived in her idealist world and saw life not as it was but as she wanted it to be. I think it was her innocence which had so attracted my father. I would have been ready to swear that since

95

he had married her he had been entirely faithful to her. She would accept this as the natural course of events and not realize how very powerful was the attraction she had for him. And that was, of course, part of her innocence.

I would never have such. Perhaps it was a pity. On the other hand, it might be better to know the truth and face life as it really was.

So while we were in Paris Charles came there. We rode in the Bois together. We walked during the days. Once we rode out of the city towards St. Cloud and when we had left the town behind us we dismounted and tethered our horses and walked among the trees.

He said: "You know I'm in love with you, Lottie."

"What goes for love with you, perhaps."

"I thought we were becoming friends."

"We have seen each other fairly frequently."

"That is not what I meant. I thought there was an understanding between us."

"I think I understand *you* very well."

He stopped suddenly and caught me up in his arms. He kissed me ... once ... twice ... and went on kissing me. I was bewildered, making an attempt to hold him off—but it was rather feeble.

"Lottie, why won't you be true to yourself?" he asked.

I withdrew myself and cried: "True to myself? What does that mean?"

"Admit you like me, that you want me in the same way as I want you."

"The last thing I should want is to be one of that multitude who have ministered to your desires ... temporarily."

"You know that is not what I want. I want you permanently."

"Indeed?"

"I want marriage."

"Marriage. But you are betrothed to Sophie."

"No longer. She has rejected me ... irrevocably. Those were her words."

"And so now you would turn to me?"

"I turned to you the moment I saw you."

"I remember. You were looking for a victim at Madame Rougemont's."

96

"Didn't I rescue you? Didn't I look after you? I protected you from the wrath of your family. I have always sought to please you. I was betrothed to Sophie before I met you. You know how these marriages are arranged. But why shouldn't there be one which is a love match, and why shouldn't that be ours?"

I felt my heart leap with excitement. I could not curb my exultation. Escape from the gloomy château with its memories. Sophie in her turret, Lisette gone. One day so like another . . . and my inability to rouse myself from my lethargy and depression.

I struggled to suppress my elation.

I said: "There is Sophie."

"It is accepted now that she will never marry. It would not surprise me if she made up her mind to enter a convent. The life would suit her. But that does not mean that I must remain unmarried all my life. I have spoken to your father."

I stared at him.

"Don't look alarmed," he said. "I have had a very encouraging answer. Your mother is anxious that you shall not be forced to do anything you do not wish. But the glorious truth is that I have your father's permission to lay my heart at your feet."

I laughed at the expression and he laughed too. He had a ready wit and he was well aware—how could he be otherwise?—that I knew the sort of life he had led. Our first meeting had been indicative of that.

"So," he went on, "Mademoiselle Lottie, I hereby ask you to become my wife. At least," he went on, "you hesitate. Do you see, I feared a determined No. Not that I should have accepted it, but it is encouraging not to be refused in the first few seconds."

"You must see how impossible the whole thing would be."

"I don't. I see it as perfectly possible."

"What of Sophie?"

"Sophie has made the choice. She has left me free."

"And you think that with her in that turret, you and I . . . ."

He gripped me by the shoulders and looked into my face.

"I want you, Lottie," he said. "You will have such a wonderful time with me. You will see. I will awaken you to such delights that you never dreamed of."

"I am not interested . . ."

"Now, Lottie, I know you well. You are bursting from your shell. You long to experience that of which you have heard so much. I am sure you have had endless discussions with that girl . . . what was her name? . . . the one who came to Rougemont's with you."

"You mean Lisette. She is married now."

"And enjoying life, I'll swear. She would. She was that sort of girl. Dear Lottie, so are you. You will marry one day. Why not me? Wouldn't you rather choose for yourself than have someone chosen for you?"

"Certainly I will make my own choice."

"Well, then, having your father's permission to woo you, I shall begin now."

"Save yourself the trouble."

His answer was to pick me up in his arms and hold me, looking up at me and laughing.

"Put me down," I said. "What if we were seen?"

"Everyone will understand. A gallant gentleman and a beautiful lady. Why shouldn't they be in love?"

Slowly he lowered me until my face was on a level with his.

"Lottie," he murmured, "Oh Lottie."

And I just wanted to be held like that. I felt suddenly that life had become interesting again.

––––

It was decided that Armand should be married at Christmas, which would mean that we would spend Christmas at Brammont, Marie Louise's family home not far from Orléans.

Sophie would not come and declared her intention of staying at the château where she would be well looked after by Jeanne. Although my mother at first attempted to persuade her, she was relieved. The festive season would have been scarcely festive with Sophie hiding herself away and everyone knowing she was there.

So we made our preparations to go to Brammont without her.

After the wedding Armand and his bride would return to Aubigné and make their home there. I hoped I should get on well with Marie Louise. It would be pleasant to have another woman in the house, though she was a serious girl and very religious and I could not imagine anyone less like Lisette.

I often wondered about Lisette. I had heard nothing from her. I had asked Tante Berthe for her address as I intended to write to her, but Tante Berthe said leave it for a while for Lisette was traveling with her husband and would be away for some months.

I did discover that her husband owned land. I imagined he was a farmer.

"I hope she will be happy," I said. "I cannot imagine Lisette on a farm."

"Lisette was very contented, I do assure you," said Tante Berthe. But she would not give me the address.

"Later on," she promised. "When they are settled."

I was, of course, rather immersed in my own affairs at the time and the possibility which had arisen in connection with Charles.

My mother talked of the matter with me.

"He is very much in love with you, Lottie, and your father would be happy with the match. He says he will give you the dowry he promised Sophie. I know the Tourvilles would be very happy with the marriage."

"What of Sophie?"

"Sophie has chosen her way of life. She will expect others to do the same. Poor Sophie. It was tragic . . . and just as she was beginning to forget her shyness. But it happened. It is life. It could have happened to anyone. Oh, my darling, how relieved I am that you came safely out of all that. I want you to be as happy as I have been. I often marvel at the way things turned out for me."

"Dear Mother," I told her, "they turned out well because you are what you are. The Comte loves you because you are so different from all these people whom we meet."

She looked amazed and I realized that she did not see them as I did.

I went on quickly: "I think so much about Sophie. It would not seem right to marry the man who was to have been her husband."

"That would have been an arranged marriage."

"But she loved him very much."

"Sophie would have loved anyone who took notice of her. Poor girl, her life is tragic but she must not be allowed to stand in the way of your happiness. If you married Charles you would not live here . . . not like Armand. This is his home. The château will be his one day.

99

But you will go to your husband's house. You can build a life for yourself . . . have children . . . be happy . . . forget that terrible night. Forget Sophie."

"I wish I could."

She smiled at me and put her arm about me. "My dearest child, you know you are doubly dear to me . . . coming as you did. You brought great happiness to Jean-Louis and to me. More than anything I want to see you happy."

"And you think that if I married Charles de Tourville . . ."

"I know it because I have watched you closely. You hold back but you don't want to. As for him, I have rarely seen a man more in love."

And so it was when we went to Brammont for Armand's wedding.

———

The Brammont château was a good deal smaller than that of Aubigné but built in the same style with tall slate roofs and pepper-pot towers. It was delightful, more charming in fact than the larger castles. I was enchanted by the arabesque friezes, sculptured niches, and pinnacled windows.

There was more than the usual Christmas activity as this was to be the occasion of the wedding as well, which was to take place two days after Christmas Day. The château was filled with guests and family and I was surprised to find that the Tourvilles were there.

It was not long before Charles sought me out. He was obviously delighted because we should spend Christmas under the same roof.

We rode, we danced, we sang Christmas hymns. It was different from our Christmas in England, but I was accustomed to these celebrations now. There was no punchbowl nor wassailing, which had been such a feature of our Christmases at Clavering; but we were all celebrating the same event.

I was enjoying everything very much and was happier than I had been for some months. Verbal sparring with Charles exhilarated me and when he kissed me and held me against him—which he did whenever possible—I had to admit I was excited.

The marriage was celebrated in the château chapel and afterwards there was a banquet. Charles had been seated next to me at this for it seemed general knowledge that there was an understanding between us.

The Catholic ceremony of marriage had reminded me that I was a

Protestant. My father had not suggested that I change my religion, although the matter had never been gone into. My mother had gone through some formality before her marriage. It now occurred to me that if I married in France it would very likely be that my husband was a Catholic, and although that might not be of paramount importance, the problem would certainly arise if there were children.

When Charles was telling me how foolish I was to delay giving him an affirmative answer, before I could stop myself I blurted out: "What about the children?"

"What children?" he asked in amazement.

"Of the marriage."

"Ours, you mean. Then this is your answer. It is yes. My dearest Lottie, at last! I shall have it announced this very day."

"But I didn't say . . ."

"You said what about the children? My dear girl, you are not suggesting we have children without the blessing of clergy?"

"I was thinking aloud."

"You were thinking of us . . . our children. What were you going to say about them?"

"I am not a Catholic."

He looked serious for a moment. Then he said: "That's easy. You could become one."

"I would not do that. Don't you see, this is the reason why I cannot marry you."

"Such reasons can easily be dealt with."

"How? Would you give up your religion?"

"I have to confess that I have not much religion."

"I gathered that by your conduct."

He laughed. "Dear Lottie," he said. "Seriously, it is something of a habit. But this matter of the children." He narrowed his eyes and surveyed me. "We wouldn't let it come between us. I am a reasonable man. You wouldn't change, you say. I can see you are adamant on that point. Very well. How is this? Our first boy will be the heir. He would have to be a Catholic. But the girls we shall have, well, they will be yours. The boy for me . . . the necessity of an ancient family and all that . . . for future inheritance and so on. You understand. And the girls for you. That's fair, isn't it?"

"I suppose it is."

101

"Then why are we waiting? I shall announce our betrothal to-night."

And that was how it happened; and, in truth, it was what I wanted. It was what I had wanted for a long time.

———

Both my father and mother were delighted, and that went for the Tourvilles too. It was a happy solution to the situation. All the settlements which had been arranged for Sophie should be turned over to me. My mother said: "I am delighted. I was a little worried really because the French are so formal . . . and your birth being a little irregular . . . I know your father was concerned about that. He was considering having you legitimized. It can be done, you know. Now that you are marrying it won't be necessary. I am so happy for you, my darling. I know you love him and he is such an attractive young man. You are happy, I can see."

"Yes," I said in a rather surprised voice, "I believe I am."

My mother began making arrangements immediately.

"It is fortunate that the Tourvilles are here now," she said. "We can get everything settled. Though perhaps the wedding should not take place just yet. There ought to be a year say after that dreadful accident. I thought perhaps May. That is a lovely month for a wedding. And there is something else. I thought about having it in Paris . . . but somehow I don't think so. It would be difficult at the château because . . ."

"Because of Sophie up there in the turret."

She nodded.

"Well, the Tourvilles have come up with a suggestion and I think it is a good one. Why shouldn't you be married from their place? I know it is a bit unorthodox and it should be the bride's home . . . but in the circumstances . . ."

I could see they were planning it for me and I was content to let them do so. I was very excited at the prospect of being married to Charles, not to have to fight against my instincts any longer.

I was not sure whether I loved him. I certainly was *in love* with him, if being in love meant that everything seemed dull when he was not there.

I wanted change. I wanted excitement. I did not want to go back to Aubigné, where Sophie lived like a grim ghost in her turret . . .

haunting me. Though why I should feel a hint of blame at what happened, I did not know. It was true that during that fearsome debacle Charles had turned to me, had rescued me. But if he had left me to go to Sophie he could not have saved her.

Yet I could never stop feeling that niggling little sense of guilt when I was shut up in Aubigné with Sophie there reminding me forever.

I had to escape and Charles offered that escape. I was going to adventure—erotic adventure which I knew in a way would appeal to my senses; unknown yes, certainly unknown. But the future would solve that for me.

———

We came back to Aubigné, and all through the winter weeks I thought of my wedding.

I missed Lisette more than ever. I promised myself that when I was a married woman I would have more freedom than I possessed now and I would go and see Lisette at her farmhouse, wherever it was. Tante Berthe had come back and settled into her old post as though nothing had happened, but she had never been very communicative and I could not get an address from her which would have enabled me to write to Lisette.

She was still traveling with her husband, Tante Berthe insisted. She would be moving into her new house with the coming of spring. Finally I wrote a letter in which I explained that I was going to marry Charles de Tourville and I thought she and her husband ought to come to my wedding. I took the letter to Tante Berthe, who said that as soon as she knew Lisette's address she would send it to her.

I heard nothing and after a while began to think less of Lisette because I was so occupied with my own affairs.

We went to Paris to get my trousseau and my attention was taken up entirely with the gowns which were being prepared for me. There was my wedding dress of white brocade which was delicately trimmed with pearls; and there was a white veil which would flow down from a pearl coronet placed high on my head. All hair styles now were high so that one's hair had to be padded out to get the desired effect. This fashion had been introduced by the Court hairdressers because Marie Antoinette's high forehead made it a becoming style for her. And it certainly was becoming except when carried to extreme, which often happens with fashions sooner or later.

However, I had a pleasant time in Paris and for the first time since the accident could ride down the Champs Élysées without feeling unbearably sad.

All the clothes would be delivered to Aubigné so that we could make sure they were what I wanted and then they would be sent on to Tourville. Aubigné would no longer be my home after the wedding as I should be with my husband's people. I think at one time that would have saddened me. It no longer did. What I wanted more than anything was to escape. I wanted to get away from my childhood, to understand the emotions which Dickon had first aroused in me before I realized what they meant. I had grown up since then and I knew that Charles would be my tutor.

Often I tried on my dresses. I reveled in them. Silks and velvets, charmingly simple day dresses and an elegant riding habit in pearl gray. Excitement did something for me much as love had for Sophie.

"You can see she's in love," said one of the maids, for several of them peeped in while I was trying on my dresses.

Was I? I didn't know. But whatever it was I was pleased to be in it.

The wedding was to be in May, exactly a year since Sophie's tragedy and we should have a quiet wedding because people might remember that Charles had intended to marry Sophie.

I was longing for the day of our departure for Tourville and yet in a way I was savoring these days of preparation. How often since have I thought that anticipation is sometimes more delightful than the realization. I reveled in looking forward to the future in delicious uncertainty of what it held for me.

And so the days passed. It was the night before we were to leave. One of the maids would pack my wedding dress after we had left and it would come along after us with my other clothes. The dress was now hung in a cupboard and I was constantly peeping at it.

I went to bed early for we should be up as soon as it was light in order to begin the long journey which lay before us, and as I was tired I was soon asleep.

I awoke startled, wondering for a moment where I was as I came out of a dream, the memory of which vanished as I opened my eyes.

There was a moon that night and its light shone into my room so that it was almost as light as day.

Then suddenly I felt myself go cold. I could almost feel the hair rising on my scalp, for someone was in my room. It was like an apparition. I lay still, unable to move . . . staring at that figure. A girl . . . myself . . . for she was wearing my wedding dress. I could see the veil flowing down her back.

Then she turned and I saw her face.

I gasped in horror. The moonlight clearly showed up the hideous disfigurement, the blue smudges, and wrinkled skin by the side of her face, the scorched patch where the hair should have been.

I raised myself and whispered in a hoarse voice: "Sophie."

She was standing at the foot of my bed looking at me and I could see the cold hatred in her eyes.

"This should be my wedding dress," she said.

"Oh, Sophie," I cried. "It could have been had you wished. You yourself refused. . . ."

Then she laughed and the bitterness of her laugh was like a knife in my heart. "You wanted him from the first. You thought I didn't know. You lured him from me. You . . . what are you? A bastard! Begotten in sin! I shall never forgive you."

"It was not my fault, Sophie," I said.

"Not your fault!" She laughed and there was such pain in her voice that I winced. "You are beautiful. You know that well enough, and I was never anything much, was I? Men like you . . . men like Charles . . . even when he was betrothed to me. You lured him from me. You determined to get him. I knew you were his mistress even before . . . before . . ."

"Sophie, that is not true. I have never been anyone's mistress."

"You lie easily. I have proof."

"What proof?"

"I found your flower in his apartment. It was lying there on the floor . . . in his bedchamber."

"What are you talking about, Sophie? I have never been in his bedchamber."

"It was the day when . . ." She turned away. Then she went on: "He bought you the red one, didn't he? I had the lavender. The red flower of passion, wasn't it? I knew by the way he put it in your hair. I knew before I found out. But I tried not to believe it. I called at their *hôtel* to see his mother. It was something about the wedding arrangements.

She said, 'He is in his room. Come up with me.' So I went and there it was lying on the floor . . . where you had dropped it."

"I remember the flower . . . though I never wore it. I had forgotten it until this moment. It couldn't have been my flower. I daresay I still have it . . . somewhere."

She clenched her hands together. "Please don't lie to me. I knew . . . and that confirmed it."

"It is all imagination, Sophie. Oh, do believe me."

"You wanted this to happen." She threw back her head and turned the scarred part of her face towards me. "A pretty sight, isn't it? On that night he was with you. You left me there. He was intent on saving you. You both hoped that I would die."

"It's not true. You know it isn't true. He wanted to marry you . . . afterwards. He asked you again and again."

"He never wanted to marry me. It was arranged. He wanted you as soon as he saw you. You think I am foolish and blind. I may be . . . but not quite so blind as not to see what is right under my eyes. I will never forgive you . . . never . . . and I hope you never forget what you have done to me."

"Oh, Sophie," I cried. "Sophie . . ."

I attempted to go to her but she held up her hand.

"Don't come near me," she said.

I covered my face with my hands because I could no longer bear to look at her. I knew it was no use pleading with her, trying to make her understand. She was determined to blame me.

When I opened my eyes she had taken off the veil and was placing it reverently on its stand. The dress she hung up in the cupboard before she stepped into her own long robe.

"Sophie," I said gently.

But she waved me away and silent as a ghost glided to the door. There she paused. "Remember me," she said, looking straight at me. "All the time he is with you, remember me. I shall be thinking of you. I shall never forget what you did to me."

The door closed on her. I stared at the veil on its stand and I thought, *I shall never be able to forget either. She will always be there to haunt me.*

When I wore that dress, when I wore that veil, I should be think-

106

ing of her standing there at the foot of my bed, accusing me, blaming me.

It was unfair. She could have married him had she wished. When she had convinced herself that he did not really want her, I could guess how deeply wounded she had been, and the wounds to her heart went as deeply as those which had disfigured her face.

She had spoken bitterly of the flower. I remembered vividly the day Charles had bought it. I had forgotten it and never worn it. It must be somewhere among my things. Whose peony was it that Sophie had seen? Someone who had visited Charles? The flowers were not exactly rare. They had been sold all over Paris at that time and Charles might well have had a woman visiting him in his rooms.

I couldn't have told Sophie that. She would never understand the type of man Charles was. Poor Sophie!

She would not forget me, she had said. I could indeed tell her the same. I would always be haunted by the sight of that pathetic figure in my white wedding dress and veil.

The Return of Lisette

It was the spring of the year 1775 and four years since my marriage to Charles. I was a very different person from that girl who had traveled to Tourville for her wedding. I had grown up quickly under Charles's tuition; he taught me how to come to terms with life and I was, on the whole, grateful for that.

I would say that our marriage had been satisfactory. There was a definite physical attraction between us and I had discovered that I, no less than he, could find great satisfaction in such a relationship.

During the first months of our marriage neither of us had thought of much else than the passion that we could arouse in each other. He

107

had recognized in me what, in his cynical way, he called "a suitable companion of the boudoir," which meant a woman who was not ashamed of her own desires and who could rise to those heights of passion which he liked to scale—so that as one they could revel in the delights of physical intercourse between the two sexes.

In the beginning I had thought a great deal about Sophie and consoled myself with the certain knowledge that she would never have been able to accompany Charles in those flights of ecstasy.

He was a connoisseur of love—perhaps I should say lust—and also of women. He told me once that he could tell at a glance when a woman had—his term again—love potentialities.

"As soon as I saw you bending over that crystal ball I recognized those qualities to a large degree," he told me.

Was I in love with him? What was love? I asked myself that many times. In love as my mother and father were? No, not like that. That was some ideal state to which people came perhaps when they were old and wise and no longer bedeviled by the urgings of desire. What a contented relationship that must be! No, certainly Charles and I were not like that.

During those first months when we seemed to mean everything to each other, my heart would leap with joy when he appeared and I was always uneasy when he was away from me; I longed during the evenings when we were with his family in the long salon at the Tourville château for the moment when we should retire and be alone.

It never occurred to me to wonder then whether this excessive excitement would last. I supposed my parents had once felt like that in those long-ago days when I was conceived. Then they had parted for years and had only come together when they were middle-aged with much experience behind them, and with the raging desire no longer there to cloud their judgment. And so they reached that deeply contented perfect relationship.

Charles was certainly the perfect lover. I could be sure he did not feign his need for me. I could not for a moment doubt it. Yet somewhere in my mind I knew that it could not last . . . not at that breathtaking level at any rate; and would what was left to us be strong enough to build on it that sort of love I had seen and envied a little in my parents?

The Tourville family itself was not very exciting. Charles's father was an invalid; his mother a mild woman who adored her family. There was a sister Amelie, for whom a marriage was being arranged.

They were a wealthy family, although not nearly so rich as my father; and clearly they had been delighted with the alliance between our families. They would have preferred Sophie, of course; but it showed how much they wanted an alliance to have accepted a daughter of illegitimate birth. Moreover the dowry had been the same as that which would have gone with Sophie.

I should have found life at Tourville very dull but for Charles.

So I went on in that excited state until I became pregnant, which was about eight months after my marriage.

Everyone at Tourville was delighted and when messages were sent to Aubigné there was great rejoicing there.

During the first three months I felt wretchedly sick and after that when I began to grow bulky I was in no state for night frolics with Charles. I guessed then that he found a mistress, for he was not the sort of man to deny himself, and he would think, from what he had always been brought up to believe, that it was the natural course of events.

Strangely enough coming into motherhood had changed me too. I was absorbed now in the baby and that was enough for me.

Charles was the devoted husband, delighted that I had shown so soon evidence of my fruitfulness, and he did not show any rancor because I could no longer endure him in my bed.

My mother came over from Aubigné to be with me at the birth and the delight of everyone was great when I produced a healthy boy.

We called him Charles, which soon became Charlot, and from the moment I heard his first lusty scream he was of the utmost importance to me.

Those were some of the happiest months of my life. I remember so well sitting up in bed with my baby in my arms and people coming in to admire him and congratulate me.

Charles walked round the room with the baby in his arms.

"Clever, clever Lottie," he said, and kissed me.

My father came to see his grandson. He held the child aloft and looked at him with such pride that I laughed.

"I see you are pleased with him," I said.

Reverently he laid the child in his cradle and came to sit beside my bed.

"Dear Lottie," he said, "what a happy day it was when you came to me and now it is you who have given me my first grandchild." He took my hand and kissed it. "Your mother is so proud of you . . . and so am I."

I said: "You overrate me. It is no great achievement. Women are doing it all over the world at this moment."

"Some seem incapable of it." He sighed.

I knew he was thinking of Armand and Marie Louise. It was a great disappointment to him that there was no child of that marriage.

After the birth of my son my relationship with my husband changed. He was no longer the delighted teacher, I no longer the pupil avid to learn. I had become mature somehow.

We were lovers, but lovemaking seemed to have become a routine instead of the indescribable thrill it had once been.

I suppose marriage was like that. However, I had my son and that was contentment enough.

Spring had come and I was going to Aubigné to visit my parents. I rarely went to Aubigné and usually found some reason for not going, suggesting that my parents come to Tourville instead. They were frequent visitors for they wanted to see their grandson growing up. My father would have liked us to live at the Château d'Aubigné but that, of course, was out of the question. Tourville was Charles's home and responsibility and I was his wife.

So I continued to make the excuse that it was difficult to travel with a child and they came to us.

Charlot was two—old enough to be left to the care of his excellent nurse—and I was to make the journey to Aubigné because my mother had sprained her ankle and was unable to make the proposed spring visit to Tourville.

"She longs to see you," wrote my father. "Do try to come. I know little Charlot is too young to travel, but if you could spare us a week or so it would so please your mother."

I decided that my desire to stay away from Aubigné must be conquered. I still thought of Sophie on the night before I had left, standing at the foot of my bed, so tragic in the wedding dress she believed should have been hers, with the veil falling away from her poor scarred face. Surely over the years she had come to terms with her fate; surely common sense must tell her that I was not to blame for what had happened to her. Although I had looked I had never found the artificial flower which had caused her such distress, and presumed it had been mislaid when the maid was packing for me.

I arrived at Aubigné in the early afternoon. My parents were waiting for me and I laughingly protested to my father that he would suffocate me in his embrace. My mother looked on with that expression of pleased content which she always wore when my father and I were together.

I was showered with questions. How was I? How was Charlot? Had I had a good journey? How long could I stay?

"Soon Charlot will be old enough to travel," said my mother. "We thought you would like your old room. We haven't used it since you went. I don't like the thought of anyone else in it. Silly of me. But there are so many rooms in the castle."

She was babbling on in her excitement and I felt happy to be with them.

But I was not so happy to be in that room of memories. I hoped I should not dream of a ghostly scarred figure coming into my room.

We dined alone.

"Armand will be back tomorrow," said my father. "He is at Court. There is a great deal of trouble brewing. Last year's harvest is the cause of it. You remember how severe the weather was. It has been difficult to keep down the price of grain. The King is most disturbed. He really does seem to care. A change from his grandfather . . . that wicked old reprobate."

It was a year since Louis XV had died and young Louis with his wife, Marie Antoinette, had, so we had heard, been overcome with emotion when they had been called upon to rule. Louis had been nineteen and his Queen eighteen and it was known that they had knelt and prayed: "O God, guide us and protect us. We are too young to rule." And the whole nation had been moved by the plight of these two young people, but heartened by their realization of their duties and determination to carry them out, which was in such contrast to the old King. It had seemed that a new era was coming to France, so it was unfortunate that right at the start of the new reign there should have been such a hard winter producing a bad harvest.

"Young Louis did well in putting Turgot at the head of finances," said my father, who seemed unable to keep his thoughts from politics. "He is a good, sincere man who is eager to do his best for his country. But it is not going to be easy to keep down the price of corn and if the cost of bread goes up, which seems inevitable, that is going to make the people restive."

"Oh, dear," I sighed. "There are always these troubles. I want to hear about Aubigné. Sophie . . . ?"

There was a brief silence.

Then my mother said: "She keeps to her turret. I do wish she would be with us more. She is becoming like a hermit. Jeanne chooses which servants are to go in and clean. She really is rather autocratic. But what can we do? We have to bow to her. She is so necessary to Sophie."

"I hope I shall be able to see Sophie while I am here."

"She refuses to see people. It is very sad to think of her up there . . . her life slipping away."

"Is it possible for anything to be done for her?"

"There are lotions and creams. Jeanne is always going out to the markets and bringing things back. How effective they are I cannot say. Not very, I should think, for Sophie stays up there and it is really only Jeanne who has any communication with her."

"It would be better if she went into a convent," said my father.

"Is she likely to?"

"No, Marie Louise is more likely to do that."

"Marie Louise is a very good girl," said my mother.

"Too good for this world," answered my father shortly.

My mother lifted her shoulders. "She should never have married," she said. "She cannot have children. I think they have given up the attempt."

"One can't blame Armand," went on my father. It was clear that he had no great love for his daughter-in-law. "She is so pious. The chapel is always in use. Once a day used to be enough. Now she spends most of her time there. Her servants have to attend with her. It is most depressing. At this moment she is staying the night at the Convent de la Forêt Verte. You know it. It is only three miles from the château. She is endowing it with a new altar. Lottie, this place has changed since you left us."

"Your father longs for the days when you were here, Lottie," said my mother. "Then Sophie behaved more normally. She was always quiet and then there was that other girl . . ."

"Lisette," I cried. "I often think of her. I wrote to her but she never answered. How is Tante Berthe?"

"The same as ever."

"I do want a word with her before I go. I should really love to see Lisette again."

"She was a very pretty girl," said my mother.

"And still is, I don't doubt," I replied. "It would be so interesting to see her again. I shall certainly beard Tante Berthe in her den. She is still in the same quarters, I suppose."

"Just the same. She is very proud of them and no one is allowed to go in without an invitation."

"What a martinet she always was!"

"But an excellent manager," said my father. "We have never regretted her coming."

"I am surprised that she allowed Lisette to escape. She used to watch over her so carefully. Lisette used to be really scared of her . . . the only person she ever was scared of."

Then we talked of other matters but I went on thinking of Lisette and the fun we used to have together, thoughts that were inevitable now that I was at the château.

The next day Marie Louise came back from the convent. She was far from good looking and despised those little aids to beauty which most women seemed to use nowadays. She wore her hair very simply tied back. None of those Marie Antoinette styles for her. Her gown was dark gray and decidedly drab. When I expressed my pleasure at seeing her and said that I hoped we should be together sometime she told me she sewed for the poor every afternoon and if I would care to join her she would find some work for me to do and she could tell me about the altar she was going to build for the Forêt Verte.

I did not find the prospect very exciting and as needlework had never appealed to me I allowed the invitation to lapse.

It was pleasant to see Armand. His unsatisfactory marriage did not appear to have changed him at all. He was of a placid nature and apparently took what came to him in a philosophical way. I was sure he had a pleasant mistress somewhere—several perhaps—and he was quite content to leave matters as they were.

The Comte, however, was less ready to accept the state of affairs. My mother told me how disturbed he was by Armand's sterile marriage.

"There is the family line . . . the estates and everything. Your father is worried about that. However, he is delighted with little Charlot."

Then we talked of my son and she wanted to know what he had done and said, for he could chatter away quite intelligently now, which we both declared was miraculous; and we spent a great deal of time talking of him.

I did see Tante Berthe in her rooms when I was granted an interview. I thought how I should have laughed with Lisette afterwards, if only she had been there to laugh with me.

Tante Berthe in black bombazine, very plain but most elegantly cut and very severe, was a most dignified lady. She made tea for me, which showed how conscious she was of the ways of society, for tea drinking was becoming quite a fashion in France. It was called *le thé anglais*. In fact, my father had told me, it was now the mode to look English. The Parisian shops were full of cloth from England and long coats with triple capes were being worn with stock hats. The shop windows displayed signs. "English spoken here." Lemonade sellers were now offering *le punch,* which was said to be exactly as drunk in England.

I expressed my surprise to my father for there had never been great friendship between our countries.

"It is not a matter of friendship," said my father. "Most Frenchmen hate the English now as much as they did after Crécy and Agincourt. It is simply a fashion to turn people's minds away from the trials of the country."

In any case Tante Berthe had her tea.

"Just as the English drink it," she said. "You would know, being partly one of them."

I declared it was delicious and she asked how I was getting on and how the baby was.

I answered these questions but very quickly came to the subject of Lisette.

"I rarely hear from her," said Tante Berthe. "She is kept so busy."

"I should love to see her."

That was greeted with silence.

"Does she seem happy?"

"She has a little one now."

"A little one? A baby?"

"Yes. A little boy."

"Oh, I would love to see her. Do tell me how I can get into touch with her. I will ask her to come and visit us."

"I don't think that would be wise, Madame Lottie."

"Not wise? But we were always such friends."

"Oh, she has her life now. It is not the life of the château but she is beginning to grow content."

"Please tell me where I can find her."

"She wouldn't want that."

"I am sure she would want to see me as much as I want to see her."

"It was hard for her to get accustomed to farm life after living as she did. It was above her station. She's settling in now. Leave well alone. She is happy now. You must not remind her of the life she once had."

"It was strange that she should marry a farmer. She always used to say that she would marry into the nobility."

"Real life is different from dreams and it is real life that has to be lived."

I begged once more for knowledge of Lisette's whereabouts but Tante Berthe was adamant and refused to tell me.

"You have your life here; she has hers. She is happy now. Don't try to spoil it and make her discontented again."

"What is the name of her little boy?"

"I don't think you should bother yourself with such matters. It is better not."

"I really cannot see what harm knowing a name can do."

Tante Berthe sat back in her chair, her lips tight. Then she drained her dish of English tea and set it down so emphatically that I knew it was time for me to go.

I went riding with my father. I was gratified to see how he enjoyed being with me. There had been a strong rapport between us from the day of our first meeting but he treated me now with respect as well as affection and was so grateful to me for giving him a grandson.

He talked to me more seriously than he ever did to my mother. She was easily alarmed and I knew that she used to fret every time he was out of her sight. He told me that he was uneasy about the state of the country. Conditions had grown bad during the last reign. There was too much poverty in France; bread was too costly and in some places people were starving. Moreover the last King had lived in the utmost extravagance. "Think what it must have cost to maintain Le Parc aux Cerfs and purely for the purpose of satisfying the King's jaded appetites. Madame du Barry lived in the utmost luxury. The King never stinted himself at all, although he must have seen disaster coming. He hated the mob. That was why he rarely went to Paris and built the road from Versailles to Compiègne to bypass the capital. Such a state of affairs cannot last forever. There comes retribution. It is unjust that this should seem to be approaching now that we have a new King who appears to be ready to listen to reason."

"What are you afraid of?"

"Of the people."

"But surely there are laws to keep order."

"Sometimes such order breaks down. I happen to know that at the Palace of Versailles the King is in long and anxious conferences with his ministers—chiefly Turgot. They both see the dangers and Turgot has set up *ateliers de charité* in Limoges where bread is distributed to the poor."

"It may be that next year there will be a good harvest. Wouldn't that make everything all right?"

"It would help."

"Then let us pray for a good winter."

We rode on and came to the town. That there was something unusual going on was obvious from the moment we came into it. Little knots of people were standing about. They looked at us as we rode past in a way which I thought had a certain hostility in it.

"What's happening?" I asked.

"I don't know," replied my father. "Keep close."

We came into the market square. Someone had set up a platform and a man was standing on it. He was very tall with a lean, cadaverous face somewhat tanned by the weather. He had flashing eyes which were of a vivid shade of blue and his hair was unpowdered and cut short as some peasants wore it; his clothes were ragged and ill fitting yet he wore them with a certain distinction.

He was speaking in a deep voice which could be heard all over the square.

"Citizens," he cried, "will you let them starve us? Will you stand aside and touch your caps when the gentry pass by? Will you say, 'God bless you, my lord. 'Tis right and fitting you should sup from a laden table while I go hungry? This is the law. God put me where I am and you where you are. I am content to starve and see my children starve that you may eat to the full, my lord, and spend good money on fine clothes and drink and women. Oh, yes, my masters, you are you and therefore the land of France belongs to you. We are here to serve you, to grovel for the few sous you throw at us. We are here to eat the filthy stuff you call bread . . . if we can get it . . .' "

My father had turned white and I could see that he was growing very angry. I was very conscious of those sullen people surrounding us. I turned away believing that if I went he would follow me.

"Comrades," the man was saying, "are you going to stand aside? Are you going to let them treat you worse than cattle? Or are you going to stand up and fight for your rights? Stand up and fight, comrades. Fight for your bread. They are taking the grain along the river now. It is for the King's granaries . . . for he must have plenty, must he not? It is only you, my friends, who must starve."

"Come away," I said quickly. "Come with me. I am going now."

I knew it was the only way. I turned my horse and started to move through the crowd. I was relieved that my father was close behind me and that the people moved—albeit sullenly—to let us pass through.

We came to the edge of the town before I turned my head to look at my father.

"That rogue," he said, "is inciting the people. He is trying to raise a riot."

"And by the look of some of them it seems that he might succeed."

"He was no peasant."

"No . . . I don't think he was."

"He's an agitator. There are many about. I should have liked to take him by the scruff of his neck and expose him."

"That was what I was afraid you were going to do so I moved off to prevent you."

"You were wise. They might have killed us. This confirms what has been in my mind for some time."

117

"What is that?"

He looked at me quickly. "Don't tell your mother. It would alarm her. But for some time I have believed that there were subversive forces at work. There are men in the world whose intentions are to overthrow monarchies everywhere and the Church with them. In other words they plan revolution. Where would such men seek to begin their campaign? In the weakest place, of course. France is weak. She has suffered years of inept rule; there has been little justice in the country; the monarchy has been selfishly indulgent; the people have become poorer; some of them are indeed close to starvation. You see, France is offering these men the very ground in which to sow their seeds of revolution."

"And you think that man . . ."

"He is one of many. Very soon . . . perhaps at this moment . . . those men who were listening to him will be roused to fury. God knows what they will do. They will raid the shops . . . steal the goods . . . and they will kill any who try to prevent them."

"How glad I am we escaped."

"Oh, Lottie, I see evil times ahead for France unless we stop this rot. We have a new King; a good minister in Turgot; there will be others. We have a chance if only the people will let us take it."

We rode thoughtfully back to the château.

———

Before the day was out we knew that what we had seen in the town square was the beginning of trouble. Armand came in the late afternoon to tell us that a mob had attacked the boats which were laden with sacks of corn; they had ripped open the sacks and thrown the corn into the river.

My father was furious. "This is surely not the work of hungry men," he said. "I am becoming more and more convinced that this is an attempt at organized revolution."

Armand wanted to go out and attack the rioters but his father restrained him.

"There'll be bloodshed if these people have their way," said the Comte. "The King and his ministers must deal with the matter."

It was easier said than done, for that conflict which was to become *La Guerre des Farines* had started.

Riots broke out in several places simultaneously, which confirmed

118

the fact that they were organized. Shop windows were broken, food stolen, and several people killed.

My mother said I must stay with them until the country was quiet again, but I was very worried as to what might be happening at Tourville, and the thought of Charlot in danger terrified me. I wanted to leave at once but my father would not hear of it.

"The trouble will not be so much in the country as in Paris and Versailles," he said. "I don't think it is going to last long. Turgot and Maurepas will know how to deal with these agitators."

I pictured the young King and Queen, so newly come to the throne, confronted by a mob of screaming people. Mobs were terrifying, mindless usually, beyond reasoning, bent on destruction and spurred on by an all-consuming envy . . . surely the most deadly of the seven deadly sins, for from it were born most of the others.

My father thought he should go to Versailles; my mother begged him not to; and when I heard that the people were marching on the palace waving pieces of moldy bread, ferociously demanding that the price of food be drastically cut and threatening to burn down the palace if it were not, I was glad that he had listened to her.

There was nothing we could do. My father was in a state of gloom. He had seen this coming. He said: "What we must do is better the condition of the poor, that is true, but this is not the way. We have to seek out these people who are inciting honest workmen to revolt against their King and Parliament, against law and order. We have to stop them. We are late. We should have done it earlier. The King understands this, I believe, and is genuinely concerned with the plight of his people. But he had to reap the harvest sown by his grandfather. He is the one to blame. May God grant our young King the wit and strength and the courage to carry us through."

I was not very well versed in politics. It had never occurred to me that we were so close to disaster, but that became clear enough during those days of the little war.

The King was courageous; he faced the mob. Some said that his action at Versailles, when the infuriated mob was at his gate, in sending out the Prince de Beauvais into the courtyard to promise to lower the price of bread saved the palace and ended the war. Had they burned the palace, as they had threatened to do, that would have been the signal for the peasants all over the country to rise against those of their countrymen who were better off than they were—starting with the nobility.

It was a miracle, and discoveries were made which proved my father's theory. Many in the mob were not peasants; they were far from starving; and the bread which they carried with them when examined proved to have been treated with ashes and other substances to make it appear moldy. One so-called starving peasant was wounded and taken to a hospital and found to be a servant in the royal household. Some of the people masquerading as women turned out to be men. As more and more evidence came to light it became obvious that there was organization behind the riots.

When this became startlingly clear the leaders, not wishing to be exposed, slipped away into obscurity, and the rioters, with no one to urge them on, grew tired. Afraid that they might be caught and brought to trial, they dispersed. And quiet reigned throughout the land.

But it was a somewhat uneasy quiet.

The country settled down so quickly that it was decided that the King's coronation should go ahead as planned. This was to take place on the eleventh of June and as both my father and mother were traveling to Rheims for the ceremony, I decided that I would return to Tourville and this I did.

———

It was about a month after I returned to Tourville when I suspected I might be pregnant. I was delighted and so was Charles when this proved to be the case, and although I resented the early discomforts of my state I was happy at the prospect of another child.

It took my mind off recent events. Charles was inclined to ignore them; he certainly did not take the same serious view that my father had done.

"They should have brought out the military and dispersed them," was his comment. "If they did that it would soon put a stop to their nonsense."

I thought of the man whom I had seen preaching in the market square and I did not believe that the military would deter him and his kind. I should have liked to hear more about the people who were trying to bring revolution into France, but, of course, none knew who they were, for the success of their plans depended on their remaining

120

anonymous. My father had said that he suspected people in high places. He even mentioned the name of the Prince de Conti. Why should they want to overthrow a régime into which they were so comfortably settled? My father believed that certain men had grievances against others and the prime factor in this discontent would be envy; and in a country like France, where there were so many injustices and which had groaned for years under heavy taxation while hearing of the excesses of its rulers, that was enough to set the spark to light the fire.

However, as the weeks passed and everything seemed to have returned to normal, I forgot about *La Guerre des Farines,* although now and then the memory of that man in the square would come back to me.

I was in my apartment one day—I remember it well, a hot August day when I was feeling listless and wishing the next few months would pass quickly—when there was a tap on my door.

I called for whoever was there to enter and a maid came in to say that there was a lady downstairs who was asking for me.

"She has come a long way," said the girl. "And she has a child with her. She says she knows that you will see her."

I went down at once and when I saw who was standing in the hall I gave a cry of joy and ran to her.

"Lisette! You have come at last. I have tried so hard to find you. It is wonderful to see you."

"I knew you would say that," she answered, her lovely blue eyes glowing with affection. I had forgotten how pretty she was. Now she was rather soberly dressed, with her fair hair escaping from the pins which held it so that it made little curling tendrils on her forehead and neck, and smiling half whimsically, half tenderly, and I could think of only one thing; my friend Lisette had come back to me.

"I had to come," she said. "I had nowhere to go. I thought you would help me. I couldn't face Tante Berthe."

"I'm glad you came. This is your little boy. I heard you had one."

She laid her hand on the boy's shoulder. He looked older than Charlot. "Louis-Charles," she said, "take madame's hand as you know how."

The boy took my hand and kissed it. I thought he was charming.

"There is so much to tell you," said Lisette.

"I long to hear it," I replied. "How have you traveled? Have you come far? Are you hungry?"

"We came on horseback . . . Louis-Charles riding with me. One of the men from my neighbor's stables brought me here. I have left him in the stables. Perhaps they would give him a bed for the night. He will want to leave in the morning."

"Of course, of course," I said.

"I have so much to tell you . . . but . . . could I wash first?"

"Certainly, and eat too. I will tell them to prepare a room for you and your son."

I called to the servants. Food must be prepared . . . a room and everything for her comfort; and the groom who had come with her must be lodged and fed.

I was delighted to have her back with me and could not wait to hear all her news as soon as she had washed and eaten and the boy was sleeping. I took her into one of the smaller rooms of the château where we could be quite alone while she told me her story.

Hers had not been a happy marriage. She had made a great mistake. When she and Tante Berthe had visited their relative she had been introduced to Farmer Dubois; he had fallen in love with her so completely that she had been quite flattered and in a mad moment had agreed to marry him.

"It was a mistake," she said. "I could not be a farmer's wife. It didn't suit me at all. He adored me . . . but one gets a little tired of such devotion. I even played with the idea of running away. I thought I'd come to you and throw myself on your mercy."

"I wish you had," I said. "Oh, I have missed you so much, Lisette."

"But you are Madame de Tourville now. You have your beautiful château and your devoted husband."

I lifted my shoulders and she studied me intently.

"You are happy?" she asked.

"Oh, yes . . . yes . . . quite happy."

"I am glad. I think the most awful thing a woman can suffer is an unhappy marriage."

"But at least your Monsieur Dubois adored you. Have you left him, Lisette?"

"I am coming to that. He is dead. That is why I got away."

"Dead! Oh, Lisette."

"I know. He was a good man, but I was bored. I wanted to get away ... though I didn't want it to happen that way."

"Which way?"

"Well, I was resigned. I had made my bed, as they say, and I must lie on it. I tried to become a farmer's wife, Lottie. I tried hard but I didn't do it very well. Still, Jacques did not seem to mind and I had my little boy."

"He must have been a great consolation."

"He is indeed. I don't think I should have had the courage to come here if it had not been for him."

"My dear Lisette, why? You know I should always be glad to see you."

"We had so many good times together, didn't we? Remember the fortune teller? That was where you first met your husband. I think he fell in love with you on sight. Poor Sophie, what a tragedy! But it made the way clear for you, didn't it?"

"I don't see it like that. I often think of Sophie."

"She could have married him."

"I don't think she would have been very happy if she had done so. I can only tell myself that it was her choice."

"At least you are happy."

"Yes, with the dearest little boy. . . . And Lisette, I am to have another."

"Lottie! How wonderful. Is your husband pleased?"

"Delighted—and so are my father and mother."

"That is good news. But I have to talk to you, Lottie. I have to talk very seriously ... because I have nowhere to go."

"Nowhere to go! But you are here. You have come back. How can you say you have nowhere to go?"

"Oh, you are good to me. I knew you would be. All the way here I've been telling myself that. But we are destitute ... we have lost everything. It was those dreadful people. I don't suppose here ... in this peaceful place ... you knew much about that dreadful war."

"*La Guerre des Farines,*" I said. "Oh, yes, I know very well how frightening that could be. I heard a man preaching ... inciting the people to revolt. It was horrible."

"Horrible to be their victims . . . to be in the heart of it, Lottie." She covered her face with her hands. "I try to shut it out but you can't shut out memories by shutting your eyes. You see, he was a farmer and he had grain and corn stored in his outhouses. They came. . . . They pillaged the storehouses . . . they dragged out the grain. I shall never forget that terrible night, Lottie. The darkness lighted by torches they carried. The shouting . . . the threats. Jacques ran out to see what they were doing. He tried to stop them. One of them knocked him down. I was at a window with Louis-Charles. I saw him go down and they all fell on him with sticks and rakes and all the implements they had brought with them as weapons. His own workers were doing that . . . and he had always been good to them. He was a good man, Jacques was. I know he bored me and I longed to escape from him . . . but he was a good man. They burned down the barns and all that good corn."

"They are criminals!" I cried. "They are not interested in giving bread to the poor. They have destroyed the corn wherever they could. How can that help a bad harvest? My poor Lisette, what you have suffered!"

"I ran away with Louis-Charles to a neighbor's house, about half a mile away. I stood at one of their windows throughout the night and when dawn came I could still see the smoke rising from what had been my home. So, you see, Lottie, I lost my husband and my home and now I have nothing . . . nothing at all. I was with my neighbor for a few weeks but I could not stay there. Then I thought of you. I thought, I will go to Lottie. I will throw myself on her mercy. I will ask her if she will give me a roof over my head. I could make myself useful with you. I could be a lady's maid. I could do something . . . if only you will let me stay here with my little boy."

There were tears in my eyes as I put my arms round her and held her against me.

"Don't say any more, Lisette. Of course you will stay here. I have tried to find you. Tante Berthe wouldn't help me. But now you are here, there is nothing else to fear. You have come home."

She was so grateful. She said: "I knew you would take me in . . . but there are others. . . . You have a new family here."

"They must welcome you as I do, Lisette."

"You say they must. Can you insist?"

"I could. But it won't be necessary. Charles is very easygoing. He asked about you once or twice. And my parents-in-law are very kind ... kind and quiet. They never interfere. My father-in-law is an invalid and scarcely ever leaves his apartments now. I have a sister-in-law, Amelie, who will shortly be married. I think they will be ready to welcome you."

"And if they are not?"

"Then they will see that they must. Don't worry. It is wonderful that you have come back. We are going to be happy again. There is so much to talk about. It has been a little dull at times."

"What! With such a husband?"

"He is away now and then. And I have missed you. It will be like the old days."

"Except that you have become a wife and I am a widow."

"And we have two dear little boys. I do hope they will be friends."

Lisette and I were in the small chamber which led from the hall when Charles returned to the château. We were talking as we had been doing since her return, almost breathlessly chattering, stopping each other with reminders of something that had happened in the past, questioning each other about our lives since our parting.

Charles stood in the doorway. There were a few seconds of tense silence while he stared at Lisette. She looked at him a little defiantly. Poor Lisette, she is afraid of being turned away, I thought.

I cried: "What do you think has happened? Lisette has come."

Lisette smiled hesitantly: "You don't know me," she said.

"But I do," he replied. "You were at the fortune teller's."

"You remembered that. You rescued us both."

"Terrible things have happened to Lisette," I put in. "Her husband has been killed and her home burned down. It was the mob ... the rioters who took his grain."

"How ... shocking!" said Charles.

He seemed to have recovered from his surprise and, coming into the room sat down and looking at Lisette he said: "How did you get here?"

I answered for her. "On horseback. She came a long way with just one groom lent to her by her neighbors."

Charles nodded. "The mob," he murmured. "The mindless mob. Those who have aroused them have a lot to answer for."

125

"Thank heaven they have quietened down now," I said. I added: "Lisette has a little boy. He is charming. Such beautiful manners. I am sure Charlot will be pleased when he meets him."

Charles repeated: "A little boy . . ."

"He was worn out by the journey," I said. "He is fast asleep now."

Charles talked with us for a while, then he said: "I will leave you two to continue. You will have much to tell each other. I will see you later." He laid his hand on my arm and pressed it and bowed to Lisette.

When we were alone Lisette burst out: "I don't think he will want me to stay here."

"Whyever not?"

"He was remembering that I was the housekeeper's niece."

"Charles wouldn't care about that."

She was earnest for a moment and looked angry; her mouth looked square as though she could not control it. "Oh, yes," she said quietly. "They care very much."

"No, Lisette, you are mistaken. I never thought of it for a moment. Nor did Sophie . . . in the old days."

She was smiling now, all bitterness gone. "I always knew I had a good friend in you, Lottie," she said.

We went on talking, but she was changed, wary. Charles's coming had alarmed her. I thought she was exhausted and should retire early so I took her to her room just as I would an honored guest. I wanted to make her happy, make her forget all she had gone through. I wanted to see her merry as she had been in the old days.

I kissed her tenderly when I said good night.

"Dear Lisette," I said. "I want you to understand that you have come home." Then I went to the small bed which had been put up temporarily in her room and in which her son was sleeping.

I gazed at him and said: "I am longing to see Charlot's face when he meets Louis-Charles. That is for tomorrow."

Then I went to the room I shared with Charles.

He was already there and in a thoughtful mood. He was seated in an armchair and as I entered he said: "Lottie, come here."

I went to him and he seized me and pulled me down until I was sitting across his knees.

"So," he said, "your partner in crime has turned up it seems."

126

"Crime?" I cried. "What crime?"

"The crime of naughty little girls who disobey orders and sneak out of their homes away from their guardians to visit evil procuresses."

"Haven't you forgotten that?"

"Forgotten the first moment I saw my love?"

"Charles," I said. "I believe you are annoyed."

"About what?"

"Lisette's being here."

He shrugged his shoulders. "What will she do? Will you give her some post? I think she would make a good lady's maid. She would know the latest fashions and if not where to discover them."

"I don't want her to feel like a servant here, Charles."

"She is the niece of one."

"A very superior one. I don't think Tante Berthe would relish being called a servant."

"Well, isn't she the *femme de charge* at Aubigné?"

"Yes, but she is in a very special position. She is Queen of the Nether Regions and there is strict protocol, I do assure you. People almost have to make appointments to see her. I think that Lisette was always conscious of being not one of us . . . like Sophie and myself, I mean . . . while at the same time she was educated with us."

"That was a mistake. Education gives people ideas."

I laughed at him. "That is surely what it is meant to do."

He was silent and I put my arms round his neck. "Tell me what is on your mind," I said.

"I wonder," he replied. "I think she might be a bit of a schemer."

"A schemer! What do you mean?"

"She seems to have bewitched you."

"Charles, that's nonsense. She is my friend. She has been through a terrible ordeal. She has seen her husband murdered before her own eyes."

"Don't get excited," he said. "Of course she will have to stay here until something is found for her."

"Found for her? What do you mean?"

"Some post perhaps . . . someone's lady's maid, as you don't want her in that capacity yourself."

"Why don't you like her?"

"I neither like nor dislike her."

127

"You talk as though you don't want her here."

"My dear Lottie, we are not a hostel for waifs and strays."

"Have you some reason for disliking her?"

He drew away from me. "Why should I?" he said sharply.

"You seem so . . . hostile."

"My dear Lottie, it matters not to me. I shall not have to see her, shall I? Do you propose to treat her like an honored guest?"

"Charles, are you telling me that you don't want her in your house? Because if you don't . . ."

"You will take off with her. I know. You will go back to Aubigné . . . the two of you adventuring together. Lottie, my lovely Lottie, mother of my son and the one who will be with us ere long, I want you to be happy. I want to show you in every way that I love you. Whatever I was before I met you, whatever I am now . . . Lottie, I am yours."

"What a charming speech!" I kissed him lightly. "What on earth provoked it?"

"You, my beautiful and fruitful wife. You satisfy me completely."

"You are indeed a devoted husband tonight. And what has all this to do with Lisette?"

"It is quite apart. But what I was trying to say about her was this: Is it wise to have her here?"

"I can't see why not, and I want her to feel happy here. I am going to insist that she stays and is made welcome by everybody in this house."

He drew me towards him and kissed my neck.

"So be it," he said. "Madame has spoken."

———

I could not sleep that night. Nor, I was sure, could Charles. He was very tender and more than once assured me that he loved me. I think he was trying to make up for his rather cold reception of Lisette, of whom he knew I was very fond. We lay side by side, hands entwined, but silent.

When I awoke he was gone. It was quite early and my first thought was for Lisette. I was happy that she had come back, although in such sad circumstances, and I was flattered that in her need she had thought of me first. Then I wondered about the groom who had come with her and it occurred to me that he might like to stay for a day before undertaking the long journey back.

As soon as I was dressed I went down to the stables. As I approached I saw a man just about to go in. I saw the back of him only but it was enough to show me that he was not one of our men.

I called out: "Just a moment . . ."

He disappeared into the stables and had apparently not heard me. I guessed he was Lisette's groom and about to saddle his horse and be off. I wanted him to be given some food to take with him and was going to suggest he go to the kitchens to get it.

I glanced inside the stables but I could not see him anywhere, and just at that moment I heard someone walking across the yard. It was the chief groom, Leroux. I went to meet him.

"Good morning, Leroux," I said. "Did you look after the groom who escorted the lady who came yesterday?"

"Oh, yes, madame," was the answer. "He had a good bed for the night and his supper."

"I believe he plans to go today. I saw him go into the stables but when I looked in I couldn't see him. I thought he might like something to take with him to eat on the journey . . . some meat pie or something. And also perhaps he would like to rest here a day before starting out. He has a long way to go."

"He seemed set on going early, madame."

"I daresay he has his reasons. But I do think we ought to give him some food to take with him. He must be somewhere in the stables. I saw him go in."

"I'll find him, madame, and tell him what you say."

Just at that moment we heard the clatter of hoofs and a rider came out of the stables.

"Ho there!" called Leroux.

But the rider took no notice and went on.

"He didn't see us," said Leroux.

"He didn't appear to hear you call to him either."

"Hard of hearing perhaps, madame."

"He certainly behaved rather oddly."

"Well, he's on his way now, madame. Too late to stop him and offer him anything."

"I'm surprised he didn't see us here and make some acknowledgment."

Leroux scratched his head and walked into the stables. I went straight up to Lisette's rooms. She was still in bed, looking very pretty with her fair curls tousled and the sleep in her eyes.

"You were very tired," I said.

"Exhausted," she answered. "Oh, I can't tell you how good it is to be here . . . in a place like this . . . with you."

"You have had a terrible time."

"Poor Jacques! I can't forget the sight of him . . . falling down with all those dreadful people attacking him. And yet . . . I might still be there. . . ."

"You've got to forget that," I said. "It will do you no good to go on remembering. By the way, that's rather an odd groom you brought with you. I spoke to him and he didn't answer. Is he deaf?"

She hesitated for a moment and then said: "Yes . . . I think he is, but he won't admit it."

"I called to him and he didn't answer. I was sure he went into the stables and when I looked in I couldn't see him."

"Did you go right in?"

"Oh, no."

"I expect he was bending down examining his horse's shoe or something. He thinks a lot of his horses. And he has gone, has he?"

"Yes. He didn't look round when he came out of the stables. Leroux called to him but he just rode straight on."

"He was in a hurry to get back. They wanted him to return as soon as possible. It was good of them to let him come with me when they couldn't really spare him."

I was thinking of the man and something suddenly struck me.

"Do you know," I said, "I think I've seen him somewhere before."

"Where could you have seen him?"

"I don't know. It's just a hazy sort of idea."

"We all have doubles somewhere on earth, they say. I'd love to meet mine, wouldn't you?"

She was laughing, looking so much like the girl I had known and been fond of.

I said with heartfelt fervor: "Oh, Lisette, I am so glad you have come here."

It was a great joy to have Lisette with me. She changed my days. She herself dispersed any awkwardness which might have arisen through her presence in the house by installing herself as my lady's maid.

"A lady in your position should certainly have one," she said, "and who could perform those necessary tasks better than I."

She herself refused to take meals with us, which was what I had wanted, although I had guessed there might be protests from Charles about this. I knew that he did not greatly like the idea of Lisette's being treated as a member of the family, which was what I really wanted; I knew, too, that Lisette was very conscious of her position as she always had been at Aubigné and that it had rankled with her that she was not on the same footing as Sophie and I had been. I wanted to treat her as one of us, but she would not have it.

She and Louis-Charles had their meals in a small room adjoining her apartment and she would go to the kitchens and take the food up with her so that none of the servants waited on her.

I said this was a lot of nonsense at first, but I did realize that even in an easygoing household like that of the Tourvilles there would have been resentments and attitudes perhaps among some of the higher servants.

Lisette was tactful; she was reserved with members of the family and it was only when she and I were alone together that she became her old vivacious self.

It was an ideal arrangement for Louis-Charles, who had no inhibitions such as those which plagued his mother, and he shared Charlot's nursery, being an excellent companion for him, and the two boys played and fought happily together.

There was no objection from my parents-in-law. Charles's father spent most of his time in his apartments and his mother was with him a good deal; she had always been very affable to me, and although they seemed rather colorless, I was grateful to be left to my own devices and to be given a free hand in the household. Amelie was immediately attracted to Lisette, who did her hair for her in such a manner as delighted her, and they spent a great deal of time discussing the trousseau together. With Amelie's coming wedding the main concern of the household, Lisette's arrival passed off without too much attention being called to it and Lisette settled in comfortably and easily. I told her she looked like a pretty kitten when she lay in her bed stretching herself in a rather feline way which was a habit of hers.

"Purring away now that I have a comfortable home and am sure of my dish of cream every day," she said laughing at me.

She changed my life completely. The tedious days of pregnancy had become full of laughter. We talked of the past most of the time and the only occasions when I was sad were when I remembered Sophie.

There was a great deal of talk at that time about the American colonists who were in conflict with the English government over taxes which were, some said, being unfairly imposed. Charles said it was clear that there would soon be war between England and her colonists if the English did not come to their senses.

He took a delight in denigrating the English, which I knew was partly in fun, but I refused to take part in these discussions. In any case my thoughts were with my child who would soon be making an appearance.

The winter was passing and we were in February when my confinement began.

Lisette was constantly with me. She had no particular flair for nursing but her high spirits did me more good than anything.

And in due course my child was born. I was delighted this time to have a girl and Charles was overjoyed. We discussed her name and finally decided that she should be called Claudine.

Griselda

I was so absorbed with my baby that I did not take much interest in what was happening in the outside world. My great pleasure was in the nursery where the new baby was received with awe by Charlot and Louis-Charles. Claudine was a noisy baby with a good pair of lungs and from the first seemed to know what she wanted.

"She's different from Monsieur Charlot," said the nurse. "A will of her own, that one."

She had been born rather an ugly baby but grew more beautiful every day. She had dark fluffy hair, quite a lot of it for one so young, and eyes that were of a vivid blue.

We all adored her and when she cried it was a charming sight to see Charlot at the side of her cradle murmuring: "Hush! Hush! Charlot is here."

I was very happy with my children.

Charles talked of little else but the trouble between England and the colonists. At first I thought he was so strongly on the side of the colonists to tease me by jeering at the English. He often reminded me, rather ruefully, that I was more English than French; and this was true, for although no one could be more French than my father—and even Jean-Louis, by a strange coincidence, had been half French, having been brought up in England by my English mother, I was decidedly of that nature in my outlook, my manners—in fact in everything. Even though I now spoke fluent French and often thought in that language, Charles liked to remind me of what he called my Englishness and whenever there was a disagreement between us, he would say: "There is the Englishwoman."

Whether he really did have the Frenchman's natural antipathy to the English I was not sure, or whether it was done in a bantering way, but it continued and the war provided more verbal ammunition to hurl at me.

Without knowing very much about the situation I defended the English, which delighted him and gave him a chance to prove me wrong again and again.

"I tell you," he said on one occasion, "this could mean war between England and France."

"Surely the French would not act so out of character as to go to war for someone else's benefit?"

"It is the cause of liberty, my dear."

"There are troubles enough here in France," I said. "Why do you worry about colonists from another country far from here when your own peasants are verging on revolt and would perhaps like to see a little of that fair treatment you are talking about?"

"You talk like a rebel," said Charles.

"You talk like a fool. As if France would go to war about this matter which is the concern of another country."

"There is strong feeling here."

"For the sole purpose of embarrassing the English."

"They got themselves into this embarrassing situation. We did nothing to bring it about."

"But you seek to exploit it."

And so we went on.

About the time when Claudine was five months old there was a Declaration of Independence in America and Charles was jubilant.

"These brave people are fighting a big nation for their freedom. *Mon Dieu,* I should like to join them. Do you know there is talk of sending an army from France?"

It occurred to me then that Charles might be finding life at Tourville a little dull. He was not really meant to manage a large estate, and because I had seen something of the manner in which such places were run—there was my father for one at Aubigné and I had lived on our estates of Clavering and Eversleigh—I did realize that Charles lacked the real aptitude. There was a manager, of course, but managers, however good, did not compensate for the indifference of their owners.

I listened half-heartedly to the talk about the American War of Independence and the part France was going to play in it, but I was really absorbed by the children. Then Lisette and I spent hours talking and riding together and sometimes walking. It was always fun to be with Lisette.

In December Charles went to Paris and stayed there for several weeks. When he came back his enthusiasm for the war was at fever pitch. He had met three deputies from America—Benjamin Franklin, Silas Deane, and Arthur Lee. Everyone was talking about them, he said, and in spite of their extraordinary appearance they had been invited everywhere as the French were so eager to hear about their fight for independence.

"Their manners were so simple," he said, "and they wore their hair unpowdered and the plainest cloth suits I ever saw in my life. But Paris is in a frenzy over them. People are demanding that we go to war against the English at once."

He had been in the company of the Marquis de Lafayette earlier in the year and had been most impressed when the Marquis bought a vessel and loaded it with ammunition and after certain troubles set sail from America.

Feeling in the country was high against England but the King was adamant that France should not become involved in a war.

That was the state of affairs when a messenger arrived from Aubigné.

My mother had news from Eversleigh that my grandmother was very ill and was longing to see us. Sabrina had written that if we could possibly make the journey Clarissa would be so happy and if we did not come soon we might not have an opportunity of seeing her.

Sabrina was clearly distressed, for she and my grandmother had been close all their lives.

"Moreover," she continued, Dickon has never recovered from his wife's death. It has been a great sadness to us all. Poor Dickon. Fortunately he is very busy and spends most of his time in London, so he has plenty to occupy him which stops him brooding on his loss. . . ."

I wondered what he was like now. What would he do? Look round for a new heiress, I thought cynically. It was of no interest to me now. I was a wife and a mother.

My mother had also written. "My dear, I know it is asking a good deal to expect you to leave your home but we should not stay long . . . just long enough to see your grandmother. As Sabrina says, there might not be another chance. I shall go in any case and it would be wonderful if you came with us. Your grandmother asks particularly for you."

When I showed Charles the letter he said that of course I must go.

Lisette thought it would be interesting for me to see my old home. She longed to come with me but that was, of course, out of the question.

"Don't stay long," she implored me. "I can't imagine this place without you."

Charles's parting shot was: "See if you can persuade them over there to come to their senses. They're in for a humiliating defeat if they don't. Wait till France gets busy across the Atlantic."

"I am not going on a political mission but to see a sick grandmother," I reminded him.

"Then make sure you don't stay too long," he said. "This place is quite dull without you."

——

My feelings were very mixed as my mother and I made the journey to the coast accompanied by my father, who saw us onto the pacquet boat before leaving us. It had been sad to say good-bye to the children, to Charles and Lisette, but I was anxious about my grandmother and I could not suppress a certain excitement at the prospect of seeing Eversleigh again. I think my mother felt the same, though she was very subdued.

We had a reasonably good crossing and arrived at Dover in the afternoon so that it was evening before we reached Eversleigh.

There was the old house as I remembered it—not so imposing perhaps as the Château d'Aubigné, but grand in its own manner.

Sabrina rushed out when she heard our arrival. She embraced us fervently. "It is wonderful to see you!" she cried. "I am so delighted that you have come."

"How is my mother?" asked my mother.

"Weak . . . but so excited at the prospect of seeing you. I am sure it will do her the world of good. Oh, here's Dickon."

And there he was—Dickon, who had been so much in my thoughts for so long. He was just as I remembered him—"larger than life" as someone had once said of him; and as good looking as he ever had been. A wig covered those hyacinthine locks, which was a pity, but his eyes were even more startlingly blue than I remembered.

"Zipporah!" he cried, first to my mother. He embraced her and I noticed that she tried to hold aloof, but he appeared not to notice that and hugged her affectionately.

And then he was looking at me. He said my name softly. "Lottie . . . Lottie . . . grown-up Lottie."

I held out my hand to him but he ignored the gesture and lifted me up in his arms, laughing up at me.

"How exciting . . . Lottie is here."

Sabrina was looking at him with that mingling of admiration, tenderness, and adoration which I remembered so well. I saw my mother's lips tighten, and I thought: *Nothing has changed.*

As for myself, I had been waiting for this moment ever since I knew I was coming here.

"They must be worn out," said Sabrina. "Did you have a good journey? Your rooms are ready . . . your old rooms. I thought you would like that. But would you like to see Clarissa first?"

"Of course," said my mother. "Let's go to her at once."

Sabrina led the way up the staircase which I remembered so well.

Dickon was close to me. He put an arm around me. "Lottie," he said, "what fun that you are here."

I said coolly: "I hope my grandmother is not seriously ill."

"She is getting on in years now," said Sabrina, "and she has grown weaker these last months. That is why I thought you should come."

"You should have come before," said Dickon.

Sabrina smiled. "Of course they should. In fact we were all very put out that you went abroad."

"At least that left you Eversleigh," I said, looking at Dickon. I was telling myself: *It is different now. I know so much about you. I know you chose this place instead of me.*

I must remember that, for in these first moments I was beginning to be too much aware of the potent charm of Dickon and was filled with misgiving.

We went to my grandmother's room. She was sitting up in bed looking frail but pretty in a lacey pink bedjacket.

"Zipporah!" she cried and my mother ran to her. "And Lottie! Oh, my dears . . . how wonderful to see you. It has seemed so long. . . ."

We embraced and she made us sit on either side of the bed. "Tell me all your news," she said. "Tell me about dear little Charlot and Claudine. Oh, Lottie, it is so odd to think of you as a mother. You seem only a child yourself."

"Time passes. I am no longer a child, Grandmother."

"Dear Lottie, as lovely as ever. She is, is she not, Sabrina? Dickon?"

Sabrina nodded and Dickon said: "She's lovelier. She's Lottie-grown-up, Lottie the woman. She's even more lovely than Lottie the child."

Sabrina and my grandmother looked at him and smiled in the way I remembered so well. My mother's face had hardened and the years seemed to drop away and we were back in those days when there was conflict because Dickon wanted to marry me.

"You are a father now, Dickon," she said.

"Oh, the terrible twins," put in Sabrina indulgently. "They were

137

rather cross because they weren't allowed to sit up. You'll see them in the morning."

"They must be about eight years old now," said my mother.

"So you remember," commented my grandmother indulgently.

"You'll have a lot of time to talk," said Sabrina smiling at my grandmother. "I'm going to take them to their rooms now. You'll want to wash and have something to eat, I daresay. You'll see them again very soon, Clarissa."

My grandmother nodded and smiled contentedly while Sabrina took charge of us and led us to our rooms.

What memories came back to me in that room! And I am sure my mother felt the same in hers. She had not always been happy here and she was obviously remembering a great deal that was disturbing. We were both going to find our stay here rather upsetting. A brief glimpse of Dickon had made that certain. He had lost none of his charm and I was as conscious of him as I had ever been. I warned myself I would have to be wary.

I washed and changed and went down with my mother to a meal.

"Are you feeling all right?" I asked her.

She turned to give me a searching look. "I'm a little emotional, I'm afraid. It's coming back here. I remember so much about the place. Uncle Carl . . . and then Jean-Louis and I here together."

"Grandmother, Sabrina, and Dickon were not here then."

"No, they came when we left."

"I daresay there will be lots of differences."

"Oh, I daresay. Your grandmother does not seem as bad as I feared she might be. That's a relief. I don't think we should stay very long, do you, Lottie? I mean . . . you'll be wanting to get home . . . and your father made me promise not to stay too long."

"We have only just come," I reminded her.

But even as early as that I was telling myself that I should never have agreed to come, for Dickon was determined to take up our relationship where it had been broken off, which was characteristic of his attitude to life. I really do believe that he saw himself as the very center of existence with everything revolving round him and everyone there for his convenience. Others might be obliged to take care what they did; the same did not apply to him. If he wanted to act without

138

honor he would do so; I am sure he believed so charmingly that every-one would forgive him.

No, I told myself. Not everyone. I shall never forget that he chose Eversleigh and let me go.

As we sat at table that night he singled me out for his attention.

"Do you ride much in France, Lottie?" he asked.

"A great deal," I replied.

"Good. We'll go out tomorrow. I have just the horse for you."

Sabrina smiled. "It will do you good, Lottie. And you'll be safe with Dickon."

I wanted to burst out laughing. I should be safer even alone than with Dickon.

My mother was talking about Claudine and what an enchanting child she was. "She has a bit of a temper, the nurse tells me. Oh, I do wish I could see my grandchildren more. Little Charlot is quite a charmer."

"What would you expect of Lottie's son?" asked Dickon.

"I am wondering," I retorted, "what I am to expect of yours."

"Strange to think of us as parents, eh, Lottie?" said Dickon.

"Why? We are no longer young."

"That's nonsense," he said. "I feel young. You look young. There-fore we are young. Is that not so, dear Mother?"

"Dickon is right," said Sabrina. *Indeed,* I thought, *when in your eyes has he ever been anything else?*

My mother asked questions about the neighborhood. "What of that old house. Enderby?"

"It's empty now," Sabrina told her. "The Forsters left after the fire. They wanted to get away ... understandably. Another family came but they didn't stay long. Nobody does at Enderby. Dickon was a hero in that fire."

"My mother always sees the best of me," said Dickon.

"Yes," put in my mother coolly, "she does indeed."

"Well, isn't that the way a mother should see her offspring?" asked Dickon. "Don't you look at dear Lottie through rose-colored glasses?"

"I don't need to," retorted my mother. "Lottie pleases me very much in her natural state."

"Zipporah has indeed become the gracious lady," observed Dickon.

139

"Madame la Comtesse—no less. You must live very magnificently in your château."

"It is very pleasant," admitted my mother.

"You look younger than you did before you left England. Oh, but then, of course, you had such anxieties."

My mother did not reply. She went on quietly eating her food; but I knew she was annoyed with him and that he was deliberately stirring up memories which she would rather forget. For all that, she was determined not to let him see this, but I, who knew her so well, realized that she was feeling far from calm.

I was glad when the meal was over and we could retire. My mother said she would go straight to her room for the journey had been very exhausting indeed.

We called in on my grandmother and chatted for about a quarter of an hour and then went to our rooms.

I had not been in mine very long when there was a tap on my door. I felt my heart start to race. I thought: *No. Even he would not dare.*

A voice said: "May I come in?"

Relief flooded over me for it was Sabrina.

"Oh, Lottie," she said, "I do hope you are comfortable. I am so glad you came with your mother. Your grandmother is so delighted. She has talked of nothing else since she knew you were coming. We are all so pleased."

I said: "I am looking forward to meeting Dickon's sons."

"You'll love them. They are such rascals. Dickon says Jonathan takes after him so you have gathered that Jonathan is the more lively of the two."

"It must be great fun to have twins."

"Yes . . . and very fortunate in view of what happened. I think he still grieves for Isabel. It was so sad. It was what they wanted more than anything else—a son."

"I have heard that she was not very strong."

"She had several disappointments before. Then she succeeded and brought them into the world and ironically their coming cost her life."

"It is very sad. I gather it was a happy marriage."

"Oh, very. They were so well suited. So different too. She was so quiet. She adored him."

"So there was yet another to worship at his feet."

"Your mother always laughed at our fondness for him. You're not surprised, are you? There is something very special about Dickon. I believe you thought that once."

She was looking at me speculatively and I flushed.

"A sort of child's hero worship," I murmured.

"Dickon was quite upset when you went to France."

"I thought he was very happy to get Eversleigh. He wouldn't have had it if my mother hadn't married and gone away. That must have made up for everything else."

"Of course he loves Eversleigh and he manages it perfectly. Poor Jean-Louis was not up to it. Well, it worked out very well."

"Do you often go to Clavering?"

"Hardly ever. Dickon put in a very good manager and he himself is here most of the time when he is not in London."

"Oh, I remember you wrote and said he had his fingers in a lot of pies."

"Dickon is not the sort to shut himself away in the country. He is in London a good deal, as a matter of fact. He has friends there . . . in influential places. Isabel's father was a wealthy banker as you probably know."

"I did hear that he had married a great heiress."

"Yes. When her father died she inherited everything. So with banking interests in London and friends at Court Dickon leads a very busy life. But he was determined to be at Eversleigh when you came."

She stood up and regarded me intently. She took it for granted that I joined in this adulation for Dickon. After all, before I left England I had been as loud in my praises of him as anyone.

"You have fulfilled your early promise, Lottie. You really are beautiful."

"Thank you," I said.

"I am sure Carlotta must have been very like you. There is a portrait of her in the house. You will see for yourself that the likeness is remarkable. Oh, well, my dear, it is wonderful to see you here. I hope you are not going to run away too soon." She kissed me. "I'll say good night. Sleep well."

When she had gone I sat on the bed and thought of Dickon's marrying Isabel, the banker's daughter and heiress. He had done that soon after I had left for France. I thought cynically: *He did well out of his women.* Because of me . . . Eversleigh. And his wife Isabel had brought him a fortune as well as an interesting life in London. Court circles no less! One could trust Dickon to get the best out of life.

I could not stop thinking of him. I tried to analyze my feelings and I came to the conclusion that in many ways I felt unsafe.

I turned the key in the lock. Only thus could I feel secure.

———

During the next few days I spent a great deal of time in Dickon's company. It was impossible to avoid him. Wherever I decided to go he would be there. He regarded me with that slightly sardonic look as though to say: *It is no use trying to escape. You know you never could escape from me.*

I reminded myself a hundred times a day that he was an adventurer, that nobody was of any great account to him except himself. He was proud of his boys. I found them interesting, for they were so much alike in appearance and had an undoubted look of Dickon. They were different in character, though. David was quiet and studious; Jonathan noisy and excelling at outdoor sports. They were not close to each other as some twins are. In fact they seemed to be highly critical of each other. Jonathan was very quick to resort to fisticuffs, but David was the master of the cutting remark. There seemed to be a rivalry between them which their tutor tried hard to eradicate. Mr. Raines was a man in his early forties with a rather forbidding manner which I thought was exactly what the boys needed. They were both in awe of Dickon, clearly admired him and sought his favor. Dickon himself had little time for them and had never been inclined to pretend what he did not feel. He had two sons which pleased him. They were the heirs and necessary to propagate the line; he had employed a tutor who could deal adequately with their education until it was time to send them away to school; there his interest ended.

We spent a great deal of time with my grandmother. After all, that was the reason why we had come and our arrival had done a lot for her. She talked with my mother over old times and the happy life she and Sabrina had had together bringing up Dickon.

There was no escaping Dickon in that house. My grandmother and Sabrina talked of him constantly and whenever I was alone he contrived to find me. When I went riding he would be beside me. I knew

142

what his purpose was and I guessed it would be the same with any personable young woman. Dickon knew exactly what he wanted and he expected everyone to fall in with his wishes.

Apart from ambitions he had been strongly attracted by me and I wondered whether he had been to Isabel; and being Dickon he presumed that he was irresistible and it would only be a matter of time before he overcame my scruples and we indulged in a love affair.

I was aware of this and so was my mother; no doubt she had memories about her first meeting with my father, which had taken place near Enderby. I was determined not to be a partner in Dickon's search for temporary satisfaction. Sabrina and my grandmother believed, of course, that he was merely playing the host in his charming gracious way but to me, from our first day, his intentions were clear.

After spending most of the morning with my grandmother I went down to the stables in the early afternoon and asked one of the grooms to saddle a horse for me, which he did. I was looking forward to a nostalgic afternoon, visiting the places I remembered from all those years, and I would remind myself of what a happy life I had found in France. I loved Charles—with reservations, it was true. I saw his faults. I did not believe that he was always faithful to me; I had, in some measure, accepted the marital conventions of my new country and I realized that the basis of a happy marriage, to the French, meant one in which a woman did not probe too deeply into her husband's extramarital relationships. Some women might have said that what was in order for men might be for women too and I knew carried their beliefs into practice. But I did see that there was some point in inflicting a more rigid code on women for the simple reason that romantic interludes could result in children.

Lisette and I had discussed the matter frequently. She said it was unfair. There should be one law and one only and that should apply to both men and women. If a child was the result the man who had fathered it should be named since the woman had no alternative but to be recognized as the mother. But no. It was not like that. How many men had their clandestine relationships resulting in difficulties for the partner in them and escaped the shame, humiliation, and practical difficulties of having a child born out of wedlock?

Lisette could argue fiercely about the matter. I always enjoyed these discussions and we usually made a habit of taking opposite sides so that we could get the most out of the discussion.

Now I thought of Lisette and considered how amused she would be to see Dickon pursuing me.

I could almost hear myself talking to Lisette. Yes, I would say, he does attract me. He always did . . . I think more than anyone I ever knew. More than Charles? Well, Charles did too. There is a similarity about them. They both have that swaggering attitude to life and see themselves as the all-conquering male, and the strange thing is that while I resent it strongly, I am attracted by it. I am determined to resist submission and yet at the same time I enjoy being conquered.

It was a pity Lisette had not come with us. She would force me to be absolutely frank about my feeling for Dickon.

Right from the first I was exhilarated. It was a battle between us from which both he and I were determined to come out victorious. He saw himself as the irresistible seducer; I, as the woman, if tempted was not going to sink her pride so deeply that she forgot her marriage vows and the fact that this man had jilted her in favor of a great property.

On that afternoon I had not gone very far when I heard the sound of horse's hooves and, looking over my shoulder, was not at all surprised to see Dickon.

"Riding alone?" he said. "That won't do."

"I was finding it very pleasant."

"But so much more so with an interesting and charming companion who knows the countryside well."

"Your assessment of your character is your own, of course, and the countryside is not altogether unfamiliar to me. Remember, I lived here once."

"Don't remind me, Lottie. My life took the wrong turning when you went away."

"The wrong one? To Eversleigh, to the bank is it? . . . the life at Court, the fingers in pies. Oh, Dickon, how can you be so ungrateful to the fate which brought you all these good things!"

"I am not ungrateful. I am just telling you that the very thing which would have made my happiness complete was denied me."

"You look contented with life, Dickon. I would forget the extra flavoring and thank God for your good fortune."

"I missed you, Lottie."

"One does miss people sometimes when they go away."

"You went to France for a holiday and stayed there."

"And you came to Eversleigh. It was yours . . . the dream of your life . . . or the chief one at that time . . . come true. What more could you ask?"

"You, Lottie, with it."

"But there was a choice, wasn't there? One or the other."

"You were a child. I didn't know then . . ."

"It is strange to hear you admit ignorance. Shall we talk of something more interesting?"

"This is of the utmost interest to me."

"But not to me and it takes two to make a conversation. Tell me about affairs in London. There is a great deal of talk in France about the American colonies."

"Talk!" he said. "There is more than talk. The wretched French are helping the rebels."

"I believe some people even over here think they are right."

"There is no reason why foreigners should interfere."

"My husband is a staunch supporter of the colonists and thinks those in France who are seeking to help them are doing what is right."

"And you can live with such a traitor?"

"Traitor? He is no traitor. He is a man of opinions."

"Are you in love with him?"

I hesitated for a moment and then replied almost defiantly: "Yes."

"A convincing negative," he said. "Lottie, don't go back. Stay here."

"You must be mad. I have two children over there."

"We could send for them."

"You're joking, of course. You have a most extraordinarily high opinion of yourself. I suppose that comes of living your life with two adoring females."

"I think I see myself as I am."

I laughed. "Tall, handsome, commanding, irresistible to all women, chivalrous—in conversation—honorable, never betraying anyone unless the price is high enough. . . ."

"You are hard on me."

"I see you as you are."

"And if you were honest with yourself you would admit you like what you see."

I pressed my horse to a gallop, for at that moment we had come into open country.

He was beside me and I enjoyed the sheer exhilaration of the ride.

We came back past Enderby. It looked gloomy now. I remembered it as it had been when the Forsters had been there. They had cut away the shrubs which grew in profusion round the house; now they were overgrown again. I could see why it had a reputation for being haunted.

"Would you like to look round it?" asked Dickon. "We can get in easily through one of the ground floor windows. It has a broken latch. The place is very overrun. It has been empty for two years."

I wanted to go inside and yet on the other hand I was aware of warning within me. No, I must not go into that house. My mother had gone there with my father. Very possibly I had been conceived in that house. There was something about it which was apparent even from the outside. My mother, when she had told me about my birth, had felt that there was some spirit there . . . something which had the power to change people who entered.

Fanciful thinking, perhaps, but I would not go into that house with Dickon.

"Not now," I said. "It's getting too late."

And turning our horses away we rode back to Eversleigh.

A groom was coming round by the house as we approached, and Dickon called to him to take our horses to the stables. Dickon leaped down before I could to help me. He took me in his arms and lifted me up as he had when I arrived. A gesture, I think, which was meant to be symbolic. He was strong. I was at his mercy.

"Thank you," I said coolly. "Put me down."

But for a few moments he held me, and I did not want to meet his eyes. I saw someone at a window looking down at us. Even as I looked up, whoever it was stepped back.

As Dickon put me on the ground I said: "Who is up there?"

"Where?" he asked idly.

"That window . . . right at the top." I nodded in the direction and he looked up.

"That would be old Grissel's place."

"Old Grissel?"

"One of the servants. Griselda. The boys call her Grissel. It fits."

I went into the house, my thoughts full of Dickon and his implications so that I forgot about old Grissel until later.

———

I wanted to get to know something about Dickon's sons and one morning, when I knew it was time for their break from lessons, I went up to the schoolroom.

The boys were seated at a table with Mr. Raine, their tutor, drinking glasses of milk.

"I hope I'm not intruding on lessons," I said.

"Come in," called Jonathan.

Mr. Raine assured me that this was the morning break and that the boys would not resume lessons for another fifteen minutes.

"Then may I sit down and talk. I want to get to know you."

Jonathan grinned at me; David looked interested.

"I have a boy of my own in France," I said. "He must be about three years younger than you."

"Three years!" said Jonathan with a look of contempt.

"You were three years younger once," David reminded him.

"That was a long time ago."

"Three years to be precise," said Mr. Raine. "Now, boys, stop arguing and be civil to Madame de Tourville."

"You're French," said Jonathan, who clearly said the first thing that came into his mind.

"She knows that and doesn't want you to tell her," added David, who seemed to have an irresistible urge to irritate his brother at every turn.

"I am French," I explained, "because my father and my husband are. But I used to live here for a while before I went to France."

"That was years ago."

"Before you were born."

They looked at me in wonder.

"They are still too young to grasp the fact that there was a world here before they joined it," said Mr. Raine.

"I also have a little girl. She is very young ... little more than a baby."

They dismissed her as of no interest.

147

"What is your boy's name?" asked Jonathan.

"Charles. We call him Charlot."

"That's a funny name," commented Jonathan.

"It's French, silly," said David. "Why didn't you bring them with you?"

"We had to come quickly and my daughter is too young to travel."

"Charlot could have come."

"Yes, I suppose he could."

"I wish he had," said Jonathan. "I'd have shown him my falcon. I'm teaching him. Jem Logger is showing me."

"Jonathan spends a great deal of time in the stables with his dogs and horses," said Mr. Raine. "And now we have a falcon. He is, I am afraid, far more interested in them than he is in literature and mathematics."

David smirked and Jonathan shrugged his shoulders.

"Does Charlot have a tutor?" asked David.

"Not yet. He only has a nursery governess at the moment."

"Like Grissel?" asked David, and the boys looked at each other and laughed.

"Grissel?" I said. "Now, I believe I saw her."

"She doesn't come out much."

"But she is your nurse."

Jonathan said scornfully: "We don't have a nurse. We're too old."

"Then Grissel . . ."

"She came with the boys' mother," explained Mr. Raine. "She keeps herself very much apart, but continues to stay here. She is . . . rather strange."

The boys exchanged glances and smiled. The subject of Grissel seemed the only one they could agree about.

"She walks in her sleep," said David.

Jonathan made claws of his fingers and put on an expression of malevolence at which David laughed.

Mr. Raine changed the subject and showed me some of the boys' work. Jonathan had a talent for sketching which rather surprised me. He had done some pictures of his dogs and horses which showed that he had a really sensitive touch. I admired them which pleased him very much.

"Jonathan's one talent in the schoolroom," said Mr. Raine. "But he is a great sportsman. David, of course, has sharp wits. He's the academic."

Both boys looked very pleased with themselves and it occurred to me that Mr. Raine did not have a very easy time.

I looked at their work and listened attentively, but I would rather have heard more about Grissel.

————

I asked Sabrina.

"Oh, Grissel is a silly old woman," she said. "I wish she would go, but where would she go to? She came with Isabel. She had been her nurse and you know how fanatical these old nurses can be about their charges. When Isabel died I think it turned her head slightly. Sometimes she seems to believe that Isabel is still here. It is very disconcerting but what can we do? We can't ask her to go. She is too old to take another post."

"I know how it is with these nannies and have often thought how sad it must be for them when their children grow up and no longer need them. Then they go on to the next . . . if they are young enough . . . and it all starts again."

"Unfortunately poor Griselda is not young enough. Oh, she is all right here. She has her two little rooms there in the east wing. Her food is taken in to her and we forget her for the most part. The only trouble is that she seems to have a most extraordinary attitude towards the twins. She dotes on Jonathan and seems to dislike David. It is odd. David doesn't care. They both used to play tricks on her until that was stopped. But she is quiet most of the time."

"I saw her looking out of one of the windows when I was coming in with Dickon."

"Oh, yes. She watches Dickon all the time. He laughs at it and takes no notice. You know how he is. Your grandmother didn't like it very much. She said it was uncanny. But it is just Griselda's way."

I didn't think much more about Griselda until a few days later when I came into the house and saw what I can only describe as a shape looking over the banisters. It was there and gone in a flash so that I wondered whether I had imagined I saw something. It was

149

nothing much, just one of those occurrences which, for some reason, send a shiver down one's spine.

Then I became aware of that figure at the window watching me when I came in. I saw her once or twice before it occurred to me that she had some special interest in me.

A week had passed and we were still at Eversleigh. My mother wanted to get back but every time she suggested leaving there were protests and she was persuaded to wait another week before making plans for departure.

I was not sorry. Eversleigh was beginning to cast its spell on me—but perhaps that was Dickon. It was all very well for me to tell myself that he was making no impression on me and that I saw him clearly for what he was. Each day I awoke with a sense of excitement and it was all due to the fact that I knew I was going to be with Dickon.

Nothing had changed since those early days—except of course that I looked at him differently. I was no longer the wide-eyed innocent child. I saw him as he was, a buccaneering adventurer, determined to get the most out of life, completely self-centered and a man whose own interests would always come first. The frightening thing was that it didn't make any difference. I still wanted to be with him, the hours were dull when he was not there, and although we spent most of the time in verbal conflict, that was more exciting than the most friendly conversation with anyone else.

Our afternoon ride had become a ritual now. All the time he was trying to charm me, to lull my suspicions and to give him the opportunity of seducing me. So far I had resisted his attentions and I intended to go on doing so.

When we rode past Enderby, he said, "Why don't you come and have a look over the house?"

"Whatever for? I have no intention of buying a house so why should I want to look over it?"

"Because it's interesting. It is a house with a history. It's haunted, you know, by all the ghosts of the past . . . those who have lived such evil lives that they can't rest."

"I expect it is very dirty."

"Cobwebs. Dark shadows. Strange shapes looming up. I'd be there to protect you, Lottie."

"I would need no protection from cobwebs and shadows."

"Ah, but what about the ghosts?"

"I don't think I have anything to fear from them either. Why should they be interested in me?"

"They are interested in any who brave their domains. But I see you are afraid."

"I am not afraid."

He looked at me slyly. "Not of the house . . . but of me."

"Afraid of you, Dickon. In heaven's name, why?"

"Afraid of giving me what I want and what you so much want to give."

"What's that? You have Eversleigh, you know."

"Yourself," he said. "Lottie, you and I were made for each other."

"By whom?"

"Fate."

"Then Fate made a very poor job of it. I assure you I was certainly not made for you . . . nor you for me. You were made for Eversleigh perhaps. That's a different matter."

"You do go on about Eversleigh. You attach too much importance to it."

"No. It was you who did that."

"Thy tongue is sharp as the serpent's. Did someone say that? If they didn't they ought to have done. In any case I'm saying it now."

"And I say beware of serpents."

"Come. Admit the truth. You are afraid to step inside Enderby with me."

"I assure you I am not."

"Back up your assurance with words."

On an impulse I dismounted. He was laughing as he tethered our horses to the post. He took my hand as we advanced towards the house.

"The window with the broken latch is round there. It is quite easy to get in. Someone wanted to look at it a few weeks ago and I showed him the way in. I wonder if he made an offer for the place."

He had found the window, opened it, looked inside and helped me in. We were in the hall at the end of which was a door. It was open and we went through it into a large stone floored kitchen. The spits

151

were still there. We examined the great fireplace with its fire dogs and cauldrons. There were layers of dust on everything. I found it quite fascinating and prowled about opening cupboards and exploring.

We must have been there for about five minutes before we went back to the hall. Above us was the minstrels' gallery.

Dickon put his fingers to his lips. "The gallery is the most haunted spot. Let's explore it."

He took my hand and I was glad of the contact as the eeriness of the house began to wrap itself about me. I could well believe that at night the ghosts came to relive their tragic lives once more in such a house.

Our footsteps rang out in the silence.

"Cold, isn't it?" said Dickon. "Are you just a little scared, Lottie?"

"Of course not."

"You look a little." He put his arm about me. "There. That's better." We mounted the stairs. Some of the furniture remained, though most of it had been taken away.

"Let's go into the gallery. Defy the ghosts. Are you game?"

"Of course."

"Come then." We mounted the staircase and went into the gallery, we leaned over the balcony and looked down on the hall.

"Imagine it full of people . . . people dancing . . . long dead people . . ."

"Dickon, you know you don't really believe in ghosts."

"Not when I'm outside. In here . . . can you feel the malevolent influence?"

I did not answer. There was certainly something strange about the place. It was uncanny but I had the feeling that the house was waiting for my answer.

"Let's defy the dead," said Dickon. "Let's show them that at least we are alive."

He put his arms about me.

"Don't do that, Dickon."

His answer was to laugh. "Dear Lottie, do you think I am going to let you go now that I have you again?"

I tried to hold him off. My strength, I knew, was puny against his. He would not dare to force himself on me. He would have to be careful . . . even he. I was no village girl to be lightly raped and no questions asked. And that was not Dickon's way. He was too sure of his charms and he wanted to be gratefully accepted; he would not want reluctance . . . not from me in any case.

"Lottie," he said, "it was always you. Never anyone else. Nor was it for you. You never forgot me any more than I forgot you. We're together at last. Let's take what we've got. Lottie . . . please."

He held me fast now and I felt myself slipping away in some sort of ecstasy. I was a child again. Dickon was my lover. This was how it was always meant to be.

I was not fighting anymore. I heard him laugh triumphantly.

"No," I said. "No." But I did not make any other protest and Dickon would know that surrender was close.

But . . . just then, I heard a movement, the sound of a footstep overhead—and I was immediately brought back to sanity.

I said: "Someone is here . . . in the house."

"No," said Dickon.

"Listen."

There it was again. The definite sound of a footstep.

"Come on. We'll see who it is," said Dickon. He started out of the gallery and up the staircase. I followed.

We were in a corridor. There were many doors there. Dickon threw open one of them. I followed him into a room. There was no one there. We went into another room. There were a few pieces of furniture in this one and it took us a little time to make sure there was no one hiding there. And as he pulled back the tattered brocade curtains about a four-poster bed we heard the movement again. This time it was downstairs. There *had* been someone in the house, and whoever it was had eluded us, for he or she must at this moment be climbing throught the window by which we had come in.

We rushed down. Soon we were through the window and out among the overgrown shrubs. I felt overwhelmingly grateful to whoever it was who had saved me from Dickon and myself.

We rode silently back to the house. Dickon was clearly disappointed but not utterly dismayed. I realized he had high hopes for the future. I felt a certain elation. Never again, I promised myself.

Something in the house had saved me. It had sounded like human footsteps, but I wondered whether it was some ghost from the past. There was that ancestress of mine, Carlotta. She had had connections with the house at some time; she had actually owned it.

I had almost convinced myself that it was Carlotta returned from the dead who had saved me, and this was an indication of the state of mind into which I was falling. I had always regarded myself as a practical woman. The French are notoriously practical; and I was half French. And yet sometimes I felt as though since I had come to England I was being drawn into a web from which I would eventually be unable to escape.

It was an absurd feeling, but I had to admit that it was there.

The sensation came to me that I was being watched. When I returned to the house, if I glanced up to what I knew to be Griselda's windows there would be a hasty movement. Someone was there looking down on me and dodging back hoping not to be seen. I could put that down to an old woman's curiosity, and according to Sabrina she was a little mad in any case; but it was more than that. Sometimes I felt I was watched from the banisters, from the corridors, and sometimes I hurried to the spot where I thought I had seen or heard a movement and there was nothing there. An old woman could certainly not have been agile enough to get out of Enderby and climb through the window.

My grandmother's health had improved since we had come and my mother said it was time we thought of going home. Sabrina and my grandmother were sad at the prospect.

"It has been so wonderful to see you," said Sabrina. "It has meant so much to us all. It has kept Dickon with us. It is a long time since he has been at Eversleigh for such a stretch."

I said that our husbands would be wondering why we did not return and my mother added that they had only agreed that we should come because the visit was to be a short one.

I was determined to see Griselda before I left, and one afternoon I made my way to that part of the house where I knew her rooms to be.

It was very quiet and lonely as I ascended the short narrow staircase and came to a corridor. I had judged from where I knew the windows to be from the shadowy watcher who had looked down on me.

154

I found a door and knocked. There was no answer, so I went to the next and knocked again.

There was still no answer but I sensed that someone was on the other side of the door.

"Please may I come in?" I said.

The door opened suddenly. An old woman was standing there. Her gray hair escaped from under a cap; her face was pale and her deep-set eyes wide with the whites visible all round the pupil which gave her an expression of staring. She was dressed in a gown of sprigged muslin, high necked and tight-bodiced. She was very slight and thin.

"Are you Griselda?" I asked.

"What do you want?" she demanded.

"I wanted to meet you. I am going soon, and I did want to make the acquaintance of everyone in the house before I do."

"I know who you are," she said as though the knowledge gave her little pleasure.

"I am Madame de Tourville. I lived here once."

"Yes," she said, "before my lady came here. You were here then."

"May I come in and chat for a moment?"

Rather ungraciously she stepped back and I entered the room. I was amazed to see Jonathan rise from one of the chairs.

"Oh, hello," he said.

"Jonathan!" I cried.

"Jonathan is a *good* boy," said Griselda; and to him: "Madame de Tourville thinks she should see everybody so she called on me."

"Oh," said Jonathan. "Can I go now?"

"Yes do," she said. "And come back tomorrow."

She caught him and kissed him with emotion. He wriggled a little in her embrace and gave me an apologetic look as though to excuse himself for having been involved in such a demonstration.

As Jonathan went away, Griselda said: "He is a good boy. He looks after me and my wants."

"You never mingle with the family," I said.

"I was the nurse. I came with my lady. I would to God we never had."

"You mean the lady Isabel."

"His wife. The mother of young Jonathan."

155

"And David," I added.

She was silent and her mouth hardened; her eyes looked wider and consequently more wild.

"I've seen you," she said almost accusingly. "I've seen you ... with him."

I glanced towards the window. "I think I have seen you up there ... from time to time."

"I know what goes on," she said.

"Oh, do you?"

"With him," she added.

"Oh?"

"I'll never forgive him. He killed her, you know."

"Killed! Who killed whom?"

"He did. The master. He killed my little flower." Her eyes filled with tears and her mouth quivered. She clenched her hands and I thought she looked quite mad.

I said gently: "I don't think that is true. Tell me about Isabel."

Her face changed so suddenly that it was startling to watch her. "She was my baby from the first. I had had others but there was something about little Isabel. An only child, you see. Her mother died ... died giving birth to her just as ... Well, there she was, my baby. And him, her father, he was a good man. Never much there. Too important. Very rich. Always doing something. . . . But when he was there he loved his little daughter. But really she was mine. He never tried to interfere. He'd always say, 'You know what's best for our little girl, Griselda.' A good man. He died. The good die and the evil flourish."

"I can see that you loved Isabel very much."

She said angrily: "There should never have been this marriage. Wouldn't have been if it had been left to me. It was the one thing I can't forgive him for. He just had the notion that girls ought to marry and that Isabel would be all right just as others were. He didn't know my little girl like I did. She was frightened ... really frightened. She used to come to me and sob her heart out. There wasn't anything I could do ... though I would have died for her. So she was married, my poor little angel. She said, 'You'll come with me, Griselda,' and I said, 'Wild horses wouldn't drag me away from you, my love.'"

156

I said: "I understand how you feel. You loved her dearly just as a mother loves her child. I know. I have children of my own."

"And I had to see her brought here . . . to this house with him. He didn't care for her. What he cared for was what she brought him."

I was silent. I could agree with Griselda on that.

"Then it started. She was terrified. You see, she had got to get this son. Men . . . they all want children . . . but it would be different, eh, if they had the bearing of them. She was frightened when she knew she'd conceived . . . and then before three months had gone she had lost it. The second was even worse. That went on for six months. There was another after that. That was her life. That was all she meant to him—except, of course, the money. And when her father died he got that too. Then he was ready to be rid of her."

"You said he killed her."

"He did. They could have saved her . . . but that would have meant losing the boys. He wouldn't have it. He wanted the boys. That was it. He got them . . . and it cost her her life."

"You mean there was a choice?"

She nodded. "I was mad with sorrow. I was there with her. She would have me and even he did not try to stop that. He murdered her, just as sure as you're sitting there, madame. And now he has his eyes on you. What does he want from you, do you think?"

"Griselda," I told her, "I am a married woman. I have a husband and children in France and I intend to go back to them shortly."

She moved close to me and lifted her face to mine; her eyes seemed luminous in her wrinkled face. "He has plans for you. Don't forget it. He's one who won't see his plans go awry."

"I make my own plans," I said.

"You're with him all the time. I know him. I know his way with women. Even Isabel . . ."

"You know nothing about me, Griselda. Tell me more about Isabel."

"What more is there to tell? She was happy with me. She came here and was murdered."

"Do stop talking about murder. I know she died giving birth to the twins. You're very fond of them, aren't you?"

"David killed her," she said.

157

"David!"

"It was both of them. Him forcing that on her . . . using her . . . my little Isabel just to bear children when she wasn't capable of it. Her mother had died giving birth to her. It was a weakness in the family. She should never have been forced to try it. Then there was David. He was born two hours after Jonathan. She might have been saved. But he had to have David, you see. He wanted two sons . . . just in case something happened to one of them. Between them they murdered her . . . him and David."

"Griselda, at least you shouldn't blame David. A newly born child! Isn't that rather foolish of you?"

"Whenever I look at him, I say to myself: It was you. . . . It was your life or hers. They had Jonathan. That should have been enough."

"Griselda, what proof have you of this?"

Her wild eyes searched my face and she did not answer my question. She said: "He never married again. He's got his two sons. That leaves him free for his women. He's brought them here sometimes. I've seen them. I used to wonder whether there'd be anyone set up in Isabel's place."

"Isn't it time to forget the past, Griselda?"

"Forget Isabel? Is that what you're saying?"

"Why did you watch me?"

"I watch all of them."

"You mean . . ."

She leaned towards me again and said: "His women."

"I am not one of them."

She smiled secretly. I remembered that moment in the minstrels' gallery at Enderby and was ashamed.

I said: "Do you have helpers in your watching?"

"I can't get about," she said. "It's my rheumatics. Had them for a long time. Makes getting about very hard."

"Do you see a good deal of Jonathan?"

She nodded smiling.

"And David?"

"I don't have him here. He was never what his brother was."

"So Jonathan comes on his own. What do you talk about?"

"His mother. The past."

"Is it wise to talk about that to a child?"

"It's truth. All children should be taught truth. It says so in the Holy Book."

"Do you let Jonathan . . . do things for you?"

"He wants to," she said. "He comes in all excitement. 'What's the scheme for today, Grissel?' he says . . . the little monkey."

"So he follows his father. He . . . spies on him?"

"We all want to know if the master is going to marry again. It would make a difference to us all."

"As a nurse, don't you think it is wrong to involve a child in these things?"

"Jonathan's not a child. He was born a man . . . like his father. I know much of what goes on. I learned through Isabel. I saw him through her eyes. Have a care, madame. No one is safe from him. Remember he murdered my Isabel."

I had a great desire to get away from the scrutiny of those mad eyes. The room seemed to be stifling me. I felt I was shut in with a crazy woman. She had accused Dickon of murder because his wife died giving birth to twins. She was teaching Jonathan to spy for her. The idea of that boy following us to Enderby . . . lying in wait there to spy on us . . . revolted me.

I wondered whether I should tell Sabrina what I had discovered. I felt someone should know, and yet who? My grandmother was not in a fit state to cope with the situation. Sabrina? My mother? Dickon?

I did not feel I could confide what I had discovered to anyone in this house. Then I thought: *What harm can the old woman do with her spying?* To Jonathan it was just a game. To spy on his father and report to Griselda! There was something decidedly unhealthy about that. But there was something unhealthy about the entire matter.

While I turned all this over in my mind, preparations for our departure went on apace and a few days after my meeting with Griselda, my mother and I were on our way to the coast.

The Wager

My father was at Calais waiting for us when we landed. I was amazed and a little envious to see the overwhelming love he had for my mother, so strong that it could not be hidden. My mother took it for granted and I know felt the same towards him. I was sure she believed that this was how all married people felt towards each other. I often thought that her blind belief in such a bond was so convincing that my father, who was first of all a man of the world, was carried along in her belief. She was innocent of the world, it appeared, and here was an example of the strength of innocence. How different were Charles and myself. There was a passionate attachment, yes; we could say we loved each other with reservations. Yet I had almost succumbed to Dickon and I was sure Charles had his affairs. I accepted this as the state of marriage—the only way in which it could survive. How shocked my mother would be!

But it was heartwarming to see them together and he had a good deal of affection to spare for me. He saw me as the outcome of the great passion of his life. I was very happy to be in their company.

I stayed at Aubigné for a few days. They wanted me to stay longer, but I was eager to get home, to see Charles and my children. I remembered with pleasure that Lisette would be there too. Moreover, it was not very comfortable to be in the château in which Sophie had shut herself away.

I should have liked to see her. I wanted to tell her that Lisette was back and it was almost like the old times and how often we talked of her and wished she were with us as she used to be.

"She doesn't grow any better," my father said, "and we have now ceased to try to make her do so. She keeps in her own apartments, presumably happy enough with Jeanne."

I asked if I could pay a visit to her room but Jeanne let us know that it would not be wise and might bring back unpleasant memories for Sophie.

Armand greeted me with that special brand of cool affection and Marie Louise seemed more remote than ever. My father said her piety increased every day and there was no sign of a child and not likely to be.

Charles welcomed me boisterously and declared he had thought I was never coming back. Charlot hugged me tightly and so did Louis-Charles. As for Claudine, she had become quite a person and now and then uttered a word which was not unintelligible. She was even able to walk a few steps. The nicest thing of all was that she knew me and clucked with pleasure when I took her in my arms.

It was good to be home and I was immensely relieved that I had kept my head and my virtue. Here in my home it seemed incredible that I could ever have come near to losing them; and as the days passed, Eversleigh with its mad Griselda and Enderby with its ghosts seemed very remote. Only the memory of Dickon stayed with me and came back to me vividly in unguarded moments.

Lisette wanted to hear all about it. I told her of Griselda. I did not mention my feelings for Dickon. I felt that was something to be kept secret. She listened and said it had been very dull at Tourville without me.

Charles had lost none of his interest in the war between England and the American colonies. In fact, I told him, he talked of little else.

"Your people are fighting a losing battle," he said. "They should know themselves beaten."

"I cannot believe they are going to be beaten by colonists who are our own people in any case. It's like a civil war."

"They are the worst. Moreover, my dear, they are going to have the might of France behind them."

"I don't believe it."

"Let me tell you something. Your English suffered a massive defeat at Saratoga, and at Court they are talking of nothing else but what this means. Our Louis has made a pact with the colonists. What do you think of that?"

"Against England?"

He grinned at me. "Poor Louis, he wants peace. They had a hard task persuading him that he was not running a risk of war. I was getting into a bit of a panic, I don't mind telling you, because I was fearful that war might be declared while you were still in England."

"What would that have meant?"

"Well, communications wouldn't have been easy. You might not have been able to get back."

"You mean I should have had to stay in England?"

"Don't worry. I should have come to fetch you. But it might not have been easy. In any case we are not at war, but the British ambassador has been recalled from Paris."

"What does that mean?"

"That the English are not very pleased with us."

"I pray there won't be war between our two countries."

"You are safely home now, Lottie, and here you are going to stay."

That summer came early. Claudine was growing up. She had had her second birthday in February and could now chatter to us and run about. She was an enchanting child with a quick temper and a desire to have her own way; but she was also affectionate and her moods changed so quickly that there were dazzling smiles after tears and most of the household were her slaves.

It was the beginning of July when we had a visitor. Lisette and I were in the garden with the children when one of the maids announced that a gentleman was asking for me.

"He has come a long way, madame, and particularly asks for you."

I rose and followed her.

And there he was, smiling at me and looking certain of a welcome, making my heart leap about in an uncomfortable fashion and filling me with emotions which were hard to analyze.

"Dickon," I cried.

"Well, you look pleased to see me, Lottie. I knew you would be. I had business in Paris and being in France I knew you would never forgive me if I did not come to see you."

"You should have warned me."

"No time. It was decided that I should visit Paris so I came without delay. And here I am."

"Well, come in. They'll take your horse. You must be hungry."

"For a sight of you."

"Please Dickon," I said, "while you are here in my husband's house . . ."

162

"Point understood," he said. "I'll promise. My behavior shall be impeccable."

The maid summoned a groom while I took him into the house.

"H'm," he said. "A fine place. I fancied a glimpse of Aubigné but did not call. I had an idea that your mother would make me less welcome. She has never really been a friend of mine. In any case I want to spend as much time as I can with my delectable Lottie."

"You promised...."

"A delicate compliment to a delightful hostess, nothing more."

Even as he looked round the hall I saw the speculative look in his eyes. He was assessing the value of everything. He could not help that. That was Dickon.

I sent one of the maids to see if she could find Charles and meanwhile told them to bring some food and prepare a room.

"You will stay for a few days, I suppose," I said.

"I shall certainly do so if invited."

"As a relation, of course you are."

"Lottie, you are so beautiful. Do you know when I am away from you, I forget how beautiful you are. Then it bursts upon me suddenly when I see you and yet I tell myself that I carry an image of you in my heart forever."

"Just another example of self-deceit," I said lightly.

Food was brought and I took him into one of the small rooms which led from the hall and sat with him while he ate. I heard Charles come in and went into the hall.

"Charles," I said, "we have a visitor. You have heard of Dickon. He had to come to Paris so he has called to see us."

The two men seemed to fill the small room. I watched them intently while they took stock of each other.

Dickon was an inch or so taller and he seemed more blond than ever beside Charles's darkness. Charles's manner was faintly hostile. I thought, he is seeing Dickon as the persecutor of colonists ... but it was more than that. Dickon was smiling, summing up Charles and being rather pleased by what he saw, which I guessed meant that he was discovering defects.

In any case they were making up their minds to dislike each other.

"Welcome to Tourville," said Charles, but his tone belied his words.

"Thank you," replied Dickon, speaking French with an exaggerated English accent. "It is a great pleasure to be here and meet you. I have heard so much about you from Lottie."

"I have heard of you too," said Charles.

"Sit down, Charles," I said, "and let Dickon get on with his food. He was very hungry when he came and he has had a long ride."

Charles sat down and Dickon went on eating. Charles asked him which way he had come and how he had found Paris.

"In a state of some excitement," said Dickon. "But then it often is, is it not? They seem to fancy themselves on the brink of war. I had some black looks when certain people discovered my nationality. I was surprised and wondered how I had betrayed myself."

"It would be fairly obvious," said Charles dryly.

"Well, to tell the truth, I was hoping so. There is all this chatter. So many of them seem eager to leap into combat. I can't think why."

"The French pride themselves on a love of justice."

"Do they?" said Dickon, showing surprise and cutting himself a piece of capon. "This is delicious, Lottie. I congratulate you on your cook."

"I am glad you are enjoying it." I felt I had to change the subject from that of the war as quickly as possible, so I went on: "Tell me, how are my grandmother and Sabrina?"

They were uneasy days which followed. Dickon had some purpose and I guessed it was that he had no intention of letting me slip out of his life. He had chosen the first opportunity of coming to Tourville. I wondered if it were true that he had business in Paris and thought it might possibly be so as there had been hints of his being concerned in all sorts of affairs. He was in Court circles, Sabrina had proudly told us, and I wondered whether he was concerned in politics. He did not sit in Parliament but there were other posts ... perhaps secret ones. I could imagine Dickon's enjoying being involved in such adventures.

Lisette's comment was that he was an outstandingly attractive man. "He has come here to see you, Lottie," she said. "How lucky you are!"

"I don't think it is lucky. I don't want trouble."

"With Charles? Well, naturally husbands can't be expected to like overpowering admirers turning up and throwing themselves on their hospitality."

"Dickon is really a relation of mine."

"He behaves more like a suitor."

"You are imagining things."

Charles was suspicious of him and of me.

When we were alone in our bedroom on the first night after Dickon's arrival, he said: "You saw him in England?"

"Of course I saw him. Eversleigh belongs to him and that was where we went. It is where my grandmother lives. Remember, I went there because she was ill."

"Was he there all the time?"

"Most of the time."

"What is he doing here?"

"Oh, Charles, I am tired of this catechism. I know no more than you do. He has business in France and came to see me and the children."

"He hasn't expressed any great interest in them."

"He will. He has two fine sons of his own. Parents always want to compare."

"I don't like him very much."

"You don't know him."

"He's arrogant."

"Well, perhaps you are too."

"I wouldn't trust him. What's he doing here in France?"

"You said that a moment ago. I can only reply: Ask him."

"I might."

"All right then." I put my arms about his neck. "Shall we forget about him now?"

He kissed me then; he was very possessive that night and I felt his mood had something to do with Dickon.

———

There was danger in the air. I supposed that was inevitable with Dickon there. He seemed to generate trouble and had done so all his life. It might have been because he pursued his own way without caring very much what happened to those whom he encountered in achieving it.

I longed for him to go and yet I wanted him to stay. Every hour that he was in the house seemed fraught with danger and yet at the same time I felt I was living at twice the rate I normally did.

He went round the estate with Charles and me and made comments which I was sure were very much to the point. If he saw anything to praise—which was rare—he did so; mostly he gave veiled criticism and made comparisons between estate management in France and in England, implying the excellence of the latter. He was knowledgeable and more interested than Charles had ever been; and I realized that all the time he was showing his superiority in every possible way.

Charles was inclined to lose his temper whereas Dickon remained serenely good-natured, enjoying the situation enormously. He was maddening.

He went to the nurseries and admired the children. Both Charlot and Louis-Charles were delighted with him, and he hovered between ignoring them and treating them as grown-up individuals, which often seemed to earn the admiration of the young. His size and his overwhelming personality won their respect and even Claudine regarded him soberly when he picked her up and she tried to pull the buttons from his coat, which indicated that she liked them very much.

He charmed my parents-in-law and when Amelie and her husband called to spend the day he did the same with them. He was determined to please everyone in the house except Charles.

Lisette said: "I should beware of such a man. He is far too attractive in a wicked way . . . and they are always the worst."

"Never fear," I replied, "I am on my guard."

She knew something of him because in the past I used to confide in her. She said: "I understand why your mother wanted to keep you away from him. I can also see why you did not want her to succeed."

"I never knew anyone quite like Dickon," I admitted. "And I doubt I ever shall."

"Life with him," suggested Lisette dreamily, "would be one long adventure. Is he very rich?"

"Very . . . now, I should imagine. He owns Clavering and Eversleigh and his wife brought him a lot of money."

"And you think he is satisfied now . . . financially?"

"I should hope so."

"He isn't, I'd be ready to gamble. His sort never are. When he marries again it will be a rich woman."

"Is that a prophecy?"

"As good as," said Lisette.

166

"Do you realize," I said, "that since Dickon has come we talk of little else?"

"What else could be so interesting?"

"I shall be glad when he goes. He is causing trouble here. He does, wherever he goes, my mother used to say."

"But it is trouble which you can't help wanting. Come, be honest. You know it will be somewhat dull when he has gone."

"He irritates Charles so. Sometimes I don't know how to get through the evening."

"Dickon is enjoying himself I don't doubt."

"I am sure Charles isn't."

In the evenings they would sit up late playing a card game. They both enjoyed gambling, Charles recklessly, his face flushed, his eyes blazing; Dickon calmly, raising the stakes ridiculously high, never showing the least bit of emotion whether he lost or won; but then he always seemed to win.

I would go to bed and leave them and when Charles came up pretend to be asleep.

Charles would be angry. I would hear him banging things about before he came to bed. Sometimes he lay sleepless beside me; at others he would wake me and indulge in a kind of stormy passion which meant that he was thinking of Dickon. He knew of course of Dickon's feeling for me and that there had been some arrangement between us in my extreme youth. It didn't help.

Dickon must go soon.

There was a good deal of talk about the war.

I remember that evening well. We were at table with my parents-in-law, Charles, Dickon, and I, and Dickon, as he often did, turned the conversation to the war. The attitude of the two of them towards the war was typical of their entire relationship. It was almost a personal war. Charles delighted in the colonists' successes, which Dickon dismissed as mere skirmishes. But mostly Dickon would attack the intervention of the French and would become very eloquent in his denunciation of the folly of those who did so.

That night he sat there, his eyes a brilliant blue as they were when he was excited, his cravat a dazzling white against the blue velvet of his jacket, his strong hands with the gold signet ring on the table before him—calm and still as though to call attention to Charles's gesticulations.

He continued in the strain of the war and the folly of French intervention.

"It is beyond understanding. Here in this country . . . think of it. No one could say it is in robust health. Turgot . . . Necker . . . they have made brave attempts to grapple with finances and without very happy results. King Louis inherited disaster. Why, I have heard that his grandfather prophesied that it would come after him. It could come . . . soon. Your house is crumbling to ruin and instead of setting yourself to rebuild it, you turn your backs on it and rush off to harry your neighbors."

"The French have always been interested in just causes," said Charles. "These people overseas—mostly your own Englishmen—are being unfairly taxed. Quite rightly they revolt and every Frenchman is in sympathy with them as he must be with those who suffer from such harsh treatment."

"As I have noticed in France," cut in Dickon smiling blandly. "How long is it since we had *La Guerre des Farines* when one class of people were in revolt against the injustice meted out to them by an other. Would it not be better for the French to look first to their own before they worry so nobly about the wrongs of foreigners? Your country is verging on revolt. Can't you see it coming? Did you know that it takes very little provocation for riots to break out in your towns. It is happening all the time. We don't hear much about it because it is on a small scale . . . as yet. But it is there. It is a warning but you don't see it because your eyes are staring overseas. I would say, 'Frenchmen, put your own house in order first!'"

"I can see," said Charles maliciously, "that you are very uneasy because of the strong feeling here in favor of the oppressed colonists."

"Naturally we would rather not have those such as the Marquis de Lafayette raising men and shouting about bringing freedom to the world. At the moment the Comte de Brouillard is raising forces in Angoulême. He speaks in the square most eloquently and the crowd obediently shouts, 'Down with the English! To America!'"

"I know it," said Charles. "I have a mind to join him."

"Have you, indeed? Then why not, my friend? It is always well to follow one's inclinations if one feels them strongly enough, because if they are brushed aside they return to pester one all one's days."

Charles's eyes were shining. "It is a great cause and my heart is in it."

"Then you should go."

"So you would urge me to what you consider an act of folly?"

"I do not urge, and you do not see it as folly. It would be your act, and to you it is the way of chivalry—the strong defending the weak. If I felt as you did I should certainly go."

"Then why do you not go and fight for your King?"

"I do not feel strongly as you do. I do not speak, as you know, of the rights and wrongs of this stupid war. What I have always stressed is the folly of a country such as France—in dire financial difficulties and, even worse, creaking with social injustice—to meddle in a cause which really does not concern it."

"And I have said that oppression should be fought wherever it occurs."

"And I have said that is a noble sentiment, but it is best to begin in your own backyard."

"You seem to know a great deal about my country."

"The looker-on often sees that which is not so obvious to those who are involved. Regard me as a looker-on. I hear of the odd riot now and then in the little towns all over the country; I hear the murmurs of the people, class against class. The Queen's brother, Emperor Joseph, is a wise man. Do you know what he said when he was asked for his opinion of this cause for which you speak so nobly? He said, 'I am a royalist by profession.' He meant that it is unwise to question the authority of kings for when there is a precedent it creates uncertainty for those who come after. You are an aristocrat by profession, yet you talk of liberty . . . you stress the rightness of those who take up arms against the monarchy. That is my point."

"You take a cynical view."

"I take a realist's view which until now I thought was something the French always prided themselves on doing."

I broke in: "I have had enough of this talk of war. You two seem to think of nothing else."

Dickon looked at me reproachfully. "It is a matter of some importance to my country. If we lost, it would mean giving up our foothold in North America. But win or lose it means a great deal more to France."

"Nonsense," said Charles. "I can see the English are beginning to get very worried."

"Not beginning to," retorted Dickon. "They have been so from the start. They believed victory would be easier than it is proving to be. They did not realize how difficult it is to carry on a war so far from home."

"Come. Admit defeat."

"It is not over yet. There are many Frenchmen who are straining to go to the rescue. As you are, for instance. I can see the appeal. Lafayette, Segur, and this man in Angoulême . . . they have a point. Adventure . . . knightly, chivalrous adventure . . . a journey overseas . . . You can understand it well. I wonder you don't take the trip."

"I would not be averse to it."

"How amusing if you and I met on opposite sides of the battlefield. A little different, eh . . . from our fighting our battles across the table."

Determinedly I talked about the additions one of our neighbors was planning to make to his house. It was a subject which interested them both and I managed again to turn the conversation from the war. But they were in a strange mood and I noticed that Charles was drinking more heavily than usual.

When we rose from the table Dickon suggested cards. My parents-in-law were already nodding, as they did after a meal in the evening, but they accompanied us into the small salon where there was a card table.

I sat with the old people while the two men played. At first they played quietly and there was silence in the room. I felt an intense uneasiness which I believed was due to the conversation at the dinner table, though why I should have felt more than usually disturbed I did not know. Dickon had baited Charles no more than usual, but somehow there had been a certain intensity behind his remarks, something which I construed as motive.

Charles continued to drink a great deal; Dickon took very little, and from his occasional laugh of triumph, I guessed that he was winning. I was not unduly disturbed because I knew that Charles could pay his debts; but there was something about Dickon on that night. His eyes burned with that brilliant blue light which I had noticed in moments of excitement. It had been there in Enderby when he had thought I was on the point of surrender. It was there now. It meant triumph in battle.

He would be leaving in a few days and I must really be relieved when he went. While he was here I could not stop myself waiting for disaster to break; and it would be of his making.

Why had he come? To see me. Yet if he could not seduce me in his home, it was hardly likely that he would in mine. Perhaps the more difficult the chase, the more it appealed to him.

I think there was some other reason. He knew so much about France. His knowledge amazed me. How did he learn of these outbreaks all over the country? People did not speak much of them. I fancied that the King and his ministers had no desire for the people to know of the unrest which was growing among the peasant classes. The King wanted no trouble with England. A war would be disastrous to France at this moment, but these adventurous aristocrats with the notion of liberty for others were doing their best to provoke war. Whatever their sympathies were, they would have been wise to keep them to themselves, for as Dickon said there was trouble brewing in their own backyard. How did Dickon become so knowledgeable about this? He was involved in Court circles, and knowing his adventurous nature I could imagine in what direction he would go. It could be that he had come to France as an ordinary traveler visiting relations. There was nothing to arouse suspicion in that. At the same time he could learn a great deal about what was going on. He would discover the strength of those expeditions to the New World; he could test the opinion in France.

He had been in Paris; he had traveled through the country and seen for himself what was happening there, and, being Dickon, he had implied that he had come to see me.

I was aroused from my reverie by the talk of the two at the card table. They had stopped and were discussing stakes.

"Let us wager something other than money," suggested Dickon. "It makes the game more exciting. Some object ... your signet ring against mine."

"I wouldn't care whether I won your signet ring or not." Charles was speaking in a rather slurred tone. He had drunk too much. I would remind him that it was getting late and try to stop the game.

"There must be something that you could be interested in. Your house? Men have staked houses before. Your house against mine."

"Of what use would a house in England be to me?"

"It is hard to find something I have which you want," said Dickon. "This living in different countries makes it a little difficult. Let me think, what have you which I want?"

He had lifted his eyes and caught mine. I looked away quickly. I could not meet that brilliant blue gaze.

"I see," Dickon went on, "that we are not going to reach any satisfaction. But I do feel there is something . . . I have it!"

There was a moment of tense silence in the room. I thought they might hear the violent beating of my heart. In those seconds I was thinking: *He should never have come here. There is always trouble where he is. And what now? What does he plan?*

Dickon was speaking quietly, almost persuasively. "You said you wanted to go. I wonder whether I should too. What an adventure! I should like to see the New World. They say it is very beautiful. A variety of scenery. Tobacco . . . cotton . . . though perhaps not where we should go. This is what I suggest we play. The loser goes into battle. You to fight for the rights of the oppressed; I on the side of the oppressor."

"What a ridiculous idea!" I cried. "I never heard anything so absurd. The idea of staking such a thing . . . on a card game!"

"Alas, my friend, your wife forbids it."

There was no mistaking the pity in Dickon's voice for the man who could not choose for himself. Poor Charles, he was implying, you are not allowed a will of your own. Your wife decides for you.

He knew that would sting Charles into action.

"I think it is an amusing idea," he said.

"This is the first time you have agreed with Dickon," I reminded him. "And over such a foolish matter!"

"It excites me," said Dickon. "The fall of a card . . . and one's future changed. That is the true spirit of gambling."

"Deal the cards," said Charles.

172

"Three games," cried Dickon, "as it is such an important issue. Too much so to be decided in one."

I knew what he was doing. He wanted to be rid of Charles. But how could he be sure? Something told me that Dickon was always sure.

I looked at my father-in-law. He was asleep now. His wife was nodding. I could not take my eyes from the table.

The first game went to Charles. He was very merry.

"I don't think you are going to like it there," he said to Dickon.

"If I go I shall make the best of it," retorted Dickon. "As I am sure you will."

"One up to me," said Charles. "The next one could be decisive. I have only to win one and there will be no need for a third."

"Here's to me," said Dickon. "If you win this one it will cut short the excitement."

I said: "Of course you are not serious."

"Deadly so," replied Dickon.

The game had begun. I heard the seconds tick away and then the final cry of triumph. Dickon was the winner.

Now I found the suspense unbearable. If Dickon went to America I might never see him again. I might not in any case. I ought not to. He was dangerous. There was no peace where he was. But I did not think he would ever go to America. If he lost he would find some excuse for staying at home.

The deciding game had started. I watched them, my heart throbbing. The silence seemed to go on for a long time. And then . . . Dickon was laying his cards on the table. He was smiling at Charles. I could not understand what Charles's expression meant and neither of them spoke.

I could endure no more. I rose and went to the table.

"Well?" I demanded.

Dickon smiled at me. "Your husband will be leaving for North America to fight in the cause of justice."

I was so angry with them both that I swept the cards from the table.

Dickon stood up and looked at me ruefully.

"You should not blame the cards," he said; and taking my hand kissed it and bade me good night.

I helped Charles to bed. He was bemused both by the wine he had drunk and the wager he had made. I don't think he quite realized then what it meant.

"An evening's nonsense," I called it. I said: "I suppose it was a way of putting a bit of excitement into a card game."

Charles slept heavily and in the morning he had fully recovered. I had slept very fitfully, because although I had tried to assure myself that it was an evening's nonsense, I was not at all certain of that.

Charles sat on the bed and said: "I shall have to go."

"How ridiculous!"

"I have always paid my debts at cards. It is a matter of honor."

"This was just a bit of nonsense between you two."

"No. It was meant. I have often thought I ought to go and this has decided me. I shall go and see Brouillard today."

"You mean that man at Angoulême!"

"It will be easier to go with him. Doubtless there will be several I know among his recruits."

"Charles, are you seriously meaning to go abroad?"

"It is only for a short time. We'll get the English on the run and it will be over soon. I'd like to be in on the end."

"So you really are serious!"

"Never more."

"My God!" I cried. "How foolish can men get!"

Two days later Dickon left and Charles had already made contact with the Comte de Brouillard and was in constant touch with the noblemen who were to form part of the Comte's expedition.

Dickon was well pleased when he said *au revoir* to me. He wouldn't have good-bye. "Too final," he said. "We shall see each other soon, I promise you."

"What would you have done ... if you had lost?" I asked him. "Would you have left Eversleigh ... your exciting life in London?"

He smiled secretly. "I try to make a point of not doing what I don't want to," he said. "I can imagine nothing more dreary. To tell the truth—but just for your ears only—I am really on the side of the colonists. I think our government are behaving as foolishly as the French and should never have levied those taxes which sparked it all off. But don't tell a Frenchman that. I take back nothing of what I have said about them. Frenchmen are making another of their mistakes which could rebound. You should come home to England, Lottie. You'd be safer there. I don't like what I see here. There is a cauldron of discontent . . . simmering at the moment but there will come a time when it will boil over, and this War of Independence . . . or rather the French participation in it . . . is adding to the fuel under that pot. Foolish aristocrats like Lafayette and that husband of yours can't see it. A pity for them."

"Don't preach to me, Dickon. I believe you were determined to get him away."

"I must admit that I do not like to see him being so intimate with you."

I laughed. "He is my husband, you know. Good-bye, Dickon."

"*Au revoir,*" he said.

The next weeks were given over to Charles's preparations. He arranged for Amelie and her husband to come to the château and stay during his absence. Amelie's husband had considered himself fortunate to marry into a family as rich as the Tourvilles and was only too ready to install himself in the château. As for Amelie, she was delighted to be home again.

So within a few weeks of Dickon's visit, Charles left for North America.

———

It was several months since Charles had left and I had heard nothing from him. For some weeks I could not believe he had really gone; then I wondered why he had gone so readily. It was true that he had indulged in that foolish game of chance, but I sensed that in his heart he had wanted to go. It showed me clearly that he must have been finding our marriage vaguely unsatisfactory. He had married me and desired me greatly in the beginning; he still did, for there had been nothing perfunctory about his lovemaking, and on our last night together he had been definitely regretful, declaring again and again that he hated leaving me. On the other hand the excitement of adventure was on him and he was eager to start out on a new way of life, for a while, at any rate.

I was sure he thought he would not be away for more than six months. Yet I could not forget that he had gone with a certain amount of eagerness.

Then Dickon? What had been his motive? To separate us, I believed.

During the months I heard nothing from Dickon but Sabrina sent messages expressing the wish that I would come to Eversleigh. "Poor Clarissa, she is very weak now," she wrote. "She would love to see you."

My mother received the same appeal and perhaps if she had suggested going I would have gone with her; but she did not. My father must have persuaded her that he needed her more than anyone else. Moreover the situation between France and England was worsening, and the more help France poured into America, the more difficult it was for the English to subdue the colonists, and the greater was the rancor between our two countries.

So there were many reasons why it would not be wise for me to pay a visit to England at this time.

We had settled into the new routine at Tourville. Amelie and I had always been friendly in a mild way; her husband was a gentle person, very honored and delighted to live in the château and take over the management of the estate. His own business affairs had been small and he was able to incorporate the two without much difficulty. As for my parents-in-law, they were delighted to have their daughter back. I think they understood her more than they had Charles so his absence did not appear to concern them as much as I had thought it would.

I spent a great deal of time with the children and it was enjoyable to watch them growing up. Lisette was my constant companion and I was more in her company than that of any other of the adult inhabitants of Tourville.

I remember well, that spring day when Lisette and I sat together in the garden. Claudine was running about on the grass and the boys were out riding with one of the grooms.

We were talking about Charles and wondering what was happening in that far-off land.

"Of course," I was saying, "it is difficult to get news through. I wonder if there is much fighting."

"I imagine he will soon grow tired of it and long for the comforts of home," said Lisette.

"Well, at least he did what he said he would do."

"Dickon rather forced him to it. Have you heard from Dickon?"

"No, but from Sabrina."

"I wonder . . ."

"Yes, what do you wonder?"

"About Dickon . . . whether he just likes to stir up a little mischief or whether this is part of a great design."

"A little mischief," I said; and just at that moment I saw a maid running across the lawn and behind her a man. I stood up but I did not recognize him immediately. It was my father, and I had never seen him look as he did then. He seemed to have aged by at least twenty years, and what was so unusual for him, he was carelessly dressed and his cravat was ruffled.

I knew something terrible had happened.

"Father!" I cried.

"Lottie." There was desolation in his voice.

He took me into his arms and I cried out: "What is it? Tell me . . . quickly."

I drew away from him and saw the tears on his cheeks.

I stammered: "My mother . . ."

He nodded, but he could not speak. Lisette was beside me. She said: "Is there anything I can do?"

I replied: "Perhaps you would take Claudine and leave us. Father," I went on, "come and sit down. Tell me what has happened."

He let me lead him to the seat which Lisette had just vacated. I was vaguely aware of her taking a rather bewildered and inclined-to-protest Claudine across the grass.

"You have just arrived. You must be worn out. Why . . . ?"

"Lottie," he said, "your mother is dead."

"No!" I murmured.

He nodded. "Gone! She's gone, Lottie. I shall never see her again. I could kill them . . . every single one of them. Why her? What had *she* done? God preserve France from the rabble. I would hang them all . . . every one of them . . . but that's too good for them."

"But why . . . why my mother?" I was trying to think of her gone, but I could only think of this poor broken man who now had to live his life without her.

"Tell me what happened," I begged. "Talk . . . please . . . I must know."

"How could I have guessed how it would be? That morning she went off into the town . . . just as she had so many times before. She wanted to go to the milliner's. She talked about the hat she was having made. She asked me about the color of the feathers."

"Yes," I said soothingly. "And then she went to the milliner's . . ."

"In the carriage. She had two grooms with her and her lady's maid."

In the carriage! I remembered it. A glorious vehicle with his crest emblazoned on it in gold.

"I did not know that the day before one of the agitators had been preaching in the town. He had stirred them up to riot. It is going on all over France . . . not in any great degree and we don't hear where it is happening, but they are working the people up in the remotest places."

"Yes," I urged him. "Yes?" I felt he was putting off telling me the dreadful truth because he could not bear to speak of it.

"While she was in the milliner's the riot started. It was at the bakery. She came out and must have heard the people shouting. She and her maid got into the carriage. It was immediately surrounded by the mob."

"Oh, no," I murmured and I recalled that occasion when I had been with the Comte and we had heard a man preaching revolution. I had never forgotten the fanaticism in his eyes.

"The coachman tried to break through the crowd. It was the only thing to do."

"And then . . . ?" I asked.

He shook his head. "I can't bear to think of it. Some of those criminals seized the horses . . . tried to stop them. The carriage was overturned and the frightened horses tried to dash through the crowd. One of the grooms was saved though badly hurt. The rest . . ."

I put my arms round him. I tried to comfort him, but that was impossible. He sat for what seemed a long time, saying nothing, just staring blankly ahead.

I don't remember much of the rest of that day. A shock such as this one had stunned me as it had him.

178

It was a week since my father had come to tell me of my mother's death, but I still could not entirely believe that it had happened. I know my father tried to convince himself that he was dreaming, and that this overwhelming tragedy was a nightmare which he had conjured up out of a fevered imagination. The only comfort we could derive was from each other. We talked often of my mother, for that seemed to soothe us both and we were constantly together. I knew he could not sleep, and Amelie, who was very sympathetic and eager to do all she could to help, made soothing possets conducive to sleep and I made him take them before retiring. In this way he did get a measure of rest. Sometimes he slept late into the mornings and I was pleased because that shortened the day.

I was in his room one morning when he awoke, and for a few seconds he seemed happy, not remembering where he was. Then I glimpsed the man I had known. But for how briefly! It was tragic to watch the realization of what had happened dawn on him. I knew that he was never going to be happy again, and he was not an old man.

While he stayed on at Tourville I devoted myself to him entirely. I realized then how deeply I had loved my mother, although we had drifted apart when she had separated me from Dickon and I had nursed a grievance against her. Now she was gone, I could understand how she had felt, how she had been ready to sacrifice herself for me. I wished that I could have told her that I understood and how much I had loved her. What she would have wanted me to do more than anything was to care for my father, and this I would do. Theirs had been one of the most romantic love stories I had ever heard of. The idyllic adventure of youth, then the reunion in middle age, when they had both grown wiser and realized what they could offer each other. Their perfect love had a bitter, tragic ending. Did every good thing in life have to be paid for? I wondered.

To see him now, this poor broken man who had once been so sure of himself, wounded me almost as much as the loss of my mother. We had taken to each other on sight, and now there was a close affection between us. He had first brought me to France and looked after me when I needed special care; now it was my turn to look after him.

He seemed to be unaware of the passing of the days. He wanted to be with me all the time, to talk of my mother—of his first meeting with her, the excitement, the passion they had shared . . . and then the long years without each other. "But we never forgot, Lottie, neither of us. . . ." And then the coming together, and the perfection of that later relationship. "It was a miracle," he said, "finding her again."

I was thoughtful. She had written to him, telling him of my existence and the need to save me from an adventurer. Dickon! I thought, Dickon again. He moulded our lives. It was always Dickon.

There was comfort in thinking of him now because it took my thoughts momentarily from our tragedy.

One day, my father said: "Lottie, I wish you could come home. Come back with me . . . bring the children. I think life would be bearable if you did."

I replied: "I could come for a while, but this is my home. When Charles returns . . ."

"I know, I know," he said. "A selfish thought. But if only it could be. . . ."

"We shall see each other often. You must come here and I will come to you."

"Dear daughter," he said, "how different you are from the others. But then you are *her* daughter too."

"Perhaps this will change Sophie. Perhaps now that she knows you need company . . . your own about you . . ."

"Sophie thinks of nothing but her own hurt. Armand . . . I never had much in common with him. He goes his own way. He is indifferent to me . . . to his wife . . . to our family . . . indifferent to life, I sometimes think. I have had one child who is dear to my heart. Oh, Lottie, I wish you would come home with me."

He knew that I could not do that. I must wait here for Charles's return.

I tried to make him talk of other things, but there were so many dangerous subjects. I dared not mention the state of the country because that would remind him of that terrible scene which had resulted in my mother's death. Neither Sophie nor Armand was a happy subject. The children were a great help. Charlot delighted him and I was glad to see a friendship springing up between them. Claudine was interested in him and would sometimes allow him to pick her up when she would peer into his face and scrutinize him.

She said to him: "Are you my grandfather?"

I saw tears in his eyes when he told her that he was.

"You're crying," she accused, looking at him in horror. "Big people don't cry." She added: "Only babies do."

I took her from him because I saw his emotion was too great for him to bear. He loved the child, though. He might be proud of Charlot but I think it was Claudine, with her frank comments, who had first place in his heart.

With the three of us together I think we could have found some semblance of happiness and I wished that I could go back with him.

The next best thing was that he should stay at Tourville and this he did, seeming in those first weeks to be unaware of the passing of time.

He talked to me a great deal of his past life. There had been many women between that first encounter with my mother and the reunion. "Yet never once did I stray in deed or even thought when she was with me. Perhaps that does not seem very remarkable to you but for the man I was it was little short of a miracle." He went on: "I am pleased to see your friendship with Lisette."

"I am very fond of her," I replied. "It is not always easy for her. She was educated with Sophie and me and she was with us so much, and then there were occasions when it was brought home to her that she was only the niece of the housekeeper. I think she felt that a little."

"Perhaps I shouldn't have done what I did." He shrugged his shoulders. "It seemed best at the time."

"It was good of you to allow Tante Berthe to have her niece with her."

There was a faraway look in his eyes and he said at length: "I think perhaps I should tell you how it came about. It started years ago when Lisette's mother came to the *hôtel* to bring some gowns for my first wife. She was a seamstress employed by one of the fashionable dressmakers, and if any alterations were required, Lisette's mother used to come to the house to do them. She was very pretty . . . a dainty, slender girl. I came upon her struggling in with a bundle of materials . . . far too heavy for her. I carried them for her up the stairs to my wife's room. That was the beginning of our acquaintance. I was interested in her. Her name was Colette. The inevitable happened. I visited her. She lived in one of those little streets close to Notre Dame . . . narrow, winding, not very salubrious, where the dyers had their tubs. I was often splashed by the red, blue, and green streams which flow down the gutters. She had two rooms in a house which was run by an old crone. On those days I found it quite an adventure to visit such an area. It meant dressing as an artisan. I was quite young then, so don't judge me too harshly. I learned that Colette had come down in the world. Like many girls she had come to Paris for a life of greater excitement than she could enjoy on her father's farm. She was one of a strictly religious family and longed to escape from it, but she soon found that life in Paris was not what she expected. She could sew well but that was not enough to give her a living. She found a protector ... some tradesman who was a little better off than she was. He left her after a while and then she found another. She was not a prostitute. She just took the occasional lover to keep her going.

"She was a brave woman, Colette, but not very strong and it would have been better for her to have stayed in the country. I did not want to get very involved, being at that time concerned with another lady, but there was something about Colette's refined looks and air of vulnerability which I found appealing, and I was not, in those days, one to think of restraining myself. What I wanted I took thoughtlessly.

"So I visited Colette in the house near that nauseating Rue des Marmousets. I would stay for an hour or so and give her enough money to keep her for a month. She was delighted with the arrangement. I forgot her for a while and when she came to the house again my interest was revived, so I went to see her once more.

"While I was there I was aware of something strange. A noise ... a sort of presence. I became rather uneasy. I was in a low class area. Colette knew who I was. I began to fear that she might have someone hidden there who would take an opportunity to rob me ... or even worse. It was a most unpleasant sensation. I dressed hurriedly, gave her the money and escaped.

"But I was quite fascinated by Colette. She had an air of innocence and I could not believe that she would be a party to anything dishonest, let alone any act of violence. I had gone there simply dressed, taking with me just the money I would give to Colette, but she would have that in any case, so that ruled out robbery. Blackmail? That was laughable. No one would have been very shocked if it were learned that I visited a girl who had invited me to do so. My wife? She knew that I had many mistresses and had raised no objection. No, the thought of someone's being secreted in those two little rooms for the purpose of harming me was ridiculous. I laughed at myself and when I next met Colette she aroused the same desires in me and very soon I paid her another visit.

"I heard the strange noises again. I felt the same uneasiness, and I knew for certain that we were not alone. Suddenly I could bear it no more. I had to know. I went to the door between the two rooms. To my astonishment there was a key in it and the door was locked from the side on which I stood. I unlocked it and opened it and there looking up at me was one of the prettiest little girls I had ever seen. She was clearly terrified. She ran past me to Colette and started to cry, 'Maman, I didn't move, I didn't.' I looked from the child to Colette, who said, 'Yes, she is mine. It is a hard job to keep her. When my friends come she must stay hidden.'

"I can't tell you how moved I was. For one thing Colette was so frail, the child so pretty; and the fact that I had entertained suspicions made me ashamed of myself and filled me with pity for the brave young woman.

"After that, my relationship with Colette grew. I wanted to help the child. I bought clothes for her. She was only four years old, I learned. Colette told me that she tried to arrange to do a lot of work at home, which was often possible for a seamstress. Then she knew that the child was all right. When she had to leave her she was in a state of dreadful anxiety. I was horrified. I gave her money so that there was always enough for them to eat and so that someone could look after the child when Colette was away. That went on for about a year. Colette was embarrassingly grateful.

"She told me her story. It was not an unusual one: the coming to Paris, believing she would make her fortune there, perhaps marry a man who was wealthy by the standards she had been accustomed to. She said her family would not help her if they knew because they would be horrified to learn that she had an illegitimate child, but on consideration she thought her elder sister might. Berthe had always been the forceful member of the family and had looked after them all; she had been very upset when Colette had left home. Colette could not bear to tell them of her circumstances.

"She had not been in Paris long when she had found her tradesman.

She had believed he would marry her. He had been devoted, but when the child was born he did not care for such responsibilities and his family arranged for him to marry another tradesman's daughter. He came to see Colette for a while but the visits became less frequent, and then suddenly she learned that he had left Paris and she heard no more of him.

"So there was poor Colette with a child to support when she found it was all she could do to support herself. She tried bravely. She was a good girl, Colette, admirable in many ways. I did not realize how ill she was. She was suffering from consumption as so many of those girls do working in stuffy rooms, not having sufficient food . . . and warm clothing.

"I did not see her for some time as I had been in the country and when eventually I went to her room I found her confined to her bed. She had at last sent for her sister and that was the first time I saw Berthe. I realized that Colette was dying, for in no other circumstances would she have sent for her sister. Berthe was clearly an admirable woman—stern, not very demonstrative but one who would do her duty as she saw it.

"I talked to her and she said it would be difficult to take the child to the country. The family was strictly religious and would not take kindly to a bastard. Colette would have known that and it was only because she was desperate that she had begged Berthe to come to her and perhaps suggest some plan.

"The sick woman for whom I had some affection, the stern but worthy aunt, and the beautiful child all touched me deeply. I found the solution. It was that Berthe should come as a housekeeper. She was the sort of woman who would soon become skilled in the management of a household or anything she undertook. She should bring the child with her and the little girl could be brought up in my household.

"As soon as I made this suggestion I saw that it was the way out for us all. Colette would die in peace; Berthe would have the sort of post which appealed to her and settle her family problems at the same time; the child would be well cared for and my conscience eased. You may be surprised to hear, Lottie, that I had a conscience in those days? But I did . . . and on occasions it would make itself heard to my discomfiture."

I said: "It was good of you. And so Lisette came to the château."

He smiled faintly. "I shall never forget Colette's face when I told her what we were arranging. I was overwhelmed by her gratitude, which was embarrassing because what I was doing cost me little effort. She said I was a saint who had brought great happiness into her life and she would die in peace knowing that her little girl would be well cared for."

"It was good of you," I said, "although you could do it. Not all people bother themselves with the problems of others."

"And what did I get from it? The most excellent of housekeepers. So you see, the advantage was mine. Colette died soon after that. I saw her lying in her coffin with a look of peace on her face which I shall never forget."

"Poor Lisette! Does she know of this?"

"She wouldn't remember very much—probably vaguely those rooms in which she used to be shut away, I don't know. She couldn't have been much more than five when she was taken away. She was told that her parents were dead and that Tante Berthe had taken their place. I don't think the poor child got much pampering from Tante Berthe, but she would be given good food and brought up rather strictly—which might have been good for her. I gave orders that she was to share Sophie's lessons and when you came she was with you and Sophie. I don't know whether it was the right thing to have done. She was one of us . . . and yet not one of us. I have always been a little anxious about Lisette."

"Lisette can take care of herself, I think."

"You know her better than any of us. You and she became friends right from the time you came here . . . you and she more than Sophie."

"Lisette was always easier to know. She and I had a good deal of fun together."

"Well, you know who she is now. Lottie, I don't think it would be wise to let her know the story. Much better to let her go on believing that she is the child of a conventional marriage, which her aunt and I agreed was what she should be told."

"I shall say nothing of what you have told me. I can see no good in bringing it up now."

"No. She is a proud girl and might be upset to know she is the

185

daughter of, well . . . not a prostitute but a poor girl who took the occasional lover in order to make ends meet."

"I think you are right. Poor Lisette! But she was fortunate really. I wonder what would have happened to her if Tante Berthe had not come along, and you, too. Tante Berthe, I suppose, would have taken her to that farmhouse from which Colette ran away. One can imagine what sort of life Lisette would have had there. I think you can be pleased with what you did for Colette and her daughter."

"It has relieved me to talk to you of Lisette."

Yes, I thought, *and it has taken your mind off your own tragedy for a little while at least.*

Of course he could not stay at Tourville indefinitely, and it was with great reluctance that he left. I told him that I would bring the children to visit him and that whenever he felt the need to be with me he must come. I would welcome him at any time.

On that note he left—a poor, sad, broken man.

———

The months slipped past quickly. I went to stay at Aubigné. It was a sad house now. My father had become morose, though, Armand told me, he was in a much better mood since I had come. He and his father quarreled a good deal and it was certainly not always Armand's fault. Armand was a man deeply concerned with his personal affairs; he interested himself in the estate but not too much; he liked to go to Court; he was the sort of man who, because he had been born into the aristocracy, considered that those who had not been were beneath him. Such an attitude was not accepted as readily as it had once been; and my father told me that one or two members of the great families were beginning to wonder whether something should not be done to raise the conditions of the poor. My father was one of these people.

He was a very honest man and he admitted to me that such thoughts had not come to him until he had realized that it might be expedient to have them.

Marie Louise was still barren and entirely devoted to her religion, which took the form of long prayer sessions and frequent celebrations of Mass in the château chapel. Sophie had become more of a recluse than ever, and with those rooms in the tower being more or less apart from the rest of the household, there was beginning to be attached to them one of those legends which spring up in such places. Some of the servants said that Jeanne was a witch who had arranged for Sophie's mutilations so that she could have power over her. Others said that Sophie herself was a witch and her scars were due to intercourse with the devil.

What disturbed me was that no attempt was made on my father's part to stifle such rumors. Tante Berthe did her best and that was very good, for she was one who was accustomed to being obeyed; but although the stories were never repeated in her presence that did not mean they were not in the maids' bedrooms and the places where the servants congregated.

So it was not a very happy household.

Lisette enjoyed being there—for I had taken her with me—but she did not altogether relish coming under Tante Berthe's scrutiny. "But I am a married woman now," she said, "and even Tante Berthe must remember that." At the same time she loved the château, and said it was such a grand old place and Tourville was nothing compared with it.

My father took such pleasure in my company and talked most of the time about what he and my mother had done together; how they had been completely happy in each other's company. As though I did not know!

"We were singularly blessed to have such a daughter," he said, but I believed that when they had been together they had thought of little else but each other. It was only now that he had lost her that he turned pathetically to me.

He visited us at Tourville and I was inclined to think that he was happier there than when at Aubigné. There were not so many memories. Besides, the children were there and it was not always easy to travel with someone as young as Claudine. So I prevailed on him to come to us, which he often did.

It pleased me. It meant that I did not have to be in that grim house with Sophie brooding in her turret. The Tourville family were always happy to see him. I thought then that I had been very lucky marrying into such a family. They might not be so grand as the Aubignés but they were most certainly kindly, and the atmosphere at Tourville was in complete contrast to that of Aubigné, bland, comfortable, Lisette called it flat and unexciting, whereas at Aubigné she felt that anything might suddenly happen.

Amelie was happily married; her husband was a gentle, rather meek man, colorless but extremely kind ... rather like Amelie herself. My father-in-law, I imagine, got on better with his son-in-law than he had with his less predictable son. Charles was of a fiery temper; he might be more significant as a person but not always so easy to live with and my parents-in-law, who liked to live in peace, were very happy with present arrangements.

We talked often of Charles. We had heard nothing of him. It was not possible to get news. For one thing, he was so far away and how letters could be sent from a country engaged in war I could not imagine.

From time to time we had visitors at Tourville and some of them had returned from America so they were able to give us a little news of what was happening there. One or two of them had been with Charles, so we knew he had arrived safely.

They were earnest young men, those returning warriors. They talked enthusiastically about the struggle for independence.

"Men should be free to choose who governs them," one young man said. He was very young, idealistic, and his pleasant features glowed with enthusiasm.

My father was with us at the time this young man came and years later I was to remember the manner in which he answered him.

"I believe," said my father, "that you young men, when you return from America, preach freedom for the oppressed."

"That is so, Comte," said the young man. "There is a wonderful spirit abroad and this war has made it clear. Monarchs and governors have no right to oppress those whom they rule. The oppressed must stand up and fight for their freedom."

"And these are doctrines you are preaching here? Is that so?"

"Assuredly, sir. They are the doctrines of truth and honor."

"And the doctrines which are inciting the mobs to riot?"

The blood flamed into my father's face. I knew he was seeing my mother coming out of the milliner's shop to face the mob whose fury killed her. It seemed that everything we discussed led to that dangerous subject.

"We are only telling people that they have rights," said the young man.

"Rights to kill their betters!" cried my father.

"No, sir, no, of course not. Rights which should be given them, and if they are not . . . to fight for them as the colonists are doing."

I changed the subject hastily. It was what I had to do continually. I liked best to be with my father on our own, and if then he talked of the war I could make sure that he was not reminded of the troubles in France.

He thought Charles was a fool to have gone to fight. First, he said, the quarrel had nothing to do with France; second, it meant that Frenchmen were coming back with revolutionary ideas; and third, France was paying heavily for her support of the colonists . . . and in more than money, which it could ill afford in any case.

"He has left his family . . . all this time. How long is it? It must be over a year now. I wish we had found a better match for you, Lottie."

"I am fond of Charles and I think he is of me."

"To leave you all this time! To go and fight for a cause which has nothing to do with this country!"

"He was challenged rather . . . I think he saw it like that."

"Yes," mused my father. "I would have liked someone higher for you."

"He *was* going to marry Sophie. You approved of that."

"Sophie was not the sort to attract important men . . . as you would. I was glad to make a match for her and the Tourvilles were ready. If only . . . but then you see you were not born in wedlock, and foolish as these conventions are they have to be considered. It seemed that the Tourville marriage was a very good one for you at the time."

"It was, and then I have Charlot and Claudine."

"Those dear ones, yes. Lottie, how I should love to have them at Aubigné . . . always." He looked at me sharply. "I see you are thinking it is hardly the place for children. But they would change it, Lottie. We should forget Sophie in her tower with dragon Jeanne, and Armand who cares for nothing but his pleasure, and his psalm-singing wife who spends most of her days in prayer instead of bringing babies into the world. And then there is that old misanthrope . . . myself . . . who would be a changed man if only he could have his loved ones about him."

"One day Charles will come home," I said. "I must be here when he does."

So once again we parted and my father went back to his life of mourning and I continued to wait for news of Charles's return. Occasionally I heard news of the war. It was not yet over. There seemed to be a series of victories and defeats and I gathered the English were not doing well.

Then one day we had a visitor.

I had met the Comte de Saramand when Charles had been making his arrangements to go to America. He had been one of those who had answered the call and he had stayed at the château several times with us.

As soon as I saw him standing in the hall I knew that he had brought news of Charles and a feeling of dread swept over me.

Why was Charles not with him? They had gone together. Surely they would return together. And why had the Comte de Saramand called on me?

There was something about his demeanor which disturbed me. He looked very grave.

"Welcome, Comte," I said. "You have news of my husband?"

The Comte looked at me steadily and said: "I have bad news for you, I'm afraid."

"Charles . . ." I murmured.

"He fell at the Battle of Eutaw Springs. I was with him at the end. His last thoughts were of you. He regretted leaving you and said he never should have done so. He wanted me to tell you that he loved you . . . that you were the only one."

"Dead?" I murmured. "Charles . . . *dead.*"

"He gave me this ring which I was to return to you."

I took the ring. It was the gold ring with the lapis seal which he had always worn. There could be no doubt. Charles was dead.

Although I had come face to face with this possibility, the realization that it had actually come to pass was a great blow and shocked me deeply.

Charles . . . dead. Buried somewhere in a foreign land. Gone forever.

———

I mourned for Charles. I shut myself away to consider what his death would mean.

It was so long since I had seen him that I could not pretend the blow was as great as it would have been if he had been snatched away from me when I saw him every day. Life would go on the same at Tourville. Charles had for a long time not been a part of it, but death is shocking however it comes. Death is irrevocable. How many times had I thought, during his absence, when he comes back we must discuss this ... or plan that? And now ... no more.

Charlot scarcely remembered him. Claudine had never really known him. His parents had lost their only son but they had a substitute in their son-in-law and this meant that Amelie and her husband would live permanently at Tourville.

When I broke the news to Charlot, I said: "Charlot, your father will never be coming back."

"Oh," said Charlot, looking up from his painting, "does he live in America now?"

"He was killed in battle," I told him.

His eyes were round. "Did they shoot him with a gun?"

"I ... I think so," I faltered.

"I wish I had a gun," said Charlot and began to sketch one on the paper before him.

And that was what Charles's death meant to Charlot.

I cried to myself indignantly: *It is your fault, Charles, if your son does not care. You should never have left us.*

I felt sad and lonely at night. He would never lie there beside me again. I should never feel his arms about me. But I had been lonely so long that I had grown accustomed to sleeping alone.

"You should never have left us, Charles," I said again and again.

So I did not feel much change at Tourville.

When my father heard the news he came over at once. His first words were: "There is nothing to keep you here now."

I had to admit it was true.

"Aubigné should be your home. Do you agree, Lottie?"

I said I should need time to think.

"Please, Lottie, come home."

He, who had once been so proud, who had rarely thought to ask for what he wanted, but merely to take it as his right, was pleading with me.

I knew what it would mean to him if I went. Was it the best thing for the children? Would it be right for me?

He had taken my hand. "Lottie," he said. "Please."
And I knew that I was going to say yes.

A Tutor Comes

It was several months since we had arrived at Aubigné and it seemed more like home to me than Tourville ever had. The children loved it. I had been rather ashamed at the blithe manner in which Charlot and Claudine said good-bye to their Tourville grandparents, who had always been so kind to them. But the prospect of adventure and new places was irresistible to them and they were guileless enough not to hide this. I am sure the Tourvilles understood and were completely sincere in wishing us all every possible happiness in our new home. Louis-Charles also was excited at the prospect and as the eldest of the children he had great influence on the others, though Charlot certainly had a will of his own.

I had to stifle my emotion when the castle came into view. I had seen it many times, of course, but somehow because of the circumstances it looked different. It seemed as it had on that first time when I had come with my father and did not know then that it was to be my home. It was like a mighty fortress with its corbelled watch towers, and its stone walled parapets and buttresses proclaimed its strength. I glanced up at what I called in my mind "Sophie's Tower" and I wondered what life was going to be like at Aubigné.

Lisette was delighted to be going back. She had found life at Tourville excessively dull and she had always had a special feeling for Aubigné.

My father was overjoyed to receive us and he could not take his eyes from the children. I thought, *He is happy . . . at least as happy as he can be without my mother.* Armand welcomed us with that brand of nonchalance which could be construed as indifference, but at least he had no objection to our coming. Marie Louise was even more indifferent. My father said derisively: "She has her eyes so firmly set on her place in Heaven that she has become unaware that she is still on Earth."

Sophie kept to her tower and for a long time the children did not know of her existence.

So we settled in and the weeks passed to months. Strangely enough, bereaved widow that I was—and I still thought nostalgically of Charles and the old days although it was so long since I had known them—I felt more alive at Aubigné than I had at Tourville. Aubigné seemed closer to affairs. My father rarely went to Paris now but he said that when he did I must go with him; and I did believe that since our coming he had begun to take a more lively interest in what was happening in the country.

I had been about two months at Aubigné when Dickon arrived.

My grandmother had died. Dickon said that the death of Zipporah had been the end of her. She had gradually lost what grip she had had on life.

He talked to me more seriously than he ever had before and as he was continually striving to be alone with me these talks were frequent. Once when we were riding he suggested that we tether our horses and sit by the stream, for it was not easy to talk on horseback.

He sat there occasionally picking up a stone and throwing it into the stream.

"Poor Zipporah," he said. "That she should meet such an end! She was always such a quiet person. I was very fond of her, you know. Oh, you can look at me skeptically. I know she didn't like *me*, but I don't have to like people just because they like me, do I?"

"I really believe you think you would have to like almost the whole of the world if you did that."

He laughed. "No ... not quite. Zipporah was against me right from the start. It was understandable. I was an impossible child. I hope none of yours turn out as I did. I rather think one of mine— Jonathan—might. We shall have to watch him. Zipporah summed me up in her quiet way and put the black marks against me. Then she did the incredible herself. I don't think she ever stopped being amazed.

But look what it brought her! You ... the incomparable Lottie ... and then that wonderful romance. It was beautiful to see. A perfect love story. The passion of youth ... the separation ... and then the final reunion when they were both older, wiser, and capable of realizing what true love meant. It is an example to us all."

I guessed what he was leading up to and did not want him to say it ... yet. I felt very insecure and I doubted his intentions. I believed I would always do that. I told myself that I could never entirely trust him again.

"They were so happy together," I said. "So ideally suited. He so worldly, she so innocent. But she was an idealist and I think she made him the man she believed him to be."

"It is possible. And to die like that! The victim of fools ... for there are many fools in this country."

"Aren't there in all countries?"

"You are right. But France at this time cannot afford her fools. Can you feel it in the air? It is like the quiet before the storm."

"I can feel nothing."

"That is because you are not aware of what is going on."

"I do live here and you are a visitor."

"I travel a little in France and I watch. . . ."

"Dickon, your mother said something about fingers in pies. Are you here on a mission?"

"If I were it would be essentially secret, wouldn't it, and therefore you would not expect an honorable man to divulge it."

"I always thought there was some motive . . ."

"The main motive in my life is to be with you."

"I don't believe that."

He sighed. "How can I make you believe it?"

"You never could. There is too much behind us. You once talked of marrying me, but you took Eversleigh instead. You married soon afterwards ... most suitably."

"I made one big mistake. I should have waited for you."

"But think what Eversleigh meant to you."

"I can only think what you mean to me. Lottie, we have the example of your parents. How wise they were! Think of their idyllic life together."

194

"It would never be like that for us."

"Why not?"

"Because we are different. You will tell me that you and my father have a lot in common. But it needs two to make a perfect union and I can assure you that I am not in the least like my mother."

"Lottie, come back to me. Marry me. Let's start where we should have started all those years ago."

"I don't think it would be wise."

"Why not?"

"If I married again I should want something wonderful. I remember seeing my parents together. I have heard by father talk of his marriage to my mother . . . nothing less would satisfy me. If I cannot have that I prefer to stay as I am, free, independent."

"You shall have everything you want."

"It's too late, Dickon."

"It's never too late. You have some feeling for me."

"Yes, I have."

"You feel better for having me around."

I hesitated. "I . . . I am aware of you."

"Very much aware of me. There is a sparkle in your eyes when you see me." He turned to me and, putting his arms round me, kissed me. I could not hide the fact that I was moved, that I responded, that I wanted him to go on kissing me; but I kept seeing my mother, hearing her voice, and she was warning me against him. She seemed closer to me now that she was dead.

I pushed him away vehemently. "No, Dickon," I said. "No."

"We are both free now," he reminded me. "Why not? Let's take it up where we should have done all those years ago."

I could not deceive myself. I wanted to say yes. I knew life with Dickon would be a hazardous adventure, but I wanted to embark on it. Yet I could still see my mother warning me, as it were, from the grave; and so vivid was that image that I could not ignore it.

"You could find someone very suitable in the circles in which you move," I said. "London society, is it? Some rich woman?"

"I have a fair share of worldly goods now, you know."

"But you would still like more."

"Who can honestly say no to possessions?"

195

"Certainly not Dickon."

"Well, you would hardly be a penniless *parti*," he said lightly. "I am sure your father, who is immensely rich, would not allow that. Then you must have dues to you from Tourville."

"I see that in the midst of your devotion you have had time to calculate my worth."

"Your worth is above diamonds, which I always considered to be more worthy than rubies. The fact is, Lottie, I love you. I always have. I always knew you were the one for me ever since I set eyes on the beautiful child with the wilful ways and the passion which matched my own. Do you imagine that your romantic birth did anything to stem my love for you?"

"No, I didn't think that. The dam was Eversleigh."

"Cruel! Cruel and cutting. A man makes one mistake. Is he never to be forgiven for it?"

"Forgiven, yes. But the mistake—if mistake it was—is not easily forgotten."

My mood towards him had changed. When he talked about my father's wealth I remembered how interested he was in the estate, his speculation, his pleasure in it which he had shown when we were riding about it.

If I married again it would not be for my possessions, and although I was sure Dickon's feeling for me went deep, I knew that he could not help considering every advantage.

He desired me. I was well aware of that. But I had seen with Charles that such desire does not last and when it begins to be less urgent there must be some firm foundation on which to build a love such as that which I had seen between my mother and father.

Dickon went on pleadingly: "There are two very good reasons why you should come to England. The first is that I need you and you need me. The second is that this is a very uneasy country. You are shut away in this rural district and you forget it. Can you ever forget, though, what happened to your mother?"

I shook my head. "Never," I said vehemently.

"Why did it happen? Ask yourself why. France is in a ferment. I know that. It is my business to know it."

"Secret mission?" I asked.

"It is obvious that if there is trouble in France we on the other side of the Channel will not be very sorry about that. They deserve what is coming to them, and remember this, Lottie, it *is* coming. It's in the air. Wise people are aware of it. Look back a little. Louis the Fourteenth left a strong France but during the reign of the fifteenth Louis France's fortunes were dissipated. The extravagant excesses of that King enraged the people. They hated the Pompadour and du Barry. The finery ... the carriages in the streets ... the glittering entertainments ... the fortunes spent on dresses and jewels by the aristocrats had been noticed. And beside this are the poor ... the starving poor. Such contrasts exist in other places but in no other have the foolish people called such blatant attention to them. They are nearly bankrupt. They have a young idealistic King with an extravagant wife who is an Austrian, and the French hate foreigners. There are agitators in this country whose sole task is to promote trouble. They started with *La Guerre des Farines* but it misfired somehow and instead of becoming a revolution it was a rehearsal for one ... probably due to the courage of the King when the mob marched on Versailles—and luck, of course. He had that."

"You hate them, Dickon."

"I despise them," he answered.

"You have never forgiven them for their attitude towards the colonists. They thought they were helping the oppressed. Charles thought that."

"And he left you, the fool. He lost you ... and his life. He earned the reward of his folly. I understand why he went to fight for the colonists. I wouldn't tell any French man or woman this, but I think they were right to stand out against the imposition of taxes. But for the French to raise companies of men and go to their aid when the money was needed in their own country, and then to come back and preach republican ideas when their monarchy and the whole structure of their country is beginning to crumble, that is the utmost folly. It is more than that—it is madness."

"And you think it will have some effect?"

"Have some effect! You have seen what happened to your mother. She knew nothing of their grievances, but the mob does not care on whom it wreaks its vengeance. She was an aristocrat in a grand carriage. That was enough for them. You have never seen these agitators. You don't know how persuasive they can be."

"I did see one once. But I did not stay long to listen. I was with my father and we left immediately."

"That was wise of you. Don't make any mistakes. There is danger in the air. It could catch up with you. Come away while you are safe."

"What of my father?"

"Bring him with you."

"Do you think he would ever leave Aubigné?"

"No."

"I shall not leave him as long as he wants me. It would be too cruel to go away. It would be worse for him than my being at Tourville. At least then I was in France."

"And what of me?"

"You, Dickon? You are capable of taking care of yourself."

"You will see that I am right."

"I hope not."

"And I shall not give up. I shall continue to harry you. And one day you will realize that it is useless to hold out any longer."

"You mean you will come to France again on your secret mission."

"On my romantic mission. That is the only mission important to me."

We talked and I swayed. I believed at some times I was on the point of giving up everything for Dickon. He had that effect on me. Then I heard again the voice of my mother and I remembered that I could not leave my father. So I tried to be content and make a happy life for myself in Aubigné.

———

Time passed quickly at Aubigné. There was so much to do. Lisette had added the task of governess to that of lady's maid. She had always taught Louis-Charles when he was young and now she took over Claudine. I helped her and we enjoyed our sessions with Claudine, who was a bright child.

My father said the boys should have a tutor and he would look out for someone reliable and suitable.

The American war had come to an end and even King George had given his consent to the independence of the colony. Everyone was very pleased about that including my father, who pointed out that the

English had been soundly beaten and that as well as losing half a continent they had added millions to their national debt.

"A piece of folly," he said.

And I thought of what Dickon had said about French participation in it. It had taken Charles; it had brought a republican spirit into France; Dickon had said that it could have far-reaching consequences, and although I tried to dismiss those implications from my mind, I could not do so entirely.

I had been up to see Sophie on several occasions. I think she could bear to see me now that Charles was dead. Neither of us had him now. I believed that was how she saw it.

She managed to look quite pretty in a way. Jeanne, who was an expert seamstress, had devised a method of attaching hoods to her gowns; they always matched the color or were beautifully blended; and they were designed to hide her scars completely.

I tried to make her believe that Charles and I had not been lovers before our marriage. I insisted that the flower she had found in his room had not been dropped there by me. I wished I could have found that flower, but although I had searched, I never had been able to. Charles had given it to me so long ago and I had never given it a thought until Sophie mentioned it. I greatly regretted that it was lost and I could not show it to Sophie to prove that I was speaking the truth. But she did not want to hear any more on the subject and I knew that if I persisted I should be prevented from going again to see her and I was trying very hard to get back to that relationship which we had once shared.

The children were a safer subject, but I did not take them to see her. It occurred to me that it might make her resentful of me if she saw the children, for she would immediately think that they might have been hers. So I merely told her about Charlot's prowess at sport and how he enjoyed playing with Louis-Charles.

I knew that Lisette went to see her, and I thought it was a great breakthrough when Lisette and I went together and there were the three of us just as there used to be in the old days.

Lisette was a great asset. She could keep the conversation flowing in the right directions. She brought materials to show Jeanne and we all discussed the making of a new gown for Sophie.

I thought: One of these days we shall persuade her to come down and live like an ordinary member of the household. There was no reason why she should not. She looked rather pretty in her cleverly fashioned gowns, and the hood seemed like a charming fashion.

Jeanne would welcome us when we went up so I supposed we were making good progress.

There was a sudden change in Armand. He seemed to have become almost lively and there was a new sparkle in his eyes. It was as though he were taking a new and sudden interest in life.

I mentioned it to my father when I was sitting with him in the small room of his own apartments which he regarded as his very private sanctum. I was one of the few who were invited to join him there.

When I mentioned Armand, he smiled and said: "Yes, he has changed. So you noticed. He really is getting quite enthusiastic about this project."

"He has a project then?"

"Yes. Perhaps he is rather overreacting. But on the other hand, it is a change to see him really getting interested in something. He is gathering together quite a little band of his friends. He was deeply affected, you know, by what . . ." My father faltered and went on briskly: "By what happened to your mother."

I nodded.

"He has always had strong feelings about the rights of those born in high places, and what happened was an outrage against his class."

"So it was that which affected him so deeply, not . . ."

"Armand's feelings for people do not go very deep. But he can feel strongly for causes. People are like that. Have you noticed? Those who campaign on behalf of the masses very often have little feeling for the individuals. Armand is such a one. So what deeply affected him was the outrage against class. It has stirred him to action, and he is gathering together a number of his friends with some scheme in mind for forming an armed band to deal with those agitators who are making speeches in the towns. They seem to be the ones who are stirring up trouble. Indeed it was one of those . . ."

I put my hand over my father's. "Don't talk of it," I said.

"You are right. I should stop myself. It brings it all back more vividly. We were saying that Armand had changed and it is a change for

200

the better. It is good to know that he can show some spirit about something. I thought he never could."

"What do they plan to do?"

"I don't quite know. When they find these agitators speaking to the people they will attempt to answer them ... and if there is trouble they will be ready to deal with it."

"There really is a great deal of trouble in the country, I fear," I said.

"That is so, my dear. Sometimes I say to myself as our King did, 'Perhaps after me the deluge.' But it won't come to that. There are men like Armand all over the country. They would soon deal with a revolt. Sometimes I wish it would come to the boil so that we could deal with it. It is these undercurrents, these subversive attempts to undermine law and order, which terrify me."

I could see that the subject was dangerously near that one which could bring back such poignant memories, and although they were never far from the surface of his mind, I wanted to stop his plunging into them. So I talked of Charlot and asked how he was getting on with his chess which my father was teaching him.

"Not bad ... not bad at all. He lacks the necessary concentration ... but he might play one day."

"He enjoys being with you."

"He likes best to talk about the castle." My father smiled. "I have had to look up our family history to satisfy him."

"Claudine likes too to get into this room."

"Ah, Claudine. She is a minx."

There was no doubt what the children's presence meant to him. How could I ever go to Dickon and take them away from him!

I vowed to myself that I would never leave Aubigné while my father lived.

The castle had its effect on Lisette. I realized that before we came here there had been a vague dissatisfaction in her manner. She had never talked about her farmer husband and I had not asked because I had quickly understood that that period of her life was something of which she did not wish to be reminded. It had brought her Louis-Charles, it was true, but although she was ambitious for him, she did not show him a great deal of tenderness.

But since we had returned to the castle she had become more like the old Lisette I had known when we were young girls. She used to come to my room to dress my hair and we had a great deal of fun trying out new hairstyles. At Court, under the influence of the most extravagant of queens, they were becoming more and more ridiculous. Ladies vied with each other to build up these towers of folly on their heads, using jewels, feathers, and stuffed birds. Lisette amused herself by trying out ideas on her own and my hair.

I had always been fond of her but since my father had told me the pathetic story of her beginnings, I felt tender towards her, and when she was laughing and talking with me I often used to wonder what her life would have been like but for my father.

We talked about everything that came into our heads. We often discussed the children and I told her that now that they were growing up my father wanted to find a good tutor for the boys.

"We can manage Claudine for a little while yet," she said, "but boys in their teens certainly do need a tutor."

"I daresay my father will find someone soon. He is waiting until he goes to Paris and then he can make enquiries in certain quarters. He is most anxious to find the right sort of person."

"That is very important. And this tutor ... he will teach Louis Charles as well?"

"But of course."

I glanced at Lisette in the mirror. Her mouth had that old square look which I had noticed before. I construed it as a form of bitterness. She was very proud, I knew, and hated to accept charity.

I said quickly: "It is good for Charlot to have a companion round about his own age. I am so glad you had a son, Lisette."

"He certainly made a lot worthwhile." She had recovered and was smiling.

"Armand seems to have changed lately," she added.

"Oh, yes, he has a project. The Comte was telling me about it."

"A project? What sort of project?"

"Well, you know there is some concern about what is happening in the country."

"Is there?" said Lisette.

"Lisette, you must give some serious attention to these matters."

"Why?"

"Because they concern you."

"How could they concern *me?*"

"Remember my mother."

"Oh, yes," said Lisette quietly.

"There was an agitator in the town. It was his talk which aroused the fury of the mob."

"I know. Don't talk of it. I can't bear it. Your mother was such a charming . . . *good* lady."

"Apparently these agitators are traveling round the country. They are men with a gift for words. Well, people are getting rather worried about it. Even Armand."

"Even Armand!" She echoed my words.

"Yes, he and some friends are getting together apparently."

"What are they going to do?"

"They will try to do something about it. I don't know what."

"Oh . . . I see. Armand has certainly changed. He seems to have found something he can really care about."

"Armand was incensed by what happened to my mother. It evidently stirred him."

"To a hatred of the rabble?"

"He always had that. But this brought home to him how much damage they could do. Well he and his friends are getting together and they are going to do something. I think it's a good thing, don't you?"

"That people should be aware of what is going on, yes."

"Dickon is always talking about it."

"Dickon! I thought when he was here he talked of other things!"

"He does, but he talks a good deal about the state of affairs in France as well."

"What does he . . . the Englishman . . . know of French affairs?"

"He seems to make it his business to find out."

"Does he tell you what he finds out?"

"No. It is all rather secret, I gather. I accuse him of being on some mission."

"It would be against France, I suppose."

"I don't know. He won't talk of it."

"He is a fascinating man. I don't know how you can resist him."

I was very frank with Lisette as I had been in the past and I admitted that sometimes it was not easy.

She understood.

"What if you married him?" she said.

"I have sworn never to leave my father."

"He would not wish you to stay surely, if you would be happier married."

"It would be too much for him. If he knew I wanted to go he would say I should, I know. Think of it. I should take the children with me. It would be too cruel."

"And me . . . ? Would you take me with you?"

"But of course you would come. You and Louis-Charles."

"I think the Comte is a little bit fond of Louis-Charles. Do you agree?"

"I am sure he is. Louis-Charles is a delightful boy."

"I fancy I see the Comte's eyes on him now and then, which is rather strange, don't you think?"

"No, I don't. The Comte likes lively children. He is desperately missing my mother and the best thing that can happen to him is to have children in the house."

"His own . . . yes. But the way in which he looks at Louis-Charles . . ."

"Oh, Lisette, stop being so obsessed."

"With what?" she asked sharply.

"With position. You are always remembering that you are the niece of the housekeeper."

"Well, am I not?"

"Yes, but it is not important."

"It is . . . now," she answered. "If those agitators had their way, perhaps it would be a good thing to be the niece of the housekeeper and not such a good thing to be the daughter of a Comte."

"What an absurd conversation! How do you think my hair would look with this green feather stuck in it at a ridiculous angle?"

"Very amusing . . . and far more important than all this talk about boring matters." She snatched the green feather from me. "Here! Let's put it there, so that it sticks right up at the back. Isn't that grand?"

I gazed at my image in the mirror and grimaced at Lisette, who was watching me with her head on one side.

About a week later we had a visit from the Duc de Soissonson. This was quite unexpected and put the household in a turmoil.

Tante Berthe complained that she should have been told and immediately set to work ordering her staff in her usual efficient and peremptory manner. They were busy in the kitchens. The cook searched her prodigious memory and remembered that when the Duc had last stayed at the château, which was twelve years before, he had shown a preference for a very special potage, the recipe for which was a guarded secret known only to her family.

In appearance the Duc was quite insignificant in spite of his wealth, which I gather was immense, and his influence in the country was also great.

He chided my father for not visiting Paris nowadays.

"I heard what happened to the Comtesse," he said. "A sorry business. This rabble ... I wish we could do something about them. Did they find the ringleaders?"

My father, with great emotion, said that they had been unable to trace the agitator who was the real villain. It was impossible to accuse a mob. They had rioted and in the melée the horses had been frightened and the carriage overturned.

"We ought to put a stop to it," said the Duc. "Don't you agree?"

"With all my heart," answered my father. "If I could find those responsible ..."

I wanted to beg the Duc not to talk about it.

We sat down to dine in the great hall of the castle. Tante Berthe and the cooks had certainly made sure that all the culinary and domestic arrangements ran smoothly and I was sure there could not have been more attention to detail in the ducal establishment itself.

The Duc however did not stand on ceremony. He was friendly and easygoing and conversation at the table was far from stilted.

Inevitably it drifted to the troubles in France and my heart sank as I looked at my father.

"Something should be done about it," said Armand. I noticed he was eyeing the Duc speculatively and I wondered whether he was contemplating asking him to join his band. "These fellows are getting really dangerous."

"I agree," said the Duc. "Something should be done. But what, my dear fellow, what?"

"Well, we should stand together . . . those of us who want to keep law and order."

"Stand together . . . that is the idea," cried the Duc.

"We are not going to stand idly by," Armand told him.

"Certainly not!" went on the Duc. "Nice boys you have here, Comte. I watched them from my window. Grandsons, I suppose."

"One of them," said my father. "And I have a granddaughter too. I hope you will meet them before you leave us."

"I want to do that. Do you have a tutor for the boys?"

"Strange you should say that. We are in fact looking out for one now."

"Léon Blanchard," said the Duc.

"What's that, Soissonson?" asked my father.

"I said Léon Blanchard . . . best man in that line, my cousin's boy Jean Pierre tells me. Ought to get him for your boys, but I suppose you couldn't do that. Jean Pierre wouldn't let him go."

"I daresay we shall find a good man."

"It's not easy," said the Duc. "A bad tutor can be a disaster, a good one worth his weight in gold."

"I agree with that," said my father.

Armand put in: "There are quite a number of us. We are not going to stand by and let the mob take over in these small towns."

"Mind you," the Duc was saing, "Jean Pierre employs the man only two or three days a week now. I wonder . . ."

"You mean the tutor?" I asked.

"Yes, the tutor. He's the man. You ought to try and get hold of him. He might manage three days a week. Three days with the right man is better than the whole week with the wrong one."

"I think you are probably right," said my father.

"Leave it to me," said the Duc. "My cousin was tellling me about this man and how pleased Jean Pierre was with him. Said he and his boys were getting too old for a tutor now. They'll be going to their university soon. But they still get coaching for two or three days a week. I'll ask." He shook his finger at my father. "You will be most unwise to engage anyone else until you have seen Léon Blanchard."

"We must certainly see the man," said my father. "It is good of you, Duc, to take such an interest."

206

"Nice boys," said the Duc. "Look as if they should have the best."

The Duc de Soissonson spent three days with us. He talked a great deal to my father and continued to chide him for shutting himself away from his friends. My father presented Charlot to him, and because I felt that Lisette was more hurt to see her son left out than she had been for herself, I arranged that Louis-Charles should be presented to the Duc at the same time.

He was a little vague and seemed unsure which boy was his friend's grandson but he was very complimentary about them both. After he had gone, my father said: "I hope he doesn't forget about the tutor. He can be a little vague."

But the Duc did not forget and in less than a week after his departure, Léon Blanchard came to see us.

———

We were all impressed by Léon Blanchard. There was about him an air of dignity and a certain indifference as to whether or not he was employed, which was unusual in someone applying for a post. Not that there was anything insolent in his demeanor—far from it. His manners were impeccable. My father said to me afterwards that it was probably because several others were trying to secure his services.

His dress proclaimed him to be something of a dandy; his white wig accentuated his blue eyes, which were startling in his dark face; his high cheekbones and lean looks were quite attractive. His clothes were of good though far from gaudy material, his shoes sturdy but of fine leather. He had a pleasant voice, and because his manner and speech and everything about him suggested a man of breeding he was treated as such.

He was in my father's private sitting room when I was called in to meet him.

My father said: "You had better tell Monsieur Blanchard what will be required."

Monsieur Blanchard took my hand and bowed over it. He could have come straight from Versailles.

"I am very glad that you have come to see us Monsieur Blanchard," I said.

"I could not ignore a command from the Duc de Soissonson, madame," replied Monsieur Blanchard smiling.

"Oh, was it a command?"

"A very urgent request. The Duc is anxious that I shall be of help to you."

"Then I hope we can come to some arrangement."

We talked about the boys and what they had learned so far. He shook his head gravely, implying that they must certainly be in need of his tuition.

"It would be my pleasure to take on that task," he said. "But it may well be that your boys need a full-time tutor."

"That was what we were hoping for," I said.

"Then, madame, I cannot be of service. I have two charges whom I must see into the university. They are advanced and I spend three days at the Château de Castian. They are connections of the Duc de Soissonson, as you are probably aware. I could not desert them at this stage and in the circumstances would only have four days a week to spare here. You see how I am placed."

My father said: "These boys you are teaching . . . I understand they will in due course go to the university."

"Indeed they will, Monsieur le Comte, but until they do I am in duty bound to stay with them."

"It does not sound very difficult to me. You could spend four days of each week here and the other time with your present pupils. How would that work out?"

"Excellently, if it were not necessary to tie me down. I could come here and teach your boys for four days of the week. But there might be a time when I would feel it necessary to give an extra day to my original pupils . . . who . . forgive my saying so . . . have first claim on me."

"It does not seem an insurmountable problem," I said.

Then we laughed and chatted and it was agreed that Léon Blanchard should come to us for part of the week and if he should need a day off to spend with the boys of Castian, no obstacle would be put in the way of his taking it.

When he left we had agreed that he should start at the beginning of the next week.

After he had left my father said he thought it was an excellent arrangement. It would give us a chance to see how we liked each other.

I was pleased to see my father in an almost merry mood. I had Léon
Blanchard and the boys to thank for that.

So Léon Blanchard came into our household and he appeared to be
a great asset.

First, the boys liked him. He had a knack of making lessons interesting. He came to table with us. He, being such a gentleman, had made
that natural and the servants accepted him, which was in itself something of a miracle because they usually took umbrage if anyone, as
they would say, "stepped out of their class." I was not sure into which
class a tutor fitted, but it seemed that in Léon Blanchard's case there
was no question. He fitted naturally.

I thought Lisette might be a little put out because he took meals
with us, something which I had wanted her to do, but she had refused. However, at least she showed no resentment.

He used to sit over the dinner table and talk with my father, usually
about the state of the country. He had traveled widely and could discuss other countries with firsthand knowledge; and he could be very
entertaining. He had a wonderful gift of words and could create a
scene vividly with a few well-chosen sentences.

"I am grateful to the Duc for sending us such a man," said my father.

There was one thing he did which was the most outstanding of all.

One day he was looking for the boys and strayed up to Sophie's
turret. Thinking that part of the castle was uninhabited, he opened a
door and walked in. Sophie and Jeanne were playing a card game together.

I can imagine her horror. Fortunately she was wearing her hood and
that must have saved her considerable embarrassment.

She must have been horrified, for the rest of the household respected her wish for privacy and whenever we did attempt to see her
we did so by first asking Jeanne if it were possible.

Lisette got out of Jeanne exactly how it had happened.

"There was Mademoiselle Sophie seated at the table," said Jeanne,
"and this man was walking into the room. I stood up and asked what
he wanted. He guessed I was a servant and went straight to Mademoiselle Sophie. She got to her feet, her face scarlet with mortification,

and he took her hand and bowed and explained that he was the tutor looking for his charges and she must forgive him for the intrusion. Well, she surprised me. She asked him to be seated. He looked at her as though he was interested. She always says she is hideous but that isn't so. With her hood on she looks like a lady wearing a special fashion, and fashions, heaven knows, are crazy enough these days. She asked him to take a glass of wine with us and there she was telling him how she had got her scars. I'd never heard her talk like that with anyone before. She explained her terror when the crowds pressed in on her . . . and the pain . . . and everything.

"He listened attentively and said he could well understand her horror of crowds. People *en masse* could be terrifying. And he said he thought what a charming fashion it was to wear a hood in the way she did. It would be the rage at Court if she appeared there in it. She said she was not likely to do that, but it was clear that she enjoyed his company and when he rose to go he apologized once more for coming in so unceremoniously, and he asked if he might come again. You could have knocked me down with a feather when she said he might."

How amazing it was that this stranger had been able to break through what had seemed an impenetrable barrier.

Even Lisette was a little charmed by him, and I thought what a happy solution it would be if he married her. She needed a happy married life. Her experiences with the farmer whom, I began to understand, she had come near to loathing, had embittered her in some way. I was sure that a happy marriage with an attractive man would heal her wounds.

Lisette and I found great pleasure in riding together and we often tied up the horses and stretched ourselves on the grass and indulged in the pleasure of lighthearted conversation. Lisette was an inveterate gossip and if she could discover a hint of scandal about anyone in the neighborhood she was delighted. What she liked most was discussing the royal family. She had the Frenchwoman's dislike for Marie Antoinette and declared her belief in the rumors about her when they were scandalous. She often went into the town and once brought back two books which were allegedly about the Queen. One was *Les Amours de Charlot and 'Toinette,* which told of the supposed love affair between the Queen and her brother-in-law Charles, Comte d'Artois.

The other was even worse. This was *Essai Historique sur la Vie de Marie Antoinette* . . . a scurrilous production.

I read it with indignation and told Lisette she should burn the book. "It is obviously full of lies," I said. "It doesn't make sense."

"I think it is only fair that when queens behave immorally they should not be allowed to escape criticism. Think what happens to poor girls who are not queens. One false step and their lives are ruined."

"But this is lies. You have only to read it to see through it. It is written by someone who hates the Queen."

"It is printed in secret but that does not prevent people's seeing it. I was told that you could buy it in most of the towns, and all over the country people are reading about the private life of their Queen. So why shouldn't I?"

"No sensible people will mistake such rubbish for truth."

Lisette looked at me slyly. "I will not show you anything else," she said.

"I hope you will not show this sort of thing to anyone."

"How fierce you are! It is only a joke."

"It wouldn't be to the Queen."

"I am sure she would laugh. They say she is very frivolous."

I refused to discuss the scandals about the Queen with Lisette and she stopped talking about them. Instead she talked about Léon Blanchard and marveled that he had become quite friendly with Sophie.

"Lottie," she said one day, "do you think he might marry Sophie?"

"Marry Sophie! She would never marry."

"Why not? She allows him to visit her. Hasn't she changed since he came?"

I flushed a little. A short while ago I had been thinking he might be a suitable husband for Lisette.

"I know," went on Lisette, "he is only a tutor and not therefore of the right social standing to mate with the daughter of a Comte, but she is scarred . . . damaged goods, you might say."

"Don't talk about Sophie like that!" I said sharply.

"You are soft, Lottie. Women in families like this one are regarded as so much merchandise or bargaining counters. Marriages are made for them . . . suitable marriages. Poor Sophie is not of the same value as she once was. I am sorry if I offended you by referring to her as damaged goods, but that is really what she is."

"If she could marry and have children, it would be wonderful. She looks quite pretty in her hoods."

"But for a husband she would have to take off her hood."

"I think Léon Blanchard is a very kind man."

Lisette was silent.

"I should be happy if she married," I went on. "I would cease . . ."

"To feel guilty for marrying the one who was to have married her?"

"I know she had rejected him."

"For good reason. Oh, Lottie, you should never feel guilty in life. What happens happens and if one person's tragedy is another's good fortune that is all the luck of the game."

Sometimes Lisette made me see myself too clearly for comfort. I did feel guilty though, and if Sophie would only marry and be happy, I should be able to wash all guilty feelings from my mind.

Lisette smiled at me knowingly.

"Let us pray for a match between them . . . for her sake and for yours."

It really seemed as though this might not be impossible. Sophie had changed. She even joined us for dinner now and then. She sat next to Léon and seemed to draw comfort from him and she began to look prettier in her beautifully colored hoods, and there was a certain contentment visible on her face.

What a change since Léon Blanchard had come to our household!

Armand talked about his friends when we gathered over the meal and the servants had brought in the last of the dishes. There would be an atmosphere then almost of conspiracy.

"These agitators are doing their work more frequently now," said Armand. "There was one in Aurillac last week. The trouble is we never know when they are going to strike. It is the same procedure every time. A man suddenly gets up in the marketplace, begins to harangue the crowd, tells them how they are maltreated, rouses them to fury, and usually that starts it."

"Why is it that you cannot find out where they are likely to be?" asked Léon. "If you did . . . and your band could be there waiting for them . . ."

"We plan to have our agents watching for them, visiting the towns,

212

listening. We shall catch up with them in time. Then we shall be ready for them. You should join us, Blanchard."

"I doubt I should have the time. But if I had I should be with you."

"I am sure we could arrange something."

"Unfortunately I have to prepare lessons for my pupils. I think perhaps that in taking on two sets of them I may have given myself too much."

My father said: "Of course Monsieur Blanchard has not time to join your band, Armand. You should know better than to ask him."

Any suggestion that Blanchard might leave threw my father into a panic. He had assured himself that, having been recommended by the Duc de Soissonson, Blanchard must indeed be the best possible tutor. His coming had made such a difference to us all. The boys seemed to enjoy their lessons; they were more docile, more serious; the Comte himself enjoyed Léon's conversation and would miss his company; but perhaps above all was what he had done for Sophie. It was so much more natural that she should join us for meals and live like a normal member of the family. Shutting herself away in her turret had been most unhealthy.

"I shall see what can be done," said Léon. "I do realize the importance of your mission. It may well be that I can find a little time."

Armand was delighted and beamed his approval of Léon Blanchard. He went on to talk at length of the aims and intention of his band.

I often wondered what it was about Léon Blanchard that people seemed to find so attractive. I myself was growing interested in him but that was because I was seeing him as a possible husband for Sophie; but I did find he was in my thoughts very often.

One day when I returned from a ride I saw him going into the stables and I was suddenly aware of an extraordinary feeling, almost as though I remembered living that moment before.

It was uncanny. A kind of *déjà vue*.

Léon turned and faced me and the strange feeling vanished. He bowed with his customary graciousness and remarked that it was an excellent day for a ride.

———

That summer Dickon visited us again. He came unexpectedly and caught me completely off my guard. With characteristic aplomb, he expected to be warmly welcomed. I told him that he should have warned us, but he was behaving as though my father's château were one of the family homes.

"Anywhere you are I think of as my home," he said.

I told him he was ridiculous and I should have to make his excuses to my father.

My father, however, had taken quite a fancy to him. It was not surprising. When my father had been young he must have been a little like Dickon. They both possessed an overwhelming masculinity and therefore perhaps irresistible charm for the opposite sex; deeply rooted in this was an assurance that they would be welcome wherever they went.

Dickon told me that he had two reasons for coming to France. One he need not explain because it was obvious: myself. The other was that France was becoming the most interesting country in Europe and the eyes of the rest of the continent were fixed on it, asking: What is going to happen next? Wildly conflicting stories were circulated about the Queen's diamond necklace and the whole of Europe was agog for news. Some reports said it had been a gigantic swindle to discredit the Queen, but her enemies were sure that she had been involved in the conspiracy. The French exchequer was in a dire state and everywhere the Queen was blamed for her extravagance. The necklace was just another excuse to denigrate her. She was becoming known as Madame Deficit. In Paris there were demonstrations against her.

Dickon was very interested to meet Léon Blanchard. He regarded him intently and said: "I have heard your praises sung throughout the household, monsieur. I understand the boys profit from your excellent tuition. I have two myself so you will forgive me if I am a trifle envious. We have tutors who never seem to be able to endure my sons for more than a few months. What is your special secret?"

"I think," answered Léon, "it is to make the lessons interesting, to understand the young, and to treat them as individuals."

"Monsieur Blanchard certainly has the gift," said my father warmly.

It was obvious even at the first meal that Dickon was eager to find out all he could about what was happening in France.

"What do you think of this necklace affair?" he asked.

Léon Blanchard said: "The Queen does not understand the state of the country and the effect that her extravagances are having on the people."

Armand put in: "The people will never be satisfied. The Court has to preserve its dignity. It is quite clear that the Queen has been cheated over this matter of the necklace and rogues and vagabonds have sought to commit a great fraud and have used her name to bring it about."

"That certainly seems to be the decision of the courts," said my father.

"The people are rising against her," added Léon. "They blame her for everything."

"They have to have a scapegoat," replied Armand. "I am for harsher punishment for the rioters. We shall track them down eventually."

"Have you had any luck in discovering who the people are who are causing all this dissension?" asked Dickon.

"It's organized," said Armand. "That much we know. We don't so much want to catch members of the mob as the people who are inciting them. That is our motive."

"But what are you *doing* about it?" insisted Dickon.

"Don't imagine we are standing aside and letting them ruin this country," cried Armand. "We are going to find these people, I tell you. We are very busy doing just that."

Léon Blanchard said: "The Vicomte is deeply concerned with what is happening and has formed a band of men who share his opinions. I am happy to be one of them. We are doing very good work. I, alas, cannot be of as much use as I would wish. I have my work to consider."

"You are doing excellent work with us," said Armand.

I watched Sophie while Léon was speaking. I was surprised that she had joined us as we had a visitor. Dickon had not shown by a flicker of his eyelids that he was surprised by her presence; he had talked to her naturally, and although she was a little quiet, she appeared to be at ease. In fact, she looked pretty in a gown of pale lavender and a hood to match. I noticed how often her eyes rested on Léon Blanchard, and although I was glad to see her changed and happier, I did feel a certain apprehension as to what the future held for her. Was it really possible that he would marry her? If he would, some of the happiness she had known during her engagement to Charles might be brought back to her.

Armand was talking enthusiastically about the work he and his band were doing, gathering together noblemen from the outlying districts. "We'll get these agitators," he cried. "They'll get their just deserts and that will hit at the root of the trouble."

When we left the table Dickon said he wanted to take a walk round the ramparts and asked if I would join him.

I said I would. I took a wrap and we went to the top of the tower and walked round the path, pausing now and then to lean on the stone between the battlements and look out over the countryside.

Dickon said: "It looks deceptively peaceful, doesn't it?"

I agreed.

He put an arm round me. "You shouldn't stay here, you know. It's going to blow up at any minute."

"You have been saying that for a very long time."

"It has been simmering for a long time."

"Then perhaps it will go on for a little while yet."

"But not too long a while, and when it comes the deluge will be terrible. Marry me, Lottie. That is what you should do."

"And come to England?"

"Of course. Eversleigh awaits you and the children. My mother hopes every time I come to France that when I return you will be with me . . . you and the children to grow up with mine. Of course, I can't promise you such a paragon of a tutor as Monsieur Blanchard appears to be. Who is that man, by the way? He is a very distinctive character."

"Did you think so? You have only seen him at dinner."

"He's the sort of man who makes his presence felt. He seems to have changed the whole household. Not you, perhaps. I hope your thralldom is for one only."

I did enjoy Dickon's company. I liked the way he could be light-hearted when discussing the most serious subjects.

"I am in thrall to no one, Dickon," I answered. "You should know that."

"To my sadness, yes. But why don't you come to England? Get away from this cauldron of discontent."

"Which you have said several times is on the point of boiling over."

"It will be no joke when it does. Some will be sadly scalded. But not my Lottie. I shall not permit that. It would be much easier, though, if you summoned up your good sense and left while it is easy to do so."

"I can't go, Dickon. I won't leave my father."

"Eversleigh is a very big house. Don't underestimate it because you have passed your days in châteaux. Let him come too."

"He never would. This is his home, his country."

"A country, my dear, from which men such as he is will soon be trying to escape."

"He never would and I would not leave him."

"You care more for him than for me."

"But of course. He loves me. He brought me here to acknowledge me. I have been treated as his daughter. You chose Eversleigh."

"Will you never forget that?"

"How can I? It is there while you are there. You are Eversleigh and I was the one whom you rejected for its sake." I laid my hand on his arm. "Oh, Dickon, I have forgiven it . . . if there was anything to forgive. You were just behaving naturally as Nature designed you should. No. What I mean is that it is not important anymore. But I won't come to England while my father lives. You can see how he relies on me. If I went and took the children—and I would never go without them—what would happen to him?"

"I know his feelings for you. That is obvious. You are the one. Poor Sophie means little to him and he does not like his son overmuch. I see that. I am not surprised. Armand is a fool. What is all this about a band?"

"It's some sort of society . . . an organization. They are trying to scent out agitators."

"I gathered that, but with any success?"

"I don't think so."

"But what do they *do?*"

"They meet and talk. . . ."

"And talk and talk," said Dickon derisively. "That sort of thing should be done in secret. He should not announce his plans at the dinner table."

"Well, it is the family."

"Not entirely. There is the tutor for one."

"Oh, but he is one of them. Armand eventually persuaded him and

Monsieur Blanchard is very obliging. He likes to live on good terms with everyone. He did plead too much work at first but eventually he agreed."

"Such an obliging man. How did you come by him?"

"By recommendation. The very best. It was a great stroke of luck when the Duc de Soissonson visited us and the matter of getting a tutor came up. Monsieur Blanchard looks after the Duc's cousin's children . . . or some such relationship. He still does for a few days a week. So we have to share him."

"The gentleman seems in great demand. The Duc de Soissonson, did you say?"

"Yes. Do you know him?"

"I know of him. He is much talked of in Parisian circles."

"I have often wondered, Dickon, how you come to know so much."

"I am glad you respect my knowledge."

"Why do you come here so often?"

"Surely you know the answer to that."

"No, I don't. At least I am not sure. Dickon, I have come to the conclusion that there is much about you that I am not sure of."

"The mystery makes me more attractive, perhaps."

"No, it does not. I should like to know more about your motives. Sometimes I think you are rather pleased . . . perhaps that is not quite the right word . . . rather gratified about the troubles here."

"As an Englishman whose country has suffered a great deal at the hands of the French, what do you expect?"

"Are you by any chance engaged in work for the government of England?"

He took me by the shoulders and looked into my face. He was laughing. "Am I a spy?" he whispered. "Am I here on some secret mission? Why won't you believe that I have one purpose in my life and that is to win you?"

I hesitated. "I know that you would marry me, but I would never be first in your life, would I? There would always be other things . . . like Eversleigh. Property, possessions which mean power, I suppose. Yes, that would come first with you, Dickon, always."

"If I could convince you that nothing else mattered to me, would you alter your determination to stand out against me?"

"I would never believe it."

"There will come a day when I shall convince you."

He caught me to him and kissed me wildly, passionately, over and over again. I wanted to cling to him to tell him that I was ready to accept what he could give me, and if it were not all that I wanted, I would take what I could get. I tried to remind myself that I was a widow who had been long without a husband; and I was a woman who needed the love of a man. I had loved Charles in a way; I had missed him sorely; but I knew that what I felt for Dickon went deeper than that. It had its roots in the past when I had been a young idealistic girl, innocent and unworldly, dreaming of perfection. I drew away from him.

"That will not convince me," I said.

"When I hold you in my arms, when I kiss you, I know that you love me. It is something you cannot hide."

"I won't deny that I could deceive myself, but I won't, Dickon. I will have everything or nothing. Besides, as I have told you, I would never leave my father."

He sighed and leaned over the parapet.

"How quietly beautiful it is—the château land. The moonlight makes the river shine like silver where it catches it. Château land . . . rich land . . . all the wood of the forest and the farmlands. The Comte must be very proud of his possessions."

"He is. They have been his family's for generations."

"And to think they will go to that fool Armand! He has no notion of how to manage an estate of this size."

"There are people to do it for him just as you have at Eversleigh when you make your mysterious jaunts to the Continent."

"Still . . . a pity. But for him it might come to you."

"What do you mean?"

"Well, you are his daughter and he is very proud of the fact."

"Armand is very much alive. And in any case Sophie would come before me."

"Sophie! I wouldn't gamble on that. You are the apple of his eye. I am sure he will want to see you well provided for."

"Dickon!" I cried.

"Well?" He smiled at me lazily.

I said: "Are you calculating again?"

"I always calculate."

"And you think that my father will make me a rich woman. Oh, now I see why you are so ardent."

"I should be ardent if you were a pauper."

"But perhaps not for marriage."

"If you were a peasant in the fields I should still yearn for you."

"I know that you have yearned for many women and some of them doubtless of humble station. It is getting cold. I want to go in."

"Not until you have listened to me. Why are you so suddenly incensed?"

"Because for a moment I forgot what you are like. You want to marry me because you have somehow discovered that my father is leaving me something, and although you won Eversleigh and Clavering . . . and heaven knows what from your wife . . . you are still looking for more."

"You get so angry, Lottie. What a temper you have!"

"Good night, Dickon. I am going in."

He took my hand and pulled me towards him. "We should not part on bad terms."

I repeated wearily: "Good night."

Then he held me against him once more and in spite of the fact that I had followed the trend of his thoughts, I was moved to respond to his embrace. He was dangerous. He could catch me unaware.

I wrenched myself free.

"You have misunderstood," he said.

"No. I understand perfectly. You are following your custom of courting rich women. Well, my father is not dead yet and I pray it will be a long time before he is, but you may be sure that what he leaves me is not going to be added to what you have accumulated through your matrimonial maneuverings."

"Lottie, I have told you that if you were a peasant gleaning in the field . . ."

"You would want to make love to me, yes. I understand you perfectly, Dickon. And as you believe me to be an heiress you would like to marry me. Once more . . . Good night."

I ran off, and I was rather surprised that he did not attempt to follow me.

In my room I lay in my bed staring up at the ceiling.

"Go away, Dickon," I murmured. "Leave me alone."

I mistrusted him and yet I longed for him. He was becoming very dangerous and I should have to be wary.

———

I spent a disturbed night thinking about Dickon, trying all the time to make myself see him as he really was, and to upbraid myself for wanting him in spite of what I knew.

He, too, might have been disturbed by our conversation of the previous night because he went off during the morning on horseback on what I began to think of as his secret missions.

I walked round the gardens with my father in the morning and he told me that Léon Blanchard had taken the boys on a ramble. They were learning something about forestry and botany and finding it very interesting.

"They will be looking for specimens of various plants," said my father. "It is good for them to learn these things. Blanchard seems to have some knowledge on every subject."

I said: "Dickon is very concerned about the position here."

"Ah, yes. Who is not?"

"He thinks it is getting more dangerous."

My father smiled. "He would like you to return to England with him."

I was silent.

He insisted: "That is what he wants, is it not?"

"He has suggested it."

"And you, Lottie?"

"I am going to stay here, of course."

"Is that what you want?"

"Yes," I said determinedly.

"He interests me, that man. I have never ceased to be grateful to him, you know. It was due to him that I found you and your mother. If your mother had not been so much afraid of him she would never have written to me and I should never have known of your existence. My feelings towards him are mixed. Your mother always disliked him and was a little afraid of him, I think. But I have to say that I have strong admiration for him. In spite of everything he might well be the man for you, Lottie."

"I should have to think a great deal about that!"

"*I* have been thinking. You are too young to spend your life here like this. You should marry. You should have more children."

"Do you want to be rid of me?"

"Heaven forbid! What I want is your happiness and if that takes you away from me, then . . . so be it."

"I should never be happy away from you."

"God bless you, Lottie," he said emotionally. "Bless you for the happiness you have brought into my life. I want you to promise me that if you should long to go with him—or with anyone—you will not let any feeling of duty, or whatever you feel towards me, stand in your way. I am old; you are young. Your life is before you. Mine is finished. Remember, that more than anything I want your happiness."

"And do you know," I said, "I want yours."

He walked away from me for a moment. Then he said: "All will be well. This kingdom has stood firm in all the troubles which have beset it through the centuries. France will always be France. There has to be a future for our children. I won't deny the fact that I want Charlot to inherit Aubigné. Of course, if by any chance Armand has children it would have to go to them first . . . but that is hardly likely. After Armand, it must be Charlot. I have drawn this up with the lawyers."

"I hate all this talk of wills," I said. "I want everything to stay as it is now. You have years ahead of you yet."

"Let us wait and see," he said.

At midday Léon Blanchard and the boys came back with their specimens which they had found in the woods and the countryside. My father was very amused by the conversation at the table, which was all about the amazing things that could be found in the forest and the meadows. They were going to spend the afternoon listing their specimens. On the days when Léon Blanchard was with them, they usually worked mornings and afternoons to make up for those days when he was with his other pupils—though he always left them work to do in his absence.

Dickon came back late in the afternoon. I saw him arrive and I watched while he left the stables and sauntered into the castle.

I was still thinking of him as I dressed for dinner.

Sophie was there. She was talking to Léon Blanchard when I came in; she was flushed and smiling, almost sparkling as she did in his company. I decided to ask my father whether he would consider a match between them. I was sure he would give his approval, for he was very impressed by Léon Blanchard and, as Lisette had said, he would be very relieved to find a husband for Sophie.

Armand had not appeared and my father asked Marie Louise if he were coming down. Marie Louise looked surprised as though it was remarkable that she should be asked her husband's whereabouts. She had no idea, she said. So my father sent up one of the servants to find out.

The servant came down with the news that the Vicomte was not in his rooms. His valet said that he had laid out his clothes, for he was expecting him back, but he had not returned.

No one was very surprised, for Armand was never very precise in his movements. He had been known to go hunting and not come back until morning. Now that he was enthusiastic about his band, he sometimes stayed a night with one of the members if he had what he called "business" to do.

So the meal progressed as usual and Léon Blanchard talked about the boys' enthusiasm for botany and said he thought that it was an excellent subject for them to pursue. Sophie listened intently to him when he spoke. The change in her was growing more and more noticeable every day and I intended to speak to my father at the first opportunity.

Dickon was unusually quiet and after the meal he did not suggest we take a walk through the castle grounds or round the parapet.

I slept well that night to make up for the previous one and the next morning, when I was alone with my father, I broached the subject of Sophie and Léon Blanchard. We were sitting on the grass overlooking the moat when I said to him: "What a difference there is in Sophie nowadays."

"It is remarkable," he agreed.

"You know why. She is in love."

"Yes . . . Léon Blanchard."

"Suppose he offered to marry her?"

My father was silent.

"You have a high opinion of him," I said.

"I would never have thought a tutor a suitable husband for my daughter."

"In the circumstances . . ."

"I agree, the circumstances make a difference."

"You could not wish for a more cultured man. He is connected with the Duc de Soissonson, I believe."

"Very remotely apparently."

I turned round. Sophie was standing very near to us. I flushed scarlet because it was Sophie.

"Sophie," I cried scrambling up.

"I was taking a walk," she said.

"It's a lovely day."

Our father said: "Good morning, Sophie."

She returned the greeting and started to walk away.

"Won't you . . ." I began, but she walked on.

I sat down again. "How strange that she should appear like that. So quietly . . ."

"We wouldn't have heard the footsteps on the grass."

"I hope she didn't hear that we were discussing her."

"She should have made herself known before."

"I think she was trying to escape notice altogether."

"We were saying that she has changed, but she doesn't seem quite to have got over that ridiculous recluse attitude."

"Only when Léon Blanchard is there. If the matter were raised you would not withhold your consent, would you?"

"I should be as pleased as you to see Sophie happily settled."

"I am so glad."

Then we talked of other things.

When Armand did not appear at dinner that night we began to be uneasy. My father said if he was not back on the next day he would send a man round to some of Armand's friends to see if they had news of him.

It was rather an uneasy meal for we were all wondering about Armand. Léon Blanchard said he was sure he was with one of his friends because there had been a meeting on the day Armand had left the château. He himself had been too involved in the boys' lessons to leave the château during the whole day, and from the first he had made it clear to Armand that his post with the boys came first with him.

The following day we heard the disquieting news that Armand had

224

not arrived at the meeting which had taken place at the house of one of his friends. They could not understand why he did not come as he had definitely arranged to be with them and had sent no message to say he could not come or why he had failed to turn up.

Now we were really alarmed.

"There must have been an accident," said the Comte and began questioning the servants. Armand had left on horseback in the early afternoon, the groom told us, and he seemed in excellent spirits. He had gone alone.

There was no news of him all that day. Dickon went out with the men to scour the countryside, but it was the following day before anything was discovered. It was Dickon who found Armand's horse tethered to a bush close to the river. The animal was in a state of panic, not having been fed for so long; and by the river bank was a feathered hat which we identified as Armand's.

The river was deep and fairly wide at that point but Armand was a strong swimmer. It seemed possible, however, that there had been some accident and the Comte ordered that the river be dragged. This was done but nothing came to light. We tried to conjecture what could have happened.

The Comte thought that Armand may have been near the river when he slipped, was knocked unconscious and fell into the water. It was swift flowing and could have carried his body away and eventually reached the sea.

Dickon said: "This looks like foul play. He was on an excursion with his band. Is it possible that this was known? Indeed it is impossible that it was not known. All the band seemed to do was talk, and there must have been many who were against such an organization."

"Wouldn't they have attacked the entire band?" asked my father. "We must find Armand."

A week passed and nothing came to light. Armand had completely disappeared. Dickon had a theory that someone had killed him and buried the body, and he took Léon Blanchard with him and they went out with spades to search the spot by the river.

Everyone joined in the task of trying to find Armand. There were no lessons during those days and the boys joined enthusiastically in the search.

At length we really began to accept the fact that Armand was dead. This seemed certain for Armand would never have forgotten his horse unless circumstances made it impossible for him to do otherwise.

A gloom had fallen over the house.

"It is true," said the Comte, "that we live in dangerous times. Armand should never have got involved in that band. Poor Armand, he never did succeed in anything he undertook and all this has done has brought him to his death."

"He may not be dead," I said.

"Something tells me that I shall never see him again."

The search went on. In the town, in the castle nothing else was talked of; it went on and on; there were continual searches, but the weeks passed and there was no news of Armand.

———

It was about three weeks after Armand's disappearance when a messenger came to the castle.

It was midafternoon. Dickon had gone out. He was still hoping to find some clue which would solve the mystery of Armand's disappearance. The boys were in the schoolroom because it was one of Léon Blanchard's days to be at the château, and Lisette and I were in my room. She was making a shirt for Louis-Charles and I was seated at the window looking out.

I was still hoping for news of Armand and I had a notion that Dickon might well be the one to find it.

As I sat there I saw a stranger riding towards the castle.

"I think he's coming here," I said.

Lisette dropped her sewing and came over to stand beside me.

"Who is it?" I wondered.

"We'll soon know," she said. "Why don't you go down and see?"

"I will. It might be news of Armand. Wouldn't it be wonderful if he were alive and well!"

I was in the hall when one of the grooms came in with the stranger.

"He is asking for Monsieur Blanchard, madame," said the groom.

"I think he is in the schoolroom." One of the maids had appeared and I said to her: "Go and fetch Monsieur Blanchard." I turned to the visitor. "Not bad news, I hope."

"I am afraid so, madame."

I sighed. He did not continue and I felt it would be incorrect to pry into Léon Blanchard's business.

Léon appeared on the stairs, his expression bewildered, and when he saw the man and recognized him, he was very anxious indeed.

"Jules . . ." he began.

The man said: "Ah, Monsieur Léon, Madame Blanchard is very ill. She is asking for you to come to her at once. Your brother sent me off and I have been two days getting here. It is necessary for us to leave without delay."

"*Mon Dieu,*" murmured Léon. He turned to me. "This is sad news. My mother is very ill and asking for me."

"Well, you must go to her," I said.

"I'm afraid I have no alternative. The boys . . ."

"The boys can wait until you come back." ·

Lisette was beside me. "They will need some food before they go," she said.

"Thank you," said Léon. "I think we should leave at once. We could get quite a way before nightfall and perhaps make it the next day."

"That would be the best, monsieur," said the messenger.

The boys came running into the hall.

"What's happening?" cried Charlot.

I said: "Monsieur Blanchard's mother is ill and he is going to see her."

"What about those poisonous toadstools you were going to show us, Monsieur Blanchard?"

"You can see those when Monsieur Blanchard comes back."

"When?" demanded Charlot.

"Before long, I hope," I said. "Oh, Monsieur Blanchard, I do hope you find your mother recovering when you get to her."

"She is very old," he replied sadly. "But if you will forgive me . . . I have very little time. I must prepare. I could be ready to leave within an hour."

I went to find my father to tell him the news. He was most concerned.

While we were gathered in the hall wishing Léon Blanchard godspeed, Sophie appeared on the stairs. Léon Blanchard stood very still as she came towards him.

"What has happened?" she asked.

He replied: "I have a sudden message from my brother. My mother is very ill. I have to go to her at once."

Poor Sophie! I thought. How she loves him!

"You will come back. . . ."

He nodded and taking her hand kissed it.

She was with us when we went into the courtyard to watch him ride away. Then, without a word, she went back to her tower.

When Dickon returned he was most interested to hear that Léon Blanchard had left. He said that he too must think of leaving. He had been away a long time, far longer than he had planned to be.

Two days later he left.

He took my hand and, holding me close to him, kissed me with fervor.

"I shall be back soon," he said, "and I shall keep coming until that day when I take you back with me."

When he had gone a gloom settled on the castle. There was no news of Armand. Marie Louise did not seem unduly upset but insisted that whatever had happened to her husband was God's Will. Sophie returned to her old way of life shutting herself away with Jeanne. I seemed to spend my time between Lisette and my father and I was thankful that I found the conversation of both of them lively enough to compensate for the brooding sense of doom which seemed to be settling over the castle.

Sometimes when I went out I would glance up at Sophie's turret. She was often there at the windows looking out along the road . . . waiting, I knew, for the return of Léon Blanchard.

———

Several months passed. We had now ceased to talk of Armand. It was presumed that he was dead.

My father had changed his will. I was to inherit his estate in trust for Charlot. He had left Sophie amply provided for and he said that if Léon Blanchard returned and asked for her hand he would make a handsome settlement.

Dickon came again. I was surprised to see him so soon. He looked more pleased with himself than ever.

228

He said: "I have been very busy and I have news for you."

"I am all eagerness to hear it."

"I would like to tell you in the presence of your father."

While he was washing off the grime of the journey I went to my father and told him that Dickon had come and that he wanted to see him immediately because he had news which he wanted us both to hear.

My father smiled at me. "I guessed who it was," he said. "I could tell by your face."

I was surprised and a little horrified that I should show my feelings so clearly.

"Yes," he went on indulgently, "there is a shine in your eyes . . . a softness. That is what makes me think that you and he . . ."

"Oh please, Father," I said, "I have no intention of marrying . . . not yet in any case."

He sighed. "You know I would not stand in your way."

"I know. But let us hear what Dickon has to say."

Dickon was clearly very proud of himself, but then that was habitual with him; but on this occasion he was more than usually self-congratulatory.

My father sent for wine and we settled down in his little sitting room to hear what Dickon had to say.

"You are going to be amazed," he said, "but I am not entirely surprised. I always thought it had worked out a little too neatly to be genuine."

"Dickon," I cried, "you are keeping us in suspense to shock and surprise us and show us what a clever creature you are. Please tell us."

"Let us start at the beginning. In the first place the Duc de Soissonson has no cousin whose boys require a tutor."

"That's impossible!" cried my father. "He was here himself and told us so."

Dickon smiled slyly. "I repeat, he has no relations whose boys require a tutor."

"Are you suggesting that the man who came here calling himself the Duc de Soissonson was not the Duc at all?" I asked.

"Absurd!" cried my father. "I know him well."

"Not well enough," retorted Dickon. "It was indeed the mighty Duc who came here, but there are certain aspects of his character which have escaped your notice. He is a crony of the Duc d'Orléans."

"What of that?"

"My dear Comte, have you never heard what goes on at the Palais Royal? The Queen's chief enemy is Orléans. Who knows what his motives are! Does he want to topple the monarchy and set himself up as ruler? If he did he would be the leader of the people—my Lord Equality. There is much intrigue at the Palais Royal. These men are the traitors to their own class and are more to be feared than the mob."

"Tell us what you are suggesting," said my father. "The Duc recommended Blanchard to us because . . ."

"Because," finished Dickon, "he wanted one of his men in your castle."

"A spy!" I cried. "Léon Blanchard . . . a spy!"

"Difficult as it is to believe of such a paragon . . . yes."

"But why here? We are remote from all this trouble."

"Armand was not. He had his little band, didn't he? Mind you, I don't think Orléans or Soissonson could be very alarmed about that. But they are acting with caution and they could not allow such meetings to go unnoticed."

"This is a monstrous suggestion," said my father. "What proof have you?"

"Only that Blanchard's story was false. He was not a part-time tutor. When he was not here he was carrying on the work his fellow conspirators had designed for him."

"But he was an excellent tutor."

"Of course he was. He is a clever man . . . cleverer perhaps than Soissonson and Orléans himself. But he was not a Duc, was he? Therefore he takes orders until the time comes when he will be one of those to give orders himself."

"He has promised to come back."

"We shall see if he does," said Dickon. "My bet is that he will never return to this château."

"And my son Armand . . ." said the Comte.

"It seems most likely that he was murdered."

"No!"

"Monsieur le Comte, we are living in dangerous times. What seems

230

like melodrama in one age is commonplace in another. Blanchard knew there was to be a meeting that day."

"Blanchard spent the whole day in the château. He could not have been involved in murder."

"Not in the act of carrying it out, but he could have given the information as to where Armand would be. My theory is that your son was set upon and killed, and his murderers made it appear an accident, that he had been drowned in the river and carried away by it."

"It is a fantastic story."

"Fantastic things are happening in this country now."

"I really cannot believe it," said my father.

"Then," retorted Dickon, "you must disbelieve."

"If Blanchard comes back he will be able to refute this story."

"But he has not come back, has he?"

"It might be that his mother is still very ill and he must stay with her."

"Where does he say he has gone to?"

"A place I never heard of. What was it, Lottie? Paraville. It is a good many leagues south. I trust he comes back soon. I should like to hear from his own lips that this is just wild conjecture."

"How do you explain Soissonson's lack of relatives with children?"

"Soissonson is vague. It might have been some connection . . . not exactly related."

"He doesn't appear to have anyone, and he is hand in glove with Orléans, who is doing his best to bring this country to revolution."

"My dear young man," said the Comte, "you have worked so hard and I know it is for our good. You must forgive me if I tell you I find it hard to believe that Soissonson would have a hand in murdering the son of an old friend."

"When revolution comes old friends become new enemies."

"You are very kind to take such an interest in our affairs," said my father. "I trust you will be staying with us for some little time."

"Thank you, but no," answered Dickon. "I must return to England in a few days."

He was really quite angry with my father. He had been so excited when he arrived with his news—which I had to admit, like my father,

I did not believe—that he found the reception of it a somewhat bitter anticlimax.

He was quite subdued when he dined with us and afterwards when he suggested a walk on the ramparts, I readily agreed because I was sorry for the reception he had had.

He said: "The sooner you leave this place the better. People are half asleep. They cannot see what is going on around them and when it is thrust under their noses they turn away and call it melodrama. I tell you this, Lottie: these people deserve what is coming to them. Don't be as foolish as they are. Come back with me . . . now. This is no place to be, I do assure you."

"Dickon," I said, "how can you be sure?"

"You should go to Paris. You should see the crowds every night at the Palais Royal. The gardens are full of them. They are preaching to the people . . . and who is behind all this? Orléans . . . men like Soissonson. Traitors to their own class . . . and therefore the most dangerous traitors. It is all as clear as crystal. Did it not strike you as fortuitous that Soissonson should arrive just at the time when you needed a tutor and provide one?"

"But he was such a good *tutor!*"

"Of course he was. These people know what they are doing. *They* are not half asleep. He comes because rumor has reached Orléans and his gang that bands are being formed throughout the country. I take it they have *dis*banded this little one. You might say that Armand was ineffectual, and I agree wholeheartedly with that, but men such as Orléans are too thorough to allow even the inefficient blunderers to have a little success. I see it all clearly. Blanchard comes to spy out the land. He even joins the band."

"He did not want to at first. He had to be persuaded."

"Of course he had to be persuaded! He wouldn't appear eager. His was a secret mission."

"It's too wild."

"And what of Armand?"

I was silent and he went on: "Yes. Poor foolish Armand, he will never inherit his father's estates now. I'll warrant they'll be for you."

I looked at him quickly and he went on: "For the boy, of course. That would be how the Comte's mind would work. After all, there are only you and that pathetic Sophie now. She was not considered for a moment."

I looked at him coldly. "At such a time you concern yourself with these matters. . . ."

"They are there, Lottie. You cannot ignore what is there."

I wasn't listening to him. I was thinking of Armand, going down to the river . . . a group of armed men springing out on him. But perhaps there was only one.

I felt sick and frightened.

I said: "I want to go in."

"Think about what I have said, Lottie. Marry me. I'll take care of you."

"And the estate," I said, "and Charlot's inheritance . . ."

"I'd take care of everything. You need me, Lottie, as much as I need you."

"I don't feel that need," I said. "Good night, Dickon."

He left the castle the next day. He was clearly very displeased with his reception.

———

Lisette wanted to know what had happened and as she knew something important had, I told her.

"Blanchard!" she said. "Yes, when you come to think of it, he was too good to be true. He was quite handsome, wasn't he, in a manly way. Yet he never seemed to look at anyone except Sophie. He never made the slightest attempt to be flirtatious with you, did he, Lottie?"

"Of course not."

"With no one but Sophie. That was a very gallant sort of relationship, wasn't it? It could have been because he was sorry for her. But what was I saying . . . handsome and courtly. His manners were of the very best . . . and such a good tutor recommended by a noble Duc. It was all so very satisfactory. Tell me what Dickon discovered."

I told her what I knew of the Duc d'Orléans and the Palais Royal and Soissonson's connections with them.

"Dickon tells a good story. When you come to think about it as good a one could be made up about him."

"What do you mean?"

"Well, let's allow our imaginations to run loose, shall we? Dickon wants you . . . very much he wants you but he would like you even better if you brought something substantial with you. I suppose the Comte's wealth is vast. Armand would naturally inherit the bulk . . . but if Armand were no longer there . . . well, it is likely that, Sophie's being *hors de combat,* so to say, all that wealth might descend on you."

"Stop it," I cried. "It's . . . horrible."

"You know what's coming. If Armand were out of the way, you see . . ."

I could not shut out the vivid pictures which came into my mind. Armand going to the river . . . someone waiting there for him . . . leaving the horse tethered . . . dropping the hat by the river . . . burying the body. Dickon had been out all that day, while Léon Blanchard had spent the morning with the boys in the wood and in the afternoon they had sorted out their specimens. Dickon had been out, I remembered. He had come back late.

"This is nonsense," I said.

"Of course it is. The whole thing is nonsense. You will see Léon Blanchard returning soon and all this suggestion about the Duc de Soissonson will be explained."

"There is one thing which cannot be explained," I said, "and that is Armand's disappearance . . . perhaps death."

"Yes." Lisette looked straight ahead. "It may be that one of our theories is right after all."

Soon after Dickon's departure the messenger who had come before to see Léon Blanchard arrived at the castle. He did ask to see my father but as he was out at the time left a letter for him.

When my father returned he sent for me and I went to his sitting room where I found him anxiously awaiting me.

"Come and look at this," he said and gave me the letter which the messenger had brought.

It was from Léon Blanchard and explained that he could not come back to us. He had found his mother very ill indeed when he returned, and although she had recovered, she was still in a weak condition. He had decided that he could not be so far from her and was most regretfully telling us that he was giving up his posts and was taking something near his mother's house so that he could live with her and care for her. He thanked us for the happy time he had had in the castle.

234

He had sent separate notes to the boys telling them that they must work harder, that Louis-Charles must look to his grammar and Charlot to his mathematics. He would be thinking of them and the happy relationship they had enjoyed when he was under the Comte's roof.

There could not have been more sincerely written letters.

"And we are to believe that this man was a spy sent to us by Soissonson!" said my father.

"Reading those letters it does seem improbable," I agreed.

"Well now," went on my father, "we have to look for a new tutor. I promise I shall keep Soissonson out of this!" he added with a laugh.

I wondered what Dickon would have said if he could have seen those letters.

I was sure he would have insisted that they proved his case.

———

The whole household was talking about Léon Blanchard, who was not coming back. The boys were clearly upset and Charlot said they would hate the new tutor. I explained that it was unfair to hate someone before you had seen him.

"His trouble will be that he is not Léon," said Charlot.

The servants talked continually of what a delightful man he had been. "Always the gentleman," they said.

He certainly had the power to charm.

Lisette told me that Jeanne had said Sophie was taking Léon's departure very badly.

"I think that is the really tragic part of it all," I said. "I wonder if it would have come to anything if he had stayed."

"If he had intended it should, surely he would have done something about it."

"I am not sure," I pondered. "Class distinction comes very strongly into it and I imagine a man like Léon Blanchard would be very much aware of that. Perhaps he was just being chivalrous to Sophie, and she, poor girl, longing to escape from what her life is here, imagined something which was not there."

"Poor Sophie," said Lisette. "His going is a tragedy for her."

That night I was awakened by some dream to find myself in a state of terror. I could not understand what was happening. Then I was suddenly aware that I was not alone.

235

For those first waking seconds I was transported back in time to the days before my wedding to Charles when I had been awakened in just such a way to see Sophie at the foot of my bed in my wedding veil.

I cried: "Who is that?"

Then she came out of the shadows. She stood by my bed. She had taken off her hood and her face looked grotesque in the moonlight.

"Sophie!" I whispered.

"Why do you hate me?" she asked.

"Hate you! But Sophie . . ."

"If you don't, why do you try to hurt me? Haven't I been hurt enough to please you?"

"What do you mean, Sophie?" I replied. "I would do anything I could for you. If it were in my power . . ."

She laughed. "Who are you? The bastard. You have come here and won my father from us all."

I wanted to protest. I wanted to cry: *He was never yours so how could I take him from you?*

She stood there at the end of my bed as she had done on that other night. She said: "You took Charles from me."

"No! You gave him up. You wouldn't marry him."

She touched her face. "You were there when this happened. You went off with him and left me."

"Oh, Sophie," I protested. "It was not like that."

"It is long ago," she said. "And then you told my father, did you not, that Léon wanted to marry me . . . and you persuaded him that it would not be right because he was only a tutor and I was a Comte's daughter. I heard you talking to him about me at the moat."

"It is not true. I said no such thing. I said it would be good for you and for him. I assure you, Sophie, that is what I said."

"And he was sent away. There was this story about his mother . . . and now he is to stay with her and he won't come back here. That is your doing."

"Oh, Sophie, you are quite wrong."

"Do you think I don't know? You tried to pretend first that he was a spy . . . you and your friend . . . that man . . . that Dickon. You are going to marry him, are you not . . . when my father is dead and everything comes to you? What of Armand? How did you and your lover get him out of the way?"

"Sophie, this is madness."

"Madness now, you say. Is that what you want them to say of me? I hate you. I shall never forget what you have done to me. I will never forgive you."

I got out of bed and approached her, but she put out her arms to ward me off. She walked backwards to the door, her arms stretched out before her as she went. She looked like a sleepwalker.

I cried: "Sophie ... Sophie ... listen to me. You are wrong ... wrong about everything. Let me talk to you."

But she shook her head. I watched the door shut on her. Then I went back to bed and lay there, shivering.

A Visit to Eversleigh

Gloom had descended on the castle. I could not forget Sophie's nocturnal visit and I wondered how I could ever get her to accept the truth. I had not realized how much she had resented me. It was only since the coming of Charles, of course; before that she had accepted me as her sister.

Perhaps I had been too taken up with my own affairs to give enough attention to hers. Poor girl, so fearfully maimed, and then to lose the man she was to marry and again to have lost the chance of happiness. I must try to understand.

Marie Louise announced her intention of going into a convent. She had long thought of doing so and now that it was almost certain that her husband was dead, there was nothing to keep her in the château. My father was delighted to see her go. He said he thought it would lessen the gloom a little.

He was very anxious about me.

"You are pining for Dickon," he said.

"No, no!" I protested. "Nothing of the sort. When he comes he creates . . . disturbances."

"But it is disturbance that makes life worth living for you and without it . . . is it not a little dull?"

"I have the children and you."

"The children are growing up. Claudine is nearly thirteen years old."

"So she is." When I was that age I had been overwhelmed by Dickon for sometime and had thought of marriage to him. Charlot was almost sixteen and Louis-Charles was a little older than that. It was indeed true that they were growing away from childhood.

"And you are getting older, my dear," went on my father.

"We all are, of course."

"It must be thirty-four years ago when I saw your mother for the first time. It was so romantic . . . dusk . . . and she stood there like a phantom from another world. She thought I was a ghost too. I had been hunting for a fob I had lost and I rose up suddenly on that haunting patch of land and really startled her."

"I know. You have told me."

"I should like to see it all again before I die. Lottie, you should go back. You should go to Eversleigh. You should make up your mind what to do about Dickon. I think you are in love with him. Are you?"

I hesitated. "What is love? Is it being excited by someone . . . enjoying the presence of someone . . . feeling alive when he is there and yet at the same time knowing too much about him . . . knowing that he wants power, money . . . and that he is prepared to do almost anything for them . . . not quite trusting . . . You see, I am trying to see his inadequacies. Is that love?"

"Perhaps you are looking for perfection."

"Didn't you look for it . . . and find it?"

"I never looked for it because I did not believe it existed. I stumbled on it by chance."

"It was because you loved so deeply that you found it. My mother might not have been perfect."

"Ah, but she was."

"In your eyes, as you were in hers. Were you perfect, Father?"

"Far from it."

"But she thought you were. Perhaps that is love . . . an illusion . . . seeing what is not there. And perhaps the more deeply one loves the more one deceives oneself."

"My dearest child, I should like to see you happy before I die . . . even if it means not having you with me. The greatest happiness I have known came through you and your mother. Who would have believed that a chance meeting could lead to that? It was an enchanted night . . . that one, and she was there and I was there. . . ."

I leaned over and kissed him. "I am glad that we pleased you . . . my mother and I. You pleased *us* every bit as much, you know. I loved the man I believed to be my father. He was kind and gentle . . . but you . . . you were different. You were so romantic and gallant in your castle. It was wonderful to learn that you were my father."

He turned away to hide his emotion. Then he said almost brusquely: "I don't want you to go on living here . . . growing older, wasting your youth. You are not like your mother. You are more able to take care of yourself. She was innocent. She did not see evil. You are not like that, Lottie."

"More . . . earthy," I said.

"I would say more worldly. You know more of men than she did. You would understand the imperfections and bear them, and perhaps even love the more because of them. I think often of Dickon. He is no saint. But do you want a saint? They can be hard to live with. I think you are fond of him in a special way, and will never forget him whatever happens. So he is with you. He is indeed a man full of faults, but brave and strong, I would say. I think he should be the father of a child for you . . . before it is too late."

"I am not going to leave the château. I like it here."

"In this gloomy castle with Sophie in her turret casting her own special sort of spell over the place?"

"The children are happy here."

"They will grow up and have lives of their own. I want you to go to England."

"Go to England? What do you mean? To Eversleigh?"

"I do. I want you to take the children, to see Dickon in his home, and there to decide what you really want. I think you should go there to discover."

"I shall not leave you."

"I thought you would say that. That is why I have decided that I will go with you."

I stared at him in astonishment.

"Yes," he went on, "I have promised myself. I, too, am tired of the château. I want a rest from it. I want to forget what happened to Armand. I want to forget Sophie, brooding in her tower. I want a bit of excitement. What do you say that you and I, with the children, cross the water to England?"

I just looked at him in amazement.

He said: "You have answered. I can see the joy in your face. That is good. I am going to tell the children at once. There is no reason why we should delay."

———

Charlot was wildly excited about the proposed visit to England. So was Claudine. Louis-Charles was so disconsolate that I said we must take him with us, and Lisette agreed that he might go. I was happy listening to them, making plans, talking of England which they had never seen, counting the days.

My father talked to them of what he knew of Eversleigh. Claudine would sit at his feet on a footstool, her arms clasped about her knees as she dreamily stared into space. Charlot plied him with questions; and Louis-Charles listened in the respectful silence he always showed in the presence of the Comte.

It was four days before we were due to leave when my father asked me to walk with him down to the moat. He took my arm and said slowly: "Lottie, I cannot make this journey."

I stopped and stared at him in horror.

"I have been letting myself pretend I would, shutting my eyes to truth. See how breathless I am climbing this slope? I am not young anymore. And if I were ill on the journey ... or in England ..."

"I should be there to take care of you."

He shook his head. "No, Lottie. I know. I have a pain here ... round my heart. It is because of this that I want to see you settled."

I was silent for a moment. Then I said: "Have you seen the doctors?"

He nodded. "I am no longer young, they tell me. I must accept my fate."

"I think a messenger should go to Eversleigh at once. They will be making preparations for us. And I will tell the children now that we are not going."

"No! I said *I* could not go. You and the children must."

"Without you?"

He nodded. "That is what I have decided."

"And leave you here . . . sick!"

"Listen to me, Lottie. I am not sick. I am merely old and unable to make a long and exhausting journey. That is not being sick. I don't need nursing. If you stayed here there is nothing you can do. You cannot disappoint the children. You will go with them. That is my wish. And I shall stay here. I am well looked after. I have good servants. And you will come back to us in due course."

I said: "This is a blow."

He stared at the water of the moat and I wondered whether he had ever intended to come.

———

I couldn't help being caught up in the young people's excitement. We set out on horseback, considering the carriage too cumbersome and slow. Claudine rode between the two boys; she was growing very pretty and had the look of my mother. I think that was one of the reasons why she was the Comte's favorite. She was sturdy, strong-willed and a little resentful of the protective air both boys showed towards her and the fact that they were inclined to treat her as a little girl. Charlot was handsome, dark-eyed, dark-haired with a quick, alert look; Louis-Charles might have been his brother; they were close friends and got on very well apart from the occasional disagreement which, as they were both hot tempered, would end in fisticuffs.

We stayed a night at an inn which delighted them all, the two boys sharing a room and Claudine coming in with me. She was awake at dawn, eager to get on with the journey and making me rise with her.

She said: "There is only one thing missing to make this perfect. That is Gran'père."

"Pray don't call him a thing," I said. "He would not appreciate that."

We both laughed, but sadly because he was not with us.

241

The sea crossing provided a further delight to them and when we landed on English soil they could talk of nothing but Eversleigh. Dickon was at Dover to escort us to the house and there was wild excitement when Claudine flung herself at him and hugged him while the boys stood by grinning. Over Claudine's head Dickon smiled at me, his eyes warm but I did detect a hint of triumph in them and I thought: *Even now he is thinking of winning.*

But a visit did not mean that I had made up my mind. Perhaps I had been foolish to come. I had a fear that I was going to be swept off my feet, unable to make clear decisions, and I knew I must be wary of Dickon. He had the effect on me of potent wine.

Such memories came back. It was long since I had seen Eversleigh, but it always gave me a feeling of home. I did not know why that should be so since most of my life in England had been spent at Clavering. But this was the home of my ancestors. It seemed to wrap itself around me; it seemed to say: *You have come home. Stay home. Home is the place for you.*

Sabrina was waiting with a very warm welcome. She was as excited as the young people.

"What a lovely house!" cried Charlot.

"It is not a castle," added Louis-Charles, a trifle disparagingly.

"Houses are really what you should live in," put in Claudine. "Castles are for sieges and holding out against the enemy."

"Some of our houses had to do that during the civil war," said Sabrina. "But let me show you your rooms and you can explore the house later on. I am sure you will like it. It's rambling and full of odd nooks and crannies. Your mother knows it well. It was once her home."

Dickon said he would show them round in the morning when it was light.

We went to our rooms. I had my old one. I felt a twinge of sadness as I ascended the stairs because the last time I had been here my grandmother had been alive . . . so had my mother.

Sabrina knew what I was thinking. She said: "Your grandmother died peacefully. She never really got over Zipporah's death."

"My father never has," I said.

"I know." She pressed my hand. "But, Lottie, my dear, she

242

wouldn't want you to be sad while you are here. She would be so delighted that you had come."

My old room. It must be more than ten years since I had been in it but it was still familiar to me.

Sabrina said: "Come down when you have washed and changed. We are eating almost immediately. Dickon thought you would be in need of a good meal."

I washed and changed from my riding habit, and when I went downstairs I could hear the sounds of excited talking and laughter. The others were already in the punch room close to the dining room where, I remembered, they assembled before meals. I could hear Claudine's high-pitched voice and the gruffer masculine ones.

I went in. There was a brief silence and then Dickon said: "You remember the twins, Lottie."

Dickon's sons! They must be almost twenty. Could that really be possible? I always thought of Dickon as being perpetually young. He must be forty-three. I had a sensation of time rushing past. My father was right. If we were ever going to make a life together it should be soon.

I remembered David and Jonathan well. They had the look of Dickon and there was a certain resemblance in them which one would expect of twins. Jonathan took my hand first and kissed it; then David did the same.

"I remember you came here once before," said Jonathan.

"My dear boy," said Dickon. "She lived here. It was her home."

"It must be interesting to come back to a place which was once your home, especially when you haven't seen it for so long," said David.

"It is very interesting indeed," I told him; "but best of all to see you and your family."

"Don't talk about *my* family, Lottie," protested Dickon. "It is your family as well."

"That's true," said Sabrina. "Now we are all here, shall we go in. Our cook is a little temperamental and throws a tantrum in the kitchen if we let the food get cold."

We went to the dining room with its tapestried walls and oak table lighted by two candelabra—one at each end. It looked very beautiful.

Sabrina sat at one end of it and Dickon at the other; she had placed me on Dickon's right hand. Claudine was between David and Jonathan, who, I could see, were amused by her bilingual conversation. She could speak English very well, for I had taught her, but she kept forgetting that she was in England and often broke into French with results which the twin brothers seemed to find hilarious. Louis-Charles had always been a young man who knew how to take care of himself and he and Sabrina chatted together in a mixture of bad French from Sabrina and execrable English from Louis-Charles. Dickon devoted himself to me. He was watching me intently, I knew, proud of this gracious dining room, of the meal which was served, of the fact that I had at last succumbed to his repeated requests to visit Eversleigh.

It was a happy evening and when it was time to retire, Claudine voiced the feelings of us all when she said: "It is wonderful for us to be here. But I don't think I shall ever get to sleep tonight. I am too excited."

Sabrina insisted on accompanying me to my room. She shut the door and sat down in one of the armchairs.

"I can't tell you how happy we are to have you here, Lottie. Dickon has always talked a lot about you and every time he went to France he said he was going to bring you back with him. I gather things are not very happy over there."

"There is a good deal of rumor."

She nodded. "Dickon is full of foreboding. He has been saying for some time that you ought to get out."

"I know. He has mentioned it to me."

"Well . . . this is your home, you know."

I shook my head. "My home is over there."

"I was sorry your father could not come with you."

"So were we all."

"Dickon says he is a very fine gentleman."

"Dickon is right."

"But he is getting old, of course. After all, you are English, Lottie."

"My father is French."

"Yes, but you were brought up here. There was never anyone more English than your mother."

"And never anyone more French than my father." I smiled at her.

"You see, that makes me a mixture. I love Eversleigh. I love it here . . . but my husband was French and my children are. That is my home over there."

She sighed and said: "I am very sad sometimes. Your grandmother and I were very close, you know."

"I do know that."

"Now she is gone I miss her terribly."

"I know that. But you have Dickon."

A smile illumined her face. "Oh, yes . . . Dickon. How I should love to see him completely happy. It was your grandmother's dearest wish . . ."

I interrupted her. "Yes, I know. She adored him."

"He is a wonderful person. It is a long time since poor Isabel died. People think it is strange that he did not marry again."

I said with a sudden burst of anger which Dickon could arouse in me: "Perhaps a good enough proposition did not arise. He had Eversleigh, Clavering, and a great deal, I gather, from Isabel."

Sabrina was the same as ever. In her mind, Dickon was above criticism and she did not see it even when it was blatantly expressed.

"I know why he has never married," she said.

"Well, he has his sons. That is one reason why ambitious people marry, isn't it?"

"I remember in the days long ago when you were a child staying with us at Clavering. Do you remember? You two were always together."

"I remember. That was after my mother inherited Eversleigh."

"He was so fond of you. We all were. He talked of nothing but Lottie . . . his little Lottie. And you . . . to you he was the sun, moon, and stars and the whole universe thrown in."

"Children get fancies."

"It is rather charming when they persist through life."

I said: "Dickon knows that my half brother disappeared. It is some little time ago now. His body was never found, but because of the situation in France we think he was murdered. My father is a very wealthy man. I have heard it said that he is one of the most wealthy in France. Charlot will inherit in time, but it will come to me first when my father dies."

She looked blank.

"Dickon was very interested in the estate. I always remember how he came here to Eversleigh. He was just overwhelmed by it because it was so much grander than Clavering. I imagine Aubigné is much more valuable than Eversleigh, so you see he has discovered a great affection for me."

"He admired Eversleigh. Of course he did. Who wouldn't? But he loved you, Lottie. He truly did. He never ceased to. I think he is unhappy at times. Do you know, my great desire in life is to see him happy."

"I know that," I told her. "Sabrina, you must be the most doting mother in the world."

She smiled at me and said: "Well, I am keeping you from your bed and you must be so tired." She rose from her chair. "Good night, my dear. It is lovely to have you here. We are going to do our best not to let you go from us, Lottie."

She paused at the door. "By the way, do you remember poor Griselda?"

"Yes, I do. She kept Isabel's rooms as they were at the time of her death. She was a little uncanny."

"She took a dislike to Dickon and spread tales about him and Isabel. She was so jealous of anyone who came between her and Isabel. We tried to stop her, but she was so old . . . senile really. It was a happy release when she went."

"So she is no longer with us?"

"It must be all of five years since she died. The rooms have been thoroughly cleaned out and it is all very normal up there now."

"As you say," I murmured, "a happy release."

She put her fingers to her lips and blew a kiss to me. "Good night, dear Lottie. Pleasant dreams. Don't forget we are going to do everything we can to keep you with us."

As Claudine had said, we were all too excited to sleep that night.

———

I was happy at Eversleigh. I knew I was going to miss it when I went away. There was something about the green fields and the May sunshine that was essentially England and not quite the same anywhere else in the world. I loved the way the sun would suddenly be obscured and if we were out we would have to take shelter from the sudden showers.

It was the end of May and the April showers seemed to be lingering longer than usual this year. The hedges were full of simple wild flowers and I remembered now, when I was very young, my mother had taught me how to make a daisy chain. I remembered the names of plants like silverweed, bird's-foot trefoil, and lady's-smocks. I rode a great deal with Dickon and the boys. We were a merry party.

Sabrina would come in the carriage and we would meet at some special beauty spot where we would have a picnic. We went to the sea; but I liked the country best, for the sea reminded me of that land only just over twenty miles away where my father would be counting the days until our return. The sea reminded me, too, that this was ephemeral, and I was realizing with every passing day that I wanted it to go on.

I wanted to forget that Dickon loved power and money more than anything else, that he had married Isabel for what she could bring him, and that her faithful nurse had accused him of murder; and although there was such happiness at Eversleigh, there were dark shadows too. I thought a great deal about Isabel, and those months when she was awaiting the birth of babies that did not come and the two who had killed her. How frightened she must have been, poor Isabel! It was as though her ghost had remained behind to come to me in quiet moments and sometimes very happy ones to remind me.

Dickon was constantly there. Charlot admired him very much, so did Louis-Charles, who was very happy at Eversleigh. Lisette had never really given him that deep mother love which children need; she had not wanted him and had so disliked the farmer whom she had married that she must see that period of her life often through Louis-Charles. He threw himself into the life of Eversleigh and he and Charlot often went off together and came back with stories of the inns they had visited and the towns through which they had passed.

Claudine loved Eversleigh too. She went riding with the rest of them on some days and was delighted when Jonathan taught her how to take high jumps. I was a little worried about her but Dickon said she had to learn and Jonathan would take care of her. She enjoyed the attention of both twins and I fancied rather revelled in bestowing her attentions first on one, then on the other. At Eversleigh it was brought home to me more than ever how fast my daughter was growing up.

Time was flying past.

> Gather ye rosebuds while ye may
> Old time is still a-flying
> And this same flower that smiles today
> Tomorrow will be dying. . . .

sang Sabrina, as she sat at the spinet, and I knew that she meant me to take heed.

Dickon was constantly with me, but he was clever. He did not suggest that I stay. He wanted Eversleigh to work its own magic on me.

I was conscious, too, of the peace of the countryside. There was a quietness in the air and I realized how different it was in that land from which that strip of water divided us. When I looked at those waves lapping on the shore, sometimes gray and angry, sometimes blue and gently swishing, I thought it was the great divide between this peaceful happy life and that of suspense and brooding menace.

I knew, when I was alone in my bedroom at night, that I wanted to be here, to stay here. It was my home, my country. And Dickon was here. If I were truthful I must admit I wanted Dickon.

Sabrina was watchful. To her Dickon was the whole meaning of life. She was blind to his faults; she thought he was perfect. Surely she must know what he was really like. Did she refuse to see it because she did not want to; she adjusted all his actions to fit her perfect picture of him. Her face changed when he appeared. Her eyes would follow him, her mouth curved in gentle contentment.

"Nobody," I once said to Dickon, "has any right to be adored as your mother adores you. It's irreligious. It's blasphemous. I really do believe she thinks you are greater than God."

He did refer then to his plans. He said: "There is only one thing needed to make me absolutely perfect in her eyes."

"Nonsense," I retorted. "There is nothing. You are that already."

"Yes, there is. She wants me to be happily married and nobody will be quite right for Sabrina but you."

"God is perfect . . . omnipotent, omniscient . . . and that is you in

Sabrina's eyes. Never mind whomsoever you marry, provided it is your choice, that will be good enough for Sabrina."

"It won't be. It has to be you, for she knows that you are the only one for me. Therefore you are for her. Give her her heart's desire. She is a lady who likes everything to be well ordered, neatly rounded off. She took the husband your grandmother Clarissa wanted, and although to her her marriage was perfect—you see, she finds perfection in her relationships—she was always worried because she took him from Clarissa. Now if Clarissa's granddaughter married the son of that other Dickon whom both Clarissa and Sabrina loved, it would be a neat rounding off, wouldn't it? Everyone can say amen and be happy."

I laughed. "Except perhaps the two who had to bring about this neat solution."

"They would be happiest of all. You are learning that, Lottie. I have always known it."

"Oh, I remember. You were always omniscient. I shall have to go back to my father soon."

"We will bring him over here. I assure you that in a very short time men in his position will be giving everything they have to get away from the coming storm."

That was the only time he mentioned our marriage. He let Eversleigh do the rest, and more and more every day I longed to give in.

———

One night after I had retired there was a knock on my door and Sabrina came in.

"I was afraid you might have gone to bed," she said. "I want you to have a look at this."

"What is it?"

"It's a diary."

"Oh . . . an old one? One of those family ones?"

"Not those weighty journals. This is quite a slim volume, you see. When Griselda died we found it in Isabel's room. It was caught up at the back of a drawer, otherwise I am sure Griselda would never have allowed it to fall into our hands."

"A diary! I always thought it was like prying to read other people's diaries."

"So do I. But I did read this one. I felt it was important, and I do think it is important that you should see it."

"Why me?"

She laid the book on the table beside my bed and I felt reluctant to touch it.

"Because I think you may have some misconception. This is the truth. It must be because it was written by Isabel herself."

"Has Dickon seen it?"

"No. I did not think that was necessary. I did give it to the twins, though. Griselda used to make a great deal of Jonathan. She used to have him to her room."

"Yes. I do remember that."

'She had a crazy notion that David killed Isabel. I suppose it *was* the second birth which weakened her, but Griselda—mad old woman— actually blamed David. That shows how senile she was."

"Yes. I see what you mean."

"Read it," she said. "I think it will tell you a great deal."

She kissed me and left me.

The reluctance to open the book persisted. Diaries contained private thoughts. Perhaps it held an account of Dickon's meeting with her, their early life together. In view of my own strong feelings for Dickon I found the thought of prying quite distasteful.

However I got into bed and lighted an extra candle, opened the book and started to read.

I became absorbed almost immediately. I was seeing Isabel clearly— the quiet, shy daughter of a powerful man—a man who loved her and wanted the best for her but who really did not understand what was the best.

There were references to Griselda. She was mentioned on every page. There were intimate little details. "Griselda curled my hair in rags last night. I found it hard to sleep for them, but Griselda said I must keep them in so that I had curls next day." "Griselda has put a blue fischu on my white dress. It looks rather pretty." There were accounts of assemblies she had been to. She wrote of her dread of them, her painful shyness. I went on reading until I came to the entry about Dickon.

"Today I met the most handsome man I have ever seen. He is in

250

London from the country where, my father says, he owns a large estate. He asked me to dance and I did . . . most awkwardly. He said he wasn't much of a dancer either and he didn't mind my mistakes at all. He talked a great deal so cheerily and wittily. I couldn't keep up with him. My father was very pleased.

"Yesterday my father sent for me and I knew he had something very serious to say because he called me 'Daughter.' 'Daughter,' he said, 'you have a suitor.' Then he told me it was Richard Frenshaw. It is that wonderful man who danced with me. I don't know how I feel. I am in a panic and yet it might have been that horrible old Lord Standing. Instead it is this wonderful, handsome man. 'But,' I said to Griselda, 'at least Lord Standing would not have minded that I am not clever and that my hair will not curl unless it is all night in rags, and that I stumble when I dance and am shy.' Griselda said, Nonsense. He would be lucky to get me, and he knew it. I had a great fortune coming to me and that was what men liked. Moreover she would always be with me. That was my great comfort."

There were several entries about the clothes which were being made and the announcement of the engagement at a ball given by her father. There were meetings with Dickon—brief and never alone. And then the entry: "Tomorrow I am to marry Richard Frenshaw."

Evidently after that she had not written in it for a long time. Then there were the brief entries.

"This afternoon it rained and there was some thunder." "Went to the Charletons' ball." "We had a dinner party for twenty." Just bald statements with very little hint of what she was feeling.

Then it changed. "Another disappointment. Shall I ever achieve my heart's desire? If I could have a little baby it would make up for everything. Dickon wants a boy. All men do. I wouldn't mind what it was . . . just a baby. That's what I want.

"I saw Dr. Barnaby today. He said there should be no more pregnancies and that he should speak to my husband. I begged him not to. I told him how much having a child meant to me. He shook his head and kept saying, 'No. No.' Then he said: 'You have tried and failed. You did your best. Now, no more.' They don't understand, I must have a child. If I don't I shall have lost Dickon completely. It is the only way.

"There is to be another chance. Griselda will be angry. She hates Dickon because of this. It is silly of her, but then she is silly sometimes. I know it is only because of her feeling for me, but she is so difficult. She gets so anxious and worried. She frightens me. I haven't told her yet. I haven't told anyone. I want to be sure. I am determined this time my child shall be born.

"They know. Dickon is delighted. That makes me so happy. He takes a lot of notice of me and makes me take care of myself. I could be happy if only . . . But it will be all right this time. It must be.

"Dr. Barnaby has been today. I have had a long talk with him. He is concerned about my condition. He says he should not have allowed me to dissuade him from speaking to my husband. 'However,' he said, 'it is done. You must be very careful. You must rest and rest. If you can get through the first three months we can still hope.'

"Three months . . . and all is well. How I long for the time to pass. Every morning I awake and I say to myself rather like someone in the Bible: 'I am with child. God be praised.'

"My time is getting near. I have dreams . . . sometimes nightmares. It is because of all those failures. I saw Dr. Barnaby today. I had a long talk with him. I said to him: 'I must have this child. More than anything I want it.' 'I know that,' he replied. 'Now pray don't get upset. It is bad for the little one.' 'I have had so many disappointments,' I said. 'I couldn't bear another.' 'Do as you are told,' he answered, 'and it will very likely be all right.' 'Sometimes,' I said, 'there is a choice between mother and child. If there is a choice I want it to be the child who is saved.' 'You're talking nonsense,' he said. But I knew I wasn't. I said, 'I want you to promise me. . . .' He looked exasperated and I remembered how he used to frighten me when I was a little girl and I hadn't taken my physic. 'This is nonsense,' he said sternly. 'You are worrying yourself about something which hasn't happened.' But I refused to be frightened of him. I insisted, 'But it may. I have had difficult pregnancies, all of which so far have ended in disaster. I know that if I failed this time there would not be another chance. I want you to promise me . . . that if this situation should arise you will save the child and let me go.' 'These matters are for a doctor to decide when they happen,' he said. 'I know,' I cried. 'I am saying if . . . if . . . if . . . !' 'You are getting agitated,' he said, 'and that is bad for the child.' 'I shall be more agitated until I have your promise.' 'This is

252

very unethical,' he said severely. But I would not let him go. I made him swear. I brought my Bible to him, for I knew he was a very religious man, and only when he began to get alarmed for my state, did he swear. He said, 'If such a contingency should arise—and there is no reason to believe it will—and if there should be a choice between the lives of the mother or the child, then I swear I will save the child.' He stayed by me for five minutes until he had satisfied himself that I was calm. I was calm, calm and happy, for something told me that whatever happened there would be a child."

There was one more entry. "The time is near. It could be any time now. Today I went and looked at my nursery. The cradle is ready for the child. I had a vision. It was so strange. The cradle seemed to be surrounded by light and I knew there was a healthy child in it. I did not see myself. It seemed unimportant. The child was there."

I laid down the book. I was deeply moved.

———

The next morning Sabrina looked at me expectantly, when I put Isabel's diary in her hands.

I told her how touched I had been.

"She was such a dear, good girl. I remember it so well. She was so long in labor. Jonathan was born easily enough. It was David. They had to take him away from her and she didn't survive. Dr. Barnaby was very unhappy. When I saw the diary I knew why. I often wondered if he could have saved Isabel at the cost of David. It would not have occurred to me to think so if I had not read the diary. But I wanted you to see it because of Griselda. I think it turned her brain. Isabel was her child . . . the whole meaning of life to her. When she lost her there was nothing to live for so she went back to the past. She was bitter and angry and she blamed Dickon. She had it in her mind that there had been a choice between Isabel and the baby and that Dickon had made the choice to save the child. She called him a murderer. I wondered whether Isabel had ever mentioned her own feelings to Griselda. It was clearly very much on her mind as you see from the diary. It was dreadful to live in the house with that. I wanted to turn her away but your grandmother was against it, and I don't think Griselda could have gone on living if she hadn't had Isabel's things to brood on. It was a great relief when she died."

"I understand," I said.

"There was a time when I thought she would do David some harm. And she made too much of Jonathan. It was almost as though she was trying to set the boys against each other . . . and certainly against their father. If only . . ."

She was looking at me appealingly.

"Lottie," she went on, "if you came back to us . . . it would be like a fresh start for us all. It was what we wanted, your grandmother and I. It was only your mother who was against it. You were blaming Dickon, weren't you? Griselda had told you something. But you don't believe her now, do you?"

I said: "I see clearly what happened through Isabel's diary."

"You know that there was nothing callous about Dickon's behavior to her. He was always kind to her. It wasn't his fault that he was not in love with her."

"I know."

She bent over and kissed me.

"I am glad you understand now," she said.

I did. I saw clearly that in this respect I had wronged Dickon. They were winning me over.

———

A few days later Dickon was called to London.

"I shall be away for a week at most," he said.

I asked Sabrina what sort of business he had in London.

She was vague. "Oh, he inherited a lot of property through Isabel."

"I knew she was very rich and that was the reason for the marriage."

She looked at me sharply. "Isabel's father was very eager for the marriage. So was Isabel herself. There was a very big settlement and when her father died a great deal came to Isabel."

"And now to Dickon," I said. "Is it something to do with banking?"

"Something like that," said Sabrina. "He goes often. Not so much of late because you are here, I expect. But he travels a good deal normally. He was very concerned in all that about the American war."

"Yes, I gathered that. He came to France because the French were helping the colonists."

"He came to France to see you," said Sabrina fondly.

It was only two days after Dickon had left when the messenger came bringing a letter from Lisette, and I knew that something was wrong before I opened it.

"You should leave at once," she had written. "Your father is very ill indeed. He was calling for you when he was delirious. He has said that we are not to send for you but we thought you would want to know. I think, if you want to see him before he dies, you should return at once."

Sabrina had seen the messenger arrive and came down to see what it was all about.

"It's my father," I said. "He is dangerously ill."

"Oh, my dear Lottie!"

"I must go to him at once," I said.

"Yes ... yes, of course. Dickon will be back soon. Wait and hear what he has to say."

"I must leave at once," I said firmly.

The messenger was standing by. Sabrina pointed out that he looked exhausted and called one of the servants to take him to the kitchens and give him food. He would want to rest too.

When they had gone she turned to me.

"I don't think Dickon would want you to go back. He has talked to me about the state of France and was so glad that you had left at last."

"This has nothing to do with Dickon," I said. "I am going and I shall leave tomorrow."

"Lottie, you can't!"

"I can and I must. Oh, Sabrina, I am sorry but you must understand. This is my father. He needs me. I should never have left him."

"You said that he wanted you to come, didn't you?"

"He did because ..."

"I daresay he thought you were safer here. He would know ... as Dickon did."

I wanted to stop her talking about Dickon. I was going and that was it. I could not possibly stay here while I knew my father was ill ... dying, perhaps, and calling for me.

"I am going to get ready immediately," I said.

She caught my arm. "Wait, Lottie. Don't be so hasty. Suppose I sent someone to London to tell Dickon."

"It would take too long, and this has nothing to do with Dickon."

"He will be upset if you go."

"Then he must be upset, because I am going."

"The children . . ." she said.

I hesitated. Then I made up my mind. "They can stay here if you will allow it. They can come home later. I will go alone and as quickly as I can."

"My dear Lottie, I don't like it. I don't like it at all. Dickon . . ."

"I will go and see the messenger. He can have a good night's rest and I will go back with him. We will start first thing in the morning."

"If only Dickon were here!"

"Nothing would stop me, Sabrina. The children will be happy here. They may stay?"

"Of course. Of course."

"Perhaps Dickon and you, too, will come back with them and stay for a while at the château."

She looked at me fearfully. "If you are intent on going you must take two grooms with you. There are certain things you will want to take for a journey . . . and it will be safer. You must do that. I insist."

"Thank you, Sabrina," I said and I went to the kitchens to find the messenger.

Farewell, France

I half hoped that Dickon would come back that night. I knew he would attempt to persuade me not to leave but when he saw that I was adamant, it might well be that he would come with me.

I longed for him to do that. I was terrified of what I would find when I returned to France and kept reproaching myself for leaving my father, even though it was he himself who had insisted that I should do so.

Eversleigh was not far from Dover and the journey was quickly accomplished. The crossing was smooth, for the weather was good. It was when we reached the other side of the Channel that everything seemed different.

The July sun beat down on us; there seemed to be a stillness in the air, a breathlessness, as though the country was waiting for some tremendous event. It was something in the atmosphere of the towns through which we passed. Sometimes we saw little knots of people standing together in the streets. They watched us furtively as we rode through; they seemed to be whispering together. Some of the towns were deserted and I imagined that people were peeping at us through their windows.

"Everything seems to have changed in an odd sort of way," I said to one of the grooms.

He said that he noticed nothing.

We came to the town of Evreux and I remembered how, when I had first come to France with my father, we had stayed there. It seemed very different now. There was that same air of brooding menace which I had noticed in the towns and villages through which we had passed.

I was very relieved when the château came into sight. I spurred on my horse and rode into the courtyard. One of the grooms took the horse and I hurried into the castle. Lisette, who must have been watching from one of the windows, came running into the hall.

"Lisette!" I cried.

"So you have come, Lottie."

"I want to see my father at once."

She looked at me and shook her head.

"What do you mean?" I asked quickly.

"He was buried nearly a week ago. He died the day after I sent the message to you."

"Dead! My father! It is not possible."

"Yes," she said. "He was very ill. The doctors had told him."

"When?" I cried. "When did the doctors tell him?"

"Weeks ago. Before you went away."

"Then why . . . ?"

"He must have wanted you to go."

I sat down at the big oak table and stared at the long narrow windows without seeing them. I understood now. He had known how ill he had been and he had sent me to England because of that. He had never had any intention of coming with me, but he had said he would just to make me plan to leave and then when we were on the point of departure he had said he could not accompany us.

"I should never have gone," I said.

Lisette lifted her shoulders and leaned against the table looking at me. If I had not been so stricken I might have noticed the change in her attitude. But I was too shocked, too immersed in my grief.

I went to his bedroom. She followed me there. The curtains were drawn back showing the empty bed. I knelt beside it and buried my face in my hands.

Lisette was still there. "It's no use," she said. "He has gone."

I went through his rooms. Empty. Then I went to the chapel and the mausoleum beyond. There was his tomb.

"Gerard, Comte d'Aubigné" and the date 1727 to 1789.

"It was so quick," I murmured and I saw that Lisette was behind me.

"You have been away a long time," she reminded me.

"I should have been told."

"He wouldn't have it. It was only when he was unable to give orders to prevent anyone's sending for you that I acted as I thought was right."

I went to my room. She was still with me. Then I saw that she was different and had been since my arrival. Everything had changed. I could not understand Lisette. She was not unhappy. There was something secretive in her manner. I did not know how to describe it. It was as though she was amused in some mysterious way.

I am imagining this, I told myself. I am suffering from acute shock.

"Lisette," I said, "I want to be alone for a while."

She hesitated, and for a moment I thought she was going to refuse to leave me.

Then she turned and was gone.

———

I lay in bed, unable to sleep. The night was hot . . . stifling. I was thinking of my father; I had never ceased to think of him since I had heard that he was ill and needing me.

258

Oh, why had I gone! Why hadn't I guessed? He had seemed to grow older suddenly. I had thought that was due to the fact that he had lost my mother. Indeed, I had felt he never really wanted to go on living after he had lost her. And all the time he had known how ill he was and he had wanted me to go to England . . . to marry Dickon. He had been worried about what was happening in this country and had wanted me to find a secure haven outside it.

I thought of how happy I had been at Eversleigh—the rides, the walks, the verbal tussles with Dickon . . . how I had enjoyed them all. And all the time he was here . . . dying alone.

The door of my room opened suddenly and I started up in bed to see Lisette gliding into the room. There was an air of suppressed excitement about her.

"I didn't hear you knock," I said.

"I didn't," she answered. "It has happened. At last it is here."

"What do you mean?"

"I have just had the news. Did you hear the noise in the courtyard?"

"No. Who . . . ?"

"News," she said. "News from Paris. The mobs are roaming the streets and the shopkeepers are barricading their shops."

"More riots!" I cried.

Her eyes were shining. "Great men are speaking in the Palais Royal gardens. Desmoulins. Danton. Men like that."

"Who are these men?" I asked.

She did not answer and went on: "They are wearing the colors of the Duc d'Orléans . . . red, white, and blue . . . the tricolor. And listen, Lottie, this is the most important of all. The people have taken the Bastille. They have killed the governor, de Launay, and have marched into the prison with his head on a pike. They have freed the prisoners. . . ."

"Oh, Lisette. What does it mean? This rioting . . . ?"

Again that secret smile. "I think," she said slowly, "it means the revolution has begun."

———

It seemed a long time before the morning came. I sat at the window waiting . . . waiting for what I did not know. The countryside looked

259

the same as ever—quiet and peaceful. At daybreak the household was astir. I could hear the servants excitedly talking. They shouted and laughed and I knew that they were discussing what had happened in Paris.

All through the day we waited for news. People were different. They seemed to watch me furtively and they seemed vaguely amused and secretive.

I saw nothing amusing in fearful riots when people went mad with fury and others lost their lives. Dickon had said it would come. Could it be that it already had?

An uneasy day followed by an uneasy night. I felt lonely without the children but what a relief it was that they were not here!

Something was about to break. I wondered what I should do. Should I go back to England? There was nothing to keep me here now that my father was dead.

The rioting will die down, I told myself. The military will suppress it. But the Bastille . . . to storm a prison! That was a very big riot indeed . . . very different from the looting of shops which had been going on in the little towns all over the country on and off over the last few years.

I was trying to behave as normal, but there was nothing normal about the château. How could there be when my father was no longer there?

When I arose next morning I rang as usual for hot water. I waited . . . and waited. No one came. I rang again and still I waited.

I put on a robe and went down to the kitchens. They were deserted. "Where is everyone?" I called.

It was Tante Berthe who finally came to me. She said: "Most of the servants have gone and those who haven't are getting ready to leave."

"Leaving! Why? Where have they gone?"

She lifted her shoulders. "They are saying they will never wait on anyone again. Others think they might be blamed for serving the aristocrats and get what is being planned for them."

"What is going on?"

"I wish I knew, madame. It's confusion . . . everywhere. There are rumors going round that they will march on all the châteaux and kill everyone in them."

"It's nonsense."

"You know what servants are ... without education ... ready to believe any tale."

"You will not go, will you, Tante Berthe?"

"This has been my home for years. Monsieur le Comte was very good to me and mine. He would not have expected me to run away. I'll stay and face whatever it is."

"Where is Lisette?"

Again that shrug of the shoulders.

"I have scarcely seen her since the day I arrived."

"She knows what she is doing, I'll swear. What did you come down for?"

"Hot water," I said.

"I'll get it for you."

"Who is left in the château?" I asked.

"There's the two in the turret."

"Jeanne is still here then."

"You don't think she would ever leave Mademoiselle Sophie?"

"No, I did not think that she would. Jeanne is loyal and Sophie is the most important thing in her life. Who else ... ?"

"If any of the servants are here they are on the point of going, as I said. Some talk of going to Paris to join in what they call 'the fun.' I don't think there'll be any need for them to go to Paris. They'll find it nearer at hand."

"Is it really as bad as that?"

"It's been coming for a long time. I thank God that He took Monsieur le Comte before he was able to see it."

"Oh, Tante Berthe," I cried, "what is going to happen to us all?"

"We'll wait and see," she replied calmly.

She went away to get hot water. I stood waiting while the silence of the château closed in on me.

————

It was evening of the next day. Tante Berthe had been right. All the servants had left except Jeanne and herself. There were just the few of us left in that vast château with that terrible sense of foreboding hanging over us. I would not have been surprised at anything that happened.

261

During the day I went to the watch tower and looked down. Nothing but the peace of the fields. It was difficult to believe that terrible things were happening not far away. I must go to England, to the children, to Dickon. I would take Lisette with me ... and Tante Berthe; Sophie and Jeanne, too, if they would come. I should not delay. I was well aware of that. I must talk to Lisette. We must make plans.

The silence was broken by sounds in the courtyard. We had visitors. It was with a sense of relief that I ran down, not knowing what to expect. It could be those who had come to harm us; but at least the monotony was broken. Something was about to happen at last.

Lisette was just behind me.

Two men were there. They were both dirty and unkempt. One of them was supported by the other for clearly he found it difficult to stand. They were both in a sorry state.

"Who ... ?" I began.

Then one of them spoke. "Lottie ..." he said.

I went to him and stared.

"Lottie," he said again. "I ... I have come home."

The voice was recognizable, but not the man.

"Armand?" I cried. But no, this filthy creature could not be Armand.

"It was a long way ..." he murmured.

"He needs rest ... nursing," said his companion. "We ... both do."

Lisette said: "Did you break out of prison?"

"We were let out ... by the people. The prison was stormed."

"The Bastille ...!" I cried. "So ... that is where you went!"

I saw at once that this was no time for explanations. Armand and his companion needed immediate attention. Armand's feet were bleeding and he was in great pain when he stood on them; and in any case he was in no condition to stand.

Lisette and I tended them and the practical Tante Berthe came to our aid. We washed them, removed their clothes, and got them to bed.

"We'll burn these things at once," said Tante Berthe, even at such a time determining that such garments should not sully the château.

We fed the men food in small quantities for we could see that they

262

were nearly starving. Armand wanted to talk and, weak as he was, would do so.

"I went off that day to a meeting," he said. "By the river I was met by a party of royal guards. Their captain handed me the *lettre de cachet*. I guessed it was due to the Orléans faction. I was working for the good of the country. I was no traitor. But they took me to the Bastille. The Bastille!" He shivered and could not stop shaking.

I insisted that he did not talk. He could tell us everything later when he was in a better condition to do so. We badly needed help. We had two very sick men on our hands, and there were only three of us to look after them. But there were two others in the house, and I decided that they could no longer live apart in their secluded turret. I went up the spiral staircase to Sophie's apartment.

I knocked and went in. Sophie and Jeanne were sitting at a table playing cards.

I cried out: "We need your help."

Sophie looked at me coldly. "Go away," she said.

I cried: "Listen. Armand is here. He has escaped from the Bastille."

"Armand is dead," said Sophie. "Armand was murdered."

"Come and see for yourself," I replied. "Armand is here. He was not murdered. Some traitors betrayed him and he was given a *lettre de cachet*. He has been imprisoned in the Bastille."

Sophie had turned white and the cards fell from her hands onto the table.

"It's not true," she said. "It can't be true."

"Come and see for yourself. You've got to help. You can't sit up here playing cards. Don't you know what's happening in the world? We need all the help we can get. The servants have gone. We have two men here who will die if they don't get proper nursing. They have walked all the way from Paris. They have escaped from the Bastille."

Sophie said: "Come, Jeanne."

She stood by the bed looking down at her brother. "Armand," she whispered. "It is not you."

"Yes, Sophie," he answered. "It is your brother Armand. You see what the Bastille does for a man."

She fell onto her knees beside the bed.

"But why? What did they accuse you of . . . *you* . . . ?"

"There does not have to be an accusation with a *lettre de cachet*. Someone betrayed me...."

I interrupted: "This is not the time for this talking. I need help in nursing them, Sophie, you and Jeanne must help. We have no servants now. They have all left."

"Left? Why?"

"I think," I said wryly, "it is because they believe the revolution has come."

———

Sophie worked indefatigably—and Jeanne with her; and with their help we managed to make the men reasonably comfortable. Armand was in worse shape. His skin was the color of dirty paper and his eyes completely lusterless; he had lost most of his hair and his jaws were sunken. Those years he had spent in prison had killed the young Armand and left a feeble old man in his place.

His companion, without whom he would never have been able to make the journey from Paris, was responding to treatment and although still very weak, was showing signs of recovery, which was more than we could say of Armand.

He told us that he had found Armand outside the prison when the mob trooped in and he had said that he wanted to get to Aubigné. He himself had nowhere to go so he helped Armand and together they crossed Paris. He described something of the scenes there. The people were in revolt. There were meetings everywhere and crowds formed to mobs who went about looting shops and attacking anyone who looked worth robbing, shouting as they did so, *"À bas les aristocrates."*

I wouldn't let him talk too much—and Armand not at all. It excited them and they were both desperately weak.

We couldn't have managed without the help of Jeanne and Sophie. Tante Berthe was very good at knowing what could best be done, and cooking the little food we ate. Lisette was less energetic than the rest of us but she comforted us in a way because she refused to be gloomy and insisted that in time everything would come right.

I had abandoned all thought of leaving France since the arrival of Armand and his companion. I was needed here and I doubted in any case that with the country in the state it was I should be allowed to get very far.

Nothing happened for several days and I was beginning to feel that we would be left alone. There was rioting in Paris. There was a revolution in progress, Lisette said; but here, apart from the fact that we had no servants, everything was at least peaceful.

Lisette said to me: "Let's go into the town. We might find out what is happening there and perhaps buy some food."

I agreed that it was a good idea.

"It is better for us to look like servants," she said. "Some of them left in such a hurry that they went without all their clothes. We could find something to wear."

"Do you think that is necessary?"

"A precaution."

She laughed at me in the dress which I had put on.

"It reminds me of the time we went to see Madame Rougemont. Ah, no longer the grand lady. Not the Comte's daughter but a simple serving maid."

"Well, you look the same."

"I am, after all, only the niece of the housekeeper. Come on."

We took two ponies from the stables and rode in on them. It was all there was. The grooms who had left had taken the horses with them. On the outskirts of the town we tied up the ponies and went in on foot.

Crowds were gathering.

"It looks as though it is a special sort of day," said Lisette with a smile.

We passed through the crowd in our simple dresses and the only glances which came our way were those which some men give to women who could be called young and good looking.

"It seems as if something special is about to take place," I said.

"Probably someone coming from Paris to speak to them. Look! There is a platform set up in the square."

"Shouldn't we try to buy some food?" I asked.

"Haven't you noticed most of the shops are boarded up?"

"Surely they are not afraid of a riot here!"

"Aubigné country is not sacred anymore, Lottie."

She gave a laugh as she said that and I looked at her quickly. Her eyes were shining with excitement.

There was a hush in the crowd as a man began to mount to his rostrum. I stared at him. I knew him at once. Léon Blanchard.

"But what . . . ?" I began.

"Hush," whispered Lisette. "He is going to speak."

A cheer went up in the crowd. He raised his hand and there was a deep silence. Then he began to speak.

"Citizens, the day has come. That which has long been due to us is almost within our grasp. The aristocrats who have ruled us . . . who have lived in luxury while we starved . . . the aristocrats who for generations have made us their slaves . . . are now being conquered. We are the masters now."

There was a deafening cheer. He held up his hand again.

"But we are not yet there, citizens. There is work to be done. We have to rout them out of their haunts of luxury and vice. We have to cleanse those haunts. We have to remember that God gave France to the people. What they have used for centuries now belongs to us . . . if we take it. You have lived your lives in the shadow of the great châteaux. You have slaved for your masters. They have kept you in a state of servile starvation to make you work the harder for them. You have lived in fear. Citizens, I tell you, that is over. It is your turn now. The revolution is upon us. We shall take their châteaux, their gold, their silver, their food, their wine. We shall no longer live on moldy bread for which we have to pay those hard-earned sous and of which we have often not had enough to buy even that. We will march as the good citizens of Paris have shown us how to. Citizens, it is happening all over the country. We will march on the Château d'Aubigné. We will take that which is ours by right."

While he was talking understanding flashed upon me. He was the man the Comte and I had seen all those years ago. No wonder I had felt I had seen him before. I had not completely recognized him for when I had first seen him he had been dressed like a peasant, as he was now. He wore a dark wig which slightly changed his appearance. He did not look quite like the gentleman who had come to tutor our boys. But it was the same man. Dickon had been right. He was an agitator in the service of the Duc d'Orléans, whose plan was to bring about a revolution so that he might step into the King's shoes. As Dickon had said, Blanchard was an Orléanist. The Duc de Soissonson was too, and he had come to Aubigné to investigate Armand's band,

266

which had resulted in Armand's receiving his *lettre de cachet* ... arranged no doubt by men in high places. Orléans ... Soissonson ...

"It is monstrous," I said.

"Hush!" warned Lisette.

I turned to her. She was staring at Léon Blanchard as though entranced.

I whispered: "We must get back quickly. We must warn them."

"Are you ready, citizens?" asked Blanchard; and there was a roar from the crowd.

"In good order then we will assemble here at dusk. These duties are best carried out at night."

I felt as though I were choking. I wanted to shout: This man is a traitor. My father was always good to his people. Our servants lived well. How dare you say we starved them! My father always cared for their welfare. They were never given moldy bread. And Léon Blanchard, wicked traitor that he was, lived with us ... as a member of the family ... when he deceived us and played the part of tutor.

How we had been deceived. Dickon had been right. If only we had listened to Dickon!

Lisette was gripping my arm. "Be careful," she hissed. "Don't open your mouth. Come on. Let's get out of here." She almost dragged me through the crowds. We found the ponies and rode back to the château.

"So that wicked man was a traitor all the time," I said.

"It depends what you mean by traitor," replied Lisette. "He was true to his cause."

"The cause of revolution! What are we going to do? Leave the château?"

"Where would we go?"

"Are we going to wait for them to come then?"

"The crowd didn't harm you, did it?" I looked down at my plain dress. "No," she went on, "you look like a good servant ... a woman of the right class."

"If they take the château ..." I began.

Again there was that familiar lifting of her shoulders.

"Lisette," I went on, "what's the matter with you? You don't seem to care."

We went into the château. It was very quiet. I thought of the mob listening to the traitor Blanchard and I wondered if I should ever see it like this again.

I said: "What are we going to *do?* We must warn Sophie and Jeanne."

"For what purpose?"

"And Tante Berthe . . ." I went on.

"She will be safe. After all, she is only a servant."

Lisette had followed me up to my bedroom.

I said: "Lisette, did you know that Léon Blanchard was going to be there today?"

She smiled at me mysteriously. "You were always so easily deceived, Lottie," she said.

"What do you mean?"

"Léon sent word to me. He and I were great friends . . . intimate friends. We had such a lot in common, you see."

"You . . . and Léon Blanchard!"

She nodded, smiling. "I knew him during those miserable years when I was at the farm. He brought me here."

I closed my eyes. So much was becoming clear. I remembered the groom who had brought her and that odd feeling I had had of something familiar about him.

"What does this mean, Lisette?" I demanded. "There is something you are trying to tell me. What has happened to you? You're different."

"I'm not different," she said. "I was always the same."

"You look at me now as though you hate me."

"In a way," she said reflectively, "I do. And yet I am fond of you. I don't understand my feelings for you. I always loved to be with you. We had such fun together." She began to laugh. "The fortune teller . . . yes, that was, in a way the beginning."

"Lisette," I said, "do you realize that that wicked man with his mob will be marching on the château at dusk?"

"What should I do about that, Lottie?"

"Perhaps we should get away. Hide . . ."

"Who? You and Sophie with Jeanne. What about those sick men? I don't suppose the mob will care very much about them. They look

268

like scarecrows anyway. Jeanne and Tante Berthe will have nothing to fear. Servants don't."

"I had decided we couldn't go and leave the men."

"Then we stay."

"Lisette, you seem . . . pleased."

"I'll tell you, shall I? I have wanted to so many times. It goes back a long way. We are sisters, Lottie . . . you . . . myself . . . and Sophie. The only difference is that I was never acknowledged as you were."

"Sisters! That's not true, Lisette."

"Oh, is it not? I have always known it. I remember our father from my babyhood. Why should he have brought me here if it were not so?"

"He told me who you were, Lisette."

"He told *you!*"

"Yes, he did. You are not his daughter. He didn't know you until you were three or four years old."

"That's a lie."

"Why should he lie to me? And if you had been his daughter he would have acknowledged you as such."

"He did not because my mother was a poor woman . . . not like yours . . . living in a great mansion . . . as noble as he was almost . . . and he married her."

"I know what happened, Lisette, because he told me. Your mother was his mistress, but after you were born. He first discovered you when he visited her and you were there. When your mother was dying she sent for her sister Berthe and asked her to take care of you. The Comte then brought Tante Berthe here as housekeeper and allowed you to stay here and be educated with us because of his affection for your mother."

"Lies!" she cried. "That was *his* story. He did not want to acknowledge me because my mother was only a seamstress."

I shook my head.

"Yes," she went on, "he told you those lies because he wanted to excuse himself. I was never treated quite as one of you, was I? I was always the housekeeper's niece. I wanted to be acknowledged. Who wouldn't? And then . . . Charles came along."

"You mean Charles my husband?"

"Charles. He was fun, wasn't he? But what a fool to go to America. He was going to marry Sophie until that disaster in the Place Louis XV. I thought when my father knew that I was going to have a child he would have arranged the marriage with Charles."

"The child . . ."

"Don't be so innocent, Lottie. Charles saw us both at the fortune tellers, didn't he? He always used to say he liked us both and he didn't know which one he preferred. He used to take me to those rooms which Madame Rougemont let to gentlemen and their friends. I was glad when I knew I was going to have a child. I was silly enough to think that it would make all the difference, that my father would acknowledge me and Charles would marry me. But what did they do to me? They made Tante Berthe take me away and they found a crude farmer husband for me. I shall never forget or forgive. After that I hated the Comte and all he stood for."

I was so shocked I could only mutter. "Yet you wanted more than anything to be part of it!"

"I hated it, I tell you. I met Léon when he was talking in the town near us. We became friends. My husband died when the mob led by Léon set fire to his granaries."

"So that was done . . . by Léon!"

She lifted her shoulders and gave me that smile which I was beginning to dread and fear.

"You *are* very innocent, Lottie. You would have done so much better to marry your Dickon when you had a chance. He made things uncomfortable for us. He was too clever, wasn't he? But he is far away now."

I said slowly: "Blanchard was the man you said was a groom lent by your neighbors." I was remembering the incident in the stable when I thought I had seen him before. I had been right in that.

"Of course. Léon thought I could do good work at the château. Besides, it was a home for me and your husband's son. I wonder you never saw the likeness. I could see it. Every day he reminded me of Charles. But it did not occur to you, did it, dear innocent sister?"

"Remember, you are not my sister. Lisette, how could you lie to us . . . all those years? How could you pretend?"

She wrinkled her brows as though trying to think. Then she said: "I don't know. I was so fond of you sometimes. Then I would think of all you had and that we were sisters and how unfair it was. Then I hated you. Then I forgot it and was fond of you again. It doesn't matter now."

"And you knew that Armand was in the Bastille?"

"Léon did not tell me everything . . . only what it was necessary for me to know. But I guessed and I wasn't sorry. Armand deserved what he got. He always looked down on me—he was always the high and mighty Vicomte. It is amusing to think of him in prison."

"How can you talk like that!"

"Easily," said Lisette. "If you had been humiliated as I have been you would be the same."

"And Léon Blanchard told you he was going to be in the town today?"

She nodded. "I wanted you to see and hear him. I wanted you to know how things were. I have been longing to tell you for so long. I wanted you to know that I was your sister."

Tante Berthe had come into the room. She said: "There is nothing much left in the kitchens. I have made a little soup. What is the matter?"

I said: "We have been into the town. Léon Blanchard was there preaching revolution. They will be coming to the château."

Tante Berthe turned pale. *"Mon Dieu,"* she murmured.

Lisette said: "Lottie has been telling me a tale. She says I am not the Comte's daughter. As if I did not always know I was. She says the Comte did not know me until I was three or four years old. It isn't true, is it? It isn't true?"

Tante Berthe looked steadily at Lisette. She said: "The Comte took you in because he was a good and kind gentleman. You and I owe him much. But he was not your father. Your father was the son of a tradesman and he worked in his father's shop. Your mother told me this before you were born when I came to Paris to try to persuade her to return home. She couldn't, of course, as she was to have a child. I helped her through her confinement. She insisted on keeping you and this she tried to do through her needlework. She couldn't make ends meet and started having gentlemen friends who helped her to pay the rent and feed her child."

"You mean she was a . . . prostitute."

"No, no," cried Tante Berthe fiercely. "She only had friends whom

271

she liked . . . and they helped her because they wanted to. The Comte was one of them. When she knew herself to be dying she asked me to come to her. She wanted me to take care of you. The Comte called when I was there. He was concerned about your mother's health and he talked to me about the future. He told me that when he had visited her he had discovered that she had a little girl hidden away. He was touched by this. He thought your mother a brave woman. When she died he offered me the post of housekeeper to the château and allowed me to bring you with me."

"Lies!" cried Lisette. "All lies!"

"It's the truth," said Tante Berthe. "I swear it in the name of the Virgin."

Lisette looked as though she were going to burst into tears. I knew that the dream of a lifetime was crumbling about her.

She went on shouting: "It is lies . . . all lies."

The door opened and Sophie came in.

"What's the matter?" she said. "I could hear the shouting in Armand's room."

"Sophie," I said, "we are in acute danger. The mob will come to the château at dusk. Léon Blanchard is bringing them."

"Léon . . . !"

I said gently: "What Dickon suspected was true. Léon Blanchard was not a real tutor. He was here to spy for the Orléanists. The Duc de Soissonson was one of them, too. We have just heard him inciting the mob to march on the château. When he comes with them you will see for yourself."

"Léon?" she repeated in a dazed way.

"Oh, Sophie," I said. "There has been such deceit. Terrible things are happening everywhere in France. How can we know who is with us and who against us?"

"I don't believe that Léon . . ." she began, and Lisette began to laugh hysterically.

"Then I'll tell you," she said. "Léon brought me to Lottie. He was my lover before that and when we were here . . . and still is. You see, even though your father acknowledged you as his daughter, you did not have all your own way. Léon, whom you wanted, was *my* lover. Charles, who was Lottie's husband, was *my* lover. He wasn't so particular in the bedroom whether my father called me daughter or not. But I

272

am the Comte's daughter. They are going to try to prove that I was not, but I am, I tell you. I am. I am of noble birth . . . as noble as either of you. We all have the same father . . . no matter what anyone says."

Sophie was looking at me helplessly. I went to her and put my arm about her.

"It's true, isn't it," she said, "that Léon cared about me? He did care a little."

"He was here on a mission," I said.

"But he was in love with Lisette all the time. He was only pretending . . ."

"People do pretend sometimes, Sophie. We were all deceived."

"And I blamed you. I blamed you for making up tales about him . . . tales which were not true. I said your lover murdered Armand that you might have my father's wealth. I said all this of you, Lottie, and I tried to believe it, but I think something inside me rejected it. I didn't really believe it. Perhaps I always knew that Léon could not have cared for me. It was the same with Charles. When I found that flower in his apartment I started to hate you."

"I was never there, Sophie. I lost the flower he bought for me. It was not my flower you found."

"What is all this about a flower?" asked Lisette.

I turned to her. "What does it matter now? It was all long ago. Charles bought a flower for me in the street and Sophie found one like it in his bedroom."

"A red peony," said Lisette. Then she started to laugh. There was an element of hysteria in that laugh. "It was I who left the flower behind, Sophie. I dropped it in Charles's apartment. I borrowed it from Lottie's room because it matched my dress, I remember. I forgot about it. It was only an artificial flower anyway. It is proof to you, Sophie, that he was my lover. I had his child, you know. Yes, Louis-Charles is his son."

"Stop it, Lisette," I cried. "Stop it."

"Why should I? This is the moment of truth. Let us stop deceiving ourselves. Let us all show what we really are."

The tears were running down Sophie's cheeks making her hood wet. I put my arms round her and she clung to me.

"Forgive, Lottie," she said. "Forgive . . ."

I said: "When people know, they understand. There is nothing to forgive, Sophie." I kissed her scarred cheek. "Dear Sophie," I said, "I am glad we are sisters again."

Lisette and Tante Berthe watched us. Tante Berthe's practical mind was trying to work out what we should do. Lisette still seemed bemused.

"You should really get out," said Tante Berthe. "Perhaps we all should. You certainly, Madame Lottie."

"And what of the men?" I asked.

"We can't move them."

"I shall stay here," I said.

Tante Berthe shook her head and Lisette said: "You and I have nothing to fear, Tante Berthe. You are a servant, and although I am an aristocrat, Léon Blanchard is my friend. He will see that I am safe."

"Be silent," cried Tante Berthe. She shook her head and turned away muttering: "What is best? What can be done?"

"There is nothing," I replied, "but to wait."

———

We waited through the long afternoon. The heat was intense. It seemed to me that I was seeing everything with special clarity. Perhaps that was how it was when one looked death in the face. I had seen the mob at Léon Blanchard's meeting and could picture those people marching on the château with the blood lust in their eyes. I thought of my mother's stepping out of the shop and finding herself in the midst of such a crowd. I pictured the carriage as I had so often before. I saw the frightened horses. What had she felt in those horrific moments? I had heard of the people's violence when they had smashed up the town and I knew that human life meant little to them. And as the daughter of the Comte d'Aubigné I was one of the enemy. I had heard that they had hanged one of the merchants from a lamppost because they said he had put up the price of bread.

I had never before come face to face with death; but I knew that I was facing it now. I was aware of a lightheadedness. I felt strangely remote. Fear was there, yes, but not fear of death but of what must happen before it. I knew now how people felt in their condemned cells awaiting the summons.

I looked at the others. Did they feel the same? Armand was too ill to care. He had suffered so much already. His companion was in the same condition. Sophie? I did not think she cared very much. Life was

.not very precious to her, though she had changed since Armand's return.

Lisette? I could not understand Lisette. All those years when I had believed her to be my friend she had harbored a hatred of me. I would never forget the triumphant look in her eyes when she considered how I should be made to suffer. I could not believe that she had really hated me all those years because I was recognized as the Comte's daughter and she thought she should be.

What did I know of Lisette? What did I know of anyone, even myself? People were made up of contradictions and when one nurtures a great grievance through life, that must have a lasting effect. Least of all I understood Lisette. Why did she care so much for birth? She was on the side of the revolutionaries. She hated the aristocrats and yet she insisted she was one of them.

The sound of a bee buzzing at the window caught my attention. I thought how wonderful it was to see living creatures, to look at the blue sky, to hear the gentle lap of the water of the moat against the green earth. All that I had taken for granted until I was confronted by the thought that I should never see or hear them again.

Tante Berthe said she thought we should all be together. She would bring the men to my bedroom if we would help her. They could both lie on my bed while we waited.

I nodded, and with the help of Sophie and Jeanne we brought the men in.

They looked very ill.

I told Armand what was happening. He nodded and said: "You should get away. You shouldn't stay here. Leave us."

"There is nowhere we can go, Armand," I told him. "And in any case we wouldn't leave you."

"No," said Sophie firmly, "we should not leave you."

Armand became animated then. "You must," he cried. "I have seen the mob. That day in Paris. You have no idea what they are like. They cease to be men and women. They are wild animals."

I said: "Armand, we are not going to leave you."

"You . . ." he insisted. "You should go. The servants could stay. They might be safe."

"Lie back," I commanded. "Rest while you can. The servants have already gone and we are staying."

275

It was a long afternoon.

Sophie sat at my feet on a footstool. Jeanne was close to her. I knew that Jeanne would never leave her as long as they both lived.

I said: "Sophie, you have a wonderful friend in Jeanne. Have you ever thought how lucky you are to have her?"

She nodded.

"She loves you," I went on.

"Yes, she loves me. The others . . ."

"It is over. They would never have been faithful. Charles wasn't to me, and Léon Blanchard is only faithful to a cause."

"They will take us, Lottie . . . you, Armand, and me . . . because of our father."

Lisette was listening and she said: "And they will take me, but I shall be safe because Léon will not let them hurt me."

Sophie flinched and Jeanne whispered: "I should never let you be hurt, Mademoiselle Sophie."

There was a long silence. We were all listening intently. We must all have been thinking that they might not wait until evening.

"I wish I could go back," said Sophie. "I'd be different. I would say, I lost so much" she touched her face beneath her hood "but it showed me how truly fortunate I was in Jeanne."

Jeanne said: "Don't, my precious one. Don't upset yourself. It's bad for your face when you cry."

We were silent again and I thought: If I could have foreseen . . . if I could go back . . . how differently I should act. I could see Sabrina's face. "Don't go," she had said. "Wait till Dickon comes back." I should have waited for Dickon. He had not really been out of my thoughts, although I had tried to prevent his intruding on them. Of what use was it to think of him now . . . it only meant bitter recriminations against myself for my folly.

I should have married him. Heaven knew, I had wanted to. I should have taken what I could get. I should have forgotten my doubts . . . my determination to accept nothing but perfection.

If I could only turn to him now . . . if I could shut out my thoughts of the perfidy of Lisette, the unfaithfulness of Charles, of death, if I could forget the wasted years, I would be content. But it was now too late.

"Too late," Sophie whispered it. I laid my hand on her shoulder and she leaned against my knee.

I said: "But we know now. I am glad we came to an understanding while there was still time."

It would be dark soon. The danger hour was near.

Lisette left and did not return until the darkness deepened. I gasped when I saw her. She was wearing one of my gowns—one which I had had made some time ago for a ball. It was one of the most elaborate gowns I had ever possessed. The skirt was of plum-colored velvet and chiffon of a lighter shade; the tightly fitted bodice was studded with pearls. About her neck was the diamond necklace which the Comte had given my mother on their wedding day and which was now mine.

"Lisette!" I cried as she entered.

"Are you mad?" said Tante Berthe.

Lisette laughed at us. *"I* should have had these things," she said. "I have as much right to them as Lottie has . . . more, because I am older. My father treated me badly, but now he is dead."

"Lisette," I said, "when the mob sees you like that what do you think they will do?"

"I will tell them, 'Yes, I am an aristocrat but I have always been for the people. I have worked with Léon Blanchard. Ask him. He will tell you I speak the truth.' I shall come to no harm then."

"You foolish girl!" cried Tante Berthe.

Lisette shook her head and laughed. She came and stood close to me, her hands on her hips, taunting, and I thought, *Her obsession has driven her mad.*

"I always wanted this dress," she said, "and the necklace goes with it so well. It belongs to me now. Everything here belongs to me. It is my right and Léon will see that it is given to me."

I turned away from her. I could not bear the look in her eyes. I thought, *Truly she is mad.*

———

They were coming. I could hear the shouts in the distance. I went to the window. There was a strange light out there. It came from the torches they were carrying.

I heard their chanting voices. *"Au château. À bas les aristocrates. À la lanterne."*

277

I thought of the lifeless body of the merchant hanging from the lamppost and I felt sick with fear.

They were coming nearer and nearer.

Tante Berthe said: "The drawbridge will stop them."

"Not for long," I answered.

We looked at each other fearfully and Lisette glided from the room.

"Where has she gone?" asked Sophie.

"To take off that finery if she has any sense," retorted Tante Berthe.

I said: "I am going to find her. I am going to talk to her."

I found her mounting the spiral staircase to the tower. I saw her standing on the battlements. The light from the torches had thrown a fierce glow over the scene for the mob was very close . . . right at the castle gates.

She stood there on the battlements. She looked magnificent with the diamonds sparkling at her throat.

The mob shouted when they saw her.

"Lisette," I called. "Come down. Come down."

She held up her hand and there was silence. She called out to the mob: "I am the daughter of the Comte d'Aubigné . . . an aristocrat by birth."

The mob started to shout. *"À bas les aristocrates. À la lanterne."*

She shouted above the noise and eventually they were quiet, listening.

"But I have worked for your cause. My friend is Léon Blanchard and he will confirm this. I have worked for you, my friends, against the overlords, against those who caused the price of bread to be so high, against those whose extravagances have impoverished France. I will prove to you that I am your friend. I will let down the drawbridge so that you may enter the castle."

There was a roar of applause.

She dashed past me. I thought of trying to stop her. She would let them in, but did it matter? They would not allow the drawbridge to stop them for very long.

She would save herself at the cost of Sophie's life and mine. It was the final act of hatred.

I went back to the room. They were all waiting expectantly. It would not be long now. The mob would soon be storming the castle.

Jeanne did a strange thing. She untied Sophie's hood and took it off

278

so that the hideous disfigurement was displayed. "Trust me," she whispered to Sophie who had gasped with dismay. "I know these people. I think it best. Trust me."

I could hear sounds of ribald laughter, the noise of falling furniture. The mob was in the château.

Lisette had joined us. Her eyes were shining with triumph. "They have come," she said.

The door burst open. It was a horrific moment—the one for which we had all been waiting. They were here.

In those terrifying moments I was surprised to recognize among the people who burst into the room three shopkeepers whom I knew slightly—respectable men—not the kind I should have expected to be involved in such an outrage; but mob madness could spring up everywhere.

Lisette faced them. "I am the daughter of the Comte," she repeated. "I am of aristocratic birth, but I have always worked for you and the revolution."

A man was staring at the diamonds at her throat. I thought he was going to snatch them. Then one of the shopkeepers pushed him roughly aside.

"Be careful," he growled. There was about him a hint of leadership and I felt a faint touch of relief. I sensed that this man was uneasy . . . wary, and it occurred to me that he could command a certain respect and perhaps hold the more bloodthirsty of the raiders in check.

His words certainly had an effect, for the men who had entered the room ignored us for a few seconds and went round the room examining everything. They looked at the men lying on the bed. Both Armand and his companion regarded them with indifference.

"Who are they?" asked one of the men.

"They are half dead," said another.

Jeanne and Tante Berthe faced them squarely. "We are servants here. We are not aristocrats," said Tante Berthe. "You don't want us."

Jeanne had her arm about Sophie and I saw the men staring at her scarred face.

One of them took Lisette by the shoulders.

"Take your hands from me," said Lisette haughtily.

"Ah, be careful of Madame la Comtesse," said one of the men ironically.

"I am the Comte's daughter," said Lisette, "but I am with you. I worked with Monsieur Léon Blanchard."

"They are on our side now it is good to be so," said another of the men. "It used to be a different story."

They started to hustle Lisette out of the room. She turned and pointed to me: "That is the acknowledged daughter of the Comte," she cried.

"Yes," said one of the men. "I know her. I've seen her with the Comte. Don't take any notice of her dress. That is put on to deceive us."

I realized then that I was still wearing the servant's dress which I had put on that morning and what a contrast I must make to Lisette in her finery.

The men were looking at the others in the room. They shrugged their shoulders. Then, dragging Lisette and me with them, they went out of the room.

What happened afterwards still bewilders me.

I can remember being dragged through the crowds; I remember the abuse, most of it directed towards Lisette. How foolish she had been to dress up as she had!

The flare of the torches, the sight of dark, menacing eyes, the dirty clenched fists which were brandished close to my face, the painful grip on my arms, the moment when someone spat in my face . . . they are scenes from a nightmare which would spring up suddenly and carry me back all through my life to that fearful night.

We were forced into a wagonette which was drawn by a mangy-looking horse.

And thus we drove through the mob into the town.

———

There followed the strangest night I have ever spent. We were driven to the *mairie* and there hustled out of the cart and taken to a small room on the first floor which looked down on the street.

We were fortunate in as much as these people were unaware of their power at this time. The revolution which had been rumbling for so long had only just broken out and among those men who carried us to the *mairie* were some who, a short time before, had been known as respectable citizens of the town . . . shopkeepers and the like. They were unsure of what reprisals might be taken. They knew that there were risings all over Paris but they must have wondered what would happen to them if the risings were suppressed and the aristocrats were in power again.

The mob would have taken us to the lamppost and hanged us right away, but there were several who advised a certain restraint. The mayor himself was uncertain. For centuries the Aubigné family had been the power in the neighborhood. It was early days and they could not be sure that that power was broken; they were not yet accustomed to the new order. And the more sober men of the town were very much afraid of retaliation.

The mob had surrounded the *mairie* and were demanding that we be brought out. They wanted to see our bodies swinging on the lanterns.

I wondered what was happening back at the château.

Were they safe there? Armand and his friend were not recognizable; poor Sophie's face had probably saved her. This was a revolt against those who had what the mob wanted. Nobody wanted what those sickly men or poor scarred Sophie had. There was nothing to envy in them. It was different with Lisette and me. They did not believe Lisette. She had miscalculated badly, and if she had not been so anxious to prove herself an aristocrat she would have realized what a very dangerous position she was placing herself in.

There were no chairs in the room, so we lay on the floor.

"I wish that scum would stop shouting," said Lisette.

"You have been so stupid," I told her. "There was no need for it. You could be back at the château now."

"I am who I am and will bear the consequences for that."

"Poor Lisette, why do you care so much?"

"Of course I cared. I was one of you. The fact that I wasn't recognized doesn't change that. Léon will save me, you see, and there will be those who have to answer for the way they have treated me."

I did not reply. There was nothing to say. Lisette cared more for her birth than she did for her life since she was ready to risk it to convince herself that she was of noble parentage.

I saw clearly then how it had obsessed her, how she had believed it—perhaps forced herself to believe it—all those years. She had let the resentment build up to such an extent that it was beyond everything else. She could not face the fact now that she must know it not to be true. She had to go on believing ... even if it cost her her life.

The noise outside seemed to have abated a little. I stood up and looked out. I turned away quickly. They were still there, waiting for us to be brought out.

"Lisette," I said, "tell them the truth. They may believe you. It is madness to go on proclaiming that you are an aristocrat and are proud of it. You are saying you are their enemy. They hate us. Don't you see? They hate us because we have what they have always wanted. Don't you understand that?"

"Yes," she said, "I see it, but it doesn't alter anything."

"I shall never forget the way they looked at Sophie and Armand. True aristocrats ... legitimately born aristocrats ... not like us, Lisette ... the bastards. But they took both of us. Why? Because we are young and healthy, because they envy us. The foundation of this revolution is built on envy. Is its purpose, do you think, to make France a better, happier country? No. It is not that at all. I saw it clearly tonight. It is an attempt by people who have not to take from those who have those luxuries which they want for themselves. When they have them they will be as selfish and careless of others as the rich have been in the past. It is not a better country that these people are destroying for. It is to turn it round so that those who did not have, now have, and those who had, now have not."

Lisette was silent and I went on: "Is that not so with you, Lisette? You are a true daughter of the revolution. You were envious. Admit it. You have let envy color your whole life. You have built up a picture that was based on falsehood from the beginning. I can see how it came about. It was a natural inference. Then you were Charles's mistress and that was gratifying because he was going to marry Sophie. Did you deliberately leave the flower in his apartment so that she could suspect me? You always liked to create a drama, didn't you? But you must have been very pleased to have been his mistress while he was engaged to Sophie. But when there was a child ..."

Lisette burst out: "He should have married me. I thought he would. I thought he would make the Comte admit that I was his daughter. Why shouldn't he have done so? *You* married Charles."

"I *was* the Comte's daughter, Lisette."

"I was too. I was ... I was ..."

I sighed. It was no use talking to her. She would not let go of her obsession, although she knew in her heart that what I and Tante Berthe had told her was true. She must go on believing; and I could see that belief had been her lifeline. She clung to it. She was not going to let it go. Even in the face of the bloodthirsty mob she stood up and said: "I am an aristocrat."

Oh, what a foolish woman she was!

But was I any wiser? I had prevaricated. I had been afraid. I had yearned for Dickon—how far away dear Eversleigh seemed now!—and I had refused to go to him. I had allowed my fears and my suspicions to grow. I had always known that there was nothing of the saint about Dickon. Far from it. But it was the Dickon he was whom I had wanted; and something perverse within me had refused to let me go to him, to take him for what he was ... which is what one must always do with others. One cannot mold them; one loves for what a person is ... faults and all, and that was how I had loved Dickon.

I tried to think of him now. Would he have returned to Eversleigh? What would he have said when he found that I had gone?

I thanked God that my father had died before this happened. I thanked God, too, that the children were in England, saved from this holocaust.

The noise had stopped. I went to the window and looked out. I saw him clearly riding through the crowd. Léon Blanchard! I wondered if he was coming to the *mairie*. Perhaps he would say what was to be done and order them to release Lisette.

"Lisette," I cried. "Look. It is Léon Blanchard."

She was beside me. "He has come for me," she cried. "Léon. Léon," she shouted; but he could not hear, nor did he look towards the windows of the *mairie*.

"I must get down to him," she said. "I must."

She ran to the door. It was locked. She came back to the window. She battered at it with her hands. I saw the blood on the plum-colored velvet. She had broken through and stood on the balcony. I heard her agonized cry: "Léon. Léon. I am here, Léon. Save me from this rabble."

I couldn't see Léon Blanchard now. The crowd was staring up at the balcony. I saw Lisette leap and she was gone.

There was a hushed silence in the crowd. The mob seemed to stampede forward. There was deafening noise and screaming. The torches threw a grisly light on the scene. I saw a bloody hand come up and in its grasp was a diamond necklace.

I waited at the window.

I was there when they carried away a broken body.

———

It was quieter down below. Sickened by what I had seen, I wanted to lie down on that hard floor and drift into oblivion. I wanted to shut out the horror of it all. I felt that if ever I should escape from this peril I should be haunted all my life by the memory of Lisette with the fanatical gleam in her eyes. Life had become a nightmare and I believed that the end of it was very near.

I was cramped lying on the floor. I felt desperately alone. A great urge came over me to weep for Lisette. All those years of resentment ... and she had been Charles's mistress. ... Had she continued to be when I was in England and she was there with him alone? Was it going on then? It didn't matter now. Why wonder about it? Soon they would come for me.

I went to the window and looked out. My eyes went to the lamp post with its faint light which showed me the dark liquid running over the cobbles. I saw that it came from the wine shop into which the mob had broken. Some men were squatting on the cobbles scooping up the puddles with their hands and holding their hands to their lips. I heard a woman start to sing in a high-pitched quavering voice and a man brusquely and crudely telling her to shut up.

Many of them were drunk. Some were propped up against walls. But they were keeping their vigil at the *mairie*. They had had one spectacle tonight and they were waiting in anticipation for another. The signal would come and they would storm the *mairie*.

I could not bear to look at them. I sat down and leaned against the wall with my eyes closed. If only I could sleep away the time until they came for me. ...

I wondered how long it took for death to come.

"Quickly, please God," I prayed.

———

The door opened quietly. A man came in. I started to my feet, a sick feeling of horror enveloping me. The moment had come.

284

It was the mayor who faced me.

He said: "You are to leave here."

"Leave here . . ."

He put his fingers to his lips. "Don't speak. Obey orders. The mob is quieter now but still in an ugly mood. I don't want to have to tell them that you are being taken to a prison outside the town. They would not allow you to go. They are determined to hang you. Here . . . follow me."

"But where . . . where am I going?"

"I told you to be silent. If the mob get wind that you are leaving they will tear you to pieces. They are bent on seeing the end of Aubigné."

I followed him down the stairs. We were in a courtyard at the back of the *mairie* where a coach was waiting. It was shabby and enclosed. A bearded driver wearing a coat and muffled up about the neck, in spite of the weather, was seated in the driving seat. He was holding a whip in his right hand and did not turn as I came out of the *mairie*.

"Get in," said the mayor.

"I want to know where you are taking me."

I was given a rough push. "Be silent," hissed the mayor. "Do you want to bring the mob down on you?"

I was pushed inside the coach and the door shut on me. The mayor lifted his hand and the coach jolted forward.

We had to come round to the front of the *mairie* and as the coach rattled into the square a cry went up.

"A carriage? Who rides in a carriage?"

The driver whipped up the horses. I heard the shouts of rage and guessed that the mob was trying to stop the coach.

I lurched from side to side. The driver drove like a madman.

Someone called out: "Who is this rogue? Who is in the carriage?"

For a few terrifying moments I thought we were going to be brought to a halt. I could imagine the fury of the people if they discovered who was inside and that an attempt was being made to cheat them of their spectacle.

The driver was silent. He just drove on. We were through the square. The coach gathered speed. Some of the people were running after us. Glancing through the window, I caught a glimpse of angry faces very close.

The coach lurched and trundled on; and the shouts of the people grew fainter. We had left the town behind. Still the driver went on driving at a furious speed so that I was thrown from side to side of the padded vehicle.

Suddenly we stopped. We were close to a wood from which a man emerged leading two horses.

The driver leaped down from his seat and pulled open the door of the coach. He signed for me to get out, which I did. I could scarcely see his face, so heavily bearded was he, and he wore a scarf high round his neck.

He looked back the way we had come. The country road seemed very quiet and the first streak of dawn was in the sky.

Then he took off his scarf and pulled at the hair about his face. It came off in his hand and he grinned at me.

"Dickon!" I said.

"I thought you might be rather pleased to see me. Now, no time to lose. Get on that horse," he said to me; and to the man: "Thank you. We'll get off now for the coast as fast as we can."

A wild exhilaration had taken possession of me. I felt faint with emotion; the transformation from terrible despair to wild joy was too sudden. Dickon was here. I was safe and Dickon had saved me.

We rode all through the morning. He would say little except: "I want to be out of this accused country by tomorrow. With luck we'll catch the pacquet. It means riding through the night but we can make it."

So we rode. My body was in a state of exhaustion but my spirits were uplifted. There came the time when we had to rest the horses and ourselves. Dickon decided when and where. We were not going through any of the towns, he told me. He had a little food with him and we must make do with that. In the late afternoon of the first day we came to a lonely spot by a river. There was a wood nearby where he said we could sleep for an hour. We had to. We needed the rest, and there was a long way to go. First he took the horses to the river and they drank and then he tethered them in the wood. We lay down under a tree and he held me in his arms.

He told me a little then of what had happened. When he had returned to Eversleigh and discovered I had left for France he had followed me at once.

"I knew that the revolution would begin soon," he said. "I was determined to bring you away. Abduct you if necessary. I went to the château. They had made a mess of it. But Armand was there with the others. Sophie was looking after him with her servant and that older one. They told me that you and Lisette had been taken. I had to act quickly. You see, Lottie, what it means to have friends in the right places. You have despised me for my interest in worldly goods and money chiefly, but see what useful purposes it can be put to. I have been coming over here now and then. I had business over here, as you know. There were many French who did not like the way things were going ... friends of England, you might say. The mayor, by great good fortune, was one of them. I took the precaution of bringing money with me ... plenty of it. I knew I was going to need it. So I came. I was there in the mob. I saw what happened to that girl Lisette. I was waiting for them to get the carriage for me. I would have fought them with my bare fists if they had touched you. But this was the best method. You can't fight against the mob. It would have been the end of us both. Never mind. I have got you so far. The rest is child's play in comparison. Now rest ... sleep ... though that is difficult for me lying here holding you in my arms."

"Dickon," I said, "thank you. I shall never forget what I owe you."

"I have made up my mind that I shall never let you."

I smiled. He had not changed. He never would and I was glad.

We were so tired that we slept and when we awoke evening had come. We mounted the horses and rode on all through the night, stopping only for brief respites.

We came into Calais on the afternoon of the second day. We left the horses at an inn. Only once were we challenged as escaping aristocrats.

Dickon answered that he was an Englishman who had been traveling in France with his wife and had no interest in French politics and quarrels.

His haughty and somewhat bellicose manner intimidated our accusers and it was clearly obvious that he was indeed an Englishman. So trouble was avoided.

We boarded the pacquet. Soon we should be home.

We stayed on deck, so eager were we for a sight of land.

"At last," said Dickon, "you are coming home to stay. Do you realize that had you come earlier, had you not dashed back to France, you could have saved us a good deal of trouble?"

"I did not know that I should find my father dead."

"We have wasted a lot of time, Lottie."

I nodded.

"Now," he went on, "you'll take me for what I am. Ambitious, ruthless, eager for possessions . . . and power, wasn't it?"

"There is something you have forgotten," I reminded him. "If you married me you would be marrying a woman who has absolutely nothing. I am penniless. The vast fortune which my father left in trust to me will all be lost. It will be taken by the revolutionaries. I don't think you have thought of that."

"Do you imagine I should not have thought of such an important detail?"

"So Dickon . . . what *are* you thinking of?"

"You, and how I shall make up for the lost years. And you, Lottie, what are you thinking? This man on whom I have foolishly turned my back for many years is ready to marry me — penniless as I am. And he was foolish enough to be ready to give up all he had acquired through a long life of ruthless scheming . . . and all for me."

"How was that?"

"Lottie, when we drove through that square we were within an inch of being stopped, of being dragged from our coach and hung on the lamppost . . . both of us. If that had happened I should have lost all my possessions, for it is a sobering thought that when you die you cannot take them with you."

"Oh, Dickon," I said, "I know what you did for me. I shall never forget . . ."

"And you'll take me in spite of what I am."

"Because of it," I said.

He kissed my cheek gently.

"Look," he said. "Land. The sight of those white cliffs always uplifts me . . . because they are home. But never in all my life did I feel such joy in them as I do at this moment."

I took his hand and put it to my lips and I held it there as I watched the white cliffs come nearer.